WADI DALIYEH

I

DISCOVERIES IN THE JUDAEAN DESERT

EMANUEL TOV, EDITOR-IN-CHIEF

MICHAEL D. COOGAN, VOLUME EDITOR

DISCOVERIES IN THE JUDAEAN DESERT · XXIV

WADI DALIYEH
I

THE WADI DALIYEH SEAL IMPRESSIONS

BY

MARY JOAN WINN LEITH

CLARENDON PRESS · OXFORD

1997

Oxford University Press, Great Clarendon Street, Oxford OX2 6DP
Oxford New York
Athens Auckland Bangkok Bogota Bombay
Buenos Aires Calcutta Cape Town Dar es Salaam
Delhi Florence Hong Kong Istanbul Karachi
Kuala Lumpur Madras Madrid Melbourne
Mexico City Nairobi Paris Singapore
Taipei Tokyo Toronto Warsaw
and associated companies in
Berlin Ibadan

Oxford is a trade mark of Oxford University Press

Published in the United States
by Oxford University Press Inc., New York

British Library Cataloguing in Publication Data
Data available

Library of Congress Cataloging in Publication Date
Data available

ISBN 0–19–826935–8

1 3 5 7 9 10 8 6 4 2

Printed in Great Britain on acid-free paper by
St Edmundsbury Press, Bury St Edmunds

CONTENTS

TABLE OF PLATES

Plates I–XXII present Wadi Daliyeh bullae in the Rockefeller Museum, Jerusalem (museum numbers beginning with WD). Plates XXIII and XXIV present a significant selection of related bullae formerly in the collection of Reuben and Edith Hecht (Hecht Group, see INTRODUCTION, p. 3), now in the collections of the Israel Museum, Jerusalem (museum numbers beginning with IM) and the Reuben and Edith Hecht Museum, The University of Haifa (museum numbers beginning with HM).

FOREWORD

THE present volume of the seal impressions from Wadi Daliyeh is the first of three volumes presenting the written material and artifacts from that site. Mary Joan Leith's much revised dissertation, *Greek and Persian Imagery in Pre-Alexandrine Samaria* (Harvard University 1990), written under the supervision of F. M. Cross, contains the basis for this volume.

Professor Michael Coogan kindly read the whole volume and commented to the author on matters of content.

The volume was typeset in Jerusalem by Eva Ben David on the basis of computer files provided by the author and was copy-edited by Janice Karnis. Ariel Tov proofread the bibliography and the bibliographical references. The camera-ready copy was produced by Sarah Presant-Collins. The production was co-ordinated by Claire Pfann.

We are grateful to the Oxford University Press for its professional production of the manuscript and the plates.

As always, we are very much indebted to Gen. (ret.) Amir Drori, director of the Israel Antiquities Authority (IAA), and the staff of the IAA for their substantial efforts on behalf of the publication of the *Discoveries in the Judaean Desert* series.

The Qumran Project of the Oxford Centre for Hebrew and Jewish Studies is to be thanked for its support for the typesetting of this volume and for the work of the international Dead Sea Scrolls Publication Project as a whole.

This volume is dedicated to the presidents—past and present—of the Oxford Centre and to the Administrator of the Qumran Project in gratitude for their unfailing and enthusiastic support and encouragement in the publication of this series.

Jerusalem
April 1997

EMANUEL TOV
EDITOR-IN-CHIEF

PREFACE

I WISH to express my gratitude first of all to the Helyn and Hess Kline Foundation and its representative, Stephen Judson. Their generous assistance was instrumental in bringing this project to fruition. I am also indebted to Stonehill College and its Academic Dean, Louis Manzo, for publication support.

To thank all those friends and colleagues who have helped me in this long-standing project would be an impossible task; I can only hope that those whom I neglect here will forgive me.

In the early stages of my work, I briefly visited John Boardman and Roger Moorey at the Ashmolean Museum, Oxford. These two scholars treated me, a stranger to them and a neophyte in the world of glyptic art, with generosity and encouragement.

In Jerusalem, I was made welcome at the Rockefeller Museum by Curator Joseph Zias. Dr. Yaakov Meshorer, Chief Curator of the Israel Museum, freely provided me with photographs of the Israel Museum's bullae from the Hecht Collection. From the Reuben and Edith Hecht Museum of the University of Haifa I received information about the bullae in their collection. The photographs of the bullae themselves, without which my work would have been impossible, were made many years ago in Jerusalem by Mr. Albina. Nancy Lapp shared with me her own Wadi Daliyeh photographs. Prof. Albert Henrichs imparted numerous arcane bibliographical references from his rich store of knowledge and a dose of caution when my fancy tried to lead me too far astray.

At the production level, the talented Cathy Alexander cleaned up my drawings. Claire Pfann's questions and guidance kept me on my toes, and I am the happy beneficiary of the meticulous copy-editing of Janice Karnis. My debt to Emanuel Tov, who knows well how much I owe to his patience and editorial advice, is immeasurable.

I have been privileged to work with four remarkable scholars and equally special human beings. Miranda Marvin taught me never blindly to accept received wisdom, but to keep an open and questioning mind. David Mitten was always forthcoming with his wide-ranging knowledge of Greek archaeology and respect for English grammar. My colleague and friend Michael Coogan spent dozens of hours combing through the manuscript as it neared completion, providing criticism of the most constructive kind. His scrupulous attention to detail on every level enhanced the coherence of the narrative, the accuracy of the data, and usefulness of this volume. And finally, ever since my sophomore year when I took his introductory Old Testament course, Frank M. Cross, Jr. has nurtured my fascination with the Ancient Near East and taught me how to begin to fathom its mysteries. Not least, he introduced me to the Wadi Daliyeh bullae.

To all these beneficient daimones I owe my gratitude. The deficiencies of this volume are my own and should not be laid at anyone else's door.

My mother, Dr. Barbara Peters Winn, and my father, William E. Winn, have always shown me by their example how being an eternal student gives life its zest. Finally, I thank my husband, Rob, for almost twenty-one years now of constant love and joyous companionship.

April 1997   MARY JOAN WINN LEITH

ABBREVIATIONS

AASOR	*Annual of the American Schools of Oriental Research*
ABD	*The Anchor Bible Dictionary*, ed. David Noel, Freedman (New York, 1992).
AGDS	*Antike Gemmen in deutschen Sammlungen*
AJA	*American Journal of Archaeology*
	E. Akurgal, 'Les Fouilles de Daskyleion', *Anatolia* 1 (1956).
AMI	*Archäologische Mitteilungen aus Iran*
Ashmolean/*ANES III*	Briggs Buchanan and P. R. S. Moorey, *Catalogue of Ancient Near Eastern Seals in the Ashmolean Museum, Volume III, The Iron Age Stamp Seals* (Oxford, 1988).
Ashmolean/*EGFR*	John Boardman and Marie-Louise Vollenweider, *Catalogue of the Engraved Gems and Finger Rings: Greek and Etruscan* (Ashmolean Museum, Oxford, 1978).
Avigad, *Bullae and Seals*	N. Avigad, *Bullae and Seals from a Post-Exilic Judean Archive*, Qedem 4 (1976).
Avigad, *Hebrew Bullae*	N. Avigad, *Hebrew Bullae from the Time of Jeremiah* (Jerusalem, 1986).
Avigad, 'Hebrew Seals'	N. Avigad, 'Hebrew Seals and Sealings and their Significance for Biblical Research', *Congress Volume*, VTSup 40, ed. J. A. Emerton (Leiden, 1988) 7–16.
BA	*Biblical Archaeologist*
Balkan, 'Inscribed Bullae'	Kemal Balkan, 'Inscribed Bullae from Daskyleion-Ergili', *Anatolia* 4 (1959) 124–7.
BAR	*Biblical Archaeology Review*
Barnett-Mendleson, *Tharros*	R. D. Barnett and C. Mendleson, eds., *Tharros: A Catologue of Material in the British Museum from Phoenician and Other Tombs at Tharros, Sardinia* (British Museum, London, 1987).
BASOR	*Bulletin of the American Schools of Oriental Research*
Beazley, *Lewes House*	John D. Beazley, *The Lewes House Collection of Ancient Gems* (Oxford, 1920).
Betlyon, *Coinage*	John Betlyon, *The Coinage and Mints of Phoenicia: The Pre-Alexandrine Period*. Harvard Semitic Monographs (Chico, CA, 1982).
Boardman, *ABV*	John Boardman, *Athenian Black Figure Vases, A Handbook* (New York, 1985).
Boardman, *AG Gems*	John Boardman, *Archaic Greek Gems* (London, 1968).
Boardman, *ARV*	John Boardman, *Athenian Red Figure Vases: The Archaic Period, A Handbook* (London, 1975).
Boardman, *Diffusion*	John Boardman, *The Diffusion of Classical Art in Antiquity* (Princeton, 1994).
Boardman, *GA*	John Boardman, *Greek Art* (London, 1973).
Boardman, *GGFR*	John Boardman, *Greek Gems and Finger Rings: Early Bronze to Late Classical* (London, 1970).
Boardman, *Intaglios*	John Boardman, *Intaglios and Rings: Greek, Etruscan, and Eastern: From a Private Collection* (London, 1975).
Boardman, 'Pyramidal'	John Boardman, 'Pyramidal Stamp Seals in the Persian Empire', *Iran* 8 (1970) 19–45.

Boardman, 'Scarabs'   John Boardman, 'Scarabs and Seals: Greek, Punic and Related Types',
                       *Tharros: A Catalogue of Material in the British Museum from Phoenician
                       and Other Tombs at Tharros, Sardinia* (London, 1987) 98–105.

Borchhardt, 'Herrschaft'   H. Borchhardt, 'Zur Herrschaft der Achaimeniden in der Bildkunst
                            Lykiens', *AMI Ergänzungsband* 6 (1979) 239–40.

Bordreuil, *BN*   Pierre Bordreuil, *Catalogue des sceaux ouest-sémitiques inscrits de la
                   Bibliothèque Nationale, du Musée du Louvre et du Musée biblique de Bible
                   et Terre Sainte* (Bibliothèque Nationale, Paris, 1986).

Bothmer, *Amazons*   D. von Bothmer, *Amazons in Greek Art* (Oxford, 1957).

Bregstein, *Seal Use*   Linda Bregstein, *Seal Use in Fifth Century B.C. Nippur, Iraq: A Study of
                         Seal Selection and Sealing Practice in the Murašu Archive* (Ph.D. diss.,
                         University of Pennsylvania, 1993).

Brett, 'Aphlaston'   A. B. Brett, 'The Aphlaston, Symbol of Naval Victory or Supremacy on
                      Greek and Roman Coins', *Transactions of the International Numismatic
                      Congress*, eds. J. Allen, H. Mattingly, and E. S. G. Robinson (London,
                      1938) 23–31.

Brommer, *Satyrspiele*   F. Brommer, *Satyrspiele* (Berlin, 1944).

Burkert, *Greek Religion*   W. Burkert, *Greek Religion* (Cambridge, MA, 1985).

Canby, Ancient Near East   J. V. Canby, The Ancient Near East in the Walters Art Gallery (Baltimore,
                            1974).

CBQ   *Catholic Biblical Quarterly*

CHI II   I. Gershevitch, ed., *The Cambridge History of Iran, II: The Median and
            Achaemenian Periods* (Cambridge, 1985).

Childs, *City Reliefs*   W. Childs, *The City Reliefs of Lycia* (Princeton, 1978).

CHJ I   W. D. Davies and Louis Finkelstein, *The Cambridge History of Judaism,
           Volume I: Introduction; The Persian Period* (Cambridge, 1984).

Collon, *First Impressions*   Dominique Collon, *First Impressions: Cylinder Seals in the Ancient Near East*
                               (Chicago, 1987).

Cook, *Persian Empire*   J. M. Cook, *The Persian Empire* (New York, 1983).

Cross, 'Aspects'   F. M. Cross, Jr., 'Aspects of Samaritan and Jewish History in Late Persian
                    and Hellenistic Times', *HTR* 59 (1966) 201–11.

Cross, 'Coins'   F. M. Cross, Jr., 'Coins', *Discoveries in the Wâdi ed-Dâliyeh*, eds. P. Lapp
                  and N. Lapp (AASOR XLI; 1974) 57–9.

Cross, 'Dâliyeh'   F. M. Cross, Jr., 'Papyri of the Fourth Century B.C. from Dâliyeh', *New
                    Directions in Biblical Archaeology*, eds. D. N. Freedman and J. C.
                    Greenfield (Garden City, NY, 1969) 45–69.

Cross, 'Discovery'   F. M. Cross, Jr., 'The Discovery of the Samaria Papyri', *BA* 26 (1963) 110–
                      121.

Cross, 'Historical'   F. M. Cross, Jr., 'The Historical Importance of the Samaria Papyri', *BAR* 4
                       (1978) 25–7.

Cross, 'Papyri'   F. M. Cross, Jr., 'The Papyri and their Historical Implications,' *Discoveries
                   in the Wâdi ed-Dâliyeh*, eds. P. Lapp and N. Lapp (AASOR XLI; 1974)
                   17–29.

Cross, 'Report'   F. M. Cross, Jr., 'A Report on the Samaria Papyri', *Congress Volume:
                   Jerusalem 1986, Supplements to Vetus Testamentum* 40 (1988) 17–26.

Cross, 'Samaria'   F. M. Cross, Jr., 'Samaria and Jerusalem: The Early History of the
                                Samaritans and their Relations with the Jews' (Hebrew), *The Restoration –*
                                The Persian Period (ההיסטוריה של עם ישראל), ed. H. Tadmor (Jerusalem,
                                1983) 148–58.

Cross, 'Samaria Papyrus 1'   F. M. Cross, Jr., 'Samaria Papyrus 1: An Aramaic Slave Conveyance of 335
                                B.C.E. found in the Wâdi ed-Dâliyeh', *ErIsr* 18 (1985) 7*–17*.

Crowfoot, Crowfoot, Kenyon   J. W. Crowfoot, G. M. Crowfoot, and K. M. Kenyon, *Samaria-Sebaste III:*
   Samaria-Sebaste   *The Objects* (London, 1957).

Delaporte, *Catalogue*   Louis Delaporte, *Catalogue des cylindres orientaux et des cachets Assyro-*
                                Babyloniens, Perses et Syro-Cappadociens de la Bibliothèque Nationale
                                (Paris, 1910).

Dörig, 'Tarentinischen'   J. Dörig, 'Tarentinischen Knöchelspielerinnen', *Museum Helveticum* XCI
                                (1959) 29–58.

DWD   P. Lapp and N. Lapp, eds., *Discoveries in the Wâdi ed-Dâliyeh* (AASOR
                                XLI; 1974) 29–58.

EAEHL   Michael Avi-Yonah, *Encyclopedia of Archaeological Excavations in the Holy*
                                Land (Jerusalem, 1975).

Elayi, 'Phoenician Cities'   J. Elayi, 'The Phoenician Cities in the Persian Period', *JANESCU* 12 (1980)
                                13–28.

Elayi, 'Studies'   J. Elayi, 'Studies in Phoenician Geography during the Persian Period',
                                JNES 41 (1982) 83–110.

ErIsr   *Eretz-Israel*

Förschner, *Münzen*   G. Förschner, *Die Münzen der Griechen in Italien und Sizilien, Kleine*
                                Schriften des Historischen Museums, Frankfort am Main 27 (1986).

Frankfort, *Art*   H. Frankfort, *The Art and Architecture of the Ancient Orient*[4]
                                (Baltimore/London, 1969).

Furtwängler, *AG*   Adolf Furtwängler, *Die antiken Gemmen: Steinschneidekunst in klassischen*
                                Altertum (Leipzig/Berlin, 1900).

Furtwängler, *Beschreibung*   Adolf Furtwängler, *Beschreibung der geschnittenen Steine in Antiquarium*
                                (Berlin, 1896).

Galling, 'Bildsiegel'   K. Galling, 'Beschriftete Bildsiegel des ersten Jahrtausends v. Chr.,
                                vornehmlich aus Syrien und Palästina', *ZDPV* 64 (1941) 121–202.

Garrison, *Seal Workshops*   M. Garrison, *Seal Workshops and Artists in Persepolis: A Study of Seal*
                                Impressions Preserving the Theme of Heroic Encounter on the Persepolis
                                Fortification and Treasury Tablets (Ph.D. diss., University of Michigan,
                                1988).

Glynn, 'Achilles'   R. Glynn, 'Achilles and Penthesilea: An Iconographic Study of an Engraved
                                Gem', *Oxford Journal of Archaeology* I (1982) 169–78.

Von Graeve,   V. von Graeve, *Der Alexandersarcophag und seine Werkstatt, Istanbuler*
   Alexandersarcophag   *Forschungen* 28 (1970).

Green, 'Note'   A. Green, 'A Note on the Assyrian "Goat-Fish," "Fish-Man" and "Fish-
                                Woman"', *Iraq* 48 (1986) 25–30.

Gropp, *Samaria Papyri*   D. M. Gropp, *The Samaria Papyri from Wadi Daliyeh, The Slave Sales*
                                (Ph.D. diss., Harvard University, 1986).

Gubel, 'Syro-Cypriote'   E. Gubel, '"Syro-Cypriote" Cubical Stamps: The Phoenician Connection',
                                SP 5 (1987) 195–224.

Henrichs, 'Myth'   A. Henrichs, 'Myth Visualized: Dionysos and his Circle in Sixth-Century
                               Attic Vase-Painting', *Papers on the Amasis Painter and his World*
                               (J. Paul Getty Museum, Malibu, 1987) 92–124.

Herrmann, *Shadow*   John J. Herrmann, Jr., *In the Shadow of the Acropolis: Popular and Private
                               Art in 4th Century Athens*. A loan exhibition from the Department of
                               Classical Art, Museum of Fine Arts, Boston, at the Brockton Art
                               Museum/Fuller Memorial, September 1984–August 1987.

Hestrin, Dayagi-Mendels,   R. Hestrin and M. Dayagi-Mendels, *Inscribed Seals: First Temple Period,*
   Inscribed Seals   *Hebrew, Ammonite, Moabite, Phoenician and Aramaic* (Israel Museum,
                               Jerusalem, 1979).

Hill, *BMC Coins*   G. F. Hill *et al.*, *British Museum Catalogue: Greek Coins* (London, 1873–
                               1927).

Hitzl, *Sarkophage*   I. Hitzl, *Die griechische Sarkophage des archaischen und klassischen Zeit*
                               Studies in Mediterranean Archaeology and Literature 104 (1991).

Holloway, *Art and Coinage*   R. Holloway, *Art and Coinage in Magna Graecia* (Bellinzona, 1978).
Hornblower, *Greek World*   S. Hornblower, *The Greek World, 479–323 BC* (New York, 1983).
Hornblower, *Mausolus*   S. Hornblower, *Mausolus* (Oxford, 1982).
Horster, *Statuen*   G. Horster, *Statuen auf Gemmen* (Bonn, 1970).
HTR   *Harvard Theological Review*
IDB   Interpreter's Dictionary of the Bible, ed., G. A. Buttrick (Nashville, 1962).
IEJ   *Israel Exploration Journal*
IGCH   M. Thompson, O. Mørkholm, and C. M. Kraay, eds., *An Inventory of*
Greek   *Coin Hoards* (New York, 1973).
JANESCU   *Journal of the Ancient Near East Society of Columbia University*
JAOS   *Journal of the American Oriental Society*, New Haven.
JBL   *Journal of Biblical Literature*
Jenkins, *Coins*   G. K. Jenkins, *Ancient Greek Coins* (London, 1972).
JHS   *Journal of Hellenic Studies*, London
JNES   *Journal of Near Eastern Studies*
Johns, 'Excavations'   C. N. Johns, 'Excavations at 'Atlit (1930–31): The Southeast Cemetery',
                               QDAP 2 (1933) 41–104.

Keel, 'Ancient Seals'   O. Keel, 'Ancient Seals and the Bible. A Review Article', *JAOS* 106 (1986)
                               307–11.

Keel, 'Tell Keisan'   O. Keel, 'La glyptique de Tell Keisan 1971–1976' *Studien zu den*
                               Stempelsiegeln aus Palästina/Israel, III, eds. O. Keel, M. Shuval, and C.
                               Uehlinger (Freiburg, 1990) 163–260.

Keel-Uehlinger, *Göttinnen*   O. Keel and C. Uehlinger, *Göttinnen, Götter und Gottessymbole* (Freiburg,
                               1992).

Klein, *Child Life*   A. E. Klein, *Child Life in Greek Art* (New York, 1932).
Koch, *Dareios*   H. Koch, *Es kündet Dareios der König . . . Vom Leben im persischen*
                               Grossreich (Mainz, 1992).

Kraay, *Coins*   Colin M. Kraay, *Archaic and Classical Greek Coins* (California, 1976).
Lapp, 'Account'   P. Lapp, 'An Account of the Discovery', *DWD*, 1–6.
Lapp, 'Cave'   P. Lapp, 'The Cave Clearances', *DWD*, 7–12.

Lawlor, 'Maenads'   L. B. Lawlor, 'The Maenads: A Contribution to the Study of the Dance in
                           Ancient Greece', *Memoirs of the American Academy in Rome* VI (1927) 69–
                           112.

Legrain, *Culture*   Leon Legrain, *The Culture of the Babylonians from their Seals in the
                           Collections of the Museum* (Philadelphia, 1925).

Legrain, *Ur*   Leon Legrain, *Seal Cylinders, Ur Excavations* X (Pennsylvania, 1951).

Leith, *Imagery*   Mary Joan Leith, *Greek and Persian Imagery in Pre-Alexandrine Samaria*
                           (Ph.D. diss., Harvard University, 1990).

LIMC   *Lexicon Iconographicum Mythologiae Classicae* (Munich, 1981 and ongoing).

Lippold, *Gemmen*   Georg Lippold, *Gemmen und Kameen des Altertums und der Neuzeit* (Stuttgart,
                           1922).

Lullies-Hirmer, *Sculpture*   Reinhard Lullies (photographs by Max Hirmer), *Greek Sculpture* (New
                           York, 1960).

Marshall, *BMC*   F. H. Marshall, *Catalogue of the Finger Rings, Greek, Etruscan and Roman,
                           in the British Museum* (London, 1907).

Marvin, *Studies*   Miranda Marvin, *Studies in Greco-Persian Gems* (Ph.D. Thesis, Harvard
                           University, 1973).

Meshorer-Qedar,   Yaᶜakov Meshorer and Shraga Qedar, *The Coinage of Samaria in the Fourth
     Coinage of Samaria   Century BCE* (Jerusalem, 1991).

Metzger, *Recherches*   Henri Metzger, *Recherches sur l'imagerie athénienne* (Paris, 1965).

Metzger, *Représentations* Henri Metzger, *Les représentations dans la céramique attique du IVe siècle*
                           (Paris, 1951).

Miller, *Perserie*   Margaret Miller, *Perserie: The Arts of the East in Fifth-Century Athens*
                           (Ph.D. Thesis, Harvard University, 1985).

Moorey, 'Metalwork'   P. R. S. Moorey, 'Metalwork and Glyptic', *CHI II,* 856–69.

Monsters and Demons   A. Farkas et al., eds., *Monsters and Demons in the Ancient and Medieval
                           Worlds: Papers Presented in Honour of Edith Porada* (Mainz, 1987).

Mørkholm-Zahle, 'Coinage'   O. Mørkholm and J. Zahle, 'The Coinage of Kprlli', *Acta Archaeologica*
                           XLIII (1972) 57–113.

Moscati, *Phoenicians*   S. Moscati (Dir.), *The Phoenicians*. Catalogue of the exhibition held at the
                           Palazzo Grassi, Venice in 1988 (New York, 1988).

OCD   *Oxford Classical Dictionary*

Petrie, Mackay, Wainwright, W. M. Flinders Petrie, E. Mackay, and G. Wainwright, *Meydum and
     Meydum   Memphis (III)* (BSAE 18: London, 1910).

Porada, *Ancient Art*   E. Porada, *Ancient Art in Seals*, ed. E. Porada (Princeton, 1980).

Porada, *Art*   E. Porada, *The Art of Ancient Iran: Pre-Islamic Cultures* (New York, 1965).

Porada, 'Greek Coin'   E. Porada, 'Greek Coin Impressions of Ur', *Iraq* XXII (1960).

Porten, *Archives*   Bezalel Porten, *Archives from Elephantine* (Berkeley, 1968).

QDAP   *Quarterly of the Department of Antiquities of Palestine*

Raeck, *Barbarenbild*   W. Raeck, *Zum Barbarenbild in der Kunst Athens in 6 und 5 Jahrhundert v.
                           Chr* (Bonn, 1981).

RB   *Revue Biblique*

REA   *Revue des Études anciennes*

Reisner, Fisher, Lyon,   G. A. Reisner, C. S. Fisher, and D. G. Lyon, *Harvard Excavations at
     Harvard   Samaria 1908–1910* (Cambridge, MA, 1924).

Richter, *EGGE*   Gisela M. A. Richter, *The Engraved Gems of the Greeks, Etruscans and
                          Romans, Part One: Engraved Gems of the Greeks and the Etruscans, A
                          History of Greek Art in Miniature* (London, 1968).

Richter, MMA   Gisela M. A. Richter, *Catalogue of the Engraved Gems Greek Etruscan and
                          Roman* (Metropolitan Museum of Art, Rome, 1956).

de Ridder, *Collection*   A. de Ridder, *Collection de Clercq, Les bijoux et les pierres gravées,* vol.
                          VII/2 (Paris, 1911).

RHR   *Revue de l'Histoire des Religions*

Ridgway, *Fifth Century* B. S. Ridgway, *Fifth Century Styles in Greek Sculpture* (Princeton,
                          1981).

Robinson, *Metal*   S. M. Robinson, *Metal and Minor Miscellaneous Finds, Excavations at
                          Olynthus* X, *Johns Hopkins University Studies in Archaeology* XXXI
                          (Baltimore, 1941).

Root, 'Heart'   M. C. Root, 'From the Heart: Powerful Persianisms in the Art of the Western
                          Empire', *Achaemenid History VI* (1991) 1–29.

Root, *King*   M. C. Root, *The King and Kingship in Achaemenid Art: Essays on the
                          Creation of an Iconography of Empire,* Acta Iranica 19 (Leiden, 1979).

Root, 'Persepolis'   M. C. Root, 'The Persepolis Perplex: Some Prospects Borne of Retrospect',
                          Ancient Persia: The Art of an Empire, ed. D. Schmandt-Besserat
                          (Malibu, 1980) 5–21.

Roscher, *Lexikon*   W. H. Roscher, *Ausführliches Lexikon des griechischen und römischen
                          Mythologie* (1884).

Rose, *Handbook*   H. J. Rose, *A Handbook of Greek Mythology* (New York, 1959).

Rubensohn, *Elephantine* O. Rubensohn, *Elephantine-Papyri* (Berlin, 1907).

Schauenburg, *Perseus*   K. Schauenburg, *Perseus in der Kunst des Altertums* (Bonn, 1960).

Schefold, *Klassischen*   Karl Schefold, *Die Göttersage in der klassischen und hellenistischen Kunst*
                          (Munich, 1981).

Schefold, *GHGK*   Karl Schefold, *Götter- und Heldensagen der Griechen in der spätarchaischen
                          Kunst* (Munich, 1978).

Schefold-Jung, *Urkönige* K. Schefold and F. Jung, *Die Urkönige, Perseus, Bellerophon, Herakles und
                          Theseus in der klassischen und hellenistischen Kunst* (Munich, 1988).

Schmidt, *Persepolis II* Erich Friedrich Schmidt, *Persepolis II: Contents of the Treasury and other
                          Discoveries,* Oriental Institute Publications LXIX (Chicago, 1957).

Seals and Sealings   McGuire Gibson and R. D. Biggs, eds., *Seals and Sealings in the Ancient
                          Near East* (Bibliotheca Mesopotamia VI; Malibu, 1977).

Shepard, *Monster*   K. Shepard, *The Fish-Tailed Monster in Greek and Etruscan Art* (New York,
                          1940).

SNG-ANS   *Sylloge Nummorum Graecorum-American Numismatic Society*

SP   *Studia Phoenicia*

Spier, *Ancient Gems*   J. Spier, *Ancient Gems and Finger Rings, Catalogue of the Collections, The
                          J. Paul Getty Museum* (Malibu, 1992).

Starr, 'Greeks'   Chester G. Starr, 'Greeks and Persians in the Fourth Century B.C.' Parts 1
                          and 2, *Iranica Antiqua 11–12* (1975, 1977) 39–99/49–115.

Stern/Hecht, 'Hoard'   Ephraim Stern, 'A Hoard of Persian Period Bullae from the Vicinity of
                          Samaria', *Michmanim* 6 (Hecht Museum, Haifa; 1992 [Hebrew]) 7–30,
                          English summary, 41*.

Stern, *Material Culture*   Ephraim Stern, *Material Culture of the Land of the Bible in the Persian
                                Period: 538–332 B. C.* (Jerusalem, 1982).

Stern, 'Persian'   Ephraim Stern, 'The Persian Empire', *CHJ I*, 70–87.

Stern, 'Phoenician'   Ephraim Stern, 'A Phoenician Art Centre in Post-Exilic Samaria', *Atti del I.
                                congresso internazionale di studi fenici e punici I* (Rome, 1983) 211–12.

Stern, 'Seal Impressions'   Ephraim Stern, 'Seal Impressions in the Achaemenid Style in the Province of
                                Judah', *BASOR* 202 (1971) 6–16.

Stucky, *Tribune*   Rolf A. Stucky, *Tribune d'Echmoun: ein griechischer Reliefzyklus des 4.
                                Jahrhunderts v. Chr. in Sidon, Antike Kunst Beiheft 13* (Basel, 1984).

Walters, *BMC*   H. B. Walters, *Catalogue of the Engraved Gems and Cameos, Greek, Etruscan
                                and Roman in the British Museum* (London, 1926).

Webster, *Potter*   T. B. L. Webster, *Potter and Patron* (London, 1972).

Winter, 'Phoenician'   I. Winter, 'Phoenician and North Syrian Ivory Carving in Historical
                                Context: Questions of Style and Distribution', *Iraq* 38 (1976) 1–23.

Wiseman, *Cylinder*   D. J. Wiseman, *Cylinder Seals of Western Asia* (London, 1959).

Zagdoun, *Fouilles*   Mary-Anne Zagdoun, *Fouilles de Delphes 4:6, Monuments Figurés: Sculpture*
                                (1977).

Zazoff, *AG*   Peter Zazoff, *Die antiken Gemmen* (Munich, 1983).

Zettler, 'Chronological'   R. Zettler, 'On the Chronological Range of Neo-Babylonian and
                                Achaemenid Seals', *JNES* 38 (1979) 257–70.

A. INTRODUCTION

INTRODUCTION

THE Wadi Daliyeh bullae are the clay sealings originally affixed to legal documents of the fourth century BCE written on papyrus. These documents, composed in the official Aramaic of the Achaemenid Persian Empire, were drawn up and sealed in the provincial capital city of Samaria (in the central hill country of Palestine), hence their designation as the 'Samaria Papyri'.[1] This is a catalogue and analysis of the legible sealings ('bullae' or 'seal impressions') and two gold seal rings, purchased first indirectly, then directly from the Taʿamireh Bedouin in November 1962 and August 1963.[2] A hoard of approximately forty additional bullae apparently from the same corpus was published in 1992.[3]

The Discovery and Recognition of the Wadi Daliyeh Bullae

When the Taʿamireh Bedouin discovered the Dead Sea Scrolls, the discovery changed their lives; it was only natural to dream of finding yet more 'treasure' in yet more caves. As excavator P. Lapp reports in his account of the Wadi Daliyeh excavations,[4]

---

[1] Unless otherwise specified, all dates in antiquity are BCE.

[2] Most of the bullae are stored in the Rockefeller Museum, Jerusalem; a few, including WD **22** (the 'Sanballat' sealing), are in the Israel Museum. The latter group could not be examined. Gold rings A and B are currently missing; see S. A. Reed, *Dead Sea Scroll Inventory Project: Lists of Documents, Photographs and Museum Plates, Fascicle 12, Wadi ed Daliyeh* (Claremont, CA: Ancient Biblical Manuscript Center, 1991) 6.

WD **22**, the palaeo-Hebrew 'Sanballat' sealing (attached to Samaria Papyrus 16), is discussed by the present editor only in passing. It was published by Cross in 'Papyri of the Fourth Century B.C. from Dâliyeh', *New Directions in Biblical Archaeology,* eds. D. N. Freedman and J. C. Greenfield (Garden City, NY, 1969) 47, figs. 34–5, and in 'The Papyri and their Historical Implications', *Discoveries in the Wâdi ed-Dâliyeh (DWD),* eds. P. Lapp and N. Lapp, AASOR XLI (1974) 18, pl 61.

Two barely legible bullae recovered from the ASOR excavations were published by Cross in 'Papyri', 28, pl 62. They were unavailable for inspection in the Rockefeller Museum, and their photographs allow only a tentative interpretation. In the case of a few other bullae which were unlocated or inaccessible, the catalogue entry is based solely on photographs and so noted in the entry.

In addition to WD **22** ('Sanballat') and the two excavated bullae, Cross published thirteen of the purchased bullae (Cross, 'Papyri', 28–9, pls 62–3): WD **3A**, WD **4**, WD **10A**, WD **11B**, WD **12**, WD **14**, WD **17**, WD **24–6**, WD **42**, WD **46** and WD **51**; WD **4**, WD **14** and WD **25** are also illustrated in Cross, 'Dâliyeh', illus. 37–9; all are included in this catalogue.

[3] E. Stern, 'A Hoard of Persian Period Bullae from the Vicinity of Samaria', *Michmanim* 6 (Hecht Museum, Haifa, 1992). They were bought by R. Hecht and are now divided between the Hecht Museum (Haifa University) and the Israel Museum, Jerusalem. Photographs of five of the Hecht bullae published in Stern/Hecht, 'Hoard' and one in private hands are included in Y. Meshorer and Sh. Qedar, *The Coinage of Samaria in the Fourth Century BCE* (Jerusalem, 1991) 12, 36 and 81; see pls XXIII and XXIV for an extensive sampling of the Hecht bullae initially published by Stern in Stern/Hecht, 'Hoard'. This group of bullae is designated the 'Hecht Group' in this catalogue.

[4] P. Lapp, 'An Account of the Discovery', *DWD*, 1. Cf. also F. M. Cross, 'Aspects of Samaritan and Jewish History in Late Persian and Hellenistic Times', *HTR* 59 (1966) 201–11 and Cross's detailed analyses: 'Dâliyeh', 45–69; 'Papyri', 17–29, and 'Coins,' *DWD*, 57–9. See also F. M. Cross, 'The Historical Importance of the Samaria

those Taʿamireh who were still living as Bedouin in the dry winter of 1961/2 had travelled farther north than usual and by February had camped chiefly around Khirbet Fasâyil, fifteen miles up the Jordan Valley rift from Jericho. A few tents were pitched along the Wadi Daliyeh, five miles to the west. Naturally, enterprising Bedouin investigated the caves in the heart of the wadi. According to Lapp's reconstruction of the course of events, the Samaria Papyri were found by a hunting party of seven men at the back of the main corridor of a cave which they called Mughâret ʾAbu Shinjeh ('Cave of the Father of the Dagger'). One of the men had spotted a gold ring and 'the hunt was on'.[5] They pillaged through bat dung, ancient garments and mats, as well as the bones of over 200 men, women and children, in their search for the gold they expected to find. Then someone noticed that pieces of the matting had writing on them.

Upon learning that such 'matting' was actually fragmentary papyrus documents that could be worth something, the hunters returned to the cave for a more systematic exploration. They were rewarded with portions of a number of fragmentary papyrus scrolls. Most of these quickly found their way into the hands of Khalil Iskander Shahin, known as 'Kando', the 'notorious middle man for the Dead Sea Scrolls'.[6]

By April of 1962, a sample of the papyri came to the attention in Jerusalem of Père R. de Vaux of the École Biblique and Y. Saad, Curator of the Palestine (now Rockefeller) Archaeological Museum; they in turn showed the piece of 'worm-eaten papyrus with Aramaic written on both sides'[7] to P. Lapp at the American School of Oriental Research. Overnight, Lapp studied the script and the next day suggested that its palaeography dated to c.375. The text, he said, seemed to mention Samaria and relate to a military administration.

A fund had only recently been established within the American Schools of Oriental Research to purchase publication rights to manuscripts such as the Samaria Papyri.[8] Frank Cross, as chairman of the administering committee, flew to Jerusalem and entered into negotiations to purchase the papyri. On November 19, Cross was able to purchase all of the badly broken and worm-eaten papyrus documents he was offered as well as some associated finds.[9] Cross's purchase consisted of 'many . . . [papyrus] fragments, some small rolls of papyrus, one still sealed with seven sealings, a collection of several dozen sealings bearing distinct Persian and Greek figures, and a few coins',[10] and the two gold seal rings.[11] Lacking further funding, he was obliged to forego the

---

Papyri', *BAR* 4 (1978) 25–7; F. M. Cross, 'Samaria Papyrus 1: An Aramaic Slave Conveyance of 335 B.C.E. found in the Wâdi ed-Dâliyeh', *ErIsr* 18 (1985) 7*–17*; F. M. Cross, 'A Report on the Samaria Papyri', *Congress Volume: Jerusalem 1986*, Supplements to Vetus Testamentum 40, ed. J. A. Emerton (1988) 17–26.

[5] Lapp, 'Account', *DWD*, 3.

[6] Lapp, 'Account', *DWD*, 4.

[7] Lapp, 'Account', *DWD*, 5.

[8] This was the Dead Sea Scrolls Fund of the American Schools of Oriental Research.

[9] And thanks to the generosity of E. Hay Bechtel.

[10] Lapp, 'Account', *DWD*, 5.

[11] Cross, 'Dâliyeh', 51.

acquisition of a significant amount of jewellery and coins.[12] Later, in August of 1963, a new, but small, collection of fragments and sealings was also purchased, this time from the middleman of the Taʿamireh tribesmen.[13] A total of 128 clay sealings were recovered by these purchases and in the subsequent excavations.[14]

The Samaria Papyri are 'the last remnants of a very large corpus of [Aramaic] legal and administrative documents'.[15] Indeed, they are 'the first legal papyri of ancient date found in Palestine'.[16] All were apparently written in the province or city of Samaria, the only place name found in any of the documents.[17] Among the many fragments or groups of fragments, Cross isolated eighteen discrete documents with the possibility of nine more; the majority—seventeen—record slave sales.[18] None seems to relate to the official bureaucracy of the Persian province or to communications between the local Samarian rulers and their satrapal superiors, Persian military authorities, or the Persian court.

Of the greatest importance are the date formulae preserved on many of the papyri keyed to the Persian kings' regnal years. Most of the documents come from the reign of King Artaxerxes III (Ochus) (358–337), but the earliest dated papyrus, frg. 22, 'belongs between the thirtieth and fortieth year of King Artaxerxes II (Memnon), that is, between 375 and 365 B.C.E.'.[19] Papyrus 1 carries the latest recorded date, corresponding to March 19, 335, year two of the usurper King Artaxerxes IV (Arses) and the succession year of Darius III (Codomannus), on the eve of Alexander's conquest in 332.[20] The latest coin—a Tyrian issue—comes from 334, the fifteenth year of Azemilkos of Tyre.[21] Thus the papyri and the bullae which sealed them date

---

[12] Cross, personal communication; cf. 'Report', 17, and 'Dâliyeh', 54 n. 10. The coins, which made their way into the antiquities trade, are known on the market as the 'Nablus Hoard' (cf. *IGCH* no. 1504, to be published by A. Spaer and S. Hurter). Although he was unable to purchase most of the coins, Cross was permitted to study them briefly and to record many of their inscriptions. His notes tally with the legends on the 'Nablus Hoard' coins which have since appeared (the present editor is indebted to S. Hurter for her generous assistance with information about the Nablus Hoard).

Meshorer-Qedar, *Coinage of Samaria*, recently published many Samarian coins from the Nablus Hoard now in scattered private collections, as well as all of a second coin hoard ('the Samaria Hoard') with numerous Samarian issues. F. Cross (personal communication) suspects this 'hoard' comes from the same findspot as the Nablus Hoard, namely the Mughâret ʾAbu Shinjeh Cave. See also Y. Meshorer, *Ancient Jewish Coinage,* vol. 1: *The Persian Period through Hasmonaeans* (Dix Hills, 1982) 31–2.

Meshorer-Qedar, *Coinage of Samaria*, 65 contains one photograph of jewellery found with the Samaria Hoard.

[13] Cross, 'Dâliyeh', p. 51.

[14] Cross, 'Papyri', p. 19.

[15] Cross, 'Dâliyeh', 46; there may originally have been over one hundred documents in the cave, most of which were probably devoured by worms (p. 51).

[16] Cross, 'Samaria Papyrus 1', *7.

[17] Cross, 'Samaria Papyrus 1', *7.

[18] Cross, 'Samaria Papyrus 1', *7 and D. M. Gropp, *The Samaria Papyri from Wadi Daliyeh, The Slave Sales* (Ph.D. dissertation, Harvard University, 1986) vii.

[19] Cross, 'Dâliyeh', 48; cf. also 'Samaria Papyrus 1', *10.

[20] Cross, 'Samaria Papyrus 1', *10. Because Artaxerxes IV died in his second regnal year, Papyrus 1 actually bears a second date formula as well, year one of Darius III (Codomannus), the last Achaemenid ruler.

[21] Cross, 'Dâliyeh', 53–6.

between 375 and not long after 334, solidly within the middle third of the fourth century.

The contents of the papyri suggest that the persons who applied their seals to these legal documents were wealthy citizens of Samaria who administered the city and province for their Persian overlords. While 'a sizable number' of foreign names reflect the mixed population of Samaria in the mid-fourth century, the majority of theophoric elements in the names are Yahwistic, implying continued veneration of the God of Israel.[22]

Without a good archaeological context, the coins, papyri and sealings (few still attached to their documents) had only limited scholarly value. As part of the purchase agreement, the location of the findspot was revealed by the Taʿamireh to be Mughâret ʾAbu Shinjeh. In January 1963, the American Schools of Oriental Research launched an arduous winter excavation, directed by P. Lapp; a second season's work took place in February of the following year. The excavators concentrated on two caves perched precariously in cliffs along the Wadi Daliyeh: Mughâret ʾAbu Shinjeh (the cave of the papyri) and, nearby, ʿArâq en-Naʿsâneh, which proved to have Middle Bronze I and Roman Second Revolt (c.135 CE) occupation.[23]

On the third day of excavation in Mughâret ʾAbu Shinjeh, the excavators found their first papyrus fragments, confirming that this was indeed the site of the manuscript finds.[24] In areas with undisturbed stratigraphy, the pottery horizon was solidly mid-fourth century.[25] Among other items, both the disturbed and undisturbed areas yielded cloth (some embroidered), matting, date and olive pits, balsa nuts, beads, a comb, and heaps of human bones, including the skulls of thirty-one males and sixteen females.[26] The Taʿamireh, however, had told of some 300 human skeletons lying in the cave.[27]

Cross has reconstructed the probable sequence of events which brought so many Samarians to Mughâret ʾAbu Shinjeh and their deaths.[28] After capturing Tyre late in 332, Alexander proceeded immediately to Egypt. According to Josephus, the Samarians

---

[22] Cross, 'Dâliyeh', 52. Cross lists the divine names *Qôs* (Edomite), *Kemoš* (Moabite), *Baʿl* (Canaanite/ Phoenician), *Nabū* (Babylonian) and *Śahar* (Aramaic). For Isis (Egyptian) see Gropp, *Samaria Papyri*, 118 (Papyrus 8.12).

[23] *DWD* is the final report on the two seasons of excavation under the direction of P. Lapp. Preliminary accounts of the excavations include, F. M. Cross, 'The Discovery of the Samaria Papyri', *Biblical Archaeologist* 26 (1963) 110–21 and P. W. Lapp, 'The Samaria Papyri', *Archaeology* XVI (1963) 204–6. Individual campaign preliminary reports were published in the American Schools of Oriental Research *Newsletter*, February 1, 1963 and March 14, 1964.

[24] P. Lapp, 'The Cave Clearances', *DWD*, 8. Lapp (p. 11) also reports that one of the Taʿamireh told him of finding five silver coins in a specific part of the cave; the description matched the coins offered for sale with the Samaria Papyri. Cf. Cross, 'Dâliyeh' p. 50, which notes that, while none of the papyri from the excavation joined any purchased fragments, all were of the same date and 'left no doubt that the original provenience of the main lot had been found'. Cf. also p. 53 n. 9.

[25] N. Lapp, 'The Late Persian Pottery', *DWD*, 30–32.

[26] W. M. Krogman, 'Cranial Material', *DWD*, 89.

[27] Lapp, 'Cave', 8, 11. In 'Dâliyeh', p. 50, Cross writes that 'perhaps two hundred men, women and children lost their lives at Dâliyeh'.

[28] Cross, 'Dâliyeh', 57–8.

at first welcomed Alexander's annexation of Palestine.[29] Curtius, however, reports that as soon as Alexander left for Egypt and his strange encounter with the oracle of Ammon, the Samarians burned alive Alexander's prefect in Syria.[30] This was clearly an act of rebellion. According to Curtius, Alexander took vengeance on the Samarian rebels. Other late sources tell of his destroying Samaria or settling it with Macedonians.[31] Cross writes:

> The leaders in Samaria who were implicated in the rebellious acts that led to the prefect's death fled Samaria on learning of Alexander's rapid march on the city. Presumably they followed the main road down the Wadi Far'ah into the wilderness, and found temporary refuge in the Wadi Daliyeh cave. A great number fled, whole families, fairly well supplied with food. Their origin and status are well attested by their seals and their legal documents. They were discovered in their hiding place by the Macedonians, either by assiduous search or, more likely, through betrayal by their fellows who remained in Samaria, and mercilessly slaughtered to a man.[32]

The Persian Period and Samaria

From 539 to 332, Samaria and the rest of Syria-Palestine including coastal Phoenicia and Cyprus belonged to the fifth satrapy—called Abar Nahara—of the Achaemenid Persian Empire.[33] The Achaemenid political policy of self-interested *laissez faire* largely enabled subject communities to operate within their traditional governing forms, to decide local religious issues and to regulate their own membership; satraps (Persian viceroys) concentrated on effective taxation (i.e. tribute), and foreign and military

---

[29] *Ant.* 11.297–345.

[30] Q. Curtius Rufus, *Hist. Alex.* 4.8.9–10.

[31] Cross, 'Dâliyeh', 57 n. 21.

[32] Cross, 'Dâliyeh', 58. Cross mentions a theory of P. Lapp (cf. Lapp, 'Cave', *DWD*, 8) that the refugees had been suffocated by a fire built at the mouth of the cave by their pursuers.

[33] The precise boundaries of this province are difficult to ascertain; they also seem to have shifted several times over the two centuries of Persian control. See J. M. Cook, *The Persian Empire* (New York: 1983) 81, 173–6, and E. Stern, 'The Persian Empire and the Political and Social History of Palestine in the Persian Period', *CHJ* I, 78–9; also T. Petit, *Satrapes et satrapies dans l'empire achéménide de Cyrus le Grand à Xerxes Ier* (Paris, 1990) 205.

The essential source for the archaeological record of the Persian period in Palestine (a neglected era even in recent archaeological handbooks) is E. Stern, *The Material Culture of the Land of the Bible in the Persian Period, 538–332 B.C.* (Jerusalem, 1982). See Stern's summary articles in *CHJ I*. Note also H. Weippert, *Palästina in vorhellenistischer Zeit, Handbuch der Archäologie, Vorderasien II, Band I* (Munich, 1988) 682–718 with additional numismatic notes by L. Mildenberg, 721–8, and E. M. Yamauchi, *Persia and the Bible* (Grand Rapids, Mich., 1990). Standard histories of ancient Israel also cover the Persian period.

For general histories of the period which make use of both the Greek and non-Greek sources, see Chester G. Starr's important 'Greeks and Persians in the Fourth Century B.C. (Part 1)', *Iranica Antiqua* 11 (1975) 39–99, and 'Part 2', *Iranica Antiqua* 12 (1977) 49–115, and S. Hornblower, *The Greek World, 479–323 BC* (New York, 1983).

For histories of the Achaemenid period, see A. T. Olmstead, *History of the Persian Empire* (Chicago, 1948); I. Gershevitch, ed., *The Cambridge History of Iran, II (CHI II): The Median and Achaemenian Periods*, (Cambridge, 1985); Cook, *Persian Empire*; R. N. Frye, 'History of Ancient Iran', *Handbuch der Altertums-wissenschaft III*[7] (Munich, 1984); R. Ghirshman, *Persia from the Origins to Alexander the Great* (London, 1964). The journal *Achaemenid History* is also an important source.

Articles on the Phoenicians in this period have appeared regularly in *Studia Phoenicia*. See also J. Elayi's series of books and articles (see below).

matters.[34] Herodotus brings to life this age when foreigners travelled regularly to the western regions of the Persian Empire, the era of Athens' clashes with Darius and Xerxes, when Greek mercenaries served the highest bidder—Greek, Egyptian, Sicilian, Carthaginian, Cypriot or Persian.[35] Among the artisans at both Pasargadae and Persepolis in the Persian heartland were Egyptians and Ionian Greeks.[36] In the late fifth century, the devastations of the Peloponnesian War forced artists on the Greek mainland (many of whom had previously come there from Ionia) to migrate west to Magna Graecia and Sicily, east to the urban Greek and Persian regions of coastal Asia Minor, and south to Phoenicia.[37]

Throughout the Persian period, the seafaring Phoenicians were technically Persian subjects providing their overlords with ships and sailors for the Persian navy. However, they also prospered mightily by their own extensive commercial relations with the Mediterranean world.[38] Phoenicia proper, as well as important southern Levantine coastal cities such as Dor, Joppa, and Ashkelon, and settlements occupied or administered by Sidon and Tyre[39] must surely have been Samaria's window onto the larger world, just as a half-millennium before, Phoenician artisans were called upon to build the palace and temple of King Solomon.

Economically, in the eastern Mediterranean, particularly Phoenicia and the cities of Asia Minor, the fourth century was a time of marked prosperity. Starr points out that the large fourth-century hoards of Cilician and other coins found in areas along the southern coast of Asia Minor often contain Phoenician and Cypriot issues, a good

---

[34] J. M. Cook, 'The Rise of the Achaemenids and Establishment of their Empire', *CHI II*, 271ff., and Christopher Tuplin, 'The Administration of the Achaemenid Empire', *Coinage and Administration in the Athenian and Persian Empires*, I. Carradice, ed. (BAR International Series 343; 1987) 111. Cf. also Hornblower, *Greek World*, 72, and Hornblower's far-ranging *Mausolus* (Oxford, 1982) 77 and *passim*.

Among others, P. Briant in his 'Polythéismes et empire unitaire', *Les grandes figure religieuses, Fonctionnement pratique et symbolique dans l'antiquité (Besançon 25–26 avril 1986)* (Paris, 1986) 425–43, and M. C. Root in 'From the Heart: Powerful Persianisms in the Art of the Western Empire', *Achaemenid History VI: Asia Minor and Egypt: Old Cultures in a New Empire,* eds. A. Kuhrt and H. Sancisi-Weerdenburg (Leiden, 1991) 1–29, argue that Persia's famous *laissez faire* attitude was by no means a sign of imperial indifference or passivity.

Objects clearly of Persian manufacture or style rarely come to light in Syria-Palestine (Stern, *Material Culture*, 236–7). So far, no Persian gold Darics and only a few other types of Persian imperial coins have been found in Palestine (U. Rappaport, 'Numismatics', *CHJ I*, 29).

[35] J. Elayi, 'The Phoenician Cities in the Persian Period', *JANESCU* 12 (1980) 18, notes the Phoenician use of mercenaries in the first half of the fourth century (via Diodorus 16.41.4–6). Stern, *Material Culture* (157, fig. 268) mentions Greek helmets, which presumably belonged to mercenaries of the fifth-fourth centuries, found underwater off the coasts of Ashdod and Ashkelon.

[36] C. Nylander, *Ionians at Pasargadae: Studies in Old Persian Architecture* (Uppsala, 1970) and M. Roaf, *Sculpture and Sculptors at Persepolis, Iran* 21 (London, 1983). For additional references see also Starr, 'Greeks', 57 n. 19. M. C. Root cautions against an excessive focus on Greek influence at Persepolis in 'The Persepolis Perplex', *Ancient Persia: The Art of an Empire,* ed. D. Schmandt-Besserat (Malibu, 1980) 8–11.

[37] Hornblower, *Greek World*, 171. On the subject of artists' mobility in the ancient world, see C. Zaccagnini, 'Patterns of Mobility among Ancient Near Eastern Craftsmen', *JNES* 42 (1983) 245–64, and T. S. Kawami, 'Greek Art and Persian Taste: Some Animal Sculptures from Persepolis', *AJA* 90 (1986) 259–67.

[38] Cf. A. M. Bisi, 'Ateliers phéniciens dans le monde égéen', *Studia Phoenicia* 5 (1987) 225–37.

[39] J. Elayi, 'Studies in Phoenician Geography during the Persian Period', *JNES* 41 (1982) 104; the relevant ancient source is the *Periplus* of Pseudo-Scylax (see K. Galling, 'Die syrisch-palästinische Küste nach der Beschreibung bei Pseudo-Skylax', *Zeitschrift des Deutschen Palästina-Vereins* 61 [1938] 66–96).

illustration of the connection between these areas and south coastal Asia Minor.[40] Starr further writes that:

> it would seem evident that Persian rule did not seriously impede the great progress which is evident in the coinage and physical remains of the era. Internal stability and the evolution of trading activity had produced a situation in which marked advance could occur.[41]

Under the Achaemenian Persians, the city of Samaria was the capital of an administrative province (מדינה), also called Samaria.[42] Between 375 and 335, the period of the Samaria Papyri, the Persians engaged in repeated attempts to regain control of Egypt using the Syro-Palestinian coast as the launching point.[43] How much the Satraps' Revolt of 366–360 affected Palestine is a matter of dispute;[44] Sidon was apparently sympathetic to the rebels, but how deeply Samaria and Judah were involved, if at all, is unclear. A decade later (around 350) Tennes, the king of Sidon, appears to have led a revolt against the Persians, a rebellion which was finally put down in 345 when Artaxerxes III sacked Sidon.[45]

With a dearth of both biblical and extrabiblical references to Judah and Samaria in the fourth century, it is difficult to determine how much of a role they played in these struggles between Egypt, Persia, and Phoenicia. Samaria and Judah are absent from ancient listings of participants in either the Satraps' Revolt or the Tennes Rebellion. Stern has pointed to the apparent stability of the Samarian ruling house (the Sanballat family) as a sign that 'these provinces did not suffer damage in the continuous warfare that took place in the coastal plain throughout the century'.[46]

---

[40] Starr, 'Greeks, Part 1', 96.

[41] Starr, 'Greeks, Part 1', 87. This prosperity led nevertheless to a disastrous attempt at independence by Sidon, in the mid-fourth century.

[42] There is much debate over the status of Judaea in the Persian period. See N. Avigad, *Bullae and Seals from a Post-Exilic Judean Archive*, Qedem 4 (1976); Stern, 'Persian', 82–6; E. Stern, 'New Evidence on the Administrative Division of Palestine in the Persian Period', *Achaemenid History IV: Centre and Periphery,* eds. A. Kuhrt and H. Sancisi-Weerdenburg (1990) 221–6, and K. Hoglund, *Achaemenid Imperial Administration in Syria-Palestine and the Missions of Ezra and Nehemiah* (Atlanta, 1992) 69–96.

For discussions of the Persian period in Palestine which take Samaria more fully into account, see G. W. Ahlström's idiosyncratic *History of Ancient Palestine from the Palaeolithic Period to Alexander's Conquest* (Sheffield, 1993) chap. 21; F. M. Cross, Jr., 'Samaria and Jerusalem: the Early History of the Samaritans and their Relations with the Jews' (Hebrew), *The Restoration - The Persian Period* (in the series ההיסטוריה של עם ישראל), ed. H. Tadmor (Jerusalem, 1983) 148–58, and M. Smith, *Palestinian Parties and Politics that Shaped the Old Testament*[2] (New York, 1987). See also studies of the book of Chronicles' positive attitude toward the North: H. Williamson, *Israel in the Books of Chronicles* (Cambridge [UK], 1977); R. Braun, 'A Reconsideration of the Chronicler's Attitude toward the North', *JBL* 96 (1977) 59–62; S. Japhet, 'Conquest and Settlement in Chronicles', *JBL* 98 (1979) 205–18.

[43] Attempts were made in 375, 350/1, 343. The Persians were successful in 343.

[44] R. A. Moysey, 'Observations on the numismatic evidence relating to the great satrapal revolt of 362/1 B.C.', *Revue des études anciennes* 91 (1989) 136–7.

[45] See D. Barag, 'The Effects of the Tennes Rebellion on Palestine', *BASOR* 183 (1966) 6–12. However, the destruction levels assigned by Barag to the Tennes Rebellion cannot be dated to any specific period in the fourth century or ascribed to any specific conquering power.

[46] Stern, 'Persian', 77.

In the provincial capital of Samaria, patrician Samarian families governed essentially as officials of the Persian administration.[47] During the fifth and fourth centuries, the office of governor appears to have been dynastic, belonging to the Sanballat family which remained in control until the beginning of the Hellenistic era.[48] Most renowned among the bullae from the Wadi Daliyeh is the 'Sanballat sealing' (WD **22**) which reads in palaeo-Hebrew '[Belonging to Yešaᶜ]yahu son of [San]ballaṭ, Governor of Samaria' and dates to the early reign of Artaxerxes III (358–338).[49]

The Sanballat of this sealing (Sanballat II, in Cross's reconstruction) was probably the grandson of the first Sanballat (Sanballat I) to rule as governor of Samaria.[50] The Bible describes in some detail the troubled encounters in the second half of the fifth century between Sanballat I and his southern counterpart, Nehemiah, the Governor of Judah (Neh 4:1-7 [Eng.]; 6:1-14). In spite of the foreign family name, the Sanballats appear to have been YHWH worshippers; prominent members of the Sanballat family bore such Yahwistic names as Yeshayahu, Delaiah, and Shemaiah.

Thus far there is no evidence of Persian military authorities or bureaucrats posted to the province of Samaria. No officials bearing Persian names are mentioned either in the fourth-century Samaria Papyri[51] or, earlier, in the letters sent in the fifth century to Samaria from the Jewish colony at Elephantine in Upper Egypt. Aside from the royal names Artaxerxes and Darius, Cross identified only three names with Persian elements in the Samaria Papyri.[52]

Even in a cultural hinterland like Samaria, the internationalist atmosphere of the Persian period may well have influenced one's choice of seal and seal type. Behind the remarkably varied Greek and Persian imagery displayed on the seals of these wealthy Samarians and their non-Samarian business partners there were no doubt the subtly compelling factors of prestige and/or 'cultural receptivity'.[53] Evidence both from Persepolis and from the western Persian Empire indicates that high satrapal officials and influential underlings such as local dynasts or large landowners shared a liking for Greek art.[54] In the great Anatolian satrapy whose capital was Sardis, Greek-style

---

[47] Stern, 'Persian', 81.

[48] Cross, 'Dâliyeh', 58–63.

[49] WD **22** has been sufficiently published elsewhere. See Cross, 'Dâliyeh', 47, figs. 34–5 and Cross, 'Papyri', pl 61. The sealing was found affixed to Papyrus 5.

[50] See Cross, 'Aspects' (revised version in 'A Reconstruction of the Judean Restoration', *JBL* 94 [1975] 4–18). See also *ABD*, s.v. 'Sanballat'.

[51] Cross, personal communication.

[52] Cross (personal communication) reports that the names are בנברת (Bagabart), חתן (which may have the same presumed Iranian background as the name Tattenay found in Ezra 5 and 6), and יהובגה (Yahubagah). The latter name, which means 'YHWH is God', probably belonged to an adherent of the Israelite cult of YHWH.

[53] I. Winter, 'Perspective on the "Local Style" of Hasanlu IVB: A Study in Receptivity', *Mountains and Lowlands: Essays in the Archaeology of Greater Mesopotamia, Bibliotheca Mesopotamica* 7, eds. L. D. Levine and T. C. Young, Jr. (1977) 371–86, and a companion study which discusses the preservation of ethnicity, L. Marfoe, 'Empire and Ethnicity in Syrian Society: "From Archaelogy to Historical Sociology" Revisited', *Archéologie au Levant* (Receuil Roger Saidah), *Collection de la Maison de l'Orient Méditerranéen* 12, Série Archéologique 9 (1982) 463–79.

[54] Root, 'Heart', 19–22; T. Kawami, 'Greek Art and Persian Taste'; W. S. Smith, *Interconnections in the Ancient Near East* (New Haven, 1965); S. Hornblower's *Mausolus* (Oxford, 1982) deals extensively with the issue of Hellenization in the East before Alexander (see especially p. vii); see also W. A. P. Childs, *The City Reliefs of Lycia*

remains outnumber Persian.[55] Only occasionally did the decision by Persian subjects to patronize artists working in the Greek rather than Persian style signal a rejection of Persian hegemony.[56] Conversely, non-Persian subjects of the Great King appear to have established game parks (παράδεισοι) on the Persian model for Persian-style hunting, and to have built palaces in imitation of their Persian masters.[57]

In Phoenicia, Samaria's northern neighbour, local rulers patronized artists working in both the Greek and Persian modes. In the ruins of a Persian period palace at Sidon, excavators discovered animal column capitals in the style of Persepolis.[58] Stylistic hybrids are found; from Sidon come sarcophagi and other sculpture with Phoenician or Anatolian decorative elements but which are Greek in the narrative reliefs which dominate the work.[59] The very Greek reliefs on the so-called Alexander Sarcophagus from late fourth-century Sidon show the central figure as a Greek, his royal Phoenician ally wears Persian garb,[60] and scenes with conventional imperial Persian symbolism (i.e. Persian Court Style) decorate the shield interiors of the Persian warriors.[61]

The patrician men and women[62] of Samaria probably followed upper-class Phoenicians in their tastes and inclinations.[63] The variety of imagery and the seal types attested to by the Wadi Daliyeh bullae suggest that Phoenicia was the cultural mediator between Samaria and the outside world. Even during the divided monarchy (922–587) Samaria had maintained closer relations with Phoenicia than had Judah, and the

---

(Princeton, 1978) and J. Borchhardt, 'Zur Herrschaft der Achaimeniden in der Bildkunst Lykiens', *AMI*, *Ergänzungsband* 6 (1979) 239–40.

[55] G. M. A. Hanfmann, *From Croesus to Constantine* (Ann Arbor, 1975) 15. But note also the cautionary comments of Root in 'Heart', esp. 7–15.

[56] For example, philhellene Cypriote rebels against Persia in the fourth century (Hornblower, *Greek World*, 292–3). See also J. Borchhardt, 'Herrschaft', 239–40.

[57] Hornblower, *Mausolus*, 7; J. K. Anderson, *Hunting in the Ancient World* (Berkeley, 1985) 61; M. Dunand, 'Les rois de Sidon au temps des Perses', *Mélanges de l'Université de Saint Joseph* 49 (1975–6), 491–9.

[58] Dunand, 'Les rois de Sidon', 491–9; C. H. Clermont-Ganneau, 'Le paradeisos royal achéménide de Sidon', *RB* 30 (1921) 106–8; G. Contenau, 'Deuxième mission archéologique à Sidon [1920]', *Syria* 4 (1923) 276, pls 43–4. Cf. Stern, *Material Culture*, 60, 66, fig. 65.

See entries on WD **31** and WD **18**.

[59] J. Elayi, *Pénétration grecque en Phénicie sous l'empire perse* (Paris, 1988) 31–2, 112–13; V. von Graeve, *Der Alexandersarcophag und seine Werkstatt, Istanbuler Forschungen* 28 (1970); I. Kleeman, *Der Satrapen Sarkophag aus Sidon* (Berlin, 1958); R. Stucky, *Tribune d'Echmoun: ein griechischer Reliefzyklus des 4. Jahrhunderts v. Chr. in Sidon, Antike Kunst*, Beiheft 13 (Basel, 1984); B. S. Ridgway, *Fifth Century Styles in Greek Sculpture* (Princeton, 1981) 149–51; R. Fleischer, *Der Klagenfrauensarkophag aus Sidon* (Tübingen, 1983).

[60] Von Graeve, *Alexandersarcophag*; cf. also Anderson, *Hunting*, 73.

[61] Root, 'Heart', 12–13. J. Borchhardt suggests that a fourth-century Phoenician king commissioned the Greek-style 'Satrap Sarcophagus' with iconography expressly emphasizing the Phoenician's dependence on the Persian king in 'Die Dependenz des Königs von Sidon vom persischen Grosskönig', *Beiträge zur Altertumskunde Kleinasiens, Festschrift für Kurt Bittel*, eds. R. M. Boehmer and H. Hauptman (Mainz am Rhein, 1983) 105–20.

[62] Samaria Papyrus 2 (Gropp, *Samaria Papyri*, 40) records a transaction in which a woman is the purchaser. She may well have sealed the document. There is evidence of women in ancient Israel not only possessing, but also using seals, sometimes in an official capacity (cf. the discussion of WD **21B**).

[63] For aspects of this 'Phoenician connection', see below and in discussions of individual bullae.

material culture of Persian Samaria points to the same relatively outward-looking cultural orientation in the Persian period.[64]

Seals and Sealing in the Near East and Greece: An Overview

Any discussion of the Daliyeh bullae must necessarily draw upon what is known of traditional images, seal types, and sealing practices in three areas of the ancient world: Mesopotamia, Syria-Palestine, and Greece, for in the Persian period, these cultural entities merge, overlap, and interact. The Achaemenid Persians borrowed immensely from Mesopotamia; they assimilated Babylonian administrative know-how to run their empire, and to native Neo-Elamite iconography they added the Mesopotamian visual vocabulary of power to present the Persian king to his subjects.[65] Before the arrival of the Persians in 539, Syria-Palestine, including Phoenicia, had belonged to the Neo-Babylonian Empire. The Phoenicians traded with Greece.[66] Geography and politics alike brought East Greece and satrapal Persia into frequent contact. The archaeological record indicates a distinct cultural and artistic philhellenism in western 'Persian' cities and provinces.[67]

Well into the first millennium, legal documents in Mesopotamia were inscribed in cuneiform script on clay tablets. To ensure the legality of the transaction recorded on a clay tablet, the interested parties—male and female buyers, sellers, witnesses—signed the tablet not with a signature, but with its legal equivalent, a cylinder seal (and increasingly in the Persian period, a stamp seal); cuneiform letters were likewise 'signed' with a seal.[68] Portable property—jars of provisions, for example—could also be

---

[64] Note the ornate bronze leg of what was an Achaemenid chair or throne found at Samaria. It may have been produced in Samaria itself (Stern, *Material Culture*, 143 and fig. 237). See also E. Stern, 'A Phoenician Art Centre in Post-Exilic Samaria', *Atti del I. congresso internazionale di studi fenici e punici I* (Rome, 1983) 211–12. See also Stern's 'Achaemenid Clay Rhyta from Palestine', *IEJ* 32, 37 and fig. 1.1. Note also 'Samaria' in the table of Greek pottery finds in Palestine in Stern, *Material Culture*, appendix II.

[65] M. C. Root, *The King and Kingship in Achaemenid Art: Essays on the Creation of an Iconography of Empire*, Acta Iranica 19 (Leiden, 1979) is the classic study on this subject.

[66] 'Greece' must be understood as a cultural term, encompassing the Greek mainland and the Greek settlements of Sicily and Magna Graecia, also the cities and islands of coastal Asia Minor which were periodically under Greek domination.

[67] Boardman, *Diffusion*, pp. 39–64.

[68] J. Renger, 'Legal Aspects of Sealing in Ancient Mesopotamia', *Seals and Sealings in the Ancient Near East*, eds. McGuire Gibson and R. D. Biggs (Bibliotheca Mespotamica VI; Malibu, 1977) 75–88; also W. Leemans, 'La fonction des sceaux, apposés à des contracts vieux-babyloniens', Zikir Sumim, Assyriological Studies Presented to F. R. Kraus on the Occasion of his Seventieth Birthday, eds. G. van Driel et al., (Leiden, 1982) 219–44, and D. Collon, *First Impressions: Cylinder Seals in the Ancient Near East* (Chicago, 1987) 5–7.

At different periods of history, if one had no seal, there were alternatives; one could make a nail mark, or leave in the clay an impression of the hem of one's garment (A. Finet, 'Les symboles du cheveu, du bord du vêtement et de l'ongle en Mésopotamie', *Annales du Centre d'Études des Religions, III, Eschatologie et cosmologie* [Brussels, n.d.], 101–30). Shells were apparently also used as seals (D. Homès-Fredericq, 'Coquillages et Glyptique Araméenne', *Insight Through Images*, ed. M. Kelly-Buccellati [Malibu, 1986] 111–18).

For seal production and workshops in Persian period Mesopotamia see E. Porada, 'Greek Coin Impressions of Ur', *Iraq* XXII (1960) 228–34. The guild of free artisans discussed in D. S. Weisberg, *Guild Structure and Political*

sealed. In Syria-Palestine during the first half of the first millennium where documents were written on papyrus and parchment, mostly stamp seals were similarly used as 'legal signatures' and property markers.[69] This practice was also customary in Archaic and Classical Greece.[70] Besides protecting property and assuring legality, seals were symbols of political and religious office in ancient Mesopotamia, Persia, Israel, Phoenicia, and Greece.[71] Seals were regularly used to administer royal enterprises.[72] The Mesopotamian evidence shows that seals 'were considered to be an integral part of their owners' persons'.[73] An oracle of doom in Jeremiah conveys something akin to this understanding in ancient Israel: '"I swear", says YHWH, "even though Coniah, the son of Jehoiakim, king of Judah were the seal ring (חותם) on my right hand, nevertheless, I would tear you off and give you into the hand of those who seek your life . . ."' (Jer 22:24). The same concept appears in Song of Songs 8:6.

Just as personal names in the ancient world had magico-religious significance, so did seals. They were amulets 'meant to protect the wearer and to bring good fortune'.[74] It is not surprising to find that seals in both Mesopotamia and Greece were presented to

---

Allegiance in Early Achaemenid Mesopotamia, Yale Near Eastern Researches 1 (New Haven, 1967) may have included seal engravers.

[69] N. Avigad, 'Hebrew Seals and Sealings and their Significance for Biblical Research', *Congress Volume*, VTSup 40, ed. J. A. Emerton (Leiden, 1988) 7–16.

[70] J. Boardman, *Greek Gems and Finger Rings: Early Bronze to Late Classical* (London, 1970) 428–9; G. M. A. Richter, *The Engraved Gems of the Greeks, Etruscans and Romans*, part one: *Engraved Gems of the Greeks and the Etruscans, A History of Greek Art in Miniature* (London, 1968) 1–4; cf. another example of seal usage in Xenophon *Lac. Pol.* 6.3–4.

[71] WD **22**, the 'Sanballat' seal, had such a function.
Mesopotamia: I. Winter, 'Legitimization of Authority through Image and Legend: Seals Belonging to Officials in the Administrative Bureaucracy of the Ur III State', *The Organization of Power: Aspects of Bureaucracy in the Ancient Near East*, eds. McGuire Gibson and R. Biggs (Studies in Ancient Oriental Civilization, 46; Chicago, 1987) 69–106; Collon, *First Impressions*, 123–30; even the gods had seals (*idem*, 131–4).
Israel: Avigad, 'Hebrew Seals', 9–10; the tale of Jezebel using either King Ahab's seal or her own to forge official documents (1 Kings 21:8) comes especially to mind. See also Gen 41:41-42 and Esth 3:10-12; 8:2.
Greece: Boardman, *GGFR*, 429; Richter, *EGGE*, 1–4.
Persia: R. T. Hallock, 'The Use of Seals on the Persepolis Fortification Tablets', *Seals and Sealings*, 127–33.

[72] J. C. Greenfield, 'A Group of Phoenician City Seals', *IEJ* 35 (1985) 129–34; Avigad, 'Hebrew Seals', 12–13.

[73] E. Porada, 'Introduction', *Ancient Art in Seals*, ed. E. Porada (Princeton, 1980) 5.

[74] Porada, 'Introduction', *Ancient Art*, 3, 9–10. Cf. E. Reiner, 'Magic Figurines, Amulets and Talismans', *Monsters and Demons in the Ancient and Medievl Worlds: Papers Presented in Honor of Edith Porada*, ed. A. Farkas, et al. (Mainz, 1987) 27–36, and B. L. Goff, 'The Role of Amulets in Mesopotamian Ritual Texts', *Journal of the Warburg and Courtauld Institutes* 19 (1956) 1–39.
An excellent illustration of seal rings functioning as amulets is provided by a statue of a so-called Cypriot 'temple boy', from Idalion (now in the British Museum). He wears a necklace strung with seal rings and other pendants (illustrated in V. Tatton-Brown, *Ancient Cyprus* [British Museum, London, 1987] fig. 59).
For Greece, see Richter, *EGGE*, 3 and L. Gernet's study, 'The Mythical Idea of Value in Greece', in L. Gernet, *The Anthropology of Ancient Greece*, Eng. trans., J. Hamilton and B. Nagy (Baltimore, 1981) 85–7.
In the case of Egyptian-style scarab seals in use in Palestine, the amuletic function seems to have predominated over the signatory in the Iron Age and Persian period (*Ashmolean/ANES III*, xi); cf. O. Tufnell, *Studies on Scarab Seals ii: Scarab Seals and their Contribution to the History of the early Second Millennium* (Warminster, 1984).

the gods as votive offerings.[75] In addition, seals were status symbols and ornaments, valued simply as jewellery. There is evidence of purely aesthetic appreciation of one's seal in Greece and the Near East[76] and also of the interaction between patron and seal carver.[77]

Seals and seal impressions show that in Mesopotamia and Persia, older Neo-Babylonian contest and cult scenes continued into the succeeding Persian period.[78] However, with the reign of Darius I late in the sixth century, the quasi-official Persian 'Court Style' began to take over in both large-scale and glyptic art.[79] A predominant court-style motif consists of the Persian Hero[80] worshipping at an altar or battling monsters with hand, knife, or bow; more elaborate variations introduce date palms and a hovering figure formerly identified as the Persian deity Ahura Mazda. Other Court Style seals and sealings show fantastic creatures such as sphinxes or scorpion men, all with the head of the Persian Hero, and Persian hunters on horseback or foot.[81] Alongside the 'Court Style', however, one finds scaraboids of decidedly Greek stylistic and iconographic influence and hybrids of Greek and Persian designs.[82]

The Achaemenid Persians, maintaining their vast Near Eastern empire from the late sixth to the late fourth centuries, presided over a monumental transformation in bureaucratic technology which had been initiated in the eighth century by their imperial predecessors, the Neo-Babylonians.[83] 'Old fashioned' clay tablets, the norm for over two millennia in Mesopotamian chanceries, gave way to lightweight 'high-tech' papyrus, leather, or parchment documents written in Aramaic with reed pen and ink.[84]

---

[75] Mesopotamia: Collon, *First Impressions*, 131; E. Porada, 'Of Professional Seal Cutters and Nonprofessionally Made Seals', *Seals and Sealings,* 7–14.

Greece: Boardman, *GGFR,* 428, reference to temple inventories.

[76] W. W. Hallo, 'The Seals of Assur-Remanni', *Symbolae Biblicae et Mesopotamicae Francisco Mario Theodoro de Liagre Böhl dedicatae* (Leiden, 1973) 180–84, and Richter, *EGGE,* 4.

[77] Root, 'Heart', 19–21 and M. C. Root, 'Circles of Artistic Programming: Strategies for Studying Creative Process at Persepolis', *Investigating Artistic Environments in the Ancient Near East,* ed. A. C. Gunter (Madison, Wisc., 1990) 130–31.

[78] Collon, *First Impressions*, 83; see also H. Frankfort, *Cylinder Seals: A Documentary Essay on the Art and Religion of the Ancient Near East* (London, 1939).

[79] R. Zettler, 'On the Chronological Range of Neo-Babylonian and Achaemenid Seals', *JNES* 38 (1979) 257–70. The over 1300 different seal images on the Persepolis Fortification tablets are currently being catalogued; see M. Garrison, *Seal Workshops and Artists in Persepolis: A Study of Seal Impressions Preserving the Theme of Heroic Encounter on the Persepolis Fortification and Treasury Tablets* (Ph.D. diss., University of Michigan, 1988) and M. C. Root, 'Seal Impressions on the Persepolis Fortification Tablets, a Progress Report', *DATA (Achaemenid History Newsletter)* (February 1993) 9.

[80] For more on the Persian Hero, see entry for WD **4**, p. 214ff.

[81] M. C. Root devotes considerable attention to the political nuances of the most common Court Style images; see Root, *King,* 303; note also 118–22 and chap. 8, part B. See entry on WD **4**, p. 214ff.; Moorey, 'Metalwork', 864–5.

[82] See L. Legrain, *Seal Cyclinders, Ur Excavations* X (Pennsylvania, 1951), and E. F. Schmidt, *Persepolis II: Contents of the Treasury and other Discoveries*, Oriental Institute Publications LXIX (Chicago, 1957).

[83] Renger, 'Legal Aspects', 78.

[84] A. L. Oppenheim, 'The Babylonian Evidence of Achaemenian Rule in Mesopotamia', *CHI II*, 571 (with references), notes the increasing use of leather, parchment and even papyrus-like writing materials. See also Root's

New technology tends to wipe out many materials and practices which were adjuncts of the old. The automobile displaced not only horses, but stables and carriages and blacksmiths. In Mesopotamia, as Aramaic pushed cuneiform Akkadian aside[85] and papyrus rolls supplanted clay tablets, stamp seals, not cylinders, became the seals of choice.

Aramaic was the official language of the Achaemenid chancellery, and the switch from cylinders to stamps came about partly because of the ascendancy of the Aramaic language whose alphabetic script, so much simpler and more efficient than syllabic cuneiform, could be written on papyrus. It is hardly surprising that the Neo-Babylonians and then the Persians adopted the stamp seal along with other Aramaean practices.[86]

Cylinder seals and clay tablets did not entirely disappear in the Achaemenid period, however. The administrative Persepolis Fortification and Treasury texts were written in Elamite on clay tablets.[87] Perhaps because the Persians tapped into time-honoured and prestigious Mesopotamian symbols of authority in their art and propaganda, they maintained the cylinder for official and administrative use,[88] but not to the exclusion of stamp seals in official circles.[89] Stamp seals and signet rings were certainly preferred by private individuals.

Of all ancient peoples, the Phoenicians (both east and west) were the most enthusiastic culture sponges. During the Persian period, Phoenician scarabs and scaraboids are found—occasionally bearing only an inscription, though more often with an inscription and an image or an image alone—with a dazzling mixture of Egyptian, Greek, and North Syrian/Mesopotamian iconography, often on the same seal; the so-called 'green jasper' scarabs in particular fall into this category.[90] Phoenician seals of

---

comments concerning L. Bregstein's study of the Murashu (Nippur) sealings and of R. Wellenfels's current research on Hellenistic sealings from Uruk in *DATA* (*Achaemenid History Newsletter*) (Feb. 1993) 13.

Evidence of the use of papyrus for official Persian documents is found on the sealings from Daskyleion where excavators found the remains of what may have been a satrapal archive, including some 400 clay bullae with papyrus imprints (E. Akurgal, 'Les Fouilles de Daskyleion', *Anatolia* 1 [1956] 23 and more recently, D. Kaptan-Bayburtluoglu, 'A Group of Seal Impressions on the Bullae from Ergili/Daskyleion', *Epigraphica Anatolica* [1990] 16–17). Some of these bullae are impressed with a cylinder seal bearing the name of Xerxes (K. Balkan, 'Inscribed Bullae from Daskyleion-Ergili', *Anatolia* 4 [1959] 124–7). The bullae date from the mid-fifth to mid-fourth centuries.

[85] *Ashmolean/ANES III*, xi. The process began with the Neo-Assyrians. See H. Tadmor, 'The Aramaization of Assyria: Aspects of Western Impact', *Mesopotamien und seine Nachbarn*, part 2, eds. H.-J. Nissen and J. Renger (Berlin, 1982) 449–70. Cf. J. Naveh and J. C. Greenfield, 'Hebrew and Aramaic in the Persian Period', *CHJ I*, 115–29, and Cook, *Persian Empire*, 85.

[86] *Ashmolean/ANES III*, xi and 53–64. Cf. J. C. Greenfield, 'Babylonian-Aramaic Relationship', *Mesopotamie und seine Nachbarn*, part 2, 471–82 (see above, n. 85).

[87] R. T. Hallock, 'The Evidence of the Persepolis Tablets', *CHI II*, 588 ff.

[88] Collon, *First Impressions*, 90; Moorey, 'Metalwork and Glyptic', *CHI II*, 864.

[89] Note the archival evidence from Daskyleion cited above, n. 84.

[90] Basic studies of Phoenician glyptic, especially as regards the Persian period: W. Culican, 'The Iconography of Some Phoenician Seals and Seal Impressions', *Australian Journal of Biblical Archaeology* 1 (1968–71) 50–103; *Ashmolean/ANES III*, 70–71; P. Zazoff, *Die Antiken Gemmen* (Munich, 1983) 85–98; D. Collon, 'The Green Jasper Cylinder Seal Workshop,' *Insight Through Images: Studies in Honor of Edith Porada*, eds. M. Kelly-Buccellati, P. Matthiae and M. Van Loon (Malibu, 1986) 57–70; J. Boardman, 'Scarabs and Seals: Greek, Punic and Related

the fifth and fourth centuries with Greek designs often appear to be modeled on older Archaic Greek scarabs.[91] Boardman has speculated that a workshop in Phoenicia produced simple gold rings decorated with Greek motifs.[92]

In Archaic and Classical Greece two seal types predominated: scaraboids and metal finger rings.[93] The extant evidence suggests inscribed seals were less common than in Mesopotamia or Syria-Palestine.[94] Devices on Greek seals mirror the subjects of Archaic and Classical art on a larger scale; similar compositions are found engraved on seals, painted on vases, and executed in bronze and marble sculpture. Greek seals also differ from Mesopotamian and Syro-Palestinian seals in illustrating many more identifiable figures from the Greek mythic repertoire as well as scenes of everyday life, war, and nature.

In Israel and Judah, the common seal type from the second millennium had been the stone stamp seal, usually in the form of a scarab or scaraboid, though conical stamp seals also appear frequently in the Persian period.[95] When inscribed, the face of these seals was often divided into horizontal registers engraved with the name of the seal owner and a patronymic. In marked contrast with the glyptic art of both Mesopotamia and Greece, inscribed seals from pre-exilic Israel and Judah and post-exilic Judah[96] are overwhelmingly aniconic with an occasional floral motif incorporated into the registration line. However, some inscribed Hebrew seals from both the North and South do have images—lions, winged sun disks, locusts, lyres, ships, fish—along with the names; a few of these seals were engraved in the Phoenician manner with Egyptianizing motifs.[97] Nevertheless, as Avigad has observed of inscribed seals, 'the

Types', *Tharros: A Catalogue of Material in the British Museum from Phoenician and Other Tombs at Tharros, Sardinia* London, 1987) 98–105; P. Bordreuil, *Catalogue des sceaux ouest-sémitiques inscrits de la Bibliothèque Nationale, du Musée du Louvre et du Musée biblique de Bible et Terre Sainte* (Bibliothèque Nationale, Paris, 1986) *passim*.

[91] J. Spier, *Ancient Gems and Finger Rings, Catalogue of the Collections, The J. Paul Getty Museum* (Malibu, 1992) 52.

[92] Boardman, *GGFR*, 221, Boardman's 'de Clercq group'.

[93] The three major modern studies of Greek glyptic art are, Richter, *EGGE*; Boardman, *GGFR*; and Zazoff, *AG*.

[94] Richter, *EGGE*, 4.

[95] *Ashmolean/ANES III*, xi. Avigad's studies of Hebrew and other West Semitic seals are most important. A partial bibliography of his writing on glyptics appears in *ErIsr* 18 (Nahman Avigad Volume) (1985) 62–3. See especially his article, 'Hebrew Seals'. See also E. Lemaire, 'Recherches actuelles sur les sceaux nord-ouest sémitiques', *VT* 38 (1988) 221–30. Note the regular publications on Israelite glyptic by O. Keel and his associates, among them O. Keel, 'Ancient Seals and the Bible. A Review Article', *JAOS* 106 (1986) 307–11, and the series *Studien zu den Stempelsiegeln aus Palästina/Israel* which began in 1985.

Stern summarizes the glyptic evidence from Persian-period Palestine in *Material Culture*, chap. 7, 196–214.

[96] Note the Israel Museum exhibition catalogue by R. Hestrin and M. Dayagi-Mendels, *Inscribed Seals: First Temple Period, Hebrew, Ammonite, Moabite, Phoenician and Aramaic* (Jerusalem, 1979). See also Avigad, *Bullae and Seals*.

[97] See Avigad's discussion of Hebrew seals and the Second Commandment in 'Hebrew Seals', 14–16. The evidence concerning ancient 'Hebrew seals' is ambiguous. As Keel trenchantly points out ('Ancient Seals and the Bible', 311), the vast majority of seals of all periods found in excavations at Judaean and Israelite sites are pure design seals primarily in the Egypto-Phoenician style; in other words, Hebrew-speaking Judaeans and Israelites owned such seals.

iconography of the Hebrew seals contains, except for one or two uncertain instances, no pagan cultic scenes or emblems of the kind to be found on other seals, such as the worship of astral symbols and deities'.[98]

The two seals from Wadi Daliyeh inscribed in palaeo-Hebrew (WD **22** and WD **23**) do not contradict this assertion, and indeed, there are no 'pagan cultic scenes' or 'astral symbols' on any of the Daliyeh bullae. There are, however, numerous images and scenes from decidedly non-Israelite artistic traditions; predominantly Greek and Persian. For the most part, the seals seem to have been scaraboids and rings.

It would be expected that as imperial agents the Sanballats and other Samarian nobles would conform, at least in part, to Persian bureaucratic practices.[99] The aniconic 'Sanballat' sealing (WD **22**) is clearly 'official', but differs little from Hebrew seals used by Judaean officials in late pre-exilic and post-exilic times.[100] WD **17**, WD **36**, and WD **51** with their purely Persian Court Style designs might have come from cylinders,[101] the type of seal Persian officials were liable to use.[102] The rather small size is not problematic; middle-level public officials at Nippur owned similarly tiny cylinders.[103] However, as at Nippur it is impossible to point to any particular seal image from Samaria, be it Greek or Persian, as denoting special status.[104] In fact, aside from WD **22** and WD **23** none of the Wadi Daliyeh bullae can confidently be matched up with a name on the papyri.[105] Perhaps at Samaria the private nature of the transactions recorded in the Samaria Papyri did not merit the symbolic presence of the Persian Empire in the form of 'official seals'.

The Mechanics of Sealing and the Wadi Daliyeh Bullae

While the legal formularies of fifth-century Elephantine (Egypt) and fourth-century Samaria differ,[106] the Aramaic papyri from the Jewish colony at Elephantine furnish

---

Nevertheless, on the basis of extant seal impressions, except in special cases (i.e. the winged disk as a royal Judaean symbol of the late eighth century) these anepigaphic seals seem not to have been used to seal property or documents. The functional and symbolic differences between inscribed and anepigraphic seals remains unclear.

[98] Avigad, 'Hebrew Seals', 15. On the other hand, C. Uehlinger proposes that such symbols as the sun disk and the lion on uninscribed 'Hebrew' seals relate to Israelite conceptions of YHWH (O. Keel and C. Uehlinger, *Göttinen, Götter und Gottessymbole* [Freiburg, 1992] esp. chaps. 6–10).

[99] They followed Neo-Babylonian-based Aramaic legal formularies. See Gropp, *Samaria Papyri*, viii–ix.

[100] Note the official sealings from Judaean archives published by N. Avigad, *Hebrew Bullae from the Time of Jeremiah* (Jerusalem, 1986) and *Bullae and Seals*.

[101] Pl XVII.1, 2, 3.

[102] P. R. S. Moorey, 'Metalwork and Glyptic', *CHI II*, 864.

[103] See discussion of cylinder seals in the single entry for WD **17**, **36**, and **51** (p. 209ff).

[104] Bregstein, *Seal Use*, 206–7.

[105] Cross reports (personal communication) that the preserved papyrus fragments do not contain the name 'Ishmael', which appears on three additional bullae—one each in the Hecht (pl XXIII.2) and Israel Museums published by Stern (Stern/Hecht, 'Hoard' drawing pl 1.1) and one in private hands (Meshorer-Qedar, *Coinage of Samaria*, 12).

[106] Gropp, *Samaria Papyri*, ix.

comparative information about the technicalities of sealing papyrus documents.[107] At Elephantine and Samaria the process was similar. After the document was written by a scribe and witnessed, it would be rolled up and flattened slightly; sometimes the roll would be folded in half or thirds. One or more pieces of string would be individually looped around the folded document and securely knotted. A pinch of soft clay would be rolled into a tiny ball, then formed between the fingers into a truncated cone shape. One cone of clay was pressed over the knot of each encircling string, and some or all of the parties in the transaction (witnesses, buyer, seller, etc.) applied their own seals to the clay. Sealings from Elephantine and elsewhere show that more than one seal might be pressed into a single clay bulla, sometimes as many separate seal impressions as would fit onto the bulla. However, with a few exceptions, one of which comes from Samaria Papyrus 1,[108] each preserved bulla from the Samaria Papyri bears only a single seal impression.

The principals to the transaction would of course have sealed the recording document, but the vast majority of the sealings on the Samaria Papyri must have been produced by witnesses whose listing in the papyri conventionally began with the Governor and ended with the Prefect.[109] Samaria Papyrus 1, the record of the slave sale on March 19, 335, supplies an example of fourth-century Samarian sealing practices.[110] The text preserves the names of the slave, the buyer and the seller and mentions 'trustworthy witnesses'.[111] Seven clay bullae (WD **11A**–WD **11G**), fairly evenly spaced, still adhered to the papyrus roll at the time of its purchase in 1962. The decipherable images included both Persian Court Style and Greek motifs. As preserved, the papyrus was 20 cm wide; originally its horizontal measurement was probably close to 43 cm.[112] If the preserved half of the papyrus with its seven bullae is any indication of the remainder, there could have been another seven bullae attached to Samaria Papyrus 1! Cross suggests the 'existence of a professional or publicly recognized class of witnesses who were regularly called upon to place their seals on legal documents'.[113] Unfortunately, the dearth of duplicate sealings among the bullae from Daliyeh diminishes the viability of this attractive theory.[114]

---

[107] J. D. Cooney in E. G. Kraeling, *The Brooklyn Museum Aramaic Papyri* (New Haven, 1953) 123ff; B. Porten, *Archives from Elephantine* (Berkeley, 1968), p. 214 and pl 14a in particular.

For a 'how to' drawing, cf. B. Porten, 'Aramaic Papyri in the Egyptian Museum: The Missing Endorsements', *The Word of the Lord Shall go Forth*, eds. C. L. Meyers and M. O'Connor (Winona Lake, Indiana, 1983) fig. 1. See also below, pl XII.1, 2, and Cross, 'Samaria Papyrus 1', *ErIsr* 18 (1985) pl 2, illustrating the rolled and sealed document; Avigad, *Hebrew Bullae*, 123 (figs. 1–4); O. Rubensohn, *Elephantine-Papyri* (Berlin, 1907) I (a group of early Hellenistic bullae).

[108] WD **11D**, unfortunately illegible; see also *DWD*, pl 100a (= pl 36, no. 4). See also Stern/Hecht, 'Hoard' drawing pl 2. 6 for a multiple sealing.

[109] Gropp, *Samaria Papyri*, 37.

[110] Cross, 'Samaria Papyrus 1', pl 2, and Gropp, *Samaria Papyri*, 3, 36–7.

[111] Witnesses were not always listed individually by name; a document may, as Cross observes in 'Samaria Papyrus 1', simply refer to 'trustworthy witnesses' (see Gropp, *Samaria Papyri*, 36–7).

[112] Cross, 'Samaria Papyrus 1', 7*.

[113] Cross, 'Samaria Papyrus 1', 15* and n. 56.

[114] The impression on WD **3A** repeats four more times; WD **5** and WD **16B** are duplicates. WD **11A** *might* be identical to WD **15A**. At least three Rockefeller Museum bullae may duplicate bullae from the Hecht group: WD **38**

Physically, the Daliyeh bullae are tiny; for the most part their height and width is less than 2 cm, and the actual seal impressions on them are even smaller. All the bullae are essentially truncated clay cones. Fingerprints visible on the outside edges are an expressive reminder of the people whose affairs are documented by the papyri.[115] The front of each bulla carries the seal impression, while the back almost always shows the imprint of the papyrus document it sealed.

In general, the clay is reddish brown, but thirteen bullae were partially or completely burned black.[116] When the burning is only partial, the unburnt portion of the bulla is reddish brown. It has been suggested that over the centuries, the natural decomposition of bat dung in the cave generated the heat which burned the bullae. Since the papyri do not appear to have been exposed to fire, this is puzzling. Perhaps the Taʿamireh Bedouin who found the papyri and bullae were somehow responsible for the burnt bullae. Most of the unburnt bullae were still attached to their strings. In quite a few cases, the loop of string remains uncut, as if the papyrus roll decayed and split under the string(s) which originally secured it.[117]

Actual fragments of papyrus still adhered to one or two bullae, but the front and back surfaces of many other bullae were sparsely dusted with tiny papyrus fibres.[118] Often, when one of these fibres fell away from the bulla it left a characteristic nick/impression in the clay. How did the fibres—basically papyrus dust—become embedded in the bullae? Once impressed, clay bullae could not be fired but were left to dry and harden in the air. It is also known from discoveries at Lachish and Elephantine, and from the account in Jeremiah 32, that important papyrus documents were often stored in earthenware jars.[119] Perhaps 'papyrus dust' from the older papyri accumulated in the store jars and stuck to the still-soft clay of the sealings on a newer document.

Consistently, the Daliyeh bullae show that they were impressed with the orientation of the seal design in mind. All the images are neatly parallel or perpendicular to the string.[120] However, the duplicate sealings WD **5** and WD **16B** show there is no real consistency in the choice between these two possible orientations. The string of WD **16B** is parallel to the vertical orientation of the image, while that of WD **5** is perpendicular. While this may appear to be an arcane detail, it shows that 'which side is up' on an unclear bulla cannot be determined from the placement of the string.

= 1M 82.19.941 (pl XXIII.5); WD **37** (pl XIII.2) = HM K63.K (pl XXIII.9); WD **55** (pl XIII.1 resembles HM K63.N [pl XXIII.11]).

[115] It might be useful to study the fingerprints on the legible and illegible bullae. Cf. S. A. Eriksson and P. Åström, *Fingerprints and Archaeology*, *Studies in Mediterranean Archaeology* 28 (1980).

[116] WD **7**, WD **9**, WD **24–5**, WD **27**, WD **30–4**, WD **39**, WD **52**, WD **55**.

[117] The string has yet to be analyzed.

[118] See entry for WD **1**.

[119] Y. Aharoni, *Investigations at Lachish: The Sanctuary and Residency*, *Lachish* V (Tel Aviv, 1975) 19–22 and Y. Aharoni, 'Trial Excavation in the "Solar Shrine" at Lachish', *IEJ* 18 (1968) 157ff, pl 11; Porten, *Archives*, 264; Jer 32: 6–15, 44.

[120] On five of the seven sealings on Samaria Papyrus 1, the seal outlines are still visible; all are ovals, placed with the short ends near the edges of the rolled document. Vertical seal designs appear to be oriented identically, and horizontal designs are 'on their sides.' Cf. Cross, 'Samaria Papyrus 1', pl II and Avigad, *Hebrew Bullae*, 123 (fig. 2).

The actual pressing of the seal into clay could be haphazard. For this reason, the images on a number of bullae are incomplete. Duplicate sealings demonstrate the uneven quality of the sealed image. WD **5** and WD **16B** are not equally clear; that the impression on WD **5** was produced more hastily than that on WD **16B** may be seen in the blurred lower portion of WD **5**. Uneven pressure applied during sealing will also distort the image. All these factors aggravate the natural abuses which the bullae suffered over the course of time.

The Wadi Daliyeh Bullae: Image Style and Seal Types

The search for parallels to the Near Eastern images among the bullae is a relatively simple process. Firstly, Persian period seals and seal impressions are sought out from controlled excavations at Palestinian sites,[121] for example, Tell Abu Hawam and the Phoenician cemetery at ʿAtlit. But the most fruitful sources of comparison are the numerous impressions on clay tablets from the excavations at Nippur and Ur[122] and at Persepolis.[123] Unexcavated Near Eastern seals and sealings in various museum collections, carefully considered, can also be of assistance. Locally issued coins may be usefully compared to seals.[124] At times it is helpful to examine Phoenician seals or ivories, and occasionally the present editor resorted to Persian or Phoenician reliefs or architectural ornamentation for comparisons.

The situation is somewhat more complicated in the case of the numerous Greek style seals. As with the Near Eastern bullae, glyptic parallels are best, but parallels from controlled excavations are less easily found.[125] Furthermore, the Greek glyptic repertoire is more varied than the Persian, as is emphatically the case with the Greek

---

[121] See Stern, *Material Culture*, chap. 7. For the Persian period seals at Tell Abu Hawam, cf. R. W. Hamilton, 'Excavations at Tell Abu Hawam', *QDAP* 4 (1935) 18, nos. 47–8; for seals from the fifth-fourth-century Phoenician cemetery at ʿAtlit, cf. C. N. Johns, 'Excavations at ʾAtlit (1930–31): The Southeast Cemetery', *QDAP* 2 (1933) 41–104; seals from Tell Keisan have been published by O. Keel, 'La glyptique de Tell Keisan 1971–1976', *Studien zu den Stempelsiegeln aus Palästina/Israel, III*, eds. O. Keel, M. Shuval, and C. Uehlinger (Freiburg, 1990) 163–260.

[122] Nippur: L. Legrain, *The Culture of the Babylonians from their Seals in the Collections of the Museum* (Philadelphia, 1925) pls 35–55, and L. Bregstein's study of the same sealings, *Seal Use in Fifth Century B.C. Nippur, Iraq: A Study of Seal Selection and Sealing Practice in the Murasu Archive* (Ph.D. diss., University of Pennsylvania, 1993). Ur: Legrain, *Ur*, pls 39–43.

[123] Schmidt, *Persepolis II* and M. Garrison, *Seal Workshops*. For other useful excavated Persian period corpora from within the empire, cf. W. M. Flinders Petrie, E. Mackay, and G. Wainwright, *Meydum and Memphis (III)* (London, 1910) pls 35–7; for the Daskyleion bullae see above n. 86.

[124] Most recently, Y. Meshorer, *Ancient Jewish Coinage*, vol. I (New York, 1982) and Meshorer-Qedar, *Coinage of Samaria*.

[125] Note D. M. Robinson, 'Metal and Minor Miscellaneous Finds', *Excavations at Olynthus*, part X (*Johns Hopkins University Studies in Archaeology* XXXI; Baltimore, 1941) pl XXVII. Olynthus was destroyed in 348. See also M. Crosby, *Lead and Clay Tokens: The Athenian Agora X, 2* (Princeton, 1964). Other excavated glyptic material comes from nineteenth-century excavations at Selinus ([n.i.] Fiorelli, 'Selinunte', *Notizie degli scavi di Antichità* [August, 1883] 287–301, pls 8–15) and early twentieth-century work at Elephantine (Rubensohn, *Elephantine*, pl II), as well as from Persepolis (Schmidt, *Persepolis II*, pls 12–14) and Ur (Legrain, *Ur*, pl 40). G. Bakir reports that a large group of Greek bullae were discovered in his excavations at Klazomenae, but they, like the Daskyleion bullae, have yet to be published. Comprehensive bibliographies may be found in Boardman, *GGFR* and Zazoff, *AG*.

bullae. In this search, therefore, a hierarchy of comparanda was followed. Most important, of course, are other seals—engraved gems or metal finger rings, and seal impressions, preferably from excavation. Next come coins. As Richter and others have demonstrated, engravers worked on both seals and coins.[126] There is also evidence that in the fourth century, seal engravers may occasionally have used coins as patterns for seals.[127] Designs on coins from Sicily, Magna Graecia, and East Greece are echoed among the Daliyeh bullae. Vase paintings, reliefs, and free-standing sculpture can also be of help.[128]

In describing the images on the Wadi Daliyeh bullae, Cross writes:

> Usually, the seals contain either Attic motifs in the contemporary Greek style or Persian mythic and royal motifs. A very few belong to the so-called Greco-Persian style. The sealings in the Greek style impress one with the vivacity of Greek influences of Samaria before the coming of Alexander.[129]

It is now possible to be more specific.[130] Two bullae (WD **22**, WD **23**) have palaeo-Hebrew inscriptions; they were therefore designated 'Hebrew'. Some thirty-nine different seal impressions can be labelled 'Greek',[131] and Gold Ring A is in a provincial Greek style. Some twenty-one images are Near Eastern,[132] including the design on Gold Ring B.[133] Some seals in both the 'Greek' and 'Near Eastern' categories should perhaps be designated 'Greco-Phoenician' or 'Perso-Phoenician'.

Stylistically speaking, then, in the sampling of Samarian glyptic taste provided by the Wadi Daliyeh bullae, the Greek outnumbers the Near Eastern by a ratio of nearly two to one.[134] Statistically, the traditional 'Hebrew' seals are negligible, although their numerical insignificance, in view of the Samarian source of the bullae, is inherently noteworthy.

Besides the two bullae bearing palaeo-Hebrew inscriptions (WD **22**, WD **23**), at least one other bulla, WD **54**, is inscribed, perhaps in Phoenician, although the image of

---

[126] Richter, *EGGE*, 23–5; cf. also Marvin, *Studies*, 37ff. and O. Mørkholm and J. Zahle, 'The Coinage of Kprlli', *Acta Archaeologica* XLIII (1972) 107–10; 'so often are there common features that the borderline between coin die and gem cutters seems to be quite eliminated' (110). See also Meshorer-Qedar, *Coinage of Samaria*, 32. For Boardman's more cautious assessment, see Boardman, *GGFR*, 238.

[127] Porada, 'Greek Coin', 228–34.

[128] Note that the present editor does not suggest that seal engravers habitually copied vase paintings or sculptures, but simply that the work of artists in all media reflects contemporary taste and trends.

[129] Cross, 'Dâliyeh', 51–2.

[130] The vague tallies below arise from the illegibility or near-illegibility of some bullae.

[131] In describing an object as 'Greek' it is implied only that it is stylistically Greek, not that it was necessarily produced by a Greek artist or that it comes from an area which was under Greek control.

[132] Some images are derivatives of the Persian 'Court Style' or are close to other Near Eastern glyptic traditions; it is likely that many of the seals were produced in Phoenicia. See the discussion of WD **13** and WD **41**.

[133] Among the Hecht group of bullae only one image, the winged horned bull (pl XXIII.5 = WD **38** [pl XV.3]) can be designated purely 'eastern'; the remainder are either purely Greek or hybrids (i.e. the griffins on pl XXIII.1–3).

[134] In the Hecht Group, the ratio approaches six to one. Bregstein found that West Semites, including Jews, at Nippur shared the Samarian seal preferences, favouring 'western style images, contest scenes and seals with animals' (Bregstein, *Seal Use*, 370).

Perseus is indisputably Greek.[135] WD **18**, with winged horses, may have had an inscription below the exergue, which is now lost. They may contradict the theory that only officials had inscribed seals in the Persian period.[136]

Upper class Samarians in the fourth century appear to have used a variety of seal types with a wide range of imagery.[137] Only two actual seals (Gold Rings A and B) are included in the corpus, and strangely, no impressions from these rings appear on any of the bullae. In the absence of the original seals, it can be difficult to determine what sorts of seals were used.[138] Many of the impressions show a distinctive pointed oval or leaf shape which indicates a ring bezel, not unlike the bezels of Gold Rings A and B. Occasionally, these bullae also bear a confirmatory nick from a ring hoop where it meets the bezel. The more rounded oval outlines on other bullae could come from rings, but the very common scaraboids could also yield this profile. Scaraboids must account for a number of the bullae, but their shape is too neutral for certain

---

[135] None of the letters on WD **54** is diagnostic for Phoenician, Aramaic or Hebrew. Two bullae in the Hecht group (Stern/Hecht, 'Hoard', photograph pls I.1 and III. 1,2; see here pl XXIII.2.) are inscribed 'Ishmael', according to Naveh, in palaeo-Aramaic (Meshorer-Qedar, *Coinage of Samaria*, 11–12). The image is a Greek griffin.

[136] Cross, 'Dâliyeh', 47.

[137] Earlier excavations at the site of Samaria turned up a bulla and a bronze ring perhaps comparable to the Wadi Daliyeh bullae: the former bears a leaf-shaped ring impression showing a nude figure with a caduceus and draperies (no date proposed, possibly fourth century) (G. A. Reisner, C. S. Fisher, D. G. Lyon, *Harvard Excavations at Samaria 1908–1910* [Cambridge, Mass., 1924] pl 57:f2); the latter is a 'Hellenistic' bronze ring with a nude male figure holding a staff (Reisner *et. al.*, pl 57:d9). Also from Samaria excavations came two Court Style seal impressions of the Persian period (Reisner, pl 57:h2, and J. W. Crowfoot, G. M. Crowfoot, and K. M. Kenyon, *Samaria-Sebaste III: The Objects* [London, 1957] pl 15, no. 42) and a Phoenician green jasper scarab (Crowfoot, etc., pl 15, no. 22). See the discussion of WD **4**, WD **14**, and WD **49**.

The seals and sealings from Jewish communities in Judaea, at Elephantine in Egypt, and (probably) at Nippur in Babylonia differ from each other and from the material we now have from mid-fourth-century Samaria. Clearly each community of Jews took on the colouration of the dominant local culture.

In Judaea, the aniconic tradition prevailed (see especially Avigad, *Bullae and Seals*, but also Stern, *Material Culture*, chap. 7, 'Seals and Seal Impressions'); both official and private seals were usually engraved simply with one's name and sometimes one's office. Such seals must have been locally produced. Stern has identified a group of bullae from locally made seals whose devices seem derived from Persian Court Style imagery (E. Stern, 'Seal Impressions in the Achaemenid Style in the Province of Judah', *BASOR* 202 [1971] 6–16 and further discussion in Keel-Uehlinger, *Göttinnen*, 446–8). Two unstratified oval ring impressions with Greek images (nude youth and armed warrior) from Ramat Rahel are reminiscent of the Daliyeh material and might be fourth-century types (Y. Aharoni, *Excavations at Ramat Rahel, Seasons 1961–62* [Rome, 1964] 23, pls 18.1, 2). If so, they indicate that in Judaea as well, there was some taste for foreign luxuries.

At Elephantine in the fifth century (see Porten, *Archives*, esp. pl 14A; J. D. Cooney in E. G. Kraeling, *The Brooklyn Museum Aramaic Papyri* [New Haven, 1953] 123ff., and E. Sachau, *Aramäische Papyrus und Ostraka aus einer jüdischen Militärkolonie zu Elephantine* [Leipzig, 1911]), Jews used primarily Egyptian-style seals and a few with Persian Court Style motifs. Citing Cooney, Porten notes (214 n. 48) that '[n]one of the extant seal impressions indicates an independent Jewish craft at Elephantine such as is evident in the many pre-exilic Hebrew seals'.

Some of the Persian period tablets from the Murashu Archives at Nippur (dated between 455 and 403; see Legrain, *Culture*) bear the seal impressions of Jewish merchants (see *CHJ* I, 200 and 344ff.); none of the many published bullae conforms to the Palestinian Judaean seal tradition. Bregstein's study (*Seal Use*) confirms this observation. Most of the Murashu sealings have motifs in the Persian Court Style; some sealings look Phoenician, others look Greek.

[138] On the basis of the published photographs, the Hecht Group of bullae seem to come primarily from scaraboids.

identification. Some of the Greek sealings with oval outlines no-doubt came from scaraboids. A few sealings can fairly confidently be recognized as coming from conical stamp seals, a type which became popular in Neo-Babylonian times and continued to appear in large numbers during the Persian period.[139] Tiny cylinders may have produced the three seal impressions (WD **17**, WD **36**, and WD **51**) with similar Court Style designs.

The breakdown of seal types (ring, scaraboid/stamp, cylinder) by the style of image they bear (Hebrew, Greek, Persian/Near Eastern) is interesting. The exact numbers are subject to revision, but there appear to be many more impressions made by rings than stamps.[140] Just as the Greek images outnumber the Persian, most of the rings have Greek designs.[141] Of the Greek bullae, twenty-nine are probable ring impressions (plus Gold Ring A), and ten probably come from scaraboids or other types of stamps. Among Near Eastern bullae, only three carry probable ring impressions (plus Gold Ring B); there appear to have been thirteen of these bullae impressed by stamps and, as is mentioned above, three were possibly made by cylinders (WD **17**, WD **36**, and WD **51**).[142] WD **10B**, one of the five illegible bullae, comes from a ring.

A similar correlation between Greek and Persian imagery may be made in regard to horizontality and verticality. Due no doubt to the necessary horizontality of cylinder seal devices, vertical compositions were rare in Mesopotamia (the chief influence on Persian Court Style glyptic design).[143] All the Daliyeh bullae which are classified here as Persian/Near Eastern (or Phoenician) are either horizontal or more square than vertical. This includes the three sealings among the Persian bullae which clearly came from metal finger rings (WD **3A**, WD **34**, WD **48**) and Gold Ring B, perhaps a Phoenician work. All the works which are classified as Persian/Near Eastern are either imports from the east (Mesopotamia, Persia) or are based on eastern glyptic imagery but perhaps produced in Phoenicia or even Samaria. On the other hand, most of the Greek images, whether they come from oval scaraboids or metal finger rings, are vertical compositions.

One of the two Hebrew sealings, WD **22**, appears to have come from a scaraboid of the traditional West Semitic (including Israelite) type in use throughout the Iron Age and into the Persian period. Since the inscription mentions the owner's title, 'Governor of Samaria', the seal was probably used for official purposes. This had been the standard shape and type of official seal in the First Temple Period, and, at least in Judah where the evidence is more plentiful, continued to be so in the Persian period.[144]

---

[139] In the early Persian period, Stern notes there are a few imported *Neo-Babylonian* (my emphasis) conical stamp and cylinder seals in use in Palestine (Stern, *Material Culture*, 196–7: two conical stamps from En Gedi, four from Tell es-Safi; one cylinder from Tell Jemmeh).

[140] Possible gems mounted in rings are included in the general category of rings. Bregstein similarly found that West Semites, including Jews, at Nippur tended to prefer rings to stamp or cylinder seals (*Seal Use*, 370).

[141] At Persepolis the purely Achaemenid designs usually appear on cylinder seals, the Greek images on stamp/ring seals (Schmidt, *Persepolis II*, 10, 14–15).

[142] See the entry on WD **17**, WD **36** and WD **51** for a discussion of cylinder seals in Persian-period Palestine. Stern, *Material Culture*, 198, writes that there are no cylinder seal impressions from Palestine dating to the Persian period.

[143] E. Porada, *The Art of Iran: Pre-Islamic Cultures* (New York, 1965) 175.

[144] Avigad, 'Hebrew Seals', and *idem, Bullae and Seals*.

The broad leaf-shaped outline of the second Hebrew impression, WD **23**, suggests a ring. This may be a first of sorts; to the best of the present editor's knowledge, although a Persian period gold ring with an Aramaic inscription was discovered at Gibeon,[145] there are no extant rings engraved with a palaeo-Hebrew inscription. The presence of the inscription, as well as the crudely executed device (a boar?) points to a local, perhaps Samarian, workshop.

Officials in the Persian administration, as previously noted, often used cylinder seals, usually with Persian Court Style designs. At Samaria, it is impossible to determine whether seals with such imagery (i.e. WD **4**, WD **8**, WD **17**) had more status or meaning than the 'Greek' seals.[146] The Governor used a traditional 'old-fashioned' Israelite scaraboid (WD **22**), but perhaps he owned and used more than one official seal.

Imagery and Ideology

The onomastic evidence from the Samaria Papyri suggests that many—perhaps most—of these Samarian patricians may have worshipped YHWH, the God of ancient Israel. How much positive information about the religious beliefs of the Samarians can be gleaned from the imagery on their seals? Apparently not very much. The status of one's seal as an amulet with magico-religious qualities cannot be discounted, of course, but recent attempts to relate the imagery on the tremendous number of anepigraphic—apparently private—seals found in excavations at ancient Israelite sites with ancient Israelite religion, while intriguing, remain problematic.[147] With few images in the predominantly—if not exclusively—aniconic Israelite official glyptic tradition, there may have been no overwhelming impulse in Persian-period Samaria to associate seal imagery with personal religious orientation.[148]

It is unclear how the Second Commandment was interpreted by Jews in the Persian period, but seals and coins seem to have fallen outside the Second Commandment's net.[149] What evidence there is shows that some Judaeans had seals with images, and

---

[145] Stern, *Material Culture*, 201; cf. J. B. Pritchard, *Gibeon Where the Sun Stood Still* (Princeton, 1962) fig. 79 and p. 116. This ring may not have been used as a seal since it was not engraved in reverse; however, it conforms stylistically to the traditional simple Hebrew seal type of letters in registers.

[146] At Nippur (Bregstein, *Seal Use*, p. 133), identifiable satrapal officials' seals all bore Court Style imagery, regardless of the seal type (cylinder, ring, stamp). Non-satrapal officials (i.e. canal inspectors) might use different seals each bearing a different style of imagery (*Seal Use*, p. 127).

[147] This project is particularly associated with O. Keel; cf. O. Keel, 'Iconography and the Bible', *Anchor Bible Dictionary*, ed. D. N. Freedman (New York, 1992) 372; *idem*, 'Ancient Seals and the Bible'; and Keel-Uehlinger, *Göttinnen*.

[148] Bregstein was able to isolate certain trends in seal choice by ethnic group in her study of the sealings on the Murashu tablets from Nippur where names—including Jewish names—can be confidently associated with specific sealings. While, as a group, West Semites (including Jews) were 'predisposed toward certain images and seal types', Bregstein reports no distinction between seals of Jews in particular and West Semites in general (Bregstein, *Seal Use*, 370).

[149] See Avigad, 'Hebrew Seals', 14–16.

both Persian provinces, Samaria and Judaea, minted coins bearing human and natural devices.[150]

In looking at seals and seal impressions produced during the Persian period in Greek, Phoenicio-Punic, Egyptian, Perso-Mesopotamian, Palestinian, and Egyptian styles, with the imagery common to each, it is worth noting what does not appear among the Daliyeh bullae. The lacunae are sometimes surprising and sometimes revealing.

It has already been noted that only two bullae belong to the centuries-old Israelite seal tradition. These were probably official seals; by using the 'old-style' seals, the Samarians may have consciously been making a nationalistic statement, or they may have simply been maintaining a practice begun in the time of the divided monarchies. By far the majority of the Samarian seals, however, reflect a liking for foreign things that may have carried a high prestige value.

Status notwithstanding, it appears that the Samarians consciously rejected some very common Persian, Greek, and Phoenician images; they may have felt these figures conflicted with their Yahwism and/or with their national identity. First and foremost, perhaps, among all the Persian Court Style sealings, none carries the image which, until recently, was confidently identified as Ahura Mazda, the Persian high god.[151] Whatever the significance of the royal figure within a circle or winged sun disk or the persona symbolized by the winged disk alone, no variant of the motif appears on the bullae.[152] Seals and bullae with these images have surfaced in excavations in Persia, Mesopotamia, and Egypt; occasionally the motifs appear on seals which may come from a Lydian workshop.[153] Another religious motif, the Persian fire altar, is likewise absent.[154] Thus it seems noteworthy that none of these motifs has yet materialized on bullae or seals from Samaria.[155]

---

[150] Meshorer-Qedar, *Coinage of Samaria*; Y. Meshorer, *Ancient Jewish Coinage, vol. 1: The Persian Period Through Hasmonaeans* (Dix Hills, 1982).

[151] Mary Boyce, "Ahura Mazda", *ABD*. There are also no Babylonian worship scenes (see above). Jews and other West Semites at Nippur also eschewed such scenes (Bregstein, *Seal Use*, 370).

[152] Meshorer-Qedar, *Coinage of Samaria*, 25, has noticed that a Samarian coin copied almost exactly from a Cilician prototype lacks the Cilician coin's sun disk.

[153] From excavations: Legrain, *Culture*, nos. 949–955; Legrain, *Ur*, nos. 759, 765; Petrie, Mackay, Wainwright, *Meydum*, no. 39; Schmidt, *Persepolis II* (selected examples) pl 6, nos. 14, 16–8. The Daskyleion bullae would be expected to include this image; they have yet to be fully published.

Examples from a homogeneous group of Persian period seals, possibly produced in Lydia: J. Boardman, 'Pyramidal Stamp Seals in the Persian Empire', *Iran* 8 (1970) nos. 116–7, 120, 122.

[154] The fire altar does, however, appear on at least two Samarian coins: in front of an enthroned Persian king on the obverse of two obols (Meshorer-Qedar, *Coinage of Samaria*, nos. 33 and 38; ex Nablus hoard). The first bears an enigmatic inscription that may reflect a Persian name, the second is inscribed in Greek, 'Zeus'. Another Samarian coin based on a Cilician one, however, has 'edited out' the fire altar (Meshorer-Qedar, *Coinage of Samaria*, no. 26 and p. 26). In their coinage, both Samaria and Judaea frequently imitated foreign issues which circulated locally and were considered trustworthy; the Persian authorities seem to have given these provincial mints a fairly free hand (Meshorer-Qedar, *Coinage of Samaria*, 20). It remains to be seen how much, if any, political or religious significance the coin devices had.

[155] A related motif is also absent although, in this case, the motif had probably died out by the fourth century. This is the Neo-Babylonian scene of a figure (a priest?) before an altar or before the symbols of Nabu and/or

There are several portrayals of Herakles on the bullae,[156] but the Samarians seem to have avoided images of this hero in his well-known smiting pose.[157] From at least the sixth century, Greeks and Phoenicians alike produced seals and coins showing Herakles on the attack with bow or club. The motif of a smiting god goes back in the Near East to at least the Bronze Age. In Syria-Palestine, the smiting god was commonly associated with the Canaanite storm god, YHWH's rival in the Hebrew Bible. Were the Samarians still aware of this and uncomfortable about having such an image on a seal?

While several Greek heroes—Herakles, Perseus, Achilles, and Penthesileia—make an appearance on the bullae, only three Olympians are portrayed: Aphrodite,[158] Hermes,[159] and Zeus.[160] Their divine status might have been recognized by the Samarians, but both male deities, as depicted on the bullae, also fit very nicely into two discrete categories of anonymous male figures. Hermes differs only in small iconographic details from the many nude or semi-nude youths and warriors which appear on so many of the bullae. Likewise, the figure of Zeus, lightning bolt notwithstanding, belongs with the group of chiton-clad men.[161]

Similarly lacking from these bullae are impressions from Egyptian scarabs or from the traditional Egyptianizing seals produced in Phoenicia. There are no ankhs, uraeae, Isis figures, Horus falcons, striding Pharaohs, Bes figures,[162] etc. The excavators of the 'Abu-Shinjeh cave did find one Egyptian scarab;[163] since no such scarabs seem to have been used to seal the Samaria Papyri, Cross is probably correct in identifying it as an amulet.

Egyptianizing designs are normative in Phoenician glyptic art, including the 'green jasper' scarabs,[164] but are, for the most part, rejected at Samaria. Details such as the disk and crescent, hatched or rope borders, the use of registers and bowl- (= hieroglyptic *neb*) shaped exergues which are commonly found on seals identified as Phoenician[165] and on Archaic Greek or Greco-Phoenician seals, virtually do not appear. While in past excavations at Samaria one such scarab was found,[166] none of the Daliyeh seal impressions came from Phoenician 'green jasper' or 'Tharros' gems of the sort

---

Marduk. A stamp seal with this image was found in the early Persian period strata at En Gedi. See Stern, *Material Culture*, 196–7 and fig. 314.

[156] See the discussion of WD **11C**, WD **39**, WD **42**, WD **47**, with references for the 'smiting god'.

[157] WD **33** (pl IV. 3) comes closest to the smiting pose, but the figure is not Herakles but an anonymous nude youth in a conventional Greek 'tyrant slayer' pose.

[158] In the Hecht Group (IM 82.19.939) pl XXIV.10.

[159] WD **14** (pl I.2), WD **49** (pl I.3), and at least one example (IM 82.19.926) in the Hecht Group pl XXIV.9.

[160] In the Hecht Group (IM 82.19.928) pl XXIV.12.

[161] WD **9** (pl VII.1); WD **11E** (pl VII.2); WD **20** (pl VII.3). There is also another bulla with a man draped in a chiton in the Hecht Group (IM 82.19.931) pl XXIV.7.

[162] Satyrs, whose origins may owe something to Bes, do occur. See entries for WD **2**, WD **5/16B**, WD **21B**, WD **44**. Bes appears on Samarian coins with foreign prototypes (Meshorer-Qedar, *Coinage of Samaria*, 22; nos. 43, 74–5).

[163] *DWD*, pl 36:11; pl 100a.

[164] See *Ashmolean/ANES III*, 37ff. and 70ff.

[165] *Ashmolean/ANES III*, 70.

[166] Crowfoot, Crowfoot, Kenyon, *Samaria-Sebaste*, pl 15, no. 22.

discovered especially in the Persian period strata at Tell Abu Hawam[167] and in the Phoenician (fifth- and early fourth-century) cemetery at ʿAtlit.[168] Of the bullae from Wadi Daliyeh, held in the Rockefeller Museum, only WD **13** and WD **41** exhibit any Egyptian detail, although in an unusual context; in a heretofore unattested variation, 'Persian Hero' sphinxes wear the double crown of Egypt rather than the usual Persian high dentate crown.[169] This new royal sphinx type may be a Phoenician innovation.

The general rejection of traditional Syro-Phoenician seal imagery, even though Syro-Phoenician artists probably produced many of the Samarians' Greek and Persian style seals, tallies with the pattern of seal patronage by the (presumably) western Anatolian owners of so-called Greco-Persian seals, of whom Starr writes:

> Insofar as the patrons selected the scenes, they looked only to Achaemenid and Greek prototypes. There seems to be no influence from Syrian scarabs, which were largely in the Phoenician style; nor does the earlier artistic tradition of Asia Minor, conservative as it had been, appear to have offered any subjects.[170]

Greco-Persian seals are believed to have come from workshops in Asia Minor, possibly Sardis and Cilicia.[171] They are represented among the Rockefeller bullae by only a few examples.[172] While a number of the Samarian seals bearing Greco-Persian subjects might come from Anatolian sources, most of the many seals with Greek subjects or executed in a Greek artistic style would appear to come from elsewhere. 'Elsewhere' is probably Phoenicia for the most part, but possibly also Samaria itself.

If the Wadi Daliyeh bullae are compared with the images on fourth-century coins minted locally in Palestine—including Judaean and Samarian issues—a few significant

---

[167] R. W. Hamilton, 'Excavations at Tell Abu Hawam', *QDAP* 4 (1935) 18, nos. 47–8.

[168] Johns, 'Excavations', 41–104. For additional references, see also the discussion of WD **11C**, etc. (Herakles figures) and WD **45**.

[169] Conventionally crowned Persian Court Style royal sphinxes appear on other bullae (WD **3A**, WD **15A**).

[170] Starr, 'Greeks', 70. He further writes (71), 'the most likely source of this patronage are local officials—not Persian satraps proper—and above all the rural squirarchy of Asia Minor'. Bregstein, in her study of the seal choice of Jews in Nippur has found a similar rejection of many traditional Near Eastern scenes (*Seal Use*, 370).

[171] For discussion and references, see Boardman, *GGFR*, chap. 6, 'Greeks and Persians'; Zazoff, *AG*, chap. 8, 'Graeco-persische Gemmen'; and M. Marvin, *Studies in Greco-Persian Gems* (Ph.D. diss., Harvard University, 1973) *passim*.

[172] WD **52**, from a scaraboid. Several bullae in the Hecht Group could perhaps be placed in this group; a ring impression (IM 82.19.934) pl XXIV.14 with a seated Persian women holding a bird appears on Greco-Persian seals (cf. Boardman, *GGFR*, nos. 964 [scaraboid], 991 [ring]), but the bulla also resembles a locally produced silver ring from the Phoenician harbour town of Tel Michal (M. Barak and S. Amorai-Stark, 'Seals and Seal Impressions', *Excavations at Tel Michal*, eds. Z. Herzog, G. Rapp, Jr., O. Negbi [Minneapolis and Tel Aviv, 1989] 335–6, pl 74.1) and a Samarian coin with a seated male figure holding a bird (Meshorer-Qedar, *Coinage of Samaria*, no. 19); the Samarian coin in turn has a Cilician prototype (Meshorer-Qedar, *Coinage of Samaria*, 25).

The complex composition of a winged griffin attacking a stag (Hecht Group IM 82.19.925, pl XXIII.3; from a scaraboid?) has Greco-Persian parallels (cf. Boardman, *GGFR*, nos. 847, 868). It is so like the obverse of a Samarian obol (Meshorer-Qedar, *Coinage of Samaria*, no. 61 and p. 36) that the same engraver could have produced them both, conceivably in Samaria itself; on the other hand, the coin in question has a clear Cilician prototype (Meshorer-Qedar, *Coinage of Samaria*, 27).

Hecht Group IM 82.19.919 and K63L (pl XXIII.1,2) with single winged griffins and IM 92.19.942 and 82.19.941 (pl XXIII.4,5) with running winged bulls might also be labelled Greco-Persian (cf. griffins in Boardman, *GGFR*, nos. 957–8, 978; leaping winged bulls in Boardman, *GGFR*, nos. 921–2).

correspondences may be noted.[173] These coins, which used to be called 'Philisto-Arabian' but which are now recognized simply as local Palestinian issues,[174] can bear Greek or Near Eastern devices (including Egyptianizing Bes figures and Persian Court Style). Not surprisingly, some of the stereotypical Persian Court Style images on the Samarian coins and the Daliyeh bullae are similar; however, the designs on the Greek-style bullae do not overlap with the coins except in two or three cases where the subjects might be considered 'Eastern' or the correspondence is ambiguous.[175] The large group of standing nude youths and warriors found at Samaria is apparently not represented on Palestinian coins.[176] Furthermore, the purely Greek images on the Samarian bullae, schematic as many of them may be, are artistically more accomplished than the usually crude numismatic work. If the Samarian seals—those in the Greek style in particular—are largely imports, then the circumstantial evidence points logically to nearby Phoenician cities[177] where artists were familiar with both Greek and Near Eastern artistic vernacular.

Imagery: Persian/Near Eastern

A wealth of available iconographic data helps to identify images generated by the Greek world.[178] The situation is different in the case of Near Eastern art, which in

---

[173] For Samaria, see Meshorer-Qedar, *Coinage of Samaria*; for Judah, see Y. Meshorer, *Ancient Jewish Coinage*, vol. I.

[174] A. Kindler, 'The Greco-Phoenician Coins struck in Palestine in the time of the Persian Empire, II: The Influence of Greek and Phoenician art on the die-cutters', *Israel Numismatic Journal* 2 (1963) 25–7. See also Stern, *Material Culture*, 221–4.

[175] The winged griffin attacking a stag (which has a counterpart on a Cilician coin) and the seated Persian woman, both in the Hecht Collection; the lily flanked by branches (Hecht Group K63.M, pl XXIII.14) calls to mind the same motif on Judaean coinage (Y. Meshorer, *Ancient Jewish Coinage*, vol. 1, 13, 29–30) but also glyptic examples (Boardman, *GGFR*, fig. 248).

[176] A standing bearded man draped in a chiton appears on some Samarian issues (Meshorer-Qedar, *Coinage of Samaria*, nos. 25, 61, 77, 79–80); in some instances he resembles standard portrayals of Zeus.

[177] Samaria's ongoing contacts with Phoenicia reach back to Omri's alliance with Tyre, which brought Jezebel to Samaria. Josephus (*Ant.* 12.9.1) writes that in the Second Temple Period, Samarians of Shechem called themselves 'Sidonians'.

Sidon was located at the head of two major inland routes, one to Damascus, the other to the south, skirting Mt. Hermon, entering Palestine and passing through Samaria and Jerusalem. Elayi stresses the importance for Phoenicia, especially Sidon, of maintaining trade relations with areas inland from the Phoenician coast proper and with towns in southern Phoenicia and Palestine ('The Phoenician Cities in the Persian Period', *JANESCU* 12 (1980) 16–18). For a discussion of routes by which Phoenicia and Samaria communicated, see Shimʿon Dar and Shimʿon Applebaum, *Landscape and Pattern. An Archaeological Survey of Samaria 800 B.C.E.–636 C.E.*, parts i–ii, *British Archaeological Reports International Series* 308 (1986) and D. A. Dorsey, 'Shechem and the Road Network of Central Samaria', *BASOR* 268 (1987) 57–70 (esp. p. 63) which describes the coastal highway which went north overland to Phoenicia and routes from Samaria to the Yarkon River basin (which was heavily settled in this period and may have been dominated by Phoenician cities) and to Phoenician-controlled Palestinian harbour sites such as Tell Hefer, Joppa, and Dor. For a discussion of the Sidonian economic hegemony over these towns in the fourth century, cf. Elayi, 'Studies', 98 and 102. The large Persian period ports of Joppa and Dor were equidistant, south and north respectively, from Samaria.

[178] See *LIMC*.

many instances seems prompted by a love of decorative patterns and heraldic/iconic representations of human or divine power, rather than by a narrative impulse.[179] Divinities and heroes do appear on Near Eastern seals, but there is little consensus about the mythic figures which may or may not be represented.[180] D. Hansen's comment on Sumerian glyptic iconography generally applies to later phases of Mesopotamian art as well:

> Although we are dealing in the seal impression representations with a world of heroes, demons, and animals, where the immediate symbol could stand for a wealth of religious ideas and overlapping or fused concepts, we cannot find in the myths or epics passages which explain the artistic iconography.[181]

The Near Eastern images break down into two basic groups: designs with the 'Persian Hero'[182] and designs with animals only. Subsets of the first category consist of the Persian Hero (a) battling a single opponent—a winged bull or winged lion, and (b) battling a pair of animals—lions or winged sphinxes. In the second category, animals either pose alone or in flanking pairs. On all but one bulla (WD **34**, horses) these animals are mythical: winged sphinxes (WD **13**, WD **15A**, WD **31**, WD **41**, WD **48**, WD **53**), winged horses (WD **18**), winged bulls (WD **38**),[183] winged scorpion-men (WD **25**), curled-winged griffins (Gold Ring B). WD **13** and WD **41** are eastern (Phoenician?) variations on a Court Style motif, as may also be the case with WD **15A** and Gold Ring B.

The imperial Achaemenid propaganda programme ensured the wide dispersal of conventional Court Style motifs. As noted above, coin engravers working for the Samarian minting authorities copied coins in the Court Style issued by Phoenician, Cilician, and Palestinian cities which were in circulation in Samaria,[184] and possibly some of the similar Court Style seals from Daliyeh were also engraved in Samaria:[185] (i.e. the winged, horned animal on WD **38** and on the obverse of a Samarian obol,[186] the flanking scorpion-men on WD **25** and the single version on the reverse of a hemiobol,[187] the Persian hero stabbing an upright animal on WD **4** and WD **8** and on numerous Samarian coins,[188] the Persian hero flanked by animals on WD **17**, WD **36**,

---

[179] Note E. Reiner's comments on this question in 'Magic Figurines, Amulets and Talismans', *Monsters and Demons*, 28, including her reference to D. E. Bynum, *The Daemon in the Wood* (Cambridge, 1978) 227.

[180] Porada, 'Introduction', *Ancient Art*, 9–10.

[181] D. P. Hansen, 'The Fantastic World of Sumerian Art; Seal Impressions from Ancient Lagash', *Monsters and Demons*, 62–3. Keel has been attempting to relate Syro-Palestinian glyptic imagery with mythology, including that of Israel with variable but thought-provoking results (see, e.g. Keel-Uehlinger, *Göttinnen*).

[182] For a discussion of this figure, see entry on WD **4**, p. 214ff.

[183] In the Hecht Group there are possibly two additional winged bulls (pl XXIII.4,5).

[184] Meshorer-Qedar, *Coinage of Samaria*, 20.

[185] In Samaria during the Persian period, artists working locally may have been producing objects which have Phoenician and Achaemenid characteristics (Stern, 'Phoenician', 211–2).

[186] Meshorer-Qedar, *Coinage of Samaria*, no. 83 (and perhaps no. 63).

[187] Meshorer-Qedar, *Coinage of Samaria*, no. 63.

[188] Meshorer-Qedar, *Coinage of Samaria*, 23; some inspired by Sidonian issues.

and WD **51**, and again, on several Samarian coins).[189] Did the coin directly inspire the seal (or vice versa, for priority is impossible to determine)? If the correspondences between some of the Samarian coins and bullae (especially from Court Style seals, but also one or two that might be called Greek) suggest the same artist at work locally, then it must be asked whether the artist is native-born or a travelling specialist. And who determines the seal image—the engraver or the local patron?

Imagery: Greek

A quick survey of the Wadi Daliyeh bullae discloses the preponderance of images that could be categorized as Greek in style and/or subject matter, especially in contrast with such manifestly Near Eastern motifs as the Persian Hero, winged bulls, and scorpion men. Nevertheless, particularly in the case of animal subjects, it is difficult to isolate some of the motifs on the bullae as Greek or Greco-Phoenician or even, more vaguely, Greco-Near Eastern. Human figures outnumber the animals[190] (both real and mythical) among the bullae in Greek style. There are fewer renderings of women than of men; women appear on some ten bullae; on six of these, the woman appears alone.[191]

Of all the bullae, Greek or Persian, by far the largest category consists of lone standing youths or warriors in various states of dress and undress.[192] This group of figures does not appear to be the work of any single recognizable artist or workshop. The figures seem to reflect a repose reminiscent of vase paintings from the end of the fifth and beginning of the fourth centuries in which gods and heroes assume graceful attitudes, as if they were themselves statues.[193] The 'youths' on the bullae cannot usually be identified with any particular Greek or Near Eastern deity. It is possible to identify some of the seventeen figures in this group, if only tentatively: Hermes (WD **14**, WD **49**[194]) Herakles (WD **11C**, WD **39**, WD **42**, WD **47**)[195] and Perseus (WD **32**, WD **54**, WD **56**). The closest comparanda, although not completely satisfactory, are provided by Greek rings in the de Clercq collection.[196] This is the reason for proposing Phoenicia as the probable source for many of the Samarian 'youth' seals.

---

[189] Meshorer-Qedar, *Coinage of Samaria*, 24. The seated Persian on a Hecht Group bulla (pl XXIV.14) also resembles three Samarian issues (Meshorer-Qedar, *Coinage of Samaria*, nos. 18, 21, 33).

[190] The Hecht Group includes a few more animals (see below).

[191] Bullae with female figures: WD **44** (nymph and satyr), WD **50** (Maenad), WD **43** (Achilles and Penthesilea), WD **6**, and WD **52** (Persian couple), WD **46** (Nike in quadriga), WD **I.3.22B** (Nike?). In the Hecht Group there are at least three, including possibly Aphrodite (pl XXIV.10,13,14).

[192] For examples in the Hecht collection, mostly from rings, see pl XXIV.1–5,8,9).

[193] Cf. G. Nicole, *Meidias et le style fleuri dans la céramique attique* (Geneva, 1908) pl XIII.

[194] See also from the Hecht Group, pl XXIV.9.

[195] Hecht Group, pl XXIV.8.

[196] Published in de Ridder, *Collection*, also discussed in *Ashmolean/ANES III*, 71 and Boardman, *GGFR*, 221. Boardman suggests they were made by Greeks in Phoenicia during the late fifth century; it is now apparent they are from the fourth century.

The de Clercq collection was assembled primarily in Lebanon in the late nineteenth century. The bulk of the collection is now in the Bibliothèque Nationale, Paris (see Bordreuil, *BN*). The rings, which on stylistic grounds date from the Archaic to the Hellenistic periods, occasionally have fairly good provenances, particularly the rings discovered in Phoenician sarcophagi by nineteenth-century archaeologists.

These bullae with lounging nude or semi-nude warriors and youths in largely Yahwistic Samaria are significant as a measure of the extent of Greek cultural artifacts already on hand in the early to mid-fourth century. Israelite society as reflected in the Hebrew Bible did not celebrate youth or the human body.[197] If the Samarians who owned these seals had little concept of Hellenic culture, then, given the mores of a culture which abhorred nudity or saw it as a sign of degradation,[198] one would expect the seals to have been regarded as grossly unsuitable for public use by legal witnesses. It is easier to assume that the owners had some level of exposure to alien Greek iconography, although precisely how they interpreted their seals' imagery remains obscure.[199]

A smaller heterogeneous group of single male figures includes mature men (WD **9**, WD **11E**, WD **20**),[200] a nude youth lounging on a rock (WD **15B**), and a nude youth leaning against a column (WD **57**).

The third category consists of so-called Dionysian subjects including satyrs on their own (WD **2**, WD **5/16B**, WD **21B**), a Persian dancer (WD **27**), a dancing Maenad (WD **50**), Eros (WD **40**), and the charming scene of a satyr and nymph playing knucklebones (WD **44**).[201] These bullae clearly show that such motifs were popular, but it would be highly presumptuous to infer that Samarians were participating in the cult of Dionysos in the fourth century.[202]

Human male and female figures appear together in the fourth group. Because relatively few female figures appear on the bullae, this is an intriguing category. WD **6** and WD **52** depict the same subject, a Persian couple, but in stylistically divergent ways. WD **43**, which probably depicts Achilles and the Amazon Penthesilea, is one of the most distinctive bullae of the corpus.

WD **46**, Nike driving a frontal quadriga, is the only bulla in the fifth group ('Other complex subjects').

Finally, in the sixth category are bullae with plant and animal designs. In the mythical category there are three winged griffins,[203] a hippocamp (WD **35**), a sphinx seated on a column,[204] and a winged boar forepart (WD **45**). The real animals consist of an eagle (Gold Ring A) and a dove,[205] several lions (WD **37**),[206] one scratching his ear

---

[197] In later years, one of Antiochus IV Epiphanes' most controversial acts was his establishing of a gymnasium in Jerusalem (1 Macc 1:14; 2 Macc 4:12).

[198] Egyptian and Assyrian sculpture alike, as well as the Megiddo ivory depicting a king in his court, reserves nudity for war captives.

[199] See discussion in entry for WD **1**.

[200] Hecht Group, see pl XXIV.6,7,11,12.

[201] See also entry for WD **40**.

[202] The evidence for Phoenician involvement with Dionysos is extremely limited in this period as well. It is unlikely that the Samarians would have anticipated their northern neighbours in such a religious matter.

[203] Hecht Group (see pl XXIII.1–3).

[204] Hecht Group (see pl XXIII.6).

[205] Hecht Group (see pl XXIII.13).

[206] Hecht Group (see pl XXIII.9–12).

(WD **55**),[207] another gnawing on a thighbone,[208] a horse and rider,[209] and galloping horses.[210] The only plant is a three-petalled flower flanked by leafy branches.[211]

Conclusions and Questions

The Wadi Daliyeh bullae, with their excellent mid-fourth century context (although an occasional heirloom is not ruled out), supplement the knowledge of Greek glyptic art and of the cultural milieu of fourth century Palestine.

One of the most significant aspects of this group of bullae is the large number and rich variety of roughly datable glyptic material. However unimpressive the clay bullae may appear, they are of importance because of their firmly established chronological (fourth century), geographical (Samaria, Palestine), and social (upper class) context. Too often, in the past, collector-connoisseurs appreciated engraved gems and finger rings as precious objects of vertu; their dating depended on typologies developed along art historical principles used in other branches of Greek art, rather than upon stratified sequences of seals. The provenance of many a seal turns out to be the town in which it was bought or the vague word of an antiquities dealer. The Wadi Daliyeh bullae markedly increase the amount of data on Greek and Persian seals of the fourth century; their uncertain status was described by Boardman in 1970, when he wrote:

> Achaemenid seals or impressions from cylinders securely datable to the fourth century are remarkably scarce. Even the finger ring impressions seem mainly fifth-century and there are no impressions from fourth-century Greek rings or gems until after Alexander.[212]

In actuality, there are a great many fourth-century seals and rings; the problem was that in the absence of sound chronological anchors, they were being labelled either fifth-century or Hellenistic on stylistic grounds alone. The corpus of bullae from Daliyeh now provides an anchor.

In the area of Classical Greek archaeology and art history, the ramifications of this material are diverse. In some cases, the Greek seals from Daliyeh conform to expectations from a provincial centre such as Samaria where a time-lag can be observed in taste; an older motif has survived or local artists seem to be making crude copies of imported originals. On the other hand, however risky it may be to evaluate the workmanship of the Samarians' seals on the basis of seal impressions, the obvious artistic ambitiousness of many of the engraved motifs elevates much of the work over the only other well-excavated and published corpus of Classical Greek glyptic art, the early fourth-century seals (primarly bronze rings) from Olynthus (north-east Greece).[213] This can probably be explained in part by the clear indications that the Samarian seal

---

[207] Perhaps doubled in the Hecht Group (pl XXIII.11).

[208] Hecht Group (pl XXIII.12).

[209] Hecht Group (pl XXIII.7).

[210] Hecht Group (pl XXIII.8).

[211] Hecht Group (pl XXIII.14), 'a lotus'. Boardman calls a comparable example a rose (Boardman, *GGFR*, fig. 248, p. 231).

[212] Boardman, *GGFR*, 326.

[213] Robinson, *Metal*.

owners were relatively wealthy. Many of these Samarians' seal rings were probably gold, like the two rings which have survived, and gold rings naturally would have received special attention from an artist. Unlike the Olynthus material, then, the Wadi Daliyeh bullae do not cross class lines but reflect the tastes of people who must have been local 'trend setters'.

A few of the 'ambitious' Greek images among the bullae[214] might have been categorized as Hellenistic if not for the firm mid-fourth-century context of the Daliyeh material. The Daliyeh bullae help reinforce the sense among Classical art historians of how arbitrary the date of 323 is to discussions of art and Hellenization.[215] These bullae, like the Mausoleum sculptures or the works of Praxiteles, may demonstrate Hellenistic art in the making.

With the Wadi Daliyeh material a significant number of finger ring impressions which clearly come from the fourth century and which have mainstream Greek designs are now extant. They help to fine-tune Boardman's typology of Classical Greek finger rings;[216] Boardman explained the presence of fifth-century ring types in fourth-century Phoenicia (the de Clercq group) and elsewhere in the Levant on the principle that older ring types persisted beyond the Hellenic world proper.[217] The factor of 'provincial lag' may indeed be at play here, but given the international familiarity with Greek styles and the probable presence in Phoenicia of Greek—even Attic—artists, at least some of the Wadi Daliyeh rings may be considered mainstream and not provincial.

The de Clercq gold rings considered with the Wadi Daliyeh rings suggest that there were active ring engraving workshops in Phoenicia in the fifth and fourth centuries, adapting to the different stylistic tastes of their patrons. A few designs on the Greek Wadi Daliyeh bullae are similar to devices on the de Clercq rings.[218]

Future consideration of the correspondences between the Wadi Daliyeh bullae and contemporary Samarian coinage may result in a clearer understanding of local coin and seal cutting and may even point more firmly toward a Samarian engraving workshop.

Hellenization in the Persian Empire

Students of fourth-century cultural history have increasingly recognized a pre-Alexandrine Hellenic *oikumene* of limited dimensions in the western Persian Empire.[219]

---

[214] WD **46** (Nike in a frontal quadriga), WD **43** (Achilles and Penthesilea in a pose unattested for them before the Hellenistic period), WD **44** (a nymph and satyr playing knucklebones), WD **57** (a youth leaning on a column), possibly WD **21D**.

[215] B. R. Brown, *Anticlassicism in Greek Sculpture of the Fourth Century B.C.* (New York, 1973) 1–4 with a summary of dates and bibliography. Also see F. Vannier, *Le IVe siècle grec* (Paris, 1967).

[216] Boardman, *GGFR*, fig. 217, pp. 213–15, 657–61.

[217] Boardman, *GGFR*, 221.

[218] See entries for WD **14**, WD **50**, WD **57**.

[219] S. Hornblower's *Mausolus* is an important example of such scholarship (p. ii). See also Hornblower, *Greek World*; Starr, 'Greeks'; Elayi, *Pénétration grecque*; M. Colledge, 'Greek and non-Greek Interaction in the Art and Architecture of the Hellenistic East', *Hellenism in the East,* eds. A. Kuhrt and S. Sherwin-White (Berkeley and Los Angeles, 1987) 134–9; Hanfmann, *From Croesus to Constantine* (Ann Arbor, 1975) 11, 15, and 24; R. Wenning,

Representative of this trend is S. Hornblower's assertion that 'the Hellenization of the inland Anatolian places (the coastal sites had long been under Greek influence) had already made remarkable progress in the fifty years before Alexander's arrival'.[220] Just what is meant by 'Hellenization before Alexander' in the Near East is still being defined;[221] as noted, however, singularly illustrative of this Hellenization is the presence of Greek art all over the western Persian empire: sculpture, painting, architecture, coinage, seals, etc., all executed by artists working in the Greek style.[222]

Unfortunately, it is not known to what degree Greek thought travelled with Greek art. A Hippodamic city plan was used at Phoenician Dor, and occasionally Greek architectural styles might be promoted by the ruler of a border area to signal his political leanings or alliances.[223] Or, perhaps the pre-Alexandrine 'barbarian' adoption of Greek artistic fashions could be compared to the enthusiastic Japanese absorption today of the trappings of the West, while maintaining, most emphatically, a profound grounding in their own culture.

Whatever the identity of the artists who were producing the Samarians' Greek seals—and many of the seals may have come from workshops in Phoenicia and perhaps a very few from Samaria itself—the seals reflect the engravers' direct or indirect acquaintance with a diverse assortment of artistic influences: Lysippan proportions,[224] tendencies in large-scale sculpture most evident in Magna Graecia and Sicily,[225] numismatic art from Persia and east and west Greece,[226] and themes from Greek myths (such as Perseus)[227] adopted by the Greek and Persian territories of Asia Minor along the cultural borderline, such as Ionia, Caria, Lycia and Cilicia.

J. Elayi proposes that '[t]he domination of the Greeks, whose culture had attracted the Phoenicians even before Alexander's conquest, was more powerful and uncompromising than the Achaemenid, and it progressively destroyed Phoenician

---

'Griechische Importe in Palästina aus der Zeit vor Alexander d. Gr., Vorbericht über ein Forschungsprojekt', *Boreas* 4 (1981) 29–46.

[220] Hornblower, *Mausolus*, vii.

[221] See particularly F. Millar's 'The Phoenician cities: A case-study of Hellenisation', *Proceedings of the Cambridge Philological Society* 209 (n.s. 29) (1983) 55–71 and 'The Problem of Hellenistic Syria', *Hellenism in the East*, eds. A. Kuhrt and S. Sherwin-White, esp. 110–11, 131–2; also cf. J. Hofstetter, *Die Griechen in Persien: Prosopographie der Griechen in persischen Reich vor Alexander*, *AMI Ergänzungsband* 5 (1978).

[222] After the initial exposure to Greek art, the artists need not have been Greeks, notwithstanding the assumption by many scholars that the objects with the best workmanship could only have come from Greeks. Marvin, *Studies*, 141–2 concludes that non-Greek artists could produce Greek images. Their work may be recognizable by a difference in engraving technique visible on the gems (Boardman, *GGFR*, 324). (See also the discussion of WD **43**). Ridgway, *Fifth Century*, 151, comments on the pervading influence of Attic styles and compositions even in non-Greek territory. She notes that the similarity of motifs among reliefs coming from widespread geographical areas may indicate the existence of pattern books of some kind. For Greek technical treatises (including monographs on art) of the fourth century, see Hornblower, *Greek World*, 156.

[223] Borchhardt, 'Herrschaft', 239–40. See also J. Zahle, 'Politics and Economy in Lycia during the Persian Period', *REA* 91 (1989) 169–82.

[224] See WD **57**.

[225] See WD **11C**, WD **15B**.

[226] See WD **42**, GR-A, and WD **45**.

[227] See WD **56**.

civilization'.[228] The pronounced Hellenism of the Wadi Daliyeh bullae and the clear absence of images in traditional Egypto-Phoenician mixed styles suggest that Elayi could be underestimating the extent of cultural Hellenism in Phoenicia in the decades before Alexander arrived on the scene. If citizens of an inland provincial hill-country town like Samaria were comfortable using Greek imagery on their seals, how much stronger must have been the Greek cultural influence among Phoenicians whose direct and indirect contact with Greece and Greeks was a fact of the Persian Period.

In small ways, such as their apparent predilection for Greek seals, the Samarians (if not the Judaeans) in the mid-fourth century seem to have been attracted to Greek culture, even if their experience of 'Greek culture' was not first-hand but reflective of the Phoenicians who had already interacted with Greeks for centuries.[229] Nevertheless, there can be no cultural receptivity unless the receiving culture has receptors somehow attuned to the new influences. Without this initial groundwork, the world conquered by Alexander, including Syria-Palestine, would have been far less receptive than it apparently was to the conqueror's vision of a Hellenized world.

---

[228] Elayi, 'Phoenician Cities', 28.

[229] Note the discovery, near the Sidonian Temple of Eshmun, of a fourth-century bilingual dedication written in Cypriot syllabary script and Greek, discussed in O. Masson, 'Pèlerins chypriotes en Phénicie (Sarepta et Sidon)', *Semitica* 32 (1982) 45–8.

B. NUDE YOUTHS AND WARRIORS

1. HERMES AND UNIDENTIFIED YOUTHS AND WARRIORS

WD 7. Nude Greek Youth with Chlamys

(PLATE I.1)

Mus. Inv. 962
Loose sealing
Image size: 1.4 cm (as preserved) x 0.8 cm
Bulla size: 1.7 cm x 1.6 cm
Clay colour: black (burned)
String not preserved but imprint of string remains; top and bottom of vertical image
Papyrus imprint
Seal type: engraved gem in metal ring?

WD 7 is the impression of what may have been a narrow, oval gem set in a metal ring; at the top of the sealing there appears to be a space between the edge of the gem and its mount. Another indication of a gemstone is the marked convexity of the sealing from top to bottom due to the concavity of the gemstone's surface. Metal rings are more likely to bow outward and create a concave image. In addition to the loss of the youth's feet due to breakage, the left and right edges of the image are not defined.

A Greek youth in a frontal pose looks to his right. He is nude except for a chlamys clasped at his throat, an item of clothing which appears several times on both the Rockefeller and Hecht bullae. Here it drapes the youth's shoulders, then falls behind him in vertical lines to the left and right to terminate in decorative folds from thigh to ankle. The clean-shaven youth has slightly puffy cheeks and high cheekbones; the eye and eyebrow are carefully indicated, but the mouth lacks definition or has worn away. On visual inspection, the youth proved to be bareheaded with short, wavy hair.[1] He rests his weight on his right leg, but his stance is fully frontal with genitals and navel clearly indicated. In his lowered and partially extended right hand he seems to hold an object of some sort. Whatever was beyond the youth's wrist—perhaps a *patera* for an offering—has been scraped away. The artist seems to have taken special delight in depicting the musculature; the young man's exaggerated masses of flesh—at the shoulder, arms, torso, legs—evoke nothing so much as a musclebound bodybuilder.

With his upraised left hand he casually grasps a vertical staff or spear; this pose slightly elevates the left shoulder. Due to careless sealing the bottom of the awkwardly executed staff is missing. The upper portion does not line up with the section below the youth's elbow, and the staff disappears behind the youth's shoulder so that he looks as if he is holding it behind him. This mistake occasionally afflicts Phoenician

---

[1] The apparent long locks in the photograph are actually an inclusion in the clay.

scaraboids,[2] and Archaic seals[3] and coins,[4] but is rare in the Classical period to which the provenance as well as the youth's Polykleitan hip-shot stance assign the sealing—a sign of local (Phoenician?) workmanship perhaps?

The Wadi Daliyeh corpus[5] provides a parallel of sorts to WD **7** in WD **54** (pl V.2) on which the nude Perseus' stance with a staff and lowered hand is quite similar. The Harvard excavation at Samaria discovered a bronze ring with an oval one-piece bezel which, according to the excavators, showed a nude male figure standing with a staff in his left hand. Both the photograph and the context are unclear.[6]

Another parallel for WD **7** is a middle-to-late fifth-century gold ring in Boston showing Hermes leaning on a pillar.[7] Richter says of it that '[t]he pose, with the weight of the body on the right leg, and the left flexed and set back, is in the so-called Polykleitan stance'.[8] Hermes' head is in profile, while his body is frontal, just as on WD **7**.

The decorative zigzags of the cloak may also fit with a late Classical date. They do not resemble the symmetrical swallowtails of the Archaic period[9] but the somewhat more naturalistic, although still abstract, folds of later Classical and Hellenistic seals.[10]

If the precise composition of WD **7** is unusual in extant Greek glyptic, similar figures are common enough on Greek coins and vases where gods, goddesses, and heroes may assume the hipshot pose leaning on a staff with the other hand lowered.[11] It also appears in the form of small Classical bronze votive athletes.[12]

---

[2] Cf. Bordreuil, *BN*, no. 18, a Phoenician scaraboid of the late seventh century. Also N. Avigad, 'Some Decorated West Semitic Seals', *IEJ* 35 (1985) no. IV, a Phoenician seal with Aramaic inscription of the eighth century.

[3] Richter, *EGGE*, no. 99, Staatliche Museen, Berlin, armed nude warrior, early fifth century,

[4] N. Avigad, 'Some Decorated West Semitic Seals', *IEJ* 35 [1985], n. 31, cites other examples on Greek coins and gems of the Archaic period.

[5] Note the similar stance on a number of Hecht Group bullae (pl XXIV.1–5,7).

[6] Reisner, Fisher, Lyon, *Harvard*, pl 57, d9.

[7] Boardman, *GGFR*, 663, of Boardman's Waterton Group = Richter, *EGGE*, 220 = A. Furtwängler, *Die Antiken Gemmen: Steinschneidekunst in klassischen Altertum* (Leipzig/Berlin, 1900) pl 61,32 = J. D. Beazley, *The Lewes House Collection of Ancient Gems* (Oxford, 1920) pl 3 = Boston MFA 28.598. Cf. also the figure of Herakles on the reverse of the name vase of the Niobid Painter in Paris (Louvre MNC 511), illustrated in J. Boardman, *Greek Art* (London, 1973) fig. 168 (*c*.460 BCE).

The exact composition of WD **7** is unusual in Greek glyptic. Two related seals may be mentioned here, on which the bodies of the male figures are frontal, but the heads are in profile; both, like WD **7**, reflect the Polykleitan stance. The first is a celebrated early Classical sard ringstone in Boston showing Apollo with his staff and wearing a chlamys (Boardman, *GGFR*, 455 = Richter, *EGGE*, 102 = Furtwängler, *AG*, pl 10,3 = G. Lippold, *Gemmen und Kameen des Altertums und der Neuzeit* (Stuttgart, 1922) pl 8,4 = Beazley, *Lewes House* pl 3,47 = Zazoff, *AG* pl 34,9 = BMFA 27.691). The second seal, a carnelian scaraboid, depicts an athlete holding a mattock and a strigil (Boardman, *GGFR*, 484 = *AGDS*, I,1, Munich, pl 39,331).

[8] Richter, *EGGE*, p.78.

[9] G. M. A. Richter, *Catalogue of the Engraved Gems Greek Etruscan and Roman,* Metropolitan Museum of Art, (Rome, 1956) 33–4.

[10] Richter, MMA, 87; Boardman, *GGFR*, 663,736; H. B. Walters, *Catalogue of the Engraved Gems and Cameos, Greek Etruscan and Roman in the British Museum* (London, 1926) 1395 'Greco-Roman'.

[11] For example, on a late fifth-century hydria by the Meidias Painter in the British Museum (BM E224) which portrays Herakles in the garden of the Hesperides, Herakles' companion is strikingly similar to the figure on WD **7**

As preserved, the image lacks the decisive iconography to identify the youth as a specific person, such as Apollo. His pose is similar to that of Perseus on WD **54** (pl V.2) and WD **56** (pl V.3), but without Perseus' magic sack this identification is speculative. As with so many other Wadi Daliyeh sealings, ultimately the youth remains anonymous.

(illustrated in *LIMC*, 'Herakles', fig. 2717) as is Dionysos on a late fifth-/early fourth-century oenochoe in Berlin (F 2660), illustrated in H. Metzger, *Les représentations dans la céramique attique du IVe siècle* (Paris, 1951) pl II, 3.

A sampling of coins from the Greek world: fourth-century silver coins of Side (G. F. Hill et al., *British Museum Catalogue: Greek Coins* (London, 1873–1927) 28 [Lycia], pl XXVI, 4–6) Apollo with laurel staff and patera at an altar; late fifth-century silver tetradrachms of Selinus (*SNG-ANS* 4 [New York, 1977] pl 27, 693–704) and silver litrae of Panormus (*ibid*, pl 20, 586–93).

[12] Two examples: a Severe Style athlete at Mt. Holyoke College (BOI. I, 1926, illustrated in D. G. Mitten and S. F. Doeringer, eds., *Master Bronzes from the Classical World*, Exhibition Catalogue (Cambridge, Mass., 1967) no. 83; and a bronze of 450–425 in the Cleveland Museum of Art (55.684), illustrated in A. Kozloff and D. G. Mitten, organizers, *The Gods Delight: The Human Figure in Classical Bronze*. Exhibition Catalogue of the Cleveland Museum of Art, November 16, 1988–January 8, 1989 (Cleveland Museum of Art, 1988) no. 12.

WD 14. Hermes with Aphlaston

(PLATE I.2)

Mus. Inv. No. 967

Samaria Papyrus 10; 350/49 BCE

Image size: 1.5 cm x 1 cm

Bulla size: 1.7 cm x 1.6 cm

Clay colour: orange-pink

String preserved; top and bottom of vertical image

Papyrus fibres on front and back

Papyrus imprint

Seal type: probably a metal finger ring

Published: F. M. Cross, Jr., 'Papyri', p. 28; pl 62, d; *idem,* 'Dâliyeh', p. 51 and fig. 38.

WD **14** was the only sealing still attached to Papyrus 10, the record of a slave sale made in 350/349,[1] a secure fixed date. The remarkably clear impression lacks any nick that would suggest a ring hoop, although its oval shape belongs to metal finger rings of the late fifth/early fourth century.[2] The convex surface of the sealing indicates a correspondingly concave seal surface.

A curly-haired, clean-shaven young man wearing only a chlamys fastened with a clasp at the throat stands in three-quarter view, looking to his right. His eye is large, his nose beaked, and his chin recedes. The chlamys reaches halfway down the back of his thighs. His right (far) leg carries his weight, while the left leg is bent slightly at the knee so that only the toes touch the ground. He has pulled his left elbow back with wrist and hand at hip level. In his left hand he holds a rather sketchy *kerykeion* (caduceus)—the staff of Hermes—drum-major fashion. The base of the staff extends up from his hand and under his left armpit with the top of the caduceus visible behind his left shoulder.[3] The finial of the caduceus staff does not read clearly.[4] The viewer's eye is drawn not to the caduceus, however, but to the branch-like object which the youth holds in his barely extended right hand. In the initial publication of WD **14**, Cross recognized it as an *aphlaston* or ship's stern ornament.[5]

---

[1] Papyrus 10 recorded a restricted slave contract with the notation that the slave was bought back (F. M. Cross, personal communication).

[2] Boardman, *GGFR*, 212–14.

[3] Cf. Hermes on a bell krater of *c.*350 in Paris (Louvre K238 = *LIMC*, 'Hermes', fig. 819). *LIMC*, 'Hermes' addresses the different ways of holding the caduceus (381–2, with illustrations).

[4] Note a similarly sketchy caduceus on a late Italian scarab (third century BCE, probably from southern Italy) in the British Museum (Walters, *BMC* 918 = Zazoff, *AG*, pl 90, 8).

[5] Cross, 'Papyri', 28. *Aphlaston* is the technical term (of uncertain derivation) for a ship's sternpost and the ornament atop the sternpost. *Akrostolion* and *akroterion*, both of which may refer to the sternpost of a ship, are more general terms which may also be used in non-naval contexts. Cf. L. Casson, *Ships and Seamanship in the Ancient*

The bulla demonstrates the artist's control of the planes of the composition. The parts of the image closer to the viewer are progressively more deeply carved to be more distinct. The caduceus, in particular, recedes into the background void. The chlamys folds and the 'leaves' of the *aphlaston* are distinct but more shallowly cut.

For the seafaring Greeks, the *aphlaston* symbolized a victory at sea; especially in the fifth century, victorious Greeks dedicated the stern ornaments of captured enemy ships as trophies in their temples.[6] Athena in particular appears with the *aphlaston*,[7] not only because her city was the pre-eminent Greek sea power, but also because she patronized the crafts of shipbuilding, navigation, and warfare.[8] The *aphlaston* appears clearly in her hand on a late fifth/early fourth-century sard scaraboid from Kourion (Cyprus) in the British Museum,[9] and on a red figure lekythos by the Brygos Painter in the Metropolitan Museum from late in the first quarter of the fifth century.[10] Both the vase and the seal come from areas (Cyprus and Sicily) with a significant Phoenician presence.

The WD **14** *aphlaston* fits neatly into the typology of the Classical period.[11] On vases, *aphlastoi* consist of two or more parallel curved vertical 'branches' like a thin bunch of reeds with an applied ornament such as a snake or a mask. On seals, including the Athena scaraboid (see above), the ornamentation most often resembles

---

World (Princeton, 1971) 86 (and n. 49) and 389. 'It was no mere ornament on the stern, but . . . a semaphore or signal post, consisting of a group of curving slats or boards of varied heights on which were hung the pennants or 'taenia', signals of the captain' (A. B. Brett, 'The Aphlaston, Symbol of Naval Victory or Supremacy on Greek and Roman Coins', *Transactions of the International Numismatic Congress*, eds. J. Allen, H. Mattingly and E. S. G. Robinson [London, 1938] 32). An Archaic scaraboid (*c.*500) from Phaleron in the Metropolitan Museum (Richter, *EGGE*, 144 = Richter, MMA, 42.11.21) illustrates a ship with its *aphlaston* clearly in evidence.

[6] *LIMC*, s.v. 'Athena', p. 1037 and Brett, 'Aphlaston', 32. By giving up or losing its *aphlaston* a ship signalled its submission.

[7] Brett, 'Aphlaston', *passim*, with numerous references and illustrations.

[8] H. Rose, *A Handbook of Greek Mythology* (New York, 1959) 108–9, 111–12 with references.

[9] Zazoff, *AG*, fig. 42.d = Zazoff, *AG*, pl 34,11 (best photograph) = British Museum 89.11–11.1 = Walters, *BMC*, 515 = Boardman, *GGFR*, 486 = Richter, *EGGE*, 242 = Lippold, *Gemmen*, pl XX,3 = Furtwängler, *AG*, pl IX, 33 = *LIMC*, s.v. 'Athena', fig. 614.

[10] From Gela (Sicily); J. Boardman, *Athenian Red Figure Vases: The Archaic Period, A Handbook* (London, 1975) fig. 249, Richter, MMA, 25.189.1 (= Boardman, *ARV²*, 384, 21). Cf. also Boardman, *ARV*, fig. 366, a menacing Athena with an *aphlaston* on a Nolan amphora by the Nikon Painter in the British Museum, BM E299 (= Boardman, *ARV*, 650,1).

[11] On an electrum stater of Cyzicus Athena holds an *aphlaston* like that on WD **14** (Brett, 'Aphlaston', 24 and pl IV, 2). Evagorus I, King of Salamis and ally of Athens minted at least two staters (*c.*394) with Athena sitting on the prow of a ship and holding an *aphlaston* (Brett, 'Aphlaston', p. 24, fig. 2 and pl IV, 4). The *aphlaston* here is beginning to curl into the 'shepherd's crook' shape of the later coins.

Cross, 'Papyri', 28 and Walters, *BMC*, p. 63 cite as a parallel a fourth-century silver stater of Side (Hill, *BMC Coins*, vol. 28 [Lycia], pl XXVI, 4–6), but the object in Apollo's hand bears little resemblance to an *aphlaston* of any period and is probably his laurel staff. The Hellenistic Sidonian coin cited by Cross (*BMC Coins*, vol. 25 [Phoenicia], pl XLII, 17) does show a youth holding an *aphlaston*, but of a type found only later, curved like a shepherd's crook and looking quite different from the one on WD **14**.

For an intermediate form close to WD **14** and actually attached to its ship, cf. *BMC Coins*, vol. 28 (Lycia), pl XVI, 9, a bronze coin of Phaselis minted in the fourth and third centuries.

leafy tendrils.[12] In the Hellenistic and Roman periods, several Phoenician cities adopted the *aphlaston* as a coin device: Sidon, Aradus, Marathus.[13] However, by this time it had evolved into a bushy shepherd's crook.

Besides Athena, other gods known to carry an *aphlaston* include Apollo, Poseidon, and Nike.[14] The caduceus on WD **14**, however, identifies the figure as Hermes, the gods' messenger, who usually carries his staff in his left hand.[15]

Why Hermes should carry an aphlaston or be connected to the sea is unclear.[16] If, as suspected, WD **14** is the impression of a seal made in a Phoenician workshop, it is possible that this is an example of iconographic confusion on the part of a non-Greek seal engraver whose understanding of the caduceus, the *aphlaston* and, indeed, of Hermes was not that of a Greek but of a quasi-Hellenized Phoenician. Hermes' caduceus was Phoenician before it was Greek[17] and its possibly separate Near Eastern identity continued into the Hellenistic period when, for example, it was the mint-mark of Cypriot Soli (originally founded by Phoenicians).[18]

A possible parallel with a fairly good Phoenician provenance is one of four seals depicting Hermes in the de Clercq collection assembled in Lebanon in the nineteenth

---

[12] Cf. Boardman, *GGFR*, 674 and 801, both rings decorated with a nymph holding an *aphlaston* and seated on the prow of a ship.

[13] Hill, *BMC Coins*: Vol. 25 (Phoenicia): Sidon: pls XXI,11; XLII, 17. Aradus: pls IV, 8-10; V,7. Marathus: pl XV, 2.

[14] *LIMC*, s.v. 'Athena', p. 1037. Cf. H. T. Ward-Gery, 'Note on *Akroteria*', *JHS* 53 (1933) 99–110.

[15] Greek artists in all media including glyptics often portrayed Hermes. Cf. P. Zanker, *Wandel der Hermesgestalt in der attischen Vasenmalerei*, (Bonn,1965); *LIMC*, s.v. 'Hermes'. For Hermes on Greek gems, cf. Richter, *EGGE*, 122, 160, 220; on Etruscan gems cf. Richter, *EGGE*, 728 and 733. Boardman, *GGFR* also cites Schmidt, *Persepolis II*, no. 55, which shows a nude youth whose attributes, if any, are vague.

Other heralds in Greek art carry the caduceus: Iris and Talthybios, the herald of *Iliad* I. These scenes probably borrow from the iconography of Hermes.

Cross proposed to identify the youth on WD **14** as Jason, mainly on the basis of two Etruscan scarabs, one from the Archaic period and one from the Classical (Cross, 'Papyri', 28, citing Furtwängler, *AG*, pl XVIII, 4 and pl XX, 26). Neither Etruscan seal, however, shows Jason like the WD **14** youth grasping the *aphlaston*; instead Jason stands behind the stern of the *Argo* as if literally about to push off. The *Argo*'s *aphlaston* appears in the scene, but in an entirely different context from the scenes with Athena described above. Athena holds an *aphlaston* torn from an enemy vessel as a trophy; Jason's *aphlaston* on the Etruscan scarabs is part of the intact *Argo*. The Archaic scarab (Furtwängler, *AG*, pl XVIII, 4) even includes a tiny oar on the *Argo*'s gunwhale. In all Jason's many adventures he never fought a sea battle, so he would never have had the opportunity to capture an enemy *aphlaston* and brandish it in triumph. Given the symbolism of the *aphlaston*, Jason would hardly be likely to parade his own ship's stern ornament as a trophy, nor would he have been able to, since the *Argo*'s *aphlaston* was ripped off as the ship swept through the Symplegades (Apollonius of Rhodes II, 605).

[16] Boardman, (*GGFR*, p. 310) observes that Hermes and Athena are often associated in the late fifth century and cites a scaraboid from Sardis on which Hermes converses with Athena (*GGFR*, 855, in Istanbul). The present editor is aware of only one parallel in any medium which shows Hermes with an *aphlaston*, a silver ring of the early fourth century in the Metropolitan Museum (Richter, MMA, no. 93 and p. 25); the god leans on a column with his caduceus behind him and an object before him which could be an *aphlaston* (suggested by Cross in 'Papyri', p. 28). Hermes appears on a fifth-century Etruscan scarab standing over waves of water which Walters suggests might be Acheron, the river of Death (Walters, *BMC* 656).

[17] W. Burkert, *Greek Religion* (Cambridge, Mass., 1985) 158.

[18] Brett, 'Aphlaston', p. 27.

century (often by 'excavating' Phoenician graves).[19] Stylistically, the de Clercq scaraboid is cruder than WD **14**. The messenger god wears a himation and carries the caduceus in one hand, a leafy branch held vertically in the other. It would be tempting to call the branch an *aphlaston*, but it clearly is not. But the similarity between the de Clercq branch and the WD **14** *aphlaston* is intriguing, additionally so because they come from the same geographical area.[20] As in the de Clercq collection, Hermes appears several times in the Wadi Daliyeh corpus[21] and excavators at Samaria itself found a contemporary ring impression of Hermes.[22]

Can any special significance be ascribed to the scene on WD **14**? Here the Phoenician connection is tantalizing, but only speculative. The fact that in a collection of seals with Phoenician provenances Hermes appears relatively often (albeit as part of a small group of seals which may only reflect the tastes of the collector) perhaps implies that Hermes, as well as the caduceus, had a Phoenician interpretation. Late (first century BCE) sources commonly equated Hermes with Thoth, the Egyptian god of scribes who was credited in some circles with the invention of the Phoenician alphabet.[23] Philo of Byblos in the late first century CE implies this was an equation made by the Phoenicians as well.[24] However Thoth (Philo's Taautos) in these late sources has taken on philosophical trappings, and it is uncertain whether the Phoenicians were making the same equation some three centuries earlier.

It should not be forgotten, either, that in the Persian period the Phoenicians were among the foremost sailors and merchants of the ancient world, and Phoenician ships were the backbone of the Imperial navy. Judging from their coinage in the Hellenistic period (see above) it can be assumed that the Phoenicians had already for some time recognized the *aphlaston*, a naval symbol, as an appropriate emblem for a nautical people.[25] Next, it should be kept in mind that Hermes watched over travellers, tricksters, and thieves as well as crossroads, borders, and graves.[26] Who better for a Hellenized Phoenician merchant to take as a patron than Hermes? It is conceivable that WD **14** comes from a seal with a Phoenician background, perhaps made by a

---

[19] De Ridder, *Collection*, 2812, a brown carnelian scaraboid. The other three are 2811, 2813 and 1814. On all four, Hermes has his caduceus.

[20] Another seal in the de Clercq collection (de Ridder, *Collection*, 2832) shows Nike carrying an *aphlaston*. It reportedly came from Ashkelon, and Boardman dates it to the fourth century (Boardman, *GGFR*, no. 660, p. 421); a nice parallel to WD **14** in date, *aphlaston*, and Phoenician-influenced provenance.

[21] In the Hecht Group also (pl XXIV.9).

[22] The impression of a leaf-shaped ring on a wine jar of 'Israelite-Greek' form. It showed a 'naked god standing left with a caduceus in [his right] hand and a garment over [the left, lowered] arm' (Reisner, Fisher, Lyon, *Harvard*, pl 57, f2).

[23] Cicero, *Nat. D.* 3.22 and Diodorus Siculus, 1.16.2, *apud* H. W. Attridge and R. A. Oden, Jr., *Philo of Byblos: The Phoenician History* (CBQMS 9; Washington, D.C., 1981) 72 n. 8.

[24] Attridge and Oden, p. 29 and refs.

[25] 'Phoenicia' refers to the aggregation of ethnically related city states with distinct civic identities; they were never united into a nation called 'Phoenicia'.

[26] Burkert, *Greek Religion*, 156–9. In Greek literature (reflecting Greek prejudice), Phoenicians had an unsavoury reputation as thieves—'gnawers at other men's goods' (*Odyssey* 15.415–6)—and as tricksters 'well-skilled in beguilements' (*Odyssey* 16.288–90; 15.419) (R. Lattimore trans.).

Phoenician artist for the Phoenician market. Naval symbolism would have meant little to the land-locked Samarians.[27]

---

[27] See the discussion of WD **49** (p. 47ff.).

WD 49. Hermes (?)

(PLATE I.3)

Mus. Inv. 946
Loose sealing
Image size: 1.4 cm x 0.9 cm (as preserved)
Bulla size: 2 cm x 1.4 cm
Clay colour: reddish brown
String preserved; top and bottom of vertical image
Papyrus fibres on front and back
Papyrus imprint
Seal type: metal finger ring

THE leaf-shaped oval configuration of this impression, a shape familiar from other Wadi Daliyeh bullae, was probably produced by a metal finger ring. Alhough the bulla is intact, careless sealing has distorted the image, while pits and scrapes have eliminated any fine detail.

As with WD **28** and WD **29**, a beardless youth appears in three-quarter pose with a himation draped over his shoulders (almost a mirror image of WD **28**). In this particular example the youth looks down to his right with his face in profile. His right arm hangs down beside his right thigh. His right (far) leg carries his weight; the left leg is bent slightly back. The himation drapes over the young man's left and right shoulders and hangs to mid-thigh.

With his left hand he balances a short staff against his left shoulder. The top of the staff is indistinct. The youth holds it like a sceptre rather than a trophy or weapon. Variations on the pose with the himation, hand on hip, and arm lowered may be seen on vases of the late fifth and the fourth century. Hermes, for example, on a vase by the Painter of the Karlsruhe Paris[1] resembles the figure on WD **49**, although he holds the caduceus in the lowered right hand, not as a sceptre. The figure on WD **49** bears some artistic kinship to the elegant youths of the late fifth-century master, the Meidias Painter,[2] and to the related, if more solid, figures of the Ornate Style (404–*c*.375).[3]

In determining the possible identity of the figure on WD **49**, some weight has to be given to the shortness of the staff; in Greek art, the figure who consistently carries a short staff is Hermes, whose symbol is the caduceus.[4] The messenger god usually holds

---

[1] Boardman, *GA*, fig. 179, a red figure hydria (Karlsruhe, Badisches Landesmuseum, 259).

[2] G. Nicole, *Meidias et le style fleuri dans la céramique attique* (Geneva, 1908) pl XIII.

[3] J. J. Herrmann, *In the Shadow of the Acropolis: Popular and Private in 4th Century Athens*, p. 26ff.

[4] *LIMC*, s.v. 'Hermes'. See also Metzger, *Représentations*, pl II, 3 (Berlin Pergamonmuseum F 2660); Metzger, *Représentations*, pl XXII,5 (Berlin F 2645); Boardman, *ARV*, fig. 252.1 (British Museum E65); K. Schefold, *Die Göttersage in der klassischen und hellenistischen Kunst* (Munich, 1981) fig. 25 (Tübingen 1600).

the caduceus in his left hand, as it appears also on WD **14**.[5] Besides the caduceus, this impression may show another detail of Hermes' iconography. There seems to be a wing-like shape on the figure's head, perhaps like the wing which sprouts from Iris' hair on a fourth-century hydria in Berkeley,[6] or alternately, a cap with wings, as attested on an early Classical amphora of the Alkamichos Painter[7] and on a calyx krater of c.435 by the Phiale Painter.[8] A third possibility is that the hat is the 'Robin Hood' type that Perseus wears on WD **54**, but which Hermes customarily wears on Attic vase paintings.[9]

Hermes also appears, adjusting his sandal, on a bulla in the Hecht Group.[10] Beyond the Wadi Daliyeh group of bullae, Hermes appears on a number of Classical rings.[11] The more square-set Boston Hermes leaning on a column[12] cited several times in this catalogue,[13] has a similar stance, and his chlamys folds may be compared to the himation ends on WD **49**.

Although there is no firm evidence, it is entirely within the realm of possibility that the WD **49** ring came from a workshop in Phoenicia. As mentioned in the discussion of WD **14**, Hermes with his caduceus was the subject of a ring impression found at Samaria,[14] and several sixth- through fourth-century engraved gems and rings with Phoenician provenances or associations including four examples in the de Clercq collection.[15] On two of these he wears a himation like a shawl.[16] The Bibliothèque Nationale in Paris has a large late sixth- or early fifth-century chalcedony ringstone showing a himation-draped Hermes with a ram, a common type in the Hellenistic and Roman periods.[17]

WD **49** could have come from a fifth-century heirloom, but the secure mid-fourth century context should probably take priority in determining the ring date.

---

[5] See *LIMC*, s.v. 'Hermes', 381–2 on the disposition of the caduceus.

[6] Metzger, *Représentations*, pl VIII, 1 (Berkeley 8.3316).

[7] Leningrad 2100; illustrated in Schefold, *Klassischen*, fig. 432.

[8] Vatican 16586, illustrated in Schefold, *Klassischen*, fig. 28.

[9] *LIMC*, s.v. 'Hermes', 383–5 presents the various hats Hermes wears. Cf. discussion of WD **54**.

[10] See pl XXIV.9.

[11] Boardman, *GGFR*, cf. index to Classical and Graeco-Persian subjects. All the Classical Greek seals with Hermes listed by Boardman seem to be metal finger rings.

[12] Boston 28.598 = Boardman, *GGFR*, 663 = Beazley, *Lewes House*, no. 48 = Richter, *EGGE*, 220; bought in Constantinople. G. Horster (*Statuen auf Gemmen*, [Bonn, 1970] 17–18) disagrees with Richter's and Furtwängler's fifth-century date, preferring the early fourth century.

[13] Cf. the discussion of WD **7** and WD **57**.

[14] Reisner, Fisher, Lyon, *Harvard*, pl 57, f2.

[15] De Ridder, *Collection*, 2811–14.

[16] De Ridder, *Collection*, 2812, 2814.

[17] Bordreuil, *BN*, 42, no. 37. See also *idem*, 'Nouveaux apports de l'archéologie et de la glyptique à l'onomastique phénicienne', *Atti del I congreso internazionale di studi fenici e punici, 1979*, Vol. III (Rome, 1983) 754–5.

WD 28. Nude Youth with Himation

(PLATE II.1)

Mus. Inv. 925
Loose sealing
Image size: 1.3 cm x 0.9 cm (as preserved)
Bulla size: 1.6 cm x 1.4 cm
Clay color: reddish brown
String preserved; top and bottom of vertical image
Papyrus fragments on back
Papyrus imprint
Seal type: metal finger ring (?)

WD **28** is one of two sealings—with WD **29**—which depict nude youths in a three-quarter pose, one hand on a hip and a himation over the shoulder. They fit into the large amorphous category of nude Greek youths so well represented among the Wadi Daliyeh sealings. A probable ring hoop nick above the youth's head suggests WD **28** was made by a finger ring with a rounded oval bezel. The shape is one that becomes popular on finger rings as the Classical period progresses into the fourth century.[1]

The condition of the impression is only fair; overall, the surface is quite grainy and details have been lost. From the hips up, the surface is so indistinct that details of face and gesture cannot be read with any certainty. The bottom of the sealing has broken away, taking the figure's feet with it.

A short-haired, probably beardless, nude male figure gazes down at something indistinct which he holds before him in his left hand. His right hand rests on his hip. The left (far) leg carries the man's weight while the right is bent back slightly at the knee. The general impression is one of a tall, slim youth with a very slight bend at the hips. Over his right shoulder the youth wears a himation which he has draped over his right arm (and perhaps his left, as well).

Judging by the youth's elongated proportions, the modelling of his right thigh and the folds of the himation that fall parallel to it, the carving may originally have been quite fine, although the three-quarter pose has given the artist some trouble; the torso remains frontal while everything else is in proper perspective. As for the modelling of the torso, the central ridge of the chest remains, along with a hint of the pectorals.

If the figure on WD **28** held an identifiable attribute in his hand, it is now lost and he remains nameless; or his hand may have been empty. Dionysos on a fourth-century bell krater gestures graciously, like the figure here, with an empty hand.[2]

---

[1] Boardman, *GGFR*, pp. 212–14.

[2] Cf. Metzger, *Représentations*, pl XVI, 4 and p. 147 (Madrid Museum 11080).

WD 29. Nude Youth with Himation and Branch (?)

(PLATE II.2)

Mus. Inv. 926
Loose sealing
Image size: 1.0 cm x 0.6 cm
Bulla size: 1.4 cm x 1 cm (as preserved)
Clay color: reddish brown
String preserved, loop uncut; top and bottom of vertical image
Papyrus fragments on back
Papyrus imprint
Seal type: metal finger ring

BOTH the pointed oval shape of WD **29** and the apparent ring hoop nick at the base of the impression suggest that a metal finger ring of the late fifth or early fourth century made the impression.[1] The uncut loop of string still attached to the clay signals the loss of the papyrus document that the bulla once sealed. The surface of the sealing has splayed and broken off, taking with it the top of the figure's head, his upraised left hand and the extreme top and upper right edge of the impression.

WD **29,** like WD **28,** shows a short-haired beardless youth in three-quarter pose, hand on hip, wearing only a himation and looking down at something he holds in his raised left hand, perhaps a leafy branch. This youth is shorter with a heftier build than the figure on WD **28.** The awkward angle of the (near) right leg which carries the youth's weight makes him look as if he is walking to the left but the hand on the hip and the slight curve of the body indicates that he is at rest. The artist has almost succeeded with the torso; at least the pectoral muscles slant down and away. The (far) left leg bends back at the knee so that only the toes touch the ground. The right foot seems to have worn away. One large eye is distinct as are the youth's curls. The himation drapes over his left shoulder, falling to knee level in two apparently weighted folds.

An attendant at the rebirth of Kore on a fourth-century red-figured pyxis presents a similar draping of the himation and positioning of the legs.[2] The type appears on coins of the Classical period, but usually has identifying attributes such as a crown, a branch and/or a *patera.*[3] A comparable youth, without the crown, appears on a gold ring in the de Clercq collection.[4] No clear attributes have survived to identify the subject of WD **29.** He may simply be an anonymous *ephebos.*

---

[1] Boardman, *GGFR*, pp. 212–14.

[2] Illustrated in Metzger, *Représentations*, pl VI, 2 and p. 82 (City Museum of Birmingham).

[3] I.e. Apollo on a fourth-century silver stater of Side (*BMC Coins*: Vol. 28 [Lycia] pl XXVI,7).

[4] De Ridder, *Collection*, 2826, from Amrit.

WD 57. Youth Leaning on Pillar

(PLATE II.3)

Mus. Inv. 954
Loose sealing
Image size: 1.5 cm x 0.7 cm
Bulla size: 1.7 cm x 1.5 cm
Clay colour: reddish brown
String preserved, loop uncut; top and bottom of image
Papyrus fibres on back and front
Papyrus imprint
Seal type: metal finger ring

A METAL finger ring produced WD **43**; the haft of the ring has left its mark at the top of the impression. The pointed oval/leaf outline of the impression matches Boardman's ring type II, a shape he dates to the mid- to late fifth century with the caution that his dating of finger rings is only approximate.[1] Indeed, the Wadi Daliyeh bullae show that the ring-type persists well into the fourth century on the periphery of the Greek world.

Part of the lower left quadrant of the impression and the bottom of the image have disappeared, or were never clearly impressed in the first place. A nick in the clay in the area of the lowered left hand renders it impossible to know if the figure was holding an object.

WD **57** shows a nude youth in extreme contrapposto, barely keeping upright by resting his right elbow on the capital of a short, slender pillar. In the impression, the youth is seen in three-quarter view as he looks down to his left; the youth's torso and neck suggest an attempt at modelling. His left leg supports his weight as he crooks his right leg around the front of the column. In his casually extended left hand he may be holding an object such as a patera or wreath, or he might be empty-handed.

While the motif of a man or woman leaning on a pillar often marks a work as Hellenistic, Greek vase painters of the fourth century made use of the compositional device of figures supporting themselves on pillars.[2] In the mid-fifth century, possibly following the lead of sculpture,[3] the image of a man or woman leaning on a pillar began

---

[1] Boardman, *GGFR*, pp. 212–14 and fig. 217.

[2] On an early fourth-century Kerch-style pelike, Paris makes his judgement while lounging against a pillar (K. Schefold, *Untersuchungen zu den Kertscher Vasen* [Berlin and Leipzig, 1934] no. 336, pl 37); another Kerch pelike shows Kore leaning against a slender column with a plain, flat capital (H. Metzger, *Recherches sur l'imagerie athénienne* (Paris, 1965) pl XXIV, Hermitage St. 1792). Vase paintings show free-standing pillars with statues mounted on their capitals as a visual shorthand for 'sanctuary'.

[3] G. Horster in her discussion of the 'leaning' motif in Classical glyptic (*Statuen*, pp. 17–18) sees no one work as the prototype; gem cutters, like painters, were the products of their time, and were familiar with 'statuesque' poses in general.

to appear on Greek seals.[4] Indeed, another Samarian bulla—in the Hecht Group—
shows a woman, perhaps Aphrodite, with her back to a column.[5] On a ring in Boston
variously dated to the fifth and fourth centuries, Hermes' pillar-supported stance
mirrors that of the WD **57** youth although the stout, fluted column he leans against is
Ionic.[6]

Perhaps a ring in the de Clercq collection should count as the most significant
parallel, proving that the column motif was known in Phoenicia; the ring came from a
Phoenician tomb in Gebel (Lebanon) and shows an ephebic Eros leaning on a column.[7]
Both Eros and his column are built more stockily than their counterparts on WD **57**,
but the god's pose is an almost exact mirror-image of the WD **57** figure, including an
empty, free hand. Without his wings, Eros here would be as nameless as the young
man on WD **57**.

The WD **57** ring shape also appears in Phoenicia according to the evidence of the de
Clercq group.[8] If, as is likely, WD **57** comes from the early or mid-fourth century, its
shape, as well as its imagery, would not be out of place in Phoenicia.[9]

Can the nude youth pictured on WD **57** be identified?[10] The pillar could be setting
the scene in a gymnasium or temple. On the other hand, the youth's pose is essentially
generic and continues to be so into the Hellenistic and Roman periods.[11] In the absence
of any distinguishing iconography on WD **57**, his identity remains very much in the
realm of uncertainty.

In view of the poor state of preservation of the bulla, it may seem presumptuous to
make such a claim, but the youth's slender proportions and small head relative to his
body suggest the sculptural proportions of the victorious athletes portrayed by
Lysippos in the second and third quarters of the fourth century.[12]

---

[4] Boardman, *GGFR*, p. 216. A bronze ring with a leaf-shaped bezel found at Persepolis in a fifth-century context
may show an armed figure leaning on a pillar (Schmidt, *Persepolis II*, pl 17, ring no. 231). Seals show as many or
more women leaning against a column in both the late Classical and Hellenistic periods. Fourth century: Richter,
EGGE, 252 = Boardman, *GGFR*, 768; Richter, *EGGE*, 253; Boardman, *GGFR*, 736; Boardman, *GGFR*, 857 =
Richter, *EGGE*, 245, according to Boardman, a Greco-Persian ring from Syria.

[5] See pl XXIV.10.

[6] Boston 28.598 = Boardman, *GGFR*, fig. 663 = Beazley, *Lewes House*, no. 48 = Richter, *EGGE*, 220; bought in
Constantinople. Horster (*Statuen*, 17–18) disagrees with Richter's and Furtwängler's fifth century date, preferring
the early fourth century.

[7] De Ridder, *Collection*, no. 2833, with a rounded oval bezel.

[8] Boardman, *GGFR*, p. 221.

[9] The leaning youth appears later in a decidedly Phoenician context. In the late third and second centuries BCE,
the Phoenician city of Marathus minted coins on whose reverse the semi-nude male figure of Marathus leans on a
column and holds an *aphlaston* (*BMC Coins* [Phoenicia] pl XV, 2–6).

[10] There is no evidence to support an identification of the Greek youth as Prince Absolom who set up a pillar
'for the memory of [his] name' in the King's Valley outside Jerusalem (2 Sam 18:18).

[11] Cf. the numerous examples in Richter, *EGGE*, 519–24.

[12] J. J. Pollitt, *Art in the Hellenistic Age* (Cambridge, 1986) 47–8.

WD 1. Nude Youth with Shield

(PLATE III.1)

Mus. Inv. 957
Loose sealing
Image size: 1.4 x 0.9 cm
Bulla size: 1.8 x 1.4 cm
Clay colour: deep reddish brown
String preserved; parallel to vertical image
Papyrus imprint
Seal type: metal finger ring

WD **1** bears the imprint of a leaf-shaped (pointed oval) metal finger ring. This shape, common among the Wadi Daliyeh bullae, appears among Greek seal rings in the late Archaic period and continues through the fourth century, gradually becoming a full oval.[1] Tiny papyrus fibres still adhere to the sealed surface, a frequent phenomenon in this corpus.[2]

The clay was not deeply impressed and the image is worn and chipped at the top and lower right. Nevertheless, the figure of a nude warrior can easily be made out. He stands at ease in three-quarter pose, his head turned to his left. The shield which he correctly carries on his left arm hides the arm and shoulder themselves. His right leg supports his weight. He rests his right hand on his hip and his left foot lingers slightly behind the right. On the basis of the ring shape and the analogies from vase painting, WD **1** could be dated to the early fourth century, but the archaeological context does not exclude a slightly later date.

Standing warriors and youths became a staple in Classical Greek glyptic art. Yet despite Boardman's comment that '[s]tudies of single standing figures begin to become more common from the later fifth century on . . .',[3] a glance through the plates of his handbooks turns up no clear parallels to WD **1**. Richter's two pages of Classical 'standing male figures at rest and in action'[4] bear out Boardman's point and provide a good sense of the variety here, but she includes no such warriors as WD **1**. When they appear, warriors assume different, more dramatic poses involving leaning over or reaching out.[5] The closest parallel is a bulla from Phoenician Tell Keisan, north of

---

[1] Ashmolean/*EGFR*, 29.

[2] See INTRODUCTION, pp. 18–19.

[3] Boardman, *GGFR*, p. 201.

[4] Richter, *EGGE*, figs. 218–35.

[5] The Etruscans (whose art often reflects Phoenician influences) in the fifth and fourth centuries and even later were especially fond of warrior seals, but Etruscan engravers preferred to show the warrior bending or curving to follow the outline of the seal (cf. P. Zazoff, *Etruskische Skarabaën* [Mainz,1968]; Walters, *BMC*, pl 11–12). Etruscan

Samaria on the coastal plain near Akko, with an almost identical figure—even with the same dimensions—in mirror image though apparently without the shield.[6]

As with the many other Wadi Daliyeh 'nude youth' images, both WD **1** and the Tell Keisan bulla call to mind Boardman's de Clercq group of gold finger rings[7] acquired almost exclusively in Lebanon (a few in Syria),[8] hence with a 'Phoenician connection'. Boardman thinks the de Clercq rings 'seem to represent local production, probably by Greeks'[9] but why not a Phoenician engraver working in a Greek style? The same question obviously applies to WD **1**. The de Clercq group of exclusively gold seal rings 'executed in a rather stiff and summary manner'[10] includes several parallels to WD **1**,[11] especially the clean-shaven, bare-headed warrior on a gold ring of the same shape as WD **1** dug up in Amrit;[12] he carries a spear, but holds his shield in a manner similar to WD **1**. Phoenician patrons may have had a special liking for seals in the Greek style depicting single, standing warriors and youths. If WD **1** belongs to this rather heterogeneous group, perhaps it can be speculated that it was made by a gold ring.

In Bordreuil's recent publication of the inscribed West Semitic seals in the Bibliothèque Nationale, there is another example of the motif[13] which Bordreuil dates to the second half of the fifth century—another candidate for Boardman's de Clercq Group? Enough of the image on this worn gold seal ring (inscribed with the good Phoenician-Punic name, Hanno) remains to make out a nude warrior of elongated proportions standing frontally with his weight on his right leg against which balances a shield decorated with a silen (old satyr) head.

---

seals also differ from WD **1** and the other similar WD impressions in having a pronounced border. The Etruscans did not export their native scaraboids (Zazoff, *AG*, 128–9).

    [6] Keel, 'Tell Keisan', no. 33. Keel labels it 'hellenistic', but its similarity to WD **1** suggests an earlier dating.

    [7] See INTRODUCTION and Boardman, *GGFR*, p. 221.

    [8] Bordreuil, *BN*, 7.

    [9] Boardman, *GGFR*, p. 221.

    [10] Boardman, *GGFR*, p. 221, figs. 222–4 (drawings only) = de Ridder, *Collection*, 2825, 2868, 2870 respectively.

    [11] De Ridder, *Collection*, nos. 2825–6.

    [12] De Ridder, no. 2825.

    [13] Bordreuil, *BN*, no. 32 (inscribed in Phoenician, "HN' BN 'RS"). Cf. also the Greek warrior leaning over to pick up his shield on another Phoenician seal of the late fifth century, *BN*, no. 34 (= Boardman, *AG Gems*, 308).

WD21D. Standing Nude Youth

(PLATES III.2 AND XXII.2D)

Mus. Inv. 780

Papyrus 2, December 352/January 351

Image size: [approx.] 1.3 cm x 0.7 cm

Bulla size: [approx.] 1.8 cm x 1.2 cm

Clay colour: undetermined

String preserved; top and bottom vertical image

Papyrus imprint: undetermined

Seal type: scaraboid? ring?

WD **21D**[1] along with at least three other bullae,[2] was originally attached to Samaria Papyrus 2 which 'records the sale of one male and one female slave (names unknown) to a woman ʾAbiʿadin (patronymic unknown) by Qôsnahar (patronymic unknown) for 23 sheqels';[3] according to the Persian date formula ('in the month of Tebet, the seventh year of Artaxerxes III [Ochus]') the sale occurred in December 352 or January 351.[4] There is no way of knowing which, if any, of the four attached bullae belonged to ʾAbiʿadin, whose name is probably Israelite[5] or to the apparently Edomite seller. The association of WD **21D** with a dated papyrus places it firmly in a mid-fourth century context.

Solely on the basis of a photograph it is difficult to make too definite a judgement as to the state of preservation of WD **21D**, the type of the seal which produced it or the identification of the image. No sealing outlines appear in the photograph. Since so many of the bullae from Daliyeh depicting nude youths seem to have been impressed by rings, it is not unlikely that WD **21D** may have been as well.

The photograph seems to show a nude youth standing in either a frontal or three-quarter pose. His head is obscured by an abrasion. There is a clear indication of contrapposto; the youth rests his weight on his right leg, bending his left leg gently back, a stance which forces his right hip slightly upward. The placement of the right arm seems clear; from the shoulder to the flexed elbow, it is kept close to the torso, but

---

[1] This description is based on a photograph. WD **21D** was unavailable for inspection.

[2] It is likely that Samaria Papyrus 2 was initially sealed with more than the four preserved bullae. Besides WD **21D**, two bullae from Samaria Papyrus 2 are (variably) legible; WD **21B** shows a dancing satyr, and WD **21C** probably depicted an Achaemenid contest scene or a pair of symmetrical animals (see pl XXII.2).

[3] Gropp, *Samaria Papyri*, 38–62. Preliminary publication by Cross, 'Report', 17–26.

[4] Gropp, *Samaria Papyri*, 62.

[5] Cross, 'Report', 23; ʾAbiʿadin 'is a typical feminine name', 'My (divine) father is the fertile one' (Cross, 'Report', 23). An Israelite woman, whose seal was published by N. Avigad, has a similar name, Hamiʿeden (N. Avigad, 'New Names on Hebrew Seals', *ErIsr* 12 [1975; Hebrew] 66:1).

For a discussion of women and seals, and speculation concerning Samaria Papyrus 2, see the entry on WD **21B**.

the lower arm is extended slightly forward. The left arm is indistinct but appears to be holding an upright spear (also indistinct). On the ground to the figure's right is an object which might be a circular shield, held upright with the interior decoration or supports visible. In that case, WD **21D** would depict a nude Greek warrior.

Several other Daliyeh bullae show warriors with shields,[6] but WD **21D** does not closely resemble any of them. On WD **21D**, the shield is on the ground, rather than being strapped to the warrior's arm; the spear (or staff) seems held out on a slant from beside the warrior's left foot, with an inverted triangle formed by the warrior's horizontal left forearm, his left side and the spear. While it is unusual for the staff to be in the left hand and the shield to be on the right side as they are on WD **21D**, confusion as to positive and negative on the part of the engraver could easily account for the discrepancy.

The warrior's stance with the staff and shield is most reminiscent of the Athena Parthenos, a glyptic version of which appears on a fourth-century gold ring, perhaps from Magna Graecia or Sicily.[7] An early Hellenistic ringstone (the so-called 'Neisos gem') in the Hermitage Museum provides a masculine version of the pose. Alexander the Great presents himself as a triumphant warrior at ease with his shield set upright on the ground beside him.[8]

It should also be noted, however, that an alternative identification might be Herakles. In that case, the shield disappears, and what is understood as the edge of the shield becomes an upright club.[9] If the WD **21D** youth were Herakles, he might carry his lion skin draped over his left arm, as on WD **11C**, and hold a bow. However, it would be expected that Herakles' right hand steadies the club or rests on it. In the available photograph, this seems not to be the case.

Without submitting the actual bulla to inspection, it is impossible to speculate too extensively on the decoration of WD **21D**. For the moment, the best reading of the design on WD **21D** would still seem to be that it represents a standing nude warrior, variants of which are found among the Wadi Daliyeh bullae.

---

[6] WD **1**, WD **26**, WD **32** (perhaps Perseus). On WD **1** and WD **26**, the warrior is nude; the warriors on WD **26** and WD **32** carry spears with their shields.

[7] Boardman, *GGFR*, 765, in the British Museum (Marshall, 69, pl 3). For later glyptic examples of the motif, cf. Richter, *EGGE*, 269, p. 67; the Athena on a mottled syenite scaraboid of the mid-third century in the Ashmolean Museum (Ashmolean/*EGFR*, 301 [1921.1237]) is quite similar in pose to the youth on WD **21D**.

[8] Richter, *EGGE*, 603 = Furtwängler, *AG*, pl XXXII, 11, p. 158 (Hermitage M609). Richter calls it an 'accomplished work of the late fourth or early third century'. Alexander has with him besides his shield, a sword, the aegis, an eagle and a thunderbolt but no spear. J. J. Pollitt discusses portraits of Alexander—including the Neisos Gem—and their relation to a putative Lysippan prototype in the first chapter of *Art in the Hellenistic Age* (Cambridge, 1986) esp. p. 23. If WD **21D** does, in fact, depict a warrior with shield and staff, it attests to the presence of the motif in the East before the arrival of Alexander, whose portrait tradition, no less than his deeds, provided an example for subsequent Hellenistic rulers of the East.

[9] Cf. the series of coins issued by Herakleia (Magna Graecia), discussed in connection with WD **11C** (Herakles with club, bow and lionskin), and Boardman, *GGFR*, 799, a bronze ring in the British Museum (Marshall, 1241), depicting Herakles (?) with shield and club.

WD 15B. Seated Youth

(PLATE III.3)

Mus. Inv. 766[1]
Papyrus 6
Image size: n.a.
Bulla size: n. a.
Clay colour: n.a.
String preserved; parallel to vertical image
Seal type: metal finger ring

WD **15B** is a vertically oriented leaf-shaped oval impression. WD **15B** and WD **15A**[2] were originally attached to Samaria Papyrus 6.[3] The impression seems to have been made by a metal finger ring; the haft of the ring has left its imprint at the base of the impression. Boardman assigns rings with this leaf shape (his type III) to the mid- to late fifth century,[4] at the same time cautioning that the distinctions between shapes are scarcely definitive. Boardman's classification does not rule out the possibility that this shape could also persist into the fourth century, especially outside the Greek world proper. WD **15B** probably comes from a metal finger ring of the mid-fourth century.

The image is easily read in its broad outlines. A nude youth sits on what may be a large rock. His legs are almost in profile while he twists around to his right (toward the viewer) so that his torso is in a three-quarter view and his left (far) shoulder is a little lower than his right. The left elbow is lowered by his side but anything below the elbow remains unclear. The right arm is easily visible; the gentle bend at the elbow indicates that he is supporting himself lightly with his right hand (on the surface of the rock?). He has stretched his right leg out before him; his left is retracted, with the right calf and part of the right foot forming an inverted 'y' with the straight, right leg. This fits with Greek compositional tendencies which appeared in the fifth century to 'have at least one leg retracted to provide variety'.[5] The proportions of the musculature, when indicated (or preserved), are not heavy, although some of the muscles are quite well defined—the youth's right shoulder, his pectorals, the central division of the rib cage, the groin, the right hip muscle. Unfortunately, the man's head is indistinct.

---

[1] WD **15A** was unavailable for examination. This entry is based on photographs only.

[2] WD **15A** is a sealing in the Persian Court Style.

[3] Papyrus 6 documents the sale of two slaves, one named ʾAbi-Luḥay (possibly a north Arabic name in the opinion of Cross [personal communication]); the names of the other slave and the interested parties as well as the number of witnesses and the date are not preserved (Gropp, *Samaria Papyri*, 102, 104).

[4] Boardman, *GGFR*, 213 (fig. 217), 212, and 214.

[5] Ridgway, *Fifth Century*, 236.

There seems to be a vaguely discernible division between hair and face, but even the direction of his gaze is debatable.

Judging by preserved examples of Classical Greek sculpture, seated figures, especially figures in the round, appear less often than other sculptural types, although they were hardly unknown.[6] WD **15B** does not call to mind a seated cult image[7] or any dramatic gestures and poses in Greek painting.[8] Even in its poor state of preservation, it is apparent that the figure's gaze is directed outward; he lacks the air of deep introspection which characterizes the traditional pose of the brooding man seated with elbows on knees.[9] The youth has the leisurely attitude apparent on fifth- and fourth-century Greek vases where gods and heroes pass idle hours in the pastoral countryside or on Mt. Olympos. And certainly, the combination of inactivity and nudity on WD **15B** sets it outside of Persian and even, perhaps, East Greek artistic conventions.[10]

The pose appears frequently on vases of the fourth century collected by Metzger for his studies of Athenian imagery.[11] However, if the seated youth on WD **15B** looks perfectly conventional from the standpoint of Greek art, a search among Greek seals does not turn up any exact parallel to the figure and pose on WD **15B**. Glyptic images of identifiable males sitting on furniture or on rocks and stumps include Zeus, Pan, Eros, Dionysos, or heroes such as a melancholy Philoctetes.[12] Often, however, the men are anonymous youths engaged in an identifiable leisure activity.[13]

A fifth-century scaraboid in the Ashmolean Museum provides an approximate parallel to WD **15B** in its depiction of an anonymous nude athlete idly sitting on a chest or stool.[14] As on WD **15B**, his legs are in profile, and his torso twists toward the

---

[6] Ridgway, *Fifth Century,* 121. Cult statues might represent the enthroned divinity whose suppliants could dedicate replicas of the cult image as votive offerings. An occasional funerary relief, such as the well-known Hegeso stele, in the National Museum, Athens, might show the dead man or woman seated on a chair (Ridgway, *Fifth Century,* fig. 107). Architectural friezes and pedimental sculpture provided another context for seated figures— deities especially, such as the group of three goddesses from the Athenian Parthenon's east pediment (Ridgway, *Fifth Century,* figs. 49–50).

[7] The cult image of Zeus enthroned, of the general type sculpted by Pheidias for Olympia, appears on a silver ring of the fourth century (Richter, *EGGE,* 270 = Paris, Cabinet des Médailles, no 517). Farther east, the dynasts of fourth-century Cilicia produced similar coins bearing the seated image of Baaltars, the 'Zeus of Tarsus'. A silver stater of this type minted by Mazaeus (Mazdai), satrap of Cilicia (361–333), was recovered at the Wadi Daliyeh excavation site (Cross, 'Coins', *DWD,* pl 80,2). The motif of a seated Zeus, along with related ones of Athena and local gods and goddesses, is more familiar on coins where the deity's image is a symbol with serious political content. WD **15B**, however, is probably not in the tradition of such imperial or civic symbols which made a coin into a political statement.

[8] Cf. G. Neumann, *Gesten und Gebärden in der griechischen Kunst* (Berlin, 1965).

[9] Neumann (*Gesten und Gebärden,* 125) designates it '*besorgtes Nachdenken*'. Philoctetes broods thus on an early fourth-century ringstone in Berlin (Richter, *EGGE,* 263 = Furtwängler, *AG,* pl 10, 29 [Staatliche Museen]). See also G. M. A. Richter 'Unpublished Gems in Various Collections', *AJA* 61 [1957] 267 and pl 80: 15, 17).

[10] Ridgway, *Fifth Century,* (91 and n. 30) asserts that even in East Greek territories 'nudity was considered disgraceful'. Cf. L. Bonfante, 'Nudity as a Costume in Classical Art', *AJA* 93 (1989) 543–70.

[11] Metzger, *Représentations, passim.*

[12] Richter, *EGGE,* 263, Berlin, Staatliche Museen, 'about 400 B.C.'.

[13] Cf. Richter, *EGGE,* nos. 261–70, a good selection of seated men.

[14] Boardman, *GGFR,* 636 = Richter, *EGGE,* 261, mottled jasper, said to come from Sparta (Ashmolean 1892.1485).

viewer with the left shoulder dropped. He is probably an athlete resting after his success; the wreath in his hair symbolizes victory. The youth on WD **15B**, however, seems bareheaded.

Since the man on WD **15B** is sitting on an irregular object which is probably a rock, it is likely that the sealing showed him on a cloak or pelt. On seals, coins, and vases divine visitors to the great outdoors tend to sit on rocks with a view to comfort, positioning a cloak, cushion, or animal skin between themselves and Nature's irregularities. Also, because mortal athletes tend not to sit on rocks in Classical sculpture or painting, the subject of WD **15B** should probably be identified as a god or hero.

A variety of gods, demi-gods, and heroes appear in the rocky wilds—Poseidon (in underwater landscapes), Iolaos (accompanying Herakles),[15] a hero on the Niobid Painter's name-vase.[16] Dionysos is a better possibility, given the presence among the Wadi Daliyeh bullae of maenads[17] and satyrs[18] and the wine god's predilection for the outdoors,[19] but he is represented less often on coins and seals, especially coins and seals—and vases as well—with an eastern connection, than is Herakles, the most likely candidate. A Levantine favourite, Herakles is attested several times on the Wadi Daliyeh bullae.[20] Might the lines below his right hand be his club? Of course, they might also be understood as the cloak/animal skin or the contours of his seat.

While an identification of Herakles here is quite conjectural, among numismatic parallels, there is the Herakles, nude, clean-shaven, and reclining on a boulder who appears on a silver stater (*c.*432) of the Magna Graecian town of Heraclea.[21] This composition differs from WD **15B** in that Herakles' right (far) foot rests on a higher part of the rock thus raising his right knee higher than his left. A similar seated Herakles from a source closer to Samaria appears on a four-obol coin minted at Salamis (Cyprus) by Evagoras I, *c.*400.[22] Excavators at the Levantine port site of Akko found an almost intact Attic bell krater of the early fourth century with a seated Herakles (on a himation) as its central figure.[23] He leans his elbow on his club, but his

---

[15] Metzger, *Représentations*; Poseidon: pl III, 4; Iolaos: pl XXVII, 4.

[16] Illustrated in Boardman, *GA,* fig. 168 (Louvre MNC 511), *c.*460. Cf. also E. Simon, 'Polygnotan Painting and the Niobid Painter', *AJA* 67 (1963) 43–62.

[17] WD **44**, WD **50**.

[18] WD **44**, WD **5/16B**, WD **21B**.

[19] On a Kerch style kalyx krater in Athens, Dionysos assumes a typical pose remarkably similar to that of the young man on WD **15B**; his legs cross and retract, just as on WD **15B**, as he sits on a himation and holds out a kantharos (Metzger, *Recherches*, pl XL = Athens, Nat. Mus. 12592. Cf. also Metzger, *Représentations*, pl 2, 1. On another Kerch vase, a pelike in the Hermitage Museum, Dionysos sits on a himation and supports his weight with his right arm as on WD **15B** (Metzger, *Représentations*, pl XV, 1, St. 1792).

[20] See entries for WD **11C**, WD **39**, WD **42**, WD **47**; see also pl XXIV.8.

[21] C. M. Kraay, *Archaic and Classical Greek Coins* (California, 1976) 735 = R. Holloway, *Art and Coinage in Magna Graecia* (Bellinzona, 1978) fig. 130. Holloway believes that this and related coins supplied the model for Michaelangelo's Sistine 'Adam' (p. 60).

[22] Kraay, *Coins*, 1084.

[23] R. Hachlili and R. Zommer, *Mound and Sea: Akko and Caesarea, Trading Centers* (Exhibition Catalogue no. 2, The Hecht Museum, University of Haifa, 1986) 22. Similar portrayals of Herakles are collected in Metzger, *Représentations*, pl XXXI.

legs are in the extended/retracted position reminiscent of WD **15B**. This krater attests, at least, to a close variant of the figure on WD **15B** in the person of Herakles at a site near both Samaria and Phoenicia.

WD 16A. Frontal Nude Warrior with Spear

(PLATES IV.1 AND XXII.1C)

Mus. Inv. 760
Papyrus 3
Dimensions: n.a.
Clay colour n.a.
String preserved; top and bottom of vertical image
Seal type: metal finger ring ?

WD **16A**[1] and WD **16B**[2] were found still attached to Samaria Papyrus 3 which recorded the sale of 'the slave Yehoᶜanani bar ᶜAzaryah to Yehopadayni bar Delayah and 'Ari bar Delayah by Yaqim for ten sheqels'.[3] Witnesses include Šelomi, son of Saharnatan, ᶜAnani, Yaqim and ᶜEṭir, 'sons of Delayah', a son of [D]uman and a son of Šekwi.[4] The probability is good that one or both of the preserved bullae were impressed by the seal of a YHWH-worshipper in view of the many Yahwistic elements (*Yeho*, *-yah*) in this group of names. Of the other names, only Saharnatan conveys hints of ethnicity/religion; it may be the name of an 'Aramaean or an Aramaized Arab'.[5]

The soft oval shape of the impression could have come from either an engraved seal stone or a metal finger ring of the fifth or fourth centuries. The sketchy impression suggests a seal that was shallow and worn, likely a finger ring.[6] Careless sealing has left the very bottom of the image unimpressed in the clay. A double line on the lower right of the impression may record the edge of the image, but how it relates to the rest of the impression is unclear.

The subject of WD **16A** is a nude male figure, for the most part viewed frontally. Only his left leg, bent at the knee and raised to rest on some now-indiscernible object, appears in profile, or perhaps, three-quarter view. He seems bareheaded and has the crude eyes and nose of a stick figure. Possibly he has a beard. In his left hand he holds an upright spear or lance whose lower portion disappears in the area of the raised left knee and calf. It is possible that what appears is not a spear but a large bow; a set of curved parallel lines seem to radiate out from the top of the object that the warrior

---

[1] The comments on WD **16A** are based solely on the photograph. WD **16A** was inaccessible for inspection.

[2] WD **16B** = WD **5** (pl VIII.1, 2), probably a satyr.

[3] Gropp, *Samaria Papyri*, 64; cf. the preliminary discussion by Cross, 'Report' 22. Note that a male slave with a Yahwistic name is sold to men likewise with Yahwistic names. For bullae attached to papyrus, see pl XXII.1a–d. See also entry for WD **16B**.

[4] Gropp, *Samaria Papyri*, 64.

[5] F. M. Cross, personal communication.

[6] Compare WD **16A** with WD **20**, from a worn metal finger ring.

holds. On the other hand, the lines might have been an engraved outline on the seal. The right arm probably rests at the warrior's side. In places, such as the neck, left elbow, and right hand, the outlines of the figure fade out, and this may have been the case on the seal as well.

The artist was more conscientious in his portrayal of the torso than the face, making a vague attempt at the muscles of the warrior's very triangular torso which appears to thrust forward from below the line of the shoulders and collar bone. The engraver suffered some confusion about cutting an image in the negative; this spearman carries his weapon in his left hand. With the lower edge of the image missing, the figure's feet and the object supporting the left foot (probably a rock) must remain conjectural.

The figure on WD **16A**, another Wadi Daliyeh nude warrior,[7] stands aggressively, like a sentry barring one's progress or a champion confronting an opponent; he looks challengingly out at the viewer.

Frontality is not rare in Classical Greek art,[8] but it is unusual. The occasional coin or seal will show a full figure (as opposed to a head) in a frontal position; usually the head is turned in profile or three-quarter view, as is the case with many male figures, including warriors.[9] A fourth-century bronze ring in the Getty collection portrays an almost frontal Hermes (head turned away, however) apparently flying, with a raised knee reminiscent of WD **16A**;[10] its Tunisian provenance could indicate a Phoenician/Punic owner.

A more certain Phoenician parallel is supplied by a gold ring from Phoenician Amrit in the de Clercq collection;[11] the points of comparison with WD **16A** are the warrior's nudity and total frontality, as well as the shared Levantine provenance. Another Phoenician gold ring in Paris, inscribed 'Hanno', also shows a fully frontal nude warrior;[12] this ring also produces a 'sketchy' impression like WD **16A**. The nude warriors on WD **16A** and the two rings in Paris all share the same odd separation of chest from shoulder line.

Perhaps the frontal head on WD **16A** can be explained as one of several possible Near Eastern traits grafted onto a fourth century Greek motif. As early as the first half of the second millennium in Mesopotamia, the figure of a hero with one leg up, bracing it against an opponent or resting it upon a defeated enemy is found on cylinder seals. Sometimes the hero will gaze directly out at the viewer, as on a late Neo-Babylonian carnelian cylinder in the Louvre.[13] The knee-up pose appears on an

---

[7] Compare WD **1**, WD **21D**, WD **26**, and WD **33**.

[8] In the Archaic period frontality was more common, but even then only certain classes of full-length figures (gorgons and related monsters, satyrs etc.) tended to appear with frontal faces on seals; see the discussion of WD **46** for further examination of this issue.

[9] Boardman, *GGFR*, 599, an example from the Classical period. However, one quite crude late-fourth-century bronze ring shows Herakles in a frontal pose, looking directly out at the viewer; he stands with his left foot propped on a rock and raises his right hand to his brow as if to shade his eyes (Richter, MMA, 94 [MMA 18.145.53]).

[10] Spier, *Ancient Gems*, no. 80 (83.AN.444.32).

[11] De Ridder, *Collection*, 2825.

[12] Bordreuil, *BN*, no. 34, ex. de Luynes (222).

[13] Collon, *First Impressions*, no. 381 (Louvre AO 4770) [= Delaporte A.900]), probably mid-sixth century, and see also p. 81.

Achaemenid cylinder from Borsippa,[14] although here the hero is seen in profile, as also on several Achaemenid stamp seal impressions from Nippur;[15] the Achaemenid version might derive from the canonical Egyptian portrayal of the smiting Pharaoh.[16] Could WD **16A** be a Phoenician product, combining elements of several styles? Until more exact parallels come to light, this question is left unanswered.

A number of Daliyah bullae show frontal figures, but only WD **46** (pl XI.1, Nike in frontal quadriga), WD **20** (pl VII.3, mature man in himation), a robust, if fragmentary, Herakles (?) in the Hecht Group[17] (whose threatening gesture is reminiscent of WD **16A**), a frontal woman's torso also in the Hecht Group,[18] and WD **16A** keep the face fully frontal rather than in profile. Perhaps WD **16A** and WD **20**—and the two rings in Paris—may be related to the same workshop. Unfortunately, it is difficult to determine whether the similarities between WD **16A** and WD **20**—their frontality, their comparable degree of wornness, their stick-figure faces, triangular torsos, and upper arms that seem not quite attached to their shoulders, their vague generic quality—may be traced to the same workshop, whether their resemblance is merely due to like patterns of wear, or possibly, both.

The most that can be deduced is that WD **16A** may have come from a provincial workshop of the western Persian Empire, possibly Phoenician, and belongs somewhere between the late fifth and mid-fourth century.

---

[14] Collon, *First Impressions*, no. 428 (BM 89337) = Wiseman, *Cylinder*, pl 105.

[15] Legrain, *Culture*, nos. 926–9. Cf. also K. Galling, 'Beschriftete Bildsiegel des ersten Jahrtausends v. Chr., vornehmlich aus Syrien und Palästina' *ZDPV* 64 (1941), no. 159, sixth century (J. P. Morgan Library 271).

[16] The most famous Persian version of the pose is that of Darius on the Behistun cliff (late sixth century).

[17] Pl XXIV.8.

[18] Pl XXIV.13.

WD 26. Nude Hoplite with Shield and Spear

(PLATE IV.2)

Mus. Inv. 923
Loose sealing
Image size: 1.1 cm (as preserved) x 1.1 cm high
Bulla size: 1 cm x 1.6 cm
Clay colour: reddish brown
String preserved; top and bottom of vertical image
Papyrus imprint
Published: Cross, 'Papyri', 29, pl 63, i.
Seal type: metal finger ring?

WD **26**, a loose sealing, was probably produced by a metal finger ring with a bezel in the broad oval shape popular in the fourth century. There is a tiny nick at the top of the impression that may have been made by the haft of a ring. The top half of the impression is preserved clearly, and the outline of the original ring is easily visible. On the lower left, that outline disappears, while the bottom of the image has broken away and the lower right of what remains is indistinct.

A nude Greek warrior is depicted here.[1] He advances in three-quarter view to his left, balancing a spear in his lowered right hand and a shield on his left. Both legs are flexed, the left (far) leg ahead of the right.[2] The bareheaded young warrior looks down and to his left; his head, in three-quarter view, mirrors the sharp slant of his body as he leans into his movement and draws his right arm back to lunge at an unseen enemy outside the frame. Although the impression has suffered considerable wear, the sturdy musculature of the figure's rather square torso is still apparent. Otherwise, all fine details, including facial features, have been lost.

WD **26** compares with WD **33** (pl IV.3) since both bullae display stock motifs of battle scenes on Classical Greek friezes[3] which were adapted in turn by coin-die cutters of the late fifth and early fourth centuries. For the image on WD **26**, the numismatic prototype is probably a Syracusan drachm of 410–400.[4] The helmeted local hero,

---

[1] Cf. especially WD **1** (WD **16A**, WD **21D**, WD **33**).

[2] WD **26** compares with WD **50** with a maenad/nymph in a similar stance, but with the near leg forward. In the discussion of that bulla it is noted that this pose is often assumed by Diomedes as he steals the Palladion. WD **26**, with the far leg forward shows the socially and ethically uncompromised version of a 'warrior advancing'.

[3] Cf. block 537 of the Amazonomachy frieze (British Museum) from the temple of Apollo at Bassae (late fifth or early fourth century); and Berlin Museum 1006, part of the Amazonomachy frieze from the Mausoleum of Halikarnassos dating to the mid-late fourth century.

[4] G. K. Jenkins, *Ancient Greek Coins* (London, 1972) 421. A second parallel is provided by a stater (Jenkins, *Coins*, 267) of Opuntian Lokris, home of the lesser Ajax, minted around 350. On the stater's reverse Ajax grimly advances just like Leukaspis, although with a short sword rather than a spear.

Leukaspis, advances to his left with the same arrangement of sword and shield as on WD **26**. Moving further east, Periklä, the Lycian dynast, may have copied the Syracusan figure of Leukaspis for his stater of 370–360.[5] On the Lycian version, the warrior holds his shield as usual but raises his sword overhead. Finally, King Demonikos of Cypriot Lapethos minted a stater between 380 and 360 on which Herakles advances with a bow instead of a shield, and a club rather than a spear.[6] This coin, too, is quite reminiscent of the shield-bearing warriors above.

There are a few seals with this motif. Three late Archaic/early Classical stones in Boardman's 'Group of the Leningrad Gorgon' show Athena advancing with spear and shield held as on WD **26**.[7] Boardman assigns this group to an East Greek or Cypriot workshop and notes that their style 'had its effect on Achaemenid glyptic, especially in the western satrapies of the Persian Empire'.[8] Although there are glyptic precedents with East Greek and western Persian Empire provenances and/or styles for the motif on WD **26**, the Wadi Daliyah bulla may owe more to numismatic than (extant) glyptic tradition. The closest parallels to the bulla, chronologically speaking, remain the coins.

Without a clearer impression, it is difficult to make stylistic judgements about WD **26**. It is noteworthy that Syracuse, Lycia and Cyprus had ties with the Phoenicians (Syracuse with Punic Phoenicians in particular) in the late fifth and early fourth centuries. It would not be surprising if a Phoenician, Greek or Cypriot artist— perhaps an engraver of both coins and seals—working in Phoenicia, or in places which traded with Phoenicians, adapted available coin images for seals. The connection between coins and seals is a logical one, given their similar scale and the fact that the artist of both had to carve the design in the negative.[9]

As in the case of WD **33**, the young warrior on WD **26** provides a rather watered-down version of the more aggressive figures on the coins. Possibly this may be attributed to a provincial artist (Greek or Phoenician or 'other') who created glyptic images at second- or third-hand. It could equally well indicate that the motif had become a common one, subject to the indifferent execution suffered by 'mass produced' images. Since the motif appears on the battle frieze of the mid-fourth-century 'Weeping Women Sarcophagus',[10] which may have been carved in Sidon, it is apparent that it had made its appearance in the Phoenician homeland.

The WD **26** seal belongs in the first half of the fourth century, contemporary with or a little later than the coins which are cited as parallels.

---

[5] Jenkins, *Coins*, 110; cf. *SNG-ANS Burton Y. Berry Collection II*, pl 44, 1191–2. For Lycian coins cf. also O. Mørkholm, 'Coin Hoard from Podalia', *Numismatic Chronicle* (1971) 13–15, nos. 389–447.

[6] Jenkins, *Coins*, 325.

[7] J. Boardman, *Archaic Greek Gems*, (London, 1968) 239 (Boston 27.676) = Beazley, *Lewes House*, 26, pl 2 = Boardman, *GGFR*, 381; Boardman, *AG Gems*, 240 (London, University College) from Egypt; Boardman, *AG Gems*, 245 (Walters, *BMC*, 315) from Egypt.

[8] Boardman, *AG Gems*, 91–2. Cf. Boardman, *GGFR*, 851, from the Oxus Treasure (British Museum, Western Asiatic Department) and Spier, *Ancient Gems*, no. 113 (Getty 85.AN.370.25) 'from Iran'.

[9] See INTRODUCTION, p. 21 and *passim*; also Richter, *EGGE*, 23–5 and E. Porada's article, 'Greek Coin', 228–34.

[10] R. Fleischer, *Der Klagenfrauensarkophag aus Sidon* (Tübingen, 1983) and R. Lullies and M. Hirmer, *Greek Sculpture* (New York, 1960) fig. 207.

WD 33. Smiting Nude Warrior

(PLATE IV.3)

Mus. Inv. 930

Loose sealing

Image size: 1.8 cm x 0.9 cm

Bulla size: 2 cm x 1.3 cm

Clay colour: reddish brown, partly burnt black

String not preserved, holes remain; top and bottom of vertical image

Papyrus imprint

Seal type: metal finger ring

WD **33** derives from a narrow oval bezel of a metal finger ring, a shape found occasionally in the corpus of Wadi Daliyeh bullae. Numerous cracks vein the surface of the bulla, some due, perhaps, to the burning or intense heat which this bulla apparently endured. The outline of the ring appears only at the upper right and lower left of the impression, registering just enough information to reconstruct the contour of the ring bezel. The general contours of the image survive although the details have worn away, and the upper left portion of the image was probably never very distinct.

The bulla shows another in the large group of nude, beardless youths found among the Wadi Daliyeh bullae.[1] He is advancing to his right with his right arm lifted overhead, presumably to deliver a violent blow to an opponent outside the frame of the composition. Only his shoulder and upper arm can still be seen. He probably also held a weapon, but this, too, has disappeared. The left arm hangs down and slightly behind him. His small head is bare and covered with a cap of short curly(?) hair. He himself is quite tall and lanky; his lean, taut muscles are still (barely) visible. His torso is frontal, his legs in approximately three-quarter view, and his head is in profile, focussed in the direction of his movement. He has initiated his movement with his right leg, but seems about to shift his weight onto his left leg.

Despite the poor condition of WD **33**, the composition itself is based on a stock Greek sculptural motif—the advancing figure seen from the front (usually in three-quarter view).[2] This motif of the 'leading' arm uplifted in a smiting gesture goes back in Greek sculpture to at least the beginning of the Classical period[3] and became almost *de rigueur* in the numerous Greek battle scenes.[4] As the Classical period advances, this

---

[1] See especially WD **1**, WD **21D**, WD **26** (nude warriors).

[2] See B. R. Brown's list of standard motifs in *Anticlassicism in Greek Sculpture of the Fourth Century* (New York, 1973) 6.

[3] This is known as the 'tyrant slayer' pose after the statue of Harmodios in the sculptural group erected by the Athenians in 476 (cf. M. Robertson, *A History of Greek Art* [Cambridge, 1975] 185–6).

[4] I.e. the Amazonomachy on the frieze of the Temple of Apollo at Bassae (British Museum, late fifth/early fourth century); the hunting frieze on the mid-fourth-century Weeping Women Sarcophagus from Sidon (Lullies-Hirmer,

violent posture gains in drama by an intensification of the gesture: the forward step becomes longer, arms and torso twist into sharper angles. A late fourth century example from Phoenicia is provided by a Greek warrior on an end panel of the Alexander Sarcophagus.[5]

The artist of WD **33** probably was not the first to put this motif on a seal; the composition has a generic quality which may be due to the fact that the artist is making a second- or third-hand reproduction of the composition. Nevertheless, the image is not entirely bland. While the image is confined by its oval outline, the action unfolds beyond the frame to our fighter's adversary.

While the motif is common enough in larger-scale sculpture, it is rare in Classical Greek glyptic art. Beyond a scarab in the British Museum, variously described as Etruscan or Greek of the late fifth century, on which Theseus assumes this pose to attack a boar with his club,[6] no clear parallels to WD **33** can be found. Coins of the fourth century from Stymphalos, from Chersonese, and from Tarentum provide a few numismatic examples;[7] all three towns minted coins on which Herakles swings his club over his head as he advances toward his victim.

All the above examples involve a figure with a club,[8] and it would be gratifying to be able to identify the figure on WD **33** as Herakles, a famous 'smiter' indeed. With the upper portion of the bulla so indistinct, however, it cannot even be determined whether a club would fit in the available space. In addition, the many examples of the pose on large-scale relief show that Herakles had no monopoly on this particular combat tactic. WD **33**, as preserved, simply shows a nude youth fighting an unseen enemy.

Sculpture, fig. 207); several times on the Amazonomachy frieze along the east, south, and west faces of the Mausoleum of Halicarnassus (mid-late fourth century; illus. Lullies-Hirmer, *Sculpture*, figs. 214–17).

[5] Lullies-Hirmer, *Sculpture*, fig. 237. See V. von Graeve's study, *Alexandersarcophag*.

[6] Walters, *BMC*, 668, carnelian scarab = Richter, *EGGE*, 795 = Furtwängler, *AG*, pl 18, 30. Furtwängler, *AG III*, p. 190 stated it was Etruscan; Walters (p. xliii) thought it could be Greek.

[7] Stymphalos: silver stater, *SNG-ANS: The Burton Y. Berry Collection II*, pl 33, 871 = Walters, *BMC*, 10 (Peloponnesus) pl XXXVII, 4; Herakles is about to battle the Stymphalian birds.

Chersonese: silver stater, *SNG-ANS: Berry II*, pl 34, 872 = Walters, *BMC*, 9 (Crete and the Aegean Islands), pl 4, 4; this coin is an imitation of the Stymphalian prototype (Walters, *BMC*, 9, p. xxiii).

Tarentum: silver diobols, *SNG-ANS I: Etruria-Calabria*, pl 38, 1463–7, 1469.

[8] The Theseus scarab (above) was originally labelled 'Herakles', because of the club.

B.   NUDE YOUTHS AND WARRIORS

2.   PERSEUS IN THE PERSIAN EMPIRE

Introductory Remarks: Perseus in the Persian Empire
WD **32**, WD **54**, WD **56**[1]

THE appearance of two—or perhaps three—fourth century portrayals of Perseus in this group of impressions (WD **32** [pl V.1], WD **54** [pl V.2], WD56[?] [pl V.3]) from the Phoenician-dominated area of the Persian Empire is notable in view of the numerous 'oriental' or 'barbarian' elements in the Perseus story, at least as the Greeks told it. In the first place, Perseus rescued Andromeda from the sea monster near Joppa on the Phoenician coast. Second, Andromeda had a grandfather 'Belus', whose name is transparently Phoenician.[2] Herodotus reports the tradition that Perses, son of Perseus and Andromeda, became the first ruler of the Persians.[3] The latter tradition explains why Perseus often wears the so-called Phrygian headdress in Greek art.[4] In his description of Egypt, Herodotus notes that in a town near Thebes there was an enclosure sacred to Perseus who was worshipped there as a 'native son' and who periodically made a personal appearance at the shrine.[5]

Perseus is familiar from Greek and Latin sources, but like the tales of Herakles, the Perseus myth may have ancient Near Eastern elements.[6] Herodotus even has Xerxes send a herald to the Argives before his invasion to claim that since they shared Perseus as a common ancestor, the Argives should welcome him to Greece as a long-lost relative.[7] Strabo (XVII I, 43) tells us that Alexander the Great consulted the oracle of Ammon because his ancestors, Herakles and Perseus, had done so. In Asia Minor, Sinope accorded Perseus special honors, and Tarsus believed him to be its founder.[8]

However, even if Persian subject peoples in Asia Minor, Phoenicians, and Samarians had no native Perseus tradition *per se* during the fifth and fourth centuries, a Greek seal engraver working for a Phoenician (or Persian) patron or market might well decide

---

[1] For bibliography, see *LIMC*, s.v. 'Perseus', and entry on WD **54**, below.

[2] Rose, *Handbook*, 273 and Herodotus 7.62.

[3] Herodotus 7.61.

[4] Cf. on gems, Boardman, *GGFR*, 767. For sculpture cf. J. Borchhardt, *Die Bauskulptur des Heroöns von Limyra. Das Grabmal des lykischen Königs Perikles* (Berlin, 1976) pl 49 (early/mid fourth century). For coins of Asia Minor issued by Mithradates Eupator (120–63 BCE) in Amastris, Amisus, Comana, Cabira and Sinope, cf. Borchhardt, pl 49.

[5] Herodotus 2.91. According to Herodotus this town, Chemmis, was the only place in Egypt where any Greek customs were adopted.

[6] Perseus' and Herakles' battles with monsters may relate to Ancient Near Eastern representations of heroes and gods battling monsters. Herodotus (VI, 54) claims that Perseus was an Assyrian who adopted Greek nationality. For theories concerning the Near Eastern provenance of Perseus and the conclusion that the tale of Perseus is a native Greek one, cf. K. Schauenburg, *Perseus in der Kunst des Altertums* (Bonn, 1960) 132 ff. The earliest representation of Perseus in Greek art occurs in the eighth century (Boardman, *AG Gems*, p. 38).

[7] Herodotus 7.150. Cf. P. Calmeyer ('Zur Genese altiranischer Motive VI', *AMI* 12 [1979] 310ff.) who, with Schauenburg, is skeptical of Perseus' Eastern origin.

[8] Calmeyer, 311 (see above, n. 7).

that Perseus would be a commercially viable subject. This hypothesis may be amplified
by looking at Lycia, another area which stood, as did Phoenicia, on the border between
the Greek and Persian worlds and received considerable Greek and Persian artistic
influence.[9] Lycian buildings erected during periods of Persian control exhibit both
Greek and Persian elements.[10] Many Greek artists had fled during and after the
Peloponnesian war to more prosperous regions like Lycia and Caria, working on such
expensive monumental buildings as the Nereid Monument and the Limyra Caryatids
in Lycia, the Mausoleum at Halicarnassus in Caria and the Priene temple and Ephesis
Artemesion in Ionia.[11] Lycian art in general betrays much Greek influence.[12]

Of special interest here is the large central akroterion on the Heroön of Limyra
which Borchardt dates between 370 and 350, a period largely paralleling the Wadi
Daliyeh bullae.[13] The marble akroterion consists of Perseus (in Persian headdress)
holding up the just-severed head of Medusa whose body writhes at his feet. The
akroterion was in the Greek style, in conformity with the overall conception of the
building, but various details indicate local and Persian artistic influence as well.

Indeed, Perseus and Medusa have a long tradition in Lycian sites of the Persian
period;[14] first, as the subject of one of the Greek-style wall paintings in a sixth-century
tomb at Kizilbel, Elmali, executed for a Lycian vassal of Persian overlords.[15] Second,
the Heroön at Gjölbasi Trysa has a relief of Perseus and Medusa.[16] Perhaps the
hellenized subjects of the Great King felt the subject mediated between the two
worlds. Alternately, in the case of the Heroön at the eastern Lycian city of Limyra, it
is likely that Päriklä, the powerful anti-Xanthos and anti-Persian dynast, consciously
commissioned the art on his tomb as a pro-Athenian statement, drawing on a favorite
Athenian theme of civilization triumphant over barbarianism.[17]

For a Phoenician attestation of Perseus, a century earlier than the Heroön and
roughly contemporary with the Kizilbel tomb-painting, there is a sarcophagus from
Golgoi on Cyprus, a town founded by Phoenicians.[18] Sarcophagae already had a long

---

[9] See J. Zahle, 'Politics and economy in Lycia during the Persian period', *REA* 91 (1989) 169–82.

[10] Borchhardt, 'Herrschaft', 239–40. Cf. also T. R. Bryce, 'Political Unity in Lycia during the 'Dynastic' Period',
JNES 42 (1983) 36–7.

[11] Hornblower, *Greek World*, 175.

[12] Hornblower, *Greek World*, 171, 175–6. See also Borchhardt, *Bauskulptur*, p. 21 and Childs, *City Reliefs*.

[13] Borchardt, *Bauskulptur* 82–94, pl 49. W. Childs in a review of the above (*AJA* 81 [1977], pp. 399–400)
described these Lycian sculptures as the 'only major new discovery of sculpture in Lycia in this century'.

[14] Childs, *City Reliefs*, 400.

[15] M. Mellink dates the tomb to 525 and considers it East Greek. She reported annually on the excavations at
Elmali in *AJA* 74 (1970) and following. For Perseus cf. *AJA* 74 (1972) 179, and *AJA* 77 (1973) 303. Note also
Mellink's report in *Comptes rendus de l'Académie des inscriptions et belles-lettres* (1979) 476–96. Subjects at Elmali
include the defeat of a Greek by a Persian warrior. Whatever the ethnicity of the artist, the politics of the patron
prevailed.

[16] Borchhardt, *Bauskulptur*, pl 49, 2.

[17] B. Jacobs, *Griechische und persische Elemente in der Grabkunst Lykiens zur Zeit der Achämenidenherrschaft*,
Studies in Mediterranean Archaeology 78 (1987) 65–7.

[18] Metropolitan Museum, New York (74.51.2451); see I. Hitzl, *Die griechische Sarkophage der archaische und
klassische Zeit* (Studies in Mediterranean Archaeology and Literature 104 [1991] no. 37, fig. 51). See also Childs,
City Reliefs, 99–103.

tradition of use by high-ranking Phoenicians;[19] the Golgoi example, carved in a largely Greek idiom, includes a representation of Perseus carrying off the Medusa's head in a *kibisis*.

Whatever meaning his story had for non-Greeks,[20] Perseus was an artistic subject well-represented in the transitional areas between the West and East in the Persian period. It should be no surprise, then, to find him attested on two (or perhaps, three) bullae in Samaria.

---

[19] Consider the Ahiram sarcophagus, for example (illus. in Moscati, *Phoenicians*, 293).

[20] Childs, *City Reliefs*, 101, suggests there may have been a shared understanding of Perseus iconography in the East.

WD 32. Warrior with Spear, Shield, and Sack (Perseus?)

(PLATE V.1)

Mus. Inv. 929
Loose sealing
Image size: 1.65 cm x 0.9 cm
Bulla size: 1.75 cm x 1.45 cm
Clay colour: black (burnt)
String not preserved, string holes remain; top and bottom of vertical image
Papyrus imprint and imprint of string across back
Seal type: metal finger ring [?]

WD **32** was probably produced by an oval metal finger ring, judging from the faint indentation of a pointed ring bezel at the top of the impression. Part of the outline of the ring bezel—here, the lower half of the left edge—is not visible. The clay was not very deeply impressed, but the image is sufficiently distinct to be understood. However, several cracks mar the upper half of the image. The very bottom of the image is indistinct and most of any finer details that may once have been visible have disappeared.

WD **32** shows a stocky, square-cut warrior[1] in Greek battle costume, standing in an almost frontal pose. Only enough of his facial features remain to show that they, too, are almost frontal as he looks very slightly to his right. He wears a corselet (probably of linen) over a semitransparent short tunic that barely covers his upper thighs. The shoulder straps of the corselet are clearly apparent, more so than the faint indications of the waist and the folds of the tunic below it.[2] The warrior's battle gear consists of a large round shield seen in profile with a raised central boss and a spear; the shield is (correctly) attached to his left arm; the spear, held upright in the warrior's left hand, rests on the ground. Traces of the decorative *sema* remain on the shield. The warrior's head is bare with a bowl-shaped cap of hair; his feet may have been bare as well.

There is the merest hint that the right leg might be flexed, with the left leg carrying a little more weight. The right arm rests casually by the warrior's side. In his right hand, rather than the expected sword or other weapon, he holds a ring from which is suspended what seems to be a cloth or leather sack with a pointed bottom.

The shape of WD **32**, an oval that is broader than many other Daliyeh ring impressions, is comparable to a number of fine rings which Boardman assigns to the mid- to late fifth centuries.[3] However, the fourth century context of WD **32** is secure;

---

[1] Other warriors: WD **1**, WD **16A**, WD **21D**, WD **26**, WD **33**.

[2] The corselet with rectanglar tabs at the bottom (*pteryges*) worn over a tunic also appears on WD **43**. See discussion and bibliography on pp. 145–6 below.

[3] Boardman, *GGFR*, 670, 674, pp. 216–19.

an example of provincial lag may be present here, or the shape may have continued into the fourth century; ring typologies are still subject to adjustment.

WD **32** is remarkably similar to the figure of Achilles on the fifth-century Achilles Painter's name vase, an amphora of *c*.440 in the Vatican which shows Achilles wearing precisely the same corselet and tunic as the warrior on WD **32**.[4] The hero of the *Iliad* takes a similarly frontal stance, he is bareheaded, holds a spear upright in his left hand, and his legs seem to be in the same position as the Daliyeh figure. The two men even share the chunky proportions. There are differences: instead of a shield, Achilles carries a himation draped over his left arm as he rests his right hand on his hip and looks in profile to his left. Nevertheless, the resemblance is striking.

The search for a comparable engraved gem or ring, however, turns up nothing as similar as the Vatican Achilles. Distant parallels come from Phoenicia and Daliyeh. A gold ring in the de Clercq collection[5] shows a completely frontal nude warrior carrying a shield on his left arm and an upright spear in his right hand. His rather loose-jointed legs seem to mirror Achilles' stance. WD **1** (pl III.1) also depicts a nude warrior with a shield, and his three-quarter pose is similar to the frontal pose of WD **32**.

Another difficulty lies in finding a warrior on a seal wearing the same costume as Achilles and the soldier on WD **32**; none appear among mainstream Greek seals where warriors are almost invariably nude. On Etruscan scarabs, however, whose engravers loved richly decorated surfaces,[6] soldiers do occasionally wear more elaborate battle gear. The warrior on WD **32** might fit in the ranks beside the soldiers on several such scarabs in the British Museum, probably of the late fifth century.[7]

Excavators at Judaean Ramat Raḥel, occupied during the Persian period, reported finding a stamped jar handle with the impression of a warrior in helmet, corselet, and tunic, holding a staff in his upraised right hand.[8] Aharoni describes the handle as 'unclassified, and the impression as "Hellenistic"'. The impression is indistinct but the presence of the WD **32** ring in Persian period Samaria should raise the possibility that the Ramat Raḥel impression came from a fourth-century ring.

Is the sack which the soldier carries a special type of bag, used for a specific purpose? On vase paintings, this sort of sack with a suspension ring tends to be used for carrying fish and game.[9] The only identifiable Greek hero who is specifically associated with a sack is Perseus,[10] who carried his 'game', the head of the Gorgon

---

[4] Cf. J. Beazley, 'The Master of the Achilles Amphora in the Vatican', *JHS 34* (1914) 179–226 (illustrated in J. J. Pollitt, *Art and Experience in Classical Greece* [Cambridge, 1972] fig. 47).

[5] De Ridder, *Collection*, 2825.

[6] Etruscan seal-cutters were influenced by Phoenician imagery.

[7] Walters, *BMC*, 637, seated armed hero; 685, heavily armed warrior.

[8] Y. Aharoni, *Excavations at Ramat Rahel, 1961–62* (Rome, 1964) 23 and fig. 18, 2.

[9] Boardman, *ARV*, fig. 344, a fisherman with his bag, on a pelike by the Pan Painter (Vienna, Kunsthistorisches Museum 3727); fig. 119, another fisherman, on a cup by the Ambrosios Painter (Boston, MFA 01.8024).

[10] J. Boardman, *Athenian Black Figure Vases, A Handbook* (New York, 1985) fig. 170.2, a Type-C cup by Psiax of *c*.510-100 (Hermitage Museum, Leningrad = Boardman, *ABV*, 294, 22) = K. Schefold, *Götter- und Heldensagen Spätarchaischen der Griechen in der spätarchaischen Kunst* (Munich, 1978) fig. 99; cf. also Schefold, *GHSGK*, fig. 93, a Chalcidian amphora of *c*.520 in the British Museum (B 155) with the three Graiai handing over their treasures to Perseus.

For bibliography on Perseus, see entry on WD **54**.

Medusa, in the magical *kibisis*.[11] It is likely, then, that WD **32** portrays Perseus, the Gorgon slayer.

An additional piece of logic may strengthen this identification. Fully armed warriors in Greek art carry a sword in their right hand, a shield attached to their left arm, and for parade purposes, at least, a spear held in the left hand. If there is no other weapon, the spear (or javelin), naturally, appears in the right hand. Since the figure on WD **32** has his spear in his left hand, perhaps the right hand holds some weapon or object of greater importance than the spear. Perseus' magic sack would fit this criterion.

Glyptic examples of this sack are rare. One occurs on another Wadi Daliyeh bulla, WD **54** (pl V.2), which also seems to depict Perseus. There, the bag looks fuller, but the same round 'handle' appears. A second example is in the Metropolitan Museum; a carnelian Etruscan scarab shows the *kibisis* hanging from Perseus' right arm.[12]

Stylistically, WD **32** and WD **54** seem far apart; no shared workshop is apparent here. Yet the same unusual details appear on both seals. There is even a third, rather crude, Perseus from Daliyeh, WD **56** (pl V.3). The presence of Perseus on three stylistically different Daliyeh sealings suggests workshops in the same geographical area—probably the eastern Mediterranean—were sharing an iconographic tradition which elsewhere in extant Greek art seems rare. Representations of Perseus, as noted elsewhere,[13] seem to have been relatively common in Hellenized areas of the western Persian Empire.

The closest parallels to WD **32** come from the second half of the fifth century. On the other hand, the fourth century context of the papyri, and the probability that the workshop of the WD **32** ring may have been a provincial one closer to Samaria than to the Greek mainland, allows for a more probable fourth-century date.

In the Roman period, Hermes/Mercury carries a sack, a money bag, but this is unattested before the Hellenistic era.

[11] See the discussion of WD **54**.

[12] Richter, MMA, p. 46 (second half of the fifth century) and fig. 171 (MMA 51.164.1). WD **56** (pl V.3) might provide a third example of the *kibisis*.

[13] See INTRODUCTORY REMARKS (above, p. 71) on Perseus in the Persian Empire. Also cf. WD **56**, p. 81 n. 9.

WD 54. Perseus with Sack

(PLATE V.2)

Mus. Inv. 951
Loose sealing
Image size: 1.65 cm x 0.8 cm
Bulla size: 1.7 cm x 1.5 cm
Clay colour: reddish brown
String preserved; top and bottom of vertical image
Papyrus fragments on back
Papyrus imprint
Seal type: metal finger ring
Inscribed: (in Phoenician script) '-b/d-n

THIS image belongs in the large category of nude youths in the Greek style found with the Samaria Papyri.

A slight bulge at the upper edge of WD **54** suggests the haft of a metal ring; the leaf-shaped oval outline appears frequently among the Wadi Daliyeh bullae and is a typical shape of the Classical period. In profile, the sealing shows a convex curve that also suggests a ring.

A short-haired male figure stands at rest in a three-quarters pose, head in profile looking directly to his right. Proportionally, his head is too large for his body and the part of the face below eye-level is scraped away. He rests his weight on his right leg and bends his left leg at the knee with the toes resting lightly on the ground, a stance that gives his body a markedly curved appearance. Some modelling of his pectoral and abdominal muscles survives, as does the merest hint of a very short ground line under the youth's right foot.

He wears a soft 'Robin Hood' travelling cap of the sort Hermes sometimes wears.[1] It is less clear whether the figure is wearing boots. His only other visible garment is a knee-length chlamys fastened at his throat and falling behind his shoulders; two chlamys folds appear behind him on his left.[2] In his upraised left hand he grasps a staff that rests on the ground beside his left foot, while in his lowered right hand he holds the looped handle of a triangular bag with two pendant tassels(?) that almost touch his feet. Unfortunately, the central zone of the sealing surface has been abraded.

The figure's stance, with a staff in one upraised arm and the other hand lowered, appears also on WD **7** (pl I.1) and WD **56** (Perseus [?] pl V.3). This pose has a long history on Greek coinage and may echo a large-scale bronze sculptural motif.[3]

---

[1] Not the usual *petasos*. Cf. Boardman, *ARV*, fig. 96, a red figure cup in the British Museum (E 815).

[2] The chlamys appears in the Wadi Daliyeh corpus also on WD **7** (Apollo?), WD **14** (Hermes), and WD **43** (Achilles).

[3] But not necessarily a *specific* statue. Cf. Horster, *Statuen*, 1–7.

The figure on WD **54** may with some confidence be identified as Perseus,[4] a Greek
hero who is represented sculpturally in Persia's western territories,[5] and who
occasionally appears on Greek and Etruscan seals.[6] The type of hat which the figure
seems to wear is worn by Perseus on a red figure pelike by the Pan Painter.[7] The
unusual bag on a ring is probably the *kibisis*, one of the magic gadgets that Perseus
tricked the Graiai into helping him acquire.[8] With the Cap of Darkness, the Shoes of
Swiftness and the *kibisis*, Perseus was able to kill the Gorgon Medusa, win the hand of
the princess Andromeda, and deliver his mother Danaë from starvation. Although the
form of the *kibisis*, which was hung from the shoulder to keep the arms free for battle,
can vary,[9] it appears on Greek vases depicting Perseus.[10] In some cases, it takes the
form of a sack used for game. One vase in particular, a black figure kylix in Kiel,[11]
shows Perseus carrying a bag with loosened drawstrings which somewhat resembles
WD **54**.

For the distinctive ring-handled *kibisis* on a seal, the only good parallel found is
another Wadi ed-Daliyah bulla, WD **32** (pl V.1).[12] On WD **56** (pl V.3), a far cruder
image, the putative Perseus is fully clothed and holds a small round object which might
be the *kibisis* or Medusa's severed head.

The Inscription

Three Phoenician letters are arranged vertically below Perseus' right elbow, parallel
with the staff: *ʾalep*, *bet* (or *dalet*), *nun*. The *ʾalep* is backwards, but it was not unusual
for seal engravers to forget to carve letters in reverse; the *ʾalep* is clearly a slashed
sideways 'V' as found on Sidonian and Tyrian inscriptions, including coins, of the fifth
and fourth centuries.[13] The bottom horizontal of the *bet* comes closer to a ninety-

---

[4] See *LIMC*, s.v. also Schauenburg, 'Perseus', and K. Schefold and F. Jung, *Die Urkönige, Perseus, Bellerophon,
Herakles und Theseus in der klassischen und hellenistischen Kunst* (Munich, 1988) 97–114. Also see E. Lippold, *Der
Triumphierende Perseus* (Köln, 1960) and E. Langlotz, *Perseus* (Heidelberg, 1951).

[5] See INTRODUCTORY REMARKS on Perseus in the Persian Empire, above, p. 71.

[6] Perseus on an Etruscan seal of the second half of the fifth century: Richter, MMA, p. 46 and fig. 171, carnelian
(MMA 51.164.1); see also Boardman, *GGFR*, 767 = Richter, *EGGE*, 224, a silver ring in the Museo Nazionale,
Taranto.

[7] Munich, Antikensammlungen inv. 8725 (illustrated in Boardman, *ARV*, fig. 349). As with the *kibisis* there is no
set form of hat for Perseus in Greek art. Schauenburg (*Perseus*, 119) writes of Perseus' hats that they are
'außerordentlich verschiedenartig'.

[8] Apollodorus ii. 4. 2; Hyginus: Poetic Astronomy ii. 12; Apollonios of Rhodes iv. 1513ff. Cf. Rose, *Handbook*,
273.

[9] Schauenburg, *Perseus*, 119. For the *kibisis* in art and literature, see Schauenburg, *Perseus*, 13 and 119 ff.

[10] See Schefold, *GHSGK*, fig. 93, a Chalcidian amphora of about 520 in the British Museum (B 155) with the
three Graiai (or nymphs?) giving their treasures to Perseus; and fig. 99 (= Boardman, *ABV*, 170), a bowl by Psiax of
510–500 in Leningrad, on which the *kibisis* seems to have ring handles like those on WD **54**. This attribute
disappears in Imperial Roman times (Schauenburg, *Perseus*, 120).

[11] Schauenburg, *Perseus*, pl 14 (Kiel, Universität B41).

[12] Richter, MMA, fig. 171 (see above) is an Etruscan scarab on which the *kibisis* into which Perseus stuffs
Medusa's head is a simple sack.

[13] J. B. Peckham, *The Development of the Late Phoenician Scripts* (Cambridge, Mass., 1968) pls 5 and 6.

degree angle than the Tyrian and Sidonian *bet*s that Peckham lists, but the overall squareness of the Phoenician *bet*s matches that on this impression. (There is also the possibility that the middle letter is a *dalet*). The *nun* is a little smaller than the other two letters, a not unusual phenomenon at Tyre and Sidon. Aramaic and Hebrew *nun*s tend to curve, while Phoenician *nun*s have straight lines, as found here.

ʾAlep, *bet*, *nun* (א.ב.נ) is a sound Semitic root meaning 'rock'. When it appears in a name, however, it becomes problematic; אב is the word for 'father' and appears in countless names; the *nun* may indicate the first person plural possessive suffix. Benz[14] lists three Phoenician and Punic names with the three radicals: *ʾbnbʿl*, *ʾbnšmš* and *ʾbnʾ*,[15] and he discusses a variety of interpretations.[16] Possibly the *ʾalep*, *bet*, *nun* (א.ב.נ) here is an abbreviation for a name like the first two above. From a Semitic point of view, *ʾabni*, 'my rock' would also be a possibility, shortened from a longer name, by analogy with *ʾEbenʿezer*. If a *dalet* rather than a *bet* appears, the name becomes something like *ʾAdon*, 'Lord'.

The original seal probably was carved in the early fourth century.

---

[14] F. L. Benz, *Personal Names in the Phoenician and Punic Inscriptions* (Rome, 1972) 258.

[15] The first two contain the theophoric elements respectively of the Phoenician divinities, Baʿal and Shemesh.

[16] Benz, *Personal Names*, 258 with references. It may mean 'our father', or may be an error for אדן; possibly it is a by-form of בן 'son'. Benz also records the interesting fact that there seems to have been a female deity אבן at Ugarit to whom some scholars believe the later Phoenician names may refer.

WD 56. Perseus (?)

(PLATE V.3)

Mus. Inv. 953
Loose sealing
Image size: 1.3 cm x 0.75 cm
Bulla size: 1.65 cm x 1.3 cm
Clay colour: reddish brown
String preserved; top and bottom of image
Papyrus imprint
Seal type: metal finger ring (?)

THE impression of a standing male figure on WD **56** has survived only in its general outlines, but enough remains to describe the image as rather flat and pinched. The soft transition from sealed to unimpressed clay apparent in the upper right quadrant may mean that a metal finger ring made the impression. The vertical oval shape would be right for a late fifth- or fourth-century finger ring. In the upper left portion of the impression part of the figure's shoulder, arm and spear are lacking.

WD **56** shows a male figure in three-quarter pose looking slightly down and to his left; his face is in profile. The costume as well as the exaggerated S-curve of the man's torso (totally illogical in view of the fact that both feet appear firmly planted on the ground and carry equal weight) indicate that the prototype of the seal, at least, was Greek. Additionally distracting is the oversized head and elongated left arm.

The figure on WD **56** differs from many of the standing male representations found among the Wadi Daliyeh bullae in that he is clothed. He wears a *pilos* hat and a knee-length tunic possibly caught at the waist by a belt. Parallel vertical lines both above and below the waist perhaps indicate the folds of the tunic.

The feet and calves are clearly bare, but it is an open question whether the tunic has sleeves, Greek visual shorthand for 'barbarian'.[1] The pilos helmet on the man's head and the spear which he appears to hold up in his raised right hand (the arm and hand are missing) lend a vaguely martial air to his demeanour, but the flat rendering considerably diminishes any dramatic impact the composition might have aimed for.

Most significant for a reading of the impression is the object the figure holds in his extended left hand. This could be the head of the Gorgon Medusa or the bag (the *kibisis*), in which Perseus secured the severed head.[2] However, if the Gorgon head on WD **56** ever had any detailed features, they have flaked away, leaving behind only a heart-shaped outline. The unprepossessing size of the Gorgon head fits into the

---

[1] M. Miller, *Perserie: The Arts of the East in Fifth-Century Athens* (Ph.D. Thesis, Harvard University, 1985) 256–7.

[2] For bibliography on Perseus, see WD **54** p. 77. Schauenburg (*Perseus*, 118) shows that Perseus' costume can vary greatly from one representation to the next.

typology of the fourth century, by which time Gorgons had lost most of their terrifying features.[3] On WD **54** (pl V.2) and WD **32** (pl V.1), other possible versions of Perseus in the Wadi Daliyeh corpus, the hero carries the *kibisis*.

If Perseus holds the Gorgon head here, the apparently diminutive size of his trophy is also attested on a number of Greek vases.[4] The rare glyptic parallels for this seal impression include a fleeing Perseus with Medusa head on a silver ring of the fourth century[5] and Etruscan scarabs.[6]

On the other hand, as noted, Perseus may hold a small head-shaped *kibisis*; such a *kibisis* is carried by Perseus on an early fifth century sarcophagus found at the Phoenician-founded town of Golgoi on Cyprus.[7]

On Greek vases, Perseus wears a variety of headgear. The pilos he wears on WD **56** is similar to that worn by the hero on a South Italian amphora in Berlin, on which he carries the Gorgoneion and *harpe* (sickle).[8]

Despite the provincial nature of the work, it demonstrates some familiarity with the topic outside the Greek world.[9] Keeping in mind the artistic and cultural time-lag between centre and periphery, WD **56** fits easily into the fourth century date of the papyri.

---

[3] Note Boardman's excursus on Gorgons and the East (Boardman, *AG Gems*, pp. 37–9) in which he rejects the theory that the Gorgon type is Near Eastern. Also, cf. E. Buschor, *Medusa Rondanini* (Stuttgart, 1958) on the subject of the Gorgoneion.

[4] Cf. Schauenburg, *Perseus* (Strasburg University) pl 18.1; and note especially a South Italian cup of the fourth century (pl 17.2).

[5] Boardman, *GGFR*, pl 767 and p. 228.

[6] For two Etruscan examples, cf. Richter, MMA, fig. 171 ('fifth century'), and *AGDS II* (Berlin) no. 293, pl 57 = Richter, *EGGE*, fig. 844, dated by disputing scholars between the mid-fifth and the mid-third centuries.

[7] Now in the Metropolitan Museum, New York (74.51.2451); see Hitzl, *Sarkophage*, no. 37, fig. 51.

[8] Schauenburg, *Perseus*, pl 18.1 (Berlin, Staatliche Museen, F 3022).

[9] See the INTRODUCTORY REMARKS (above, p. 71) on Perseus in the Persian Empire.

B. NUDE YOUTHS AND WARRIORS

3. HERAKLES FIGURES IN GREEK STYLE

Introductory Remarks: Herakles Figures in Greek Style
WD **11C**, WD **39**, WD **42** [WD **47**]

AT least three sealings from Wadi Daliyeh[1] depict Herakles, a purely Greek visual idiom. Multiple renderings of this hero found wherever the Phoenicians set foot during the Persian period[2] are hardly surprising in view of the popularity of Herakles[3] (and his probable Phoenician *alter ego*, Milkqart of Tyre).[4] All three impressions seem to have come from engraved metal finger rings, but each differs from the other in composition and style. All include lions—a dead one on WD **11C** (pl VI.1) and WD **39** (pl VI.2) and a live version on WD **42** (pl VI.3) which repeats a scene found on Greek coins of Herakles wrestling the Nemean lion.

Although the nude master of animals on WD **47** (pl XII.2) may be a Greco-Phoenician version of the hero, none of the Wadi Daliyeh bullae shows Herakles in the traditional Near Eastern smiting pose; instead, his weapon, the club, appears either on the ground or turned on its end and used as a support. The smiting gesture was associated with the Phoenician storm god from at least as early as the Late Bronze Age. It is possible that in the Daliyeh bullae some evidence may be detected of self-selection at work against images which could have been understood in Samaria as portraying YHWH's ancient rival. As always, however, it is impossible to say how the Samarians

---

[1] WD **11C** (pl V.1), WD **39** (pl VI.2), WD **42** (pl VI.3). Additional, less likely but possible, Herakles figures include WD **57** (pl II.3), WD **21D** (pl III.2), WD **16A** (pl IV.1), and even WD **33** (pl IV.3), but these could equally be a number of other persons. Note also the possible Herakles in the Hecht Group (pl XXIV.8).

[2] Note, however, that traditional Herakles types (whether Greek or Phoenician) do not appear on Phoenician coins, although Achaemenid images of the 'Persian Hero', which do appear on mainland Phoenician coins (Betlyon, pl 1.1,4,5; pl 2.3,9, etc.), could perhaps be likened to Herakles scenes.

The number of Graeco-Phoenician green jasper scarabs which show either Herakles or the Egypto-Phoenician Bes as Herakles is considerable (cf. Walters, *BMC*, pls 5–7).

On Punic Tharros (Sardinia) gems, cf. Boardman, 'Scarabs' 98–105, and Giovanna Quattrocchi Pisano, *I gioielli fenici di Tharros nel Museo nazionale di Cagliari* (Rome, 1974).

[3] *LIMC*, s.v. 'Herakles'. Cf. also F. Brommer, *Hercules: The Twelve Labors of the Hero in Ancient Art and Literature* (New Rochelle, NY, 1986).

[4] Cf. Boardman, *Intaglios*, p. 36; M. Yon ('Cultes phéniciens à Chypre: l'interprétation chypriote', *SP* 4 [1986] 127–52) observes, however, that there is no concrete evidence before the end of the Classical period that Herakles was equated with Melqart on Cyprus and that, in addition, 'one has to wait until the end of the Hellenistic period before one finds throughout the Phoenician world . . . bilingual inscriptions which equate Melqart with the god called Herakles in Greek' (147). Yon also notes that, at least in the third century BCE, there is evidence that Resheph could look like Herakles as well (149).

The literature on Herakles in the East and Milkqart is vast and remains to be coherently synthesized. Cf. C. Bonnet-Tsavellas, 'Le dieu Melqart en Phénicie et dans le bassin Méditerranéen: Culte national et officiel', *SP* 1/2 (1983) 195–207; J. Teixidor, 'L'interprétation Phénicienne d'Héraclès et d'Apollon', *RHR* 200 (1983) 234–55; C. Bonnet, *Melqart: cultes et mythes de l'Héraclès Tyrien en Méditerranée*, *SP* 8 (1988); R. du Mesnil du Buisson, *Nouvelles études sur les dieux et les mythes de Canaan* (Leiden, 1973) 32–87; W. Culican, 'Melqart Representations on Phoenician Scarabs', *Abr Naharain* 2 (1960–61) 41ff.; and the notes to WD **35**, p. 188ff.

interpreted the Greek Herakles imagery, that pleased them sufficiently to spend money for it.

Just as there are no smiting Herakles figures, there are also no bullae produced from seals of the Phoenician 'green jasper' type; none has an ornamental border, and none has the shape of the green jasper pieces. By contrast, the excavations at ʿAtlit on the Palestinian coast not far from Samaria uncovered at least six Greco-Phoenician (primarily 'green jasper') scarabs depicting Herakles in a series of fifth- to fourth-century tombs.[5]

In the de Clercq collection, two of the four images of Herakles[6] on gold rings of the sixth to fourth centuries from Phoenicia belong with the green jasper series, and the other two, with more naturalistic poses and bodies, come closer to the Wadi Daliyeh group.[7] Again, however, there are no exact correspondences between images of Herakles on seals owned by fourth-century Samarians—which likely were produced in Phoenician ateliers—and the Herakles figures, probably also Phoenician, in the de Clercq Group.

On the Greek side, several classicists have observed that in the fourth century Herakles' struggles with monsters, a staple of the Athenian vase painting industry for the preceding two centuries, became rarer.[8] Instead, new versions of the hero appeared: a more youthful Herakles, often in repose, accompanied by a companion or gods.[9] Herakles' victory over death grew steadily more significant than battles with mere monsters. None of these new types appears, however, on the Wadi Daliyah bullae (unless WD **15B** [pl III.3] shows Herakles). Apparently, in the Phoenician sphere of artistic influence, the older style had yet to be supplanted by the new.

---

[5] Johns, 'Excavations', pl XIV, 496,–7, 552, 643, 687, 705 (some examples illustrated in Stern, *Material Culture*, 200); *EAEHL* s.v. 'ʿAtlit', 134, 137.

[6] De Ridder, *Collection*, pl XIX, 2807, 2808. These are also probably earlier than the next two Herakles rings (see below). It must be remembered that this collection may reflect the predilections of its original owner as well as ancient Phoenician taste.

[7] De Ridder, *Collection*, pl XIX, 2809, 2810 (= Boardman, *GGFR*, fig. 222).

[8] Cf. T. B. L. Webster, *Potter and Patron* (London, 1972) 66, 259–61.

[9] Herrmann, *Shadow*, 11; Metzger, *Représentations*, 229–30.

WD 11C. Herakles with Club, Bow, and Lionskin

(PLATE VI.1)

Mus. Inv. 769
Papyrus 1, March 19, 335.[1]
Image size: 1.5 x 1 cm
Bulla size: 2 x 1.7 cm
Clay colour: n.a.
String preserved; top and bottom of vertical image.
Seal type: metal finger ring

WD **11C**[2] was one of seven clay impressions still attached to Samaria Papyrus 1; of these only four are even slightly legible.[3] SP1 records the sale of a slave named 'Yehoḥanan bar Šeʾilah to Yehonur bar Laneri by Ḥananyah bar Beyadʾel for 35 sheqels'.[4] All the first names (of buyer, seller and slave) are Yahwistic although, curiously, the patronyms are not. Of the seven sealings, only WD **11B** (pl XIX.3), possibly the sealing of Yehonur, can be associated with any of the men mentioned in the papyrus.[5]

WD **11C** was covered with incrustations, but the impression is nevertheless in good condition with a fairly clear image. It was produced by a metal finger ring with a broad leaf-shaped oval bezel, a type seen before on a number of bullae.[6] The edge of the ring is clearly defined on the upper half of the impression but fades out elsewhere, including the bottom, where the figure's right foot is impossible to see. In the lower right quadrant of the bulla, not only is the edge indistinct, but there seems to have been an overflow of clay onto the field of the image, obscuring the figure's left arm and associated details.

The presence of three iconographical details—a club, a bow, and a lionskin—indicates that the nude male figure on WD **11C** must be Herakles. With WD **39** (pl VI.2) and WD **42** (pl VI.3), WD **11C** is one of three clearly identifiable renderings of Herakles in Greek style in the Wadi ed-Daliyah corpus. Here he stands in a three-quarter pose with pronounced contrapposto, looking down to his left. It is unclear whether his relatively small and apparently bare head is in profile or three-quarter

---

[1] Gropp, *Samaria Papyri*, 1–37. See earlier Cross, 'Samaria Papyrus 1'. Corrections in Cross, 'Report'.

[2] This discussion of WD **11C** is based on photographs; it was unavailable for examination.

[3] WD **11A–G**. WD **11A** and WD **11B** show similar debased versions of the 'Persian Hero' throttling flanking monsters. WD **11D**, WD **11F** and WD **11G** are illegible. WD **11E** seems to show a mature man with a bare torso draped in a himation (along the lines of WD **9** and WD **20**).

[4] Gropp, *Samaria Papyri*, 3.

[5] See discussion of WD **3A** (= WD **11B** = WD **12** = WD **24**).

[6] Cf. WD **1**, WD **42**, WD **49**, WD **56**.

view. His left leg carries his weight, while the right (near) leg bends back slightly at the knee. He has set his club upright and tilted it towards his right thigh to support his right arm; his right hand seems to press, palm down, on the narrow end of the club, while his raised, right shoulder and his right arm, bent at the elbow, suggest that the club is a little too long to be a truly comfortable leaning post. Herakles' left shoulder drops , weighed down by the heavy lion pelt draped over his left arm and by the bow that he holds in his left hand.

Herakles, equipped with club, lion-pelt and bow, has a long history of appearances in all media of Greek art.[7] The compactness as well as the formality of Herakles' pose on WD **11C** is also appropriate to works on a small scale such as coins and seals, and it appears on both. An Archaic ancestor, *c*.500, of the WD **11C** Herakles appears on a ringstone from Aegion,[8] but the club has not yet become a support. The late fifth-/early fourth-century Etrurian Herakles on a carnelian scarab now in the British Museum[9] is remarkably similar to WD **11C** and to a slightly later series of coins, primarily silver staters, issued by Magna Graecian Herakleia;[10] Herakles usually rests one hand on his club (lethal end down) and drapes the lion skin on the other arm. The bow appears frequently, if not consistently on these coins. An early fourth-century stater minted by Issus in Cilicia,[11] however, may be the most immediate ancestor of WD **11C**; Cilician issues were copied by Phoenician and Samarian mints in the fourth century.[12]

Other seals—a rather pedestrian mid fourth-century bronze ring 'from Smyrna'[13] and a strange cornelian scaraboid found in Taranto with a lion-headed Herakles[14]— repeat the same motif. A few rings with related but less precisely similar figures of Herakles have been attributed to Magna Graecia.[15] One of the (probably) Phoenician de Clercq gold rings depicts Herakles in this pose but without the lion skin or bow.[16] WD **39** (pl VI.2) presents another variation of the pose. Bullae from later fourth and early

---

[7] Cf. *LIMC*, s.v. 'Herakles'; Metzger, *Représentations*, chap. 5 and pp. 374–5, 386, 397; Schefold-Jung, *Urkönige*, 128–229.

[8] Boardman, *GGFR*, 368 = Richter, *EGGE*, 101 = A. Furtwängler, *Beschreibung der geschnittenen Steine in Antiquarium* (Berlin, 1896) 177 = *AGDS*, 2 (Berlin) 81 = Boardman, *AG Gems*, 263.

[9] Walters, *BMC*, 667.

[10] The city was founded in 433. Cf. *SNG-ANS* 2, pl 2, 68–80 [especially 80], 82–6; pl 3, 95–8. Kraay, *Coins*, pp. 193–4 and pl 42, 739.

[11] Kraay, *Coins*, 1028, *c*.390.

[12] Meshorer-Qedar, *Coinage of Samaria*, 20.

[13] Ashmolean/*EGFR*, no. 157 (1885.404) = Boardman, *GGFR*, no. 960m (p. 426).

[14] Boardman, *GGFR*, 485 (Taranto 100024).

[15] Richter, *EGGE*, 221 = Furtwängler, *Beschreibung* no. 291 = Furtwängler, *AG*, pl 10, 42 in the Staatliche Museen, Berlin; a gold ring of the 'second half of the fifth century', according to Richter; a fourth-century Magna Graecian work, according to Furtwängler, *AG*.
Note also a silver ring in the Rheinisches Landesmuseum, Bonn = Furtwängler, *AG*, pl 61,31, according to Furtwängler, Magna Graecian of the fourth century.

[16] De Ridder, *Collection*, 2810 = Boardman, *GGFR*, fig. 222.

third century contexts excavated at Elephantine (Egypt) and Selinus (Sicily) also depict the hero in essentially the same fashion.[17]

Early in the century, Furtwängler categorized this pose as a *statuarisches Motiv*.[18] G. Horster agreed that the similarities among the seals suggested a large-scale statue of Herakles as a prototype for the glyptic examples, probably a work located in Magna Graecia.[19] The type on WD **11C** is similar to the 'Albertini Herakles', named for a Roman copy of what is supposed to have been an early fourth-century bronze original, perhaps created in South Italy.[20] Boardman describes the WD **11C** Herakles type as a 'stock figure', best known 'from copies of what is probably Myron's work of the mid [fifth] century.'[21]

WD **11C** comes from a fourth-century metal finger ring, possibly produced in Phoenicia.

---

[17] Rubensohn, *Elephantine*, no. 3 from Papyrus 1 (in Greek, dated 310/11); no. 6 from Papyrus II (285/4). 'Selinunte', *Notizie degli scavi di Antichità* (August 1883) pl 8, nos. 12, 13, 16 (the terminal date for this group of over 600 sealings is 249 BCE [Boardman, *GGFR*, p. 446]).

[18] Cf. discussion of Furtwängler, *AG*, pl 61, 31, the silver ring in Bonn (see above).

[19] Horster, *Statuen*, 16 and cf. pl III, 4 and pl IV, 1–3.

[20] Boardman, *LIMC* s.v. 'Herakles', p. 745 (with illustrations).

[21] Boardman, *GGFR*, p. 197.

WD 39. Herakles in Lionskin with Club

(PLATE VI.2)

Mus. Inv. 936
Loose Sealing
Image size: 1.8 cm x 1.3 cm
Bulla size: 1.8 cm x 1.6 cm
Clay colour: burnt black
String not preserved, string holes remain; top and bottom of vertical image
Papyrus imprint
Seal type: metal finger ring

WD **39** seems to have been made by a broad, somewhat irregularly oval metal finger ring. A nick from a probable ring haft is visible at the bottom of the impression. Both the upper and lower edges of this bulla have broken or worn away. The image is somewhat indistinct with several cracks further obscuring details of the composition.

The general outline of WD **39** is fairly clear; a sturdy, broad-chested Herakles looks to his right with his head in profile. This is one of three clearly identifiable Greek-style Herakles images in the Wadi Daliyeh corpus.[1] He has little room to move up or down since his head almost touches the upper rim of the impression, and his feet rest on a single straight ground line very near the bottom. His torso and legs are in three-quarter view. A slight degree of contrapposto is indicated by the curve of the hips away from the viewer; the hero's weight is carried by the (far) right leg, and the left leg is bent back slightly at the knee. Both feet are bare. The empty left hand, fist clenched, hangs behind him. His right hand rests lightly before him on the handle of his knobby club which he balances like a cane.

In the photograph of WD **39**, the details of Herakles' head and costume give the rather incongruous impression of an Easter Islander in a Polynesian grass skirt. His unbearded jaw seems too long, and his fine nose looks out of proportion. From the back of his head protrude several 'spikes'. The 'grass skirt' is the legs of the pelt of the Nemean lion, draped over Herakles' body. Representations of Herakles in the lionskin often show the lion's legs hanging down like tassels. Precisely how Herakles' feline trophy is draped, however, remains unclear on the bulla because of its poor state of preservation. On close examination, the 'spikes' on Herakles' head turn out to be the fur of the lion head Herakles is wearing as combination hat and mask. The apparent elongation of the hero's jaw must actually be the lion's jaw, barely discernible on the

---

[1] See WD **11C** (pl VI.1) and WD **42** (pl VI.3). See also the INTRODUCTORY REMARKS on Herakles (p. 85).

bulla, from which Herakles' face protrudes.[2] Herakles may wear his lionskin like this from the Archaic period onwards.[3]

On WD **39**, Herakles assumes essentially the stock 'statuesque' pose discussed in relation to WD **11C**. In sculpture, the type of the New York Herakles is comparable, except that WD **39** seems to lack the knot of lion legs at Herakles' throat.[4] Archaic and Classical Attic red figure vases[5] supply the best parallels, showing Herakles wearing the lionskin on his head and standing as he does on WD **39**. Herakles stands in the same way on a Punic bronze votive razor of the third century from Carthage.[6] A crude terracotta figurine of the Persian period from Lachish represents Herakles wearing the lionskin on his head.[7]

Strangely, exact glyptic and numismatic parallels are difficult to find; coins or seals with a standing Herakles in the lionskin are much rarer. There is a fifth-century stater from Kition (Cyprus) of *c*.460, but Herakles is in the smiting posture;[8] or a series of smaller issues from Thasos between 400 and 350 on which Herakles, wearing his lionskin, kneels to aim his bow.[9] The closest numismatic parallel may be a small group of fourth-century triobols (and a possible diobol) of Kroton (Magna Graecia) on which Herakles stands in profile and seems to wear the lionskin on his head.[10]

On a carnelian scaraboid found in Taranto, Herakles' head has actually turned into a lion head, but, as noted above, the hero stands as he does on WD **11C**.[11] The figure of Herakles on a bronze ring in the Ashmolean Museum[12] matches WD **39** in many particulars; the hero's pose is almost a mirror-image of the WD **39** Herakles. There is even a ground line. On the other hand, there is no sign of a lion pelt, and the ring has been dated to the Hellenistic period. Even without exact comparisons, however, the figure of Herakles, as he appears on WD **39**, was known all around the Mediterranean.

---

[2] Cf. the stater minted by Evagoras I of Salamis (Cyprus) *c*.400 with the head of Herakles wearing the lion skin on his head (Kraay, *Coins*, 1083).

[3] Boardman, *ARV*, figs. 8, 26.2, 29, 65, 145, 156 (especially), 182, 188, 231, 298, 300, 336. Cf. also *LIMC*, 'Herakles'. Boardman (ARV 226–8) comments on the reduced role of Herakles on Athenian vases in the fifth century. For fourth century Attic examples of a beardless Herakles wearing the lion head, cf. Metzger, *Représentations*, pl XVI,3, a Kerch-style bell krater at Angers, Musée Pincé; also pl XXVII,3, a kalyx krater in Paris (Petit Palais, 327); also pl XXXIX, 4, a bell krater in Naples (Naples Museum H2200).

A. Lemaire 'Nouveaux sceaux nord-ouest sémitiques', *Syria* LXIII [1986] 305–7, figs. 1a,b published an inscribed Phoenician scarab of the sixth or fifth century engraved with the figure of Herakles wearing the lion skin on his head and brandishing his club.

[4] Boardman, *LIMC*, s.v. 'Herakles', p. 753 (with illustrations); the type may have been created early in the fourth quarter of the fourth century.

[5] Such as a kylix by the Panaitios Painter (Schefold-Jung, *Urkönige*, fig. 271, *c*.490 [Richter, MMA 12. 231.2]). See also Schefold-Jung, *Urkönige*, fig. 223, Herakles on the 'Underworld Krater', *c*.450, also in New York (MMA 08. 258. 21).

[6] E. Acquaro, *I Rasoi Punici* (Rome, 1971) fig. 39, cat. 82 = Moscati, *The Phoenicians*, cat. no. 308.

[7] Stern, *Material Culture*, 172, fig. 295:1.

[8] Kraay, *Coins*, pl 64, 1103. A similar figure appears on a ring in the de Clercq collection (de Ridder, *Collection*, no. 2807).

[9] Kraay, *Coins*, pl 29, 522, 523.

[10] *SNG-ANS* 3, pl 13. 425–7.

[11] Boardman, *GGFR*, 485 (Taranto 100024).

[12] Ashmolean/*EGFR*, 169 (1910.96).

WD 42. Herakles (with Club) vs. Nemean Lion

(PLATE VI.3)

Mus. Inv. 939
Loose Sealing
Image size: 1.6 cm x 0.75 cm
Bulla size: 2 cm x 1.7 cm
Clay colour: reddish brown
String minimally preserved; top and bottom of vertical image
Papyrus fragments on back
Papyrus imprint
Seal type: metal finger ring
Published: Cross, 'Papyri', 29, Pl 62, h.

WD **42** bears the impression of a leaf-shaped oval metal finger ring, a Classical type apparently quite common in Samaria. The bulla shows Herakles wrestling the Nemean lion.[1] This is one of three securely identified Herakles images in the Wadi Daliyeh corpus; WD **11C** (pl VI.1) and WD **39** (pl VI.2) are the others. The entire image survives in outline, although most of the finer details, particularly at the top and bottom, have long since vanished. A number of tiny white inclusions like grains of sand further obscure the impression.

On WD **42** the nude, apparently beardless hero, seen in three-quarter view, wrestles the Nemean lion. On the left side of the image, Herakles half crouches to meet the attack of the lion on the right. The hero keeps both feet on the ground and bends his knees to brace himself. The lion's tail dangles between its legs, next to Herakles' left knee. He keeps his left rear paw on the ground and claws at Herakles' left thigh and knee with his right. As Herakles wraps his right arm around the lion's neck to choke him, below the hero's arm can be seen both the lion's open muzzle in profile, and the lion's front (upper) left paw scratching at the arm. A few traces of lines detailing the lion's bushy mane survive above the lion's (upper) left shoulder. Behind Herakles' back, the abandoned club, rendered in some detail, seems to lean upright against the rim of the impression.

The motif of a hero confronting a lion has Near Eastern and Phoenician roots,[2] and it is also common on pyramidal stamp seals in the Persian Court Style for an animal

---

[1] A variety of sources state that the Nemean lion (Hesiod, *Theogony*, 326ff.), which Herakles had to kill and flay as his first Labour, was impervious to iron, bronze, and stone (Apollodorus ii. 5.1), hence the need for a wooden bludgeon. In some accounts, even the club was broken, forcing Herakles to set it aside and resort to his own hands (Bacchylides, 13.53; Diodorus Siculus, 4.11; Euripides, *Herakles*, 153).

[2] E. Gubel, '"Syro-Cypriote" Cubical Stamps: The Phoenician Connection', *SP* 5 (1987) 210, on leontomachies. Note that the nude hero grappling two lions on WD **47** (pl XII.2) might be Herakles.

combatant to claw at the hero's thigh.[3] The Greek pedigree of the motif reaches at least back into the Archaic period.[4] In the late sixth century, twenty percent of scenes depicting Herakles on black figure vases showed him grappling with the Nemean lion,[5] but by the late fifth century the scene had all but disappeared from vase painting.[6] Engravers of seals and coin-dies, however, continued to portray Herakles in hand-to-paw combat with the lion. Certainly in the case of the coins, the factor of tradition played a role in perpetuating a somewhat outdated motif.

Because of the rough condition of WD **42**, it is impossible to venture any fine stylistic judgements. Nevertheless, a number of Greek seals dating from the mid-fifth to the fourth century show Herakles in the same pose, with the upright lion's head peeping out below the hero's right arm and the lion's rear (lower) paw digging into the hero's leg. A few come from areas frequented by Phoenicians or have direct or indirect 'eastern' connections.

On a sard scarab of the mid fifth century with a complicated tangle of legs, Herakles has a beard and there is no sign of the club.[7] The decorative treatment of the lion's shoulder suggests Persian influence, according to Furtwängler, while the hatched border has a vaguely Etruscan (or Phoenician?) quality.[8] Richter believes the scarab is Greek.[9] The rather vague provenance and the 'Persian' detail would seem to suggest the eastern Greek area as its source.

The second parallel, in New York, is a bronze ring (once gilded) of the second half of the fifth century on which Herakles is beardless and the club appears awkwardly between his legs, presumably lying on the ground.[10]

A third seal, probably of the mid- to late fifth century, with no provenance but bearing two Phoenician letters (ʿayin, nun), shows a horizontal version of the scene.[11] Again, the club has been set aside, and Herakles, with one knee on the ground, has the

---

[3] Boardman, 'Pyramidal', pp. 32–3. On the Nippur seal impressions (Legrain, *Culture*) of contest scenes there is no clawing; perhaps the motif is Anatolian or East Greek.

[4] Note the Archaic carnelian ringstone from Cyprus in the Museum of Fine Arts, Boston on which Herakles appears to be using judo against the lion (Boardman, *GGFR*, 366 = Beazley, *Lewes House* 22 = Furtwängler, *AG*, pl X,2 = Boardman, *AG Gems*, 254 = Boston, MFA 27.674). Boardman, *AG Gems*, 295 = Furtwängler, *AG*, IX, 7 (Bibliothèque Nationale, ex. de Luynes 214) from Tortosa, is slightly similar. Impressions of Persian period rings on tablets from Ur include this motif (Legrain, *Ur*, nos. 748, 749). Cf. Boardman, *ARV*, fig. 10, a belly amphora by the Andokides Painter in the British Museum (B 193).

[5] Richter, *EGGE*, p. 103. Cf. the black figure amphora by Psiax in the Museo Civico, Brescia (illustrated in Boardman, *GA*, fig. 88. Cf. also Boardman, *ABV*, fig. 7, a belly amphora by the Andokides Painter (private collection).

[6] Webster, *Potter*, 259–60. Webster (260) claims that Greeks grew uncomfortable with the violence of the scene.

[7] Richter, *EGGE*, 350 = Boston, MFA 27.722 (ex. Tyszkiewicz) = Beazley, *Lewes House* 86 = Furtwängler, *AG*, pl LXI, 20, 'sent from Constantinople'. Cf. the black figure amphora by Psiax in the Museo Civico, Brescia (illustrated in Boardman, *GA,* fig. 88.

[8] Richter, *EGGE*, p. 103. For two Etruscan versions of Herakles and the lion, cf. Richter, MMA, 173 and 174, both of the late fifth/early fourth century. The position of the lion is different on each seal, and neither seal really compares to WD **42**.

[9] Richter, *EGGE*, p. 103.

[10] Richter, MMA, 72 (MMA 41.160.493).

[11] Bordreuil, *BN*, no. 33 = Boardman, *AG Gems*, 308 = Lippold, *Gemmen*, pl 52.10 = Furtwängler, *AG*, pl 9.4; a chalcedony scaraboid. Boardman (*AG Gems*) incorrectly reads 'SO'.

lion in a head-lock. The inscription implies a Phoenician patron and raises no more than a possibility that the seal was produced by a Phoenician artist.

Finally, a round sard ringstone of *c*.400 from Katania (Sicily) is also of interest,[12] even though the circular arrangement of man and beast differs slightly from that on WD **42**. The design on the ringstone—the curving figures of kneeling Herakles and the lion making a round shape to fit into the frame of a coin—is 'practically identical with that on the gold coins of Syracuse (*c*.390) by Euainetos and Kimon'.[13]

The existence of the sard ringstone which seems to copy a coin helps to highlight what must have been a rather fluid relationship between numismatics and glyptics. This 'round' motif, in fact, appears slightly earlier on a series of staters from Herakleia in South Italy,[14] and in general, the coins closest to WD **42** are those minted in fourth century Herakleia. On these coins, Herakles occasionally appears as on WD **42**, braced on two legs against his foe with his club behind him.[15] The lion attacks from the rampant position, with one hind leg on the ground and the other scratching at Herakles' leg, just as on WD **42**; and the lion's head is seen pinned under Herakles' right arm. The chief divergence between the bulla and the coins is in the distance between the separately articulated combatants on the latter.

In view of WD **42**'s presence in Palestine, it is not surprising to find the western coin device copied on coins minted closer to Samaria. These include a stater, *c*.360, of Mallus (Cilicia),[16] and a similarly dated stater from an undetermined Cypriot mint.[17] Perhaps the design was perceived in the western Persian Empire as a variation on the stereotypical Achaemenid scene of the 'Persian Hero' battling a lion or monster, of which there are several examples among the Wadi Daliyeh bullae.[18]

The connection of WD **42** with fourth-century papyri dates the ring which produced it to the middle of the fourth century, as does the bulla shape, its similarity to fourth-century coins, and Herakles' beardlessness, a feature that became more and more the rule in the late fifth and fourth centuries.[19]

---

[12] Richter, MMA, 42.11.25 = Richter, *EGGE*, 308 = Boardman, *GGFR*, 528 (see discussion, pp. 200–1) = Furtwängler, *AG*, pl IX, 49 = Richter, MMA, 76.

[13] Richter, *EGGE*, p. 94. Cf. Kraay, *Coins*, 818, a gold 100 litra.

[14] Kraay, *Coins*, p. 193. Cf. *SNG-ANS* 2, pl 1.13–40. Other examples of this 'round' version of Herakles kneeling against the lion occur on an electrum stater of Cyzicus, *c*.380 (Kraay, *Coins*, 960), which Kraay (p. 263) believes copies the Syracusan gold 100 litra piece; and on diobols (between 380 and 344) of Tarentum (G. Förschner, *Die Münzen der Griechen in Italien und Sizilien, Kleine Schriften des Historischen Museums, Frankfort am Main* 27 [1986] nos. 180–84; *SNG-ANS 1*, pl 37.1387–1430). The same design appears on a series of Tarentine diobols, cf. *SNG-ANS* 1, pls 37–8. Cf. Holloway, *Art and Coinage*, 56, 131–3.

[15] The best photographs are in Holloway, *Art and Coinage*, 132 (stater, 433–330), and Jenkins, *Coins*, 469 (*c*.350). Cf. *SNG-ANS 2*, pl 1. 46–9, 51; pl 2. 52–5, 57–66.

[16] Kraay, *Coins*, 1026. Meshorer (*Coinage of Samaria*, 20) remarks on the connection between Cilician coinage and coins issued in Phoenicia and Samaria.

[17] Kraay, *Coins*, 1110.

[18] Cf. WD **4** (pl XVIII.2) , WD **8** (pl XVIII.3), WD **19** (pl XX.1).

[19] Herrmann, *Shadow*, 11. Compare also a bronze ring from Sicily in the Getty Museum (85.AN.370.16) dated by Spier to the second half of the fourth century (Spier, *Ancient Gems*, no. 85).

C.   MATURE MALE FIGURES

WD 9. Mature Man Wearing Himation

(PLATE VII.1)

Mus. Inv. 964
Loose sealing
Image size: 1.5 cm x 0.75 cm
Bulla size: 1.7 cm x 1.6 cm
Clay colour: black-brown (partially burned ?)
String preserved, including the uncut loop; top and bottom of vertical image
Fragments of papyrus on back
Papyrus imprint
Seal type: metal finger ring

A METAL finger ring with an extremely narrow oval bezel, slightly pointed at the top and bottom, produced the image on WD **9**. This shape belongs to the late Classical period[1] and accords well with the fourth century context of the Wadi Daliyeh sealings.

The contours of the image are rather indistinct, as if the ring were worn down from use. A gouge obscures the area between the figure's hips and knees. It is also unclear if there was an inscription in the small exergue below the broad groundline.

A rather long-haired bearded man with his head in profile but the rest of his body in three-quarter view walks—or stands—with a bit of a stoop to his right. His slightly hunched posture as well as the short walking-stick in the figure's right hand suggest advanced years. His large feet appear in flat-footed profile, Egyptian style. While the artist has attempted to suggest contrapposto by giving the figure a bend of the left knee and an apparent curve of the torso, this contradicts the vaguely stooping steps the man seems to be making with the aid of his stick.

There is an abundance of drapery here, but poor preservation and the crude execution of the figure combine to make it difficult to understand the gentleman's outfit in more than a general way. He seems to wear a calf-length himation, girded with an overfold at the waist. The right half of his chest and his right shoulder appear bare. The himation falls over his left shoulder to drape like a shawl in a bunch over his left arm. He holds his left hand close to his hip to keep the himation in place. Overall, there is little volume or movement. The image is a Greek one, but whoever carved this seal was perhaps not sufficiently interested or able to engrave more than the essentials of the subject.

At least four other Wadi Daliyeh bullae display mature men in himatia, WD **11E** (pl VII.2) and **20** (pl VII.3) and two bullae in the Hecht Group (pl XXIV.7, 12, and possibly 11). Each is different, although the two Hecht bullae might be by the same

---

[1] Boardman, *GGFR*, type XVI (fig. 217) and p. 230.

hand; all but one—the figure of Zeus in the Hecht Group (pl XXIV.12)—remain anonymous.

Is an old man, a little unsteady on his feet, depicted on WD **9**, or is the figure supposed to be a mature, robust man? In the Hellenistic period, if not before, the sculptural type of the bearded man in a himation became very popular and was chosen especially for statues of philosophers, writers, and some deities.[2] Gods, such as Zeus, may wear a himation arranged just as on WD **9**.[3] They have beards to attest to their maturity but also enjoy the prime of their adult vigour. It is unclear whether the perceived stooping posture of the man on WD **9** was intentional on the part of the artist, but the short cane cannot be confused with the long staffs and sceptres wielded by divinities in Classical art. Canes do not belong exclusively to old men in Greek art,[4] but it is reasonably certain that the man on WD **9** is supposed to be somewhat elderly.

Bearded men wrapped in himatia with one shoulder and part of the chest bare[5] wield staffs in several possible ways; they lean on a staff placed under an armpit as if it were a crutch, or use a shorter staff like a cane, or a longer staff like a walking stick.[6] Like the WD **9** figure, the stooped posture and bent knees of these men betray their age. They appear on stelae with one foot placed directly before the other, also a detail repeated on WD **9**. Sometimes these old men wear sandals, but not always; this question remains open in regard to WD **9**.

Reliefs and vases supply more parallels to the figure on WD **9**.[7] The figure of an old man leaning on his staff appears relatively often on Greek funerary stelae beginning in the early fifth century.[8] While some scholars have speculated on a symbolic meaning

---

[2] Cf. J. J. Pollitt, *Art in the Hellenistic Age* (Cambridge, 1986) 59ff.

[3] 'Acknowledged seniors' include Dionysos, Poseidon, Hephaistos, Nereus and Priam (Boardman, *ARV*, p. 223). For an early version of Dionysos, bearded and with a himation, cf. an Archaic rock crystal scaraboid in Cambridge (England), which Boardman places in a group of East Greek or Cypriot gems (Boardman, *AG Gems*, p. 91–2, 'the Group of the Leningrad Gorgon' = Boardman, *GGFR*, 383 = Boardman, *AG Gems*, 242). In the fourth century, Asclepios joins their number (B. Holtzmann, *LIMC,* 'Asclepius'). Hermes' caduceus can look like a walking stick or staff (*LIMC*, 'Hermes', 381–2).

[4] Rhapsodes, heralds and shepherds may have a cane (D. Mitten and S. Doehringer, *Master Bronzes from the Classical World*, Exhibition Catalog [Fogg Art Museum, 1967–8] 61). In *palaistra* scenes on red figure vases, athletic trainers (often nude) may carry a staff or a cane (Boardman, *ARV*, p. 220 and fig. 97), and a set of young (or middle-aged?) idlers in himatia have short canes on a late sixth-century statue base from Athens (National Museum 3476; illustrated in Lullies-Hirmer, *Sculpture*, pls 64–5); this composition should also be categorized as a *palaistra* scene.

[5] The occasional old man will wear a tunic under his himation; for example, Phoinix, on a cup by the Brygos Painter who was active in the 480s and 470s (Louvre G 152 = Boardman, *ARV*, fig. 245.1).

[6] M.-A. Zagdoun, *Fouilles de Delphes 4:6, Monuments figurés: Sculpture* [1977], figs. 1–9. Zagdoun (13) points out that young men with staffs generally hold them upright like spears or sceptres, and usually these men wear a chlamys or short mantle rather than a long himation.

[7] Cf. the group of men with staffs on the east frieze of the Parthenon. Cf. Zagdoun, *Fouilles*, fig. 35, a votive relief of 329/8 in the Ny Carlsberg Glypotheque [inv. 462]). For a whole group of Trojan men, old and young, with staffs, note the outside of a kylix in Boston (95.28) by the Telephos Painter from *c*.470 (illustrated in Schefold, *Klassischen*, fig. 453–4).

[8] A good mid-fourth century example: the funerary stele of a father and son, *c*.350–330, in the National Museum, Athens (illustrated in G. M. A. Richter, *A Handbook of Greek Art*[6] [London, 1969] fig. 218). Zagdoun, *Fouilles*, 15; cf. 2–15 for discussion and bibliography related to men leaning on staffs. Cf. also G. M. A. Richter, *The Archaic Gravestones of Attica* (London, 1961).

for the motif, seeing these figures as travellers to the great beyond, fifth-century taste for scenes of everyday life on funerary stelae was probably reason enough.[9]

In general, however, old men with staffs are rare on Greek seals and coins.[10] A rough parallel to WD **9** is a gold ring on which a man walking with his dog stops to adjust his sandle. He has a staff and himation; his *pilos* hat may identify him as Odysseus.[11]

To conclude, the figure on WD **9** probably is simply a man mature in years. Nevertheless, in view of the dearth of comparable images on seals and coins in both the Archaic and Classical periods it is impossible to eliminate totally the possibility that the figure is a god or hero. Provincial workmanship and ignorance of Greek artistic conventions might be obscuring the engraver's intentions.

---

[9] Zagdoun, *Fouilles*, 15.

[10] The Arcadians of Tegea between 468 and 460 minted a half-drachma with a standing Zeus on the obverse; he wears a draped himation, leans on a long staff, crutch fashion, and holds an eagle in his outstretched right hand (R. T. Williams, *The Confederate Coinage of the Arcadians in the Fifth Century* [ANS, 1965] nos. 175–7). Without the eagle and apart from his numismatic context it would be difficult to identify him as Zeus.

[11] Boardman, *GGFR*, 757 = Richter, *EGGE*, 228, in the Muzeo Nazionale, Taranto. Boardman calls it western Greek and fifth century; Richter declines to mention geography, and assigns the ring to the fourth century.

WD 11E. Mature Man in Himation and Pilos

(PLATE VII.2)

Mus. Inv. 772[1]
Papyrus 1, March 19, 335.[2]
Image size: approx. 1.1 x 0.8 cm
Bulla size: approx. 1.8 x 1.4 cm
Clay colour: n.a.
String preserved; emerging top and bottom of vertical image
Seal type: metal finger ring or scaraboid

WD **11E** is one of seven clay impressions found attached to Samaria Papyrus 1;[3] of these only four are even slightly legible.[4] Samaria Papyrus 1 records the sale of a slave named 'Yehoḥanan bar Šeʾilah to Yehonur bar Laneri by Ḥananyah bar Beyadʾel for 35 sheqels'.[5] All the first names (buyer, seller and slave) are Yahwistic while the patronyms are not. Of the seven sealings, only WD **11B** (pl XIX.3), possibly the sealing of Yehonur, can be associated with any of the men mentioned in the papyrus.[6]

The available photograph shows that the bulla has suffered considerable wear, and the lower left edge of the incompletely sealed area consists of a bulge of clay.

A mature bearded man draped in a himation and wearing a *pilos* cap looks in profile to his right. Whether the torso is frontal or in three-quarter view is difficult to determine, probably the latter. He appears to be of stocky proportions. The himation drapes over the man's left shoulder, leaving the other bare. The left arm, bent at the elbow and held horizontally across his waist, may be concealed in the folds of the cloth. His bare right arm is extended out to his right side. The right hand is not preserved; the ankles and feet have suffered a similar fate.

At least four other Wadi Daliyeh bullae depict mature men in himatia, WD **9** (pl VII.1) and **20** (VII.3) and two bullae in the Hecht Group (pl XXIV.7, 12, and possibly 11). Each is different, although the two Hecht bullae might be by the same hand; all but one—the figure of Zeus in the Hecht Group (pl XXIV.12)—are anonymous. It is possible that, like the figure on WD **9**, the gentleman on WD **11E** held a walking stick

---

[1] The following discussion is based on photographs only. WD **11E** was unavailable for inspection.

[2] Gropp, *Samaria Papyri*, 1–37. See earlier, Cross, 'Samaria Papyrus 1'. Corrections in Cross, 'Report'.

[3] WD **11A–G**. At least as many more bullae may have been attached to SP 1.

[4] WD **11A–11B** show similar debased versions of the Persian Hero throttling flanking monsters. WD **11C** shows Herakles. WD **11D**, WD **11F** and WD **11G** are illegible.

[5] Gropp, *Samaria Papyri*, 3.

[6] See discussion of WD **3A** (= WD **11B** = WD **12** = WD **24**).

in his missing right hand; the typology of older men in Classical Greek art supports this reconstruction.[7]

A walking stick is generically associated with mature Greek men, as is the himation draped over one shoulder. Rather more unusual is the presence on WD **11E** of the *pilos* cap, the only detail in the photograph which could qualify as iconographical. For comparison one notes a Classical gold ring in Taranto showing an older himation-draped man with a dog; he is leaning on the usual staff but wears a *pilos*.[8] For both Richter and Boardman, the *pilos* marks the figure as Odysseus, on the basis of iconographical parallels.[9]

Perhaps WD **11E** does portray Odysseus; on the other hand, neither Richter nor Boardman insists upon this interpretation for the Tarentine ring. Odysseus appears on few seals of the Archaic or Classical periods.[10] Another possible identification might be that of Hephaistos, who also appears in Greek art as an elderly man clothed in a tunic with one shoulder bare and wearing a *pilos*.[11] The identification remains uncertain.

---

[7] See discussion of WD **9** above, p. 97.

[8] Boardman, *GGFR*, 757 = Richter, *EGGE*, 228, found in Taranto, now in the Museo Nazionale, Taranto. Boardman calls it western Greek and fifth century; Richter declines to mention geography and assigns the ring to the fourth century.

[9] The *pilos* looks like a gently peaked skullcap and, like the *petasos*, was worn by travellers. The dog would be Argos.

[10] Cf. Boardman, *GGFR*, 534, Boardman, *GGFR*, 535 = *AGDS* (Berlin) 155, Boardman, *GGFR*, 537; Boardman, *GGFR*, p. 201 and especially the description of 535. These are identified with varying degrees of uncertainty. Boardman, *GGFR*, 535 and Odysseus are discussed briefly by J. Boardman in 'Greek Gem Engravers, Their Subjects and Style', *Ancient Art in Seals*, ed. E. Porada (Princeton, 1980) 105–6.

[11] Cf. F. Brommer, *Hephaistos: der Schmiedegott in dem antiken Kunst* (Mainz, 1978).

WD 20. Frontal Male Figure in Himation

(PLATE VII.3)

Mus. Inv. 971
Loose sealing
Image size: 0.8 cm (as preserved) x 1 cm; originally probably 1.3 cm high
Bulla size: 0.9 cm x 1 cm
Clay colour: reddish brown
String preserved; top and bottom of vertical image
Papyrus imprint
Seal type: metal finger ring

PART of WD **20** has broken away from the bottom of the bulla. It is nonetheless clear that the impression came from a worn leaf-shaped metal finger ring, a fifth-/fourth-century ring type well represented among the Wadi Daliyah bullae. A crack runs diagonally across half the image, from the lower left to the upper right.

The faint but generally legible image consists of a single front-facing male figure quite crudely rendered. He wears a himation draped over his left shoulder and bunched at his waist, and the artist has made a weak attempt to show the muscles of the man's bare torso. Beyond this, the details are vague. He seems to have a beard; his eyes and nose are those of a stick figure, and the mouth is invisible, perhaps lost in his beard. An inverted bowl shape sits atop his head. If the figure could be taken as a warrior, there would be no difficulty in identifying the 'bowl' as a plumed helmet based on conventions of frontality. However, the figure has no apparent martial qualities, so the 'bowl' probably indicates hair.

His right arm appears to bend up with the hand at shoulder level, possibly to display something. The man's left arm is hidden in the folds of the himation which he holds against his waist with his (perhaps) visible hand.

WD **20** and at least four other Wadi Daliyeh bullae display mature men in himatia: WD **9** (pl VII.1), WD **11E** (pl VII.2) and two bullae in the Hecht collection (pl XXIV.7, 12 and possibly 11). Each is different, although the two Hecht bullae might be by the same hand; all but one—the figure of Zeus in the Hecht group (pl XXIV.12)—are anonymous figures.

Portrayals of older men or even of mature gods are unusual in Archaic and Classical glyptic art.[1] The awkward frontal pose of WD **20** is unusual,[2] but otherwise, the figure on the bulla resembles mature gods in Greek art who wear their himatia thus around the waist and over one shoulder. The search for numismatic comparisons leads to some suggestive parallels, but no exact counterparts to WD **20**.

---

[1] See discussion of this genre in entry for WD **9**, above, p. 97.

[2] On frontality in general, see entry on WD **46**, below, p. 137.

The strange headdress or hair of the figure on WD **20** could be a degenerated form of the crown worn by the city god of Tarsus, 'Baaltarz', on a series of Cilician staters. These were minted at Tarsus in the fourth century by successive Persian satraps of Cilicia (Datames, Pharnabazus, Tiribazus, Mazaeus/Mazdai).[3] The city god appears enthroned and draped in a himation with his left hand at his waist. On a late issue of Mazaeus (after 361), Baaltarz sits frontally on his throne and looks directly out at the viewer.[4] The overall frontality and the rather summary treatment of the frontal torso resemble that on WD 20.[5]

Any attempt to identify the figure on WD **20** must remain tentative. Perhaps the artist of the WD **20** seal ring had an image from a coin in mind, or actually before him,[6] when he set to work. If so, the figure in the impression is probably a deity, but for us remains an anonymous one. The only conceivable piece of iconography preserved in the clay is the bowl-shaped headdress/hair possibly intended as a radiate crown of the sort Baaltarz and other deities wear on coins. However, it could also be a degraded version of a number of other hairstyles or helmets featured on coins.

---

[3] Kraay, *Coins*, 1039–46 (minted 378–333). Meshorer notes of Samaria's fourth-century coinage that at least fifteen issues are in imitation of Cilician coins (Meshorer-Qedar, *Coinage of Samaria*, 20).

[4] Kraay, *Coins*, 1044 (= *SNG-ANS: Burton Y. Berry, Vol. II*, nos. 1303–4).

[5] Another possible comparison would be with a series of late fifth-century staters issued by the Cilician city of Nagidus. A regal himation-clad Dionysos stands erect, his head in profile looking to his right, but with his bare torso facing. Unlike the draped figure on WD **20**, however, Dionysos holds a tall thyrsus, his staff of office, in his left hand, offers a bunch of grapes in his right, and has a pronounced contrapposto (*SNG-ANS; Burton Y. Berry, Vol. II*, pl 48.1283–4 = Hill, *BMC Coins*, 21 [Lycaonia, Isauria and Cilicia] pl XIX.2, 10–12 [420–400]).

[6] Cf. Porada, 'Greek Coin', 228–34.

D. DIONYSIAN SUBJECTS

WD 5 and WD 16B. Satyr

(WD 5 = PLATE VIII.2; WD 16B = PLATES VIII.1 AND XXII.1D)

WD **5**:

Mus. Inv. 960

Loose sealing

Image size: 1.5 x 1.2 cm

Bulla size: 1.6 x 1.4 cm

Clay colour: deep reddish brown

String preserved; perpendicular to vertical image

Papyrus imprint

Papyrus fibres on back and bottom edge of bulla

Seal type: metal finger ring

WD **16B**:[1]

Mus. Inv. 777

Papyrus 3 (n.d.)

Image size: 1.5 x 1.2 cm

Bulla size: 1.8 x 1.9 cm

Clay colour: n.a.

String preserved; parallel with vertical image

Seal type: metal finger ring

WD **5** and WD **16B** are duplicate impressions from the same seal.

WD **16B** is one of four bullae found attached to Samaria Papyrus 3[2] which describes the sale of 'the slave Yeho'anani bar 'Azaryah to Yehopadayni bar Delayah and 'Ari bar Delayah by Yaqim for ten sheqels'.[3] Witnesses include Šelomi, son of Šaharnatan, 'Anani, Yaqim and 'Eṭir, 'sons of Delayah', a son of [D]uman and a son of Šekwi.[4] In view of the many Yahwistic elements ('*Yeho*', '*-yah*') in this group of names, one or more of the preserved bullae could have been impressed by the seal of a YHWH-worshipper. Of the other names, only Šaharnatan conveys hints of ethnicity/religion; it may be the name of 'an Aramaean or an Aramaized Arab'.[5]

Like many other seal impressions from the Samaria Papyri, WD **5** and WD **16B** were made by a metal seal ring with a rounded oval bezel; the ring left an indentation of its rim at the top and on the right side of WD **5**. The ring bezel shape is typically

---

[1] Discussion of WD **16B** is based on photographs alone as it was unavailable for inspection.

[2] See pl XXII.1d. The other bullae are WD **16A**, nude warrior (pl IV.1), WD **16C** (illeg.) and WD **16D** (illeg.).

[3] Gropp, *Samaria Papyri*, 64; cf. the preliminary discussion by Cross, 'Report', 22. Note that a male slave with a Yahwistic name is sold to men likewise with Yahwistic names.

[4] Gropp, *Samaria Papyri*, 64.

[5] F. M. Cross, personal communication.

mid to late fifth century, but it is not surprising to find it persisting into the fourth on the fringes of the Greek world.[6]

Viewed together, these two impressions demonstrate the uneven quality of images produced in the act of sealing. The deeply incised seal made impressions in high relief, but the craftsmanship is awkward.

A stocky, bearded satyr[7] stands in a three-quarter rear view, facing the viewer's left; his head is in profile. In his left (near) hand he grasps what looks like a branch and holds it before him at waist height. WD **16B** clearly shows the left fist almost touching the left edge of the impression. Both arms bend at the elbows; the elbow of the right (far) arm is pulled sharply back. The left hip swings slightly to the side as the satyr advances. The rear-view composition creates the curious impression that the figure is bending his torso back from his waist while he thrusts his belly forward. Like the significantly less hairy satyr of WD **21B**, this figure has his near leg forward, possibly a visual signal that the figure registers low on the Greek scale of humanity.[8]

The satyr's knees and legs bend forward in an anatomical impossibility, humanly speaking. However, this satyr has furry caprid flanks which, unlike human limbs, bend forward below the knee joint. The back of his left leg sprouts feathery tufts of fur. Neither sealing shows the head or the buttocks clearly, leaving us guessing about his head (does he have animal ears and horns?) and whether he has a tail.[9]

At least one satyr appears in a three-quarter rear view on a Classical seal: a goat-tailed satyr dancing with a tambourine.[10] Another ecstatic satyr on a blue chalcedony scaraboid from Cyprus[11] waves a branch, a good Dionysian attribute which the WD **5/16B** satyr may also be carrying.

With his wrestler's build, this satyr threatens to erupt from the confines of the seal; his head and arms almost touch the border. The composition on WD **5/16B** differs from the other Wadi Daliyeh bullae in the proportionally large size of the figure as it relates to the background, a quality more typical of Archaic than of Classical seals.[12] Satyrs are also a favorite motif on Archaic seals, and one familiar to the Phoenicians as well.[13] Furtwängler long ago noted that as the Classical period progressed, gems

---

[6] Boardman, *GGFR*, fig. 217 (type III) and p. 214.

[7] S.v. 'Satyrn und Silene', *Lexikon der alten Welt* (Zürich and Stuttgart, 1965) cols. 2707–8. Cf. F. Brommer, *Satyrspiele* (Berlin, 1944).

[8] Cf. the discussion of WD **50**. below, p. 117.

[9] Satyrs do not always have tails, nor are they always bearded. Cf. 'Satyrn und Silene', *Lexicon der alten Welt* (Zürich and Stuttgart, 1965), and Brommer, *Satyrspiele*.

[10] Boardman, *GGFR*, 629, (now lost) of unknown material, published in Lippold, pl 14,2 and Boardman, *AG Gems*, fig. 99.

[11] Boardman, *GGFR*, 626 = Richter, *EGGE*, 223 = Ashmolean/*EGFR*, 1892.1489.

[12] Compare the satyrs in Boardman, *AG Gems*, figs. 84–108, for example, and discussion in Boardman, *GGFR*, p. 193. Notably, the main centres for Greek seal carving in the Archaic period were the Greek islands, Ionia, and especially Cyprus (then part of the Persian Empire; Boardman, *AG Gems*, pp. 172, 175–6; Boardman, *GGFR*, p. 141).

[13] As is mentioned in the discussion of WD **21B**, a mediating figure between Greece and the East was certainly Bes. Clay images of the Egypto-Phoenician dwarf god turn up, for example, at sites occupied by Persian mercenaries in southern Palestine in the fifth century (J. A. Blakey and F. L. Horton, Jr., 'South Palestinian Bes Vessels of the Persian period', *Levant* XVIII [1986] 111–19). Bes was a frequent subject of Phoenician seals, terracottas, and

illustrating Dionysian subjects diminished in number in contrast to the increase in the numbers of those portraying Aphrodite and Eros.[14]

But WD **5/16B** is not an Archaic work. In his more naturalistic stance, this satyr differs stylistically from Archaic satyrs with kneeling-running or stooping poses. If anything, he calls to mind some of the heavy-set servant figures on Lycian tombs carved in good Ionian Greek style[15] and in particular a rear-facing groom on the late fifth-century 'Satrap's Sarcophagus' from Sidon.[16]

The satyr on WD **5/16B** is not alone in the Wadi Daliyeh corpus. Three other bullae depict satyrs: WD **2** (pl X.2), WD **21B** (pl VIII.3) and WD **44** (pl X.3); there is also an additional Dionysian subject, a maenad (WD **50** [pl IX.2]). This does not indicate an interest in Dionysos in Samaria, but rather that some common subjects in Classical Greek art had made their way to a provincial capital of the Persian Empire by the fourth century at the latest.[17] *Mischwesen* were familiar subjects throughout the ancient Near East, but not of the naturalistic sort on WD **5/16B**. As in other cases, what knowledge the owner had of the identity of the half-goat figure on this seal is decidedly obscure.

---

ivories both in the Levantine homeland and the Punic west. It is instructive to compare a fourth century terracotta Bes figurine from Sardinia (Moscati, *Phoenicians*, no. 555) with a fifth-century Sardinian clay plaque depicting a dancing satyr (Moscati, *Phoenicians*, no. 585). Phoenician green jasper seals produced at Tharros (Sardinia) depict both Bes (Moscati, *Phoenicians*, no. 655 and Walters, *BMC*, 371) and satyrs (Walters, *BMC*, no. 393) who look very similar. Cf. also Zazoff, *AG*, pp. 89–90 with references.

[14] Furtwängler, *AG* III, p. 140 ff.

[15] Cf. C. Bruns-Özgan, *Lykische Grabreliefs des 5. und 4. Jdts v. Chr.* (Tübingen, 1987).

[16] Photograph in J. Boardman, *The Diffusion of Classical Art in Antiquity* (Princeton, 1994) fig. 3.7. See also I. Kleemann, *Der Satrapen-Sarkophag aus Sidon* (Berlin, 1958) and Hitzl, *Sarkophage*.

[17] See discussion of Dionysos in entry for WD **50**, pp. 118–19.

WD 21B. Dancing Satyr

(PLATES VIII.3 AND XXII.2B)

Mus. Inv. 767
Papyrus 2, December 352/January 351.
Image size: [approx.] 1.3 cm. x 0.7 cm
Bulla size: [approx.] 1.8 cm. x 1.2 cm
Clay colour: n.a.
String preserved; top and bottom of vertical image
Papyrus imprint: n.a.
Seal type: metal finger ring

WD **21B**[1] along with at least three other bullae,[2] was originally attached to Samaria Papyrus 2 which 'records the sale of one male and one female slave (names unknown) to a woman ꜣAbiᶜadin (patronymic unknown) by Qôsnahar (patronymic unknown) for 23 sheqels';[3] according to the Persian date formula ('in the month of Ṭebet, the seventh year of Artaxerxes III [Ochus]') the sale occurred in December 352 or January 351.[4] There is no way of knowing which, if any, of the four attached bullae belonged to ꜣAbiᶜadin, whose name is probably Israelite[5] or to Qôsnahar, the apparently Edomite seller.

The narrow oval, leaf-shaped outline of the metal finger ring which produced the image is clear; the bezel shape, narrower than usual in the Wadi Daliyeh corpus, is fourth century.[6] The satyr on WD **21B** is a common motif on Greek seals and occasionally appears on Phoenician ones as well.

The entire image has survived in outline but it seems worn, and the area around the satyr's head is particularly obscure. This sealing, as preserved, also appears to have been a second attempt on the same piece of clay; a set of lines behind the satyr seem to echo his back and left leg.

Although the photograph does not seem to show a tail, the nude figure's apparently substantial beard and his pose speak strongly for the identification of the figure as a satyr.[7] This heavy-set satyr with a human body prances in profile toward the viewer's

---

[1] This description is based on a small photograph only, as WD **21B** was unavailable for inspection.

[2] See pl XXII.2. Samaria Papyrus 2 was probably sealed with more than the four surviving attached bullae (WD **21A–D**).

[3] Gropp, *Samaria Papyri*, 38–62. Preliminarily published in Cross, 'Report', 17–26.

[4] Gropp, *Samaria Papyri*, 62.

[5] Cross, 'Report', 23; ꜣAbiᶜadin is a typical feminine name, 'My (divine) father is the fertile one' (*idem*, 23).

[6] Boardman, *GGFR*, fig. 217 and p. 213; type XVI.

[7] Satyrs do not always have tails, nor are they always bearded. Cf. 'Satyrn und Silene', *Lexikon der alten Welt* (Zürich and Stuttgart, 1965) and Brommer, *Satyrspiele*. Note also the tail-less satyr on a seal in the Bibliothèque

right. Country-dance style, he doubles up with his bent right elbow almost touching his upraised right knee. His right foot is raised to the height of his left knee which bends slightly under the weight of the satyr's exertions. He seems to have the bald head expected of satyrs; is there shaggy hair lower down the back of his skull? The (far) right arm does not appear in the photograph, nor does the photograph reveal what, if anything, the satyr holds in his upraised right hand. It is also unclear whether the figure has animal ears. The execution of the image seems to be full-bodied and assured.

Along with maenads, satyrs are Dionysos' regular companions.[8] Beginning in the Archaic period, satyrs appear often on Greek seals. They may hold drinking cups[9] or other Dionysian paraphernalia or carry off captive nymphs.[10] Perhaps the WD **21B** satyr had a kantharos in his left hand (there does not seem to be enough space for a cup in his right).

In the Wadi Daliyeh corpus this is one of several bullae with a Dionysian subject. WD **2** (pl X.2) depicts a satyr with a heron, WD **44** (pl X.3) a satyr playing knucklebones with a nymph; another, WD **5/16B** (pl VIII.1,2) portrays a single satyr; three show dancers: WD **27**, a Persian (pl IX.3), WD **50** (pl IX.2), probably a maenad and here on WD **21B**, a satyr. Dionysos did not have a strong presence in Syria-Palestine until the Hellenistic period, but at least from an artistic point of view, his mythical minions were already known prior to this era.

The best glyptic parallel for WD **21B** is a Classical seal on which a satyr with a goat's tail dances and shakes a tambourine (or waves a cup).[11] An additional parallel is provided by a blue chalcedony scaraboid 'from Larnaka'.[12] Here a satyr dances ecstatically, his head thrown back as he waves a branch. Although the Larnaka satyr does not dance the same step as that of WD **21B** and tambourine-playing satyrs, he shares a small detail of stance with them in having his near leg forward as he executes some sort of vigorous movement.[13]

Nationale, Paris (below). An early fourth-century Attic lekanis cover in Leningrad with its troupe of dancing satyrs gives a good idea of the various satyr dance poses (Metzger, *Représentations*, pl IX [Hermitage St. 2007]).

A fifth-century bronze parallel to WD **21B** is the little high-kicking satyr illustrated in the catalogue of the Kimbell Art Museum's exhibition, *Wealth of the Ancient World: The Nelson Bunker Hunt and William Herbert Hunt Collections* (Beverly Hills, 1983) no. 29.

[8] Burkert, *Greek Religion*, 166 and references.

[9] Boardman, *GGFR*, 30 = Richter, *EGGE*, 11 = Walters, *BMC*, 465, the name piece of the Master of the London Satyr, an Archaic agate scarab. The satyr's orientation on the seal has been debated. If he were viewed 'feet down', the stance would relate to WD **21B**.

[10] Boardman, *GGFR*, 305 = Boardman, *AG Gems*, no. 107, in Hanover, an Archaic rock crystal scarab. This satyr seems to resemble the WD **21B** satyr in (apparently) lacking a tail.

A. Henrichs makes the distinction between nymphs and maenads in 'Myth Visualized: Dionysos and his Circle in Sixth-Century Attic Vase-Painting', *Papers on the Amasis Painter and his World* (Malibu, J. Paul Getty Museum, 1987) 99–106.

[10] Boardman, *GGFR*, 646.

[11] Boardman, *GGFR*, 629 [now lost], published in Lippold, *Gemmen*, pl 14,2 and Boardman, *AG Gems*, fig. 99.

[12] Boardman, *GGFR*, 626 = Furtwängler, *AG*, pl 12,42 = Richter, *EGGE*, 223 = (Ashmolean 1892.1489).

[13] The possible implications of this positioning of the legs are rehearsed elsewhere (cf. discussion of WD **50** p. 119); it may mark figures who lack dignity or are less than fully human.

Boardman places these two parallels to WD **21B** in a category he calls 'Plain Eastern Gems', which he will only stipulate as Classical, without hazarding any closer dating.[14] He surmises that they may come from a single centre, 'removed from those producing the Greco-Persian gems. It is perhaps to be located in the Syria-Palestine area where, in the Classical period, many styles seem to have been current side by side—the Phoenician, Babylonian, Persian, and hybrids deriving from these'.[15] WD **21B** comes from a ring, so cannot by definition be a 'plain eastern gem', but it certainly comes from the milieu Boardman proposes for his group of gems and could perhaps have been a product of the same or a related workshop.

Sidon, the leading Phoenician city in the Persian period, apparently saw the satyr as a meaningful image, significant enough to be a city symbol on a small silver coin minted in the late fifth century on whose reverse was a facing satyr head.[16] Perhaps the Sidonians, syncretizing Phoenicians that they were, thought of Bes, the Egypto-Phoenician dwarf, when they put the satyr on their coin; Bes's lion skin with tail, for example, was not infrequently confused on Greco-Phoenician gems with the tail of a satyr.[17]

A fair number of seals depicting satyrs are connected with Phoenicia. A sixth-century example is a rock crystal scarab with a Phoenician inscription;[18] a tail-less satyr reclines with a kantharos in his hand, a cruder version of the 'London Satyr'.[19] Another Archaic satyr, tail-less and waving a branch, appears on a cubical seal found at Kourion (Cyprus), a decided mixture of Oriental and Greek motifs.[20]

Excavations in the early thirties at ʿAtlit (perhaps Adarus, a fourth-century Sidonian colony listed by Scylax[21]) on the Mediterranean coast south of Haifa unearthed a variety of Persian period seals in fifth- and fourth-century burials.[22] These, along with other finds suggest that certainly in its material culture, ʿAtlit was overwhelmingly Phoenician. One of the seals in Greek style, a carnelian scarab in an elaborate bronze and silver mounting, is almost identical to WD **21B** in its tail-less dancing satyr.[23]

The fact that a woman, ʾAbiʿadin, was the buyer named in Samaria Papyrus 2 raises the intriguing possibility that one of the bullae came from her seal. ʾAbiʿadin was probably an Israelite; her name resembles that of another Israelite woman, Hamiʿeden,

---

[14] Boardman, *GGFR*, p. 209.

[15] Boardman, *GGFR*, p. 209.

[16] J. Betlyon, *The Coinage and Mints of Phoenicia: The Pre-Alexandrine Period*, Harvard Semitic Monographs (Chico, CA, 1982) no. 6.

[17] J. Boardman, *Intaglios and Rings: Greek, Etruscan, and Eastern: From a Private Collection* (London, 1975) pp. 10 and 47. Cf. U. Sinn's discussion of Bes in the Greek world, 'Zur Wirkung des ägyptischen ,Bes' auf die griechische Volksreligion', in D. Metzler, B. Otto and Ch. Müller-Wirth, eds., *Antidoron: Festschrift für Jürgen Thimme* (Karlsruhe, 1983) 91 and n. 76. Cf. also discussion of WD **5/16B**, p. 107 above.

[18] Bordreuil, *BN*, no. 29 = Galling, 'Bildsiegel', no. 109. The imagery is Archaic Greek, probably of the sixth century.

[19] Boardman, *GGFR*, 301 (see above).

[20] Kourion Museum St. 846. The figure identified as a satyr is called an 'attendant in a sacred tree worship scene' (Gubel, 'Syro-Cypriote', 196–7, fig. 1).

[21] *EAEHL*, ʿAtlit'.

[22] Johns, 'Excavations', 41–104.

[23] Johns, 'Excavations', no. 629, fig. 49 and pl XIV (illustrated in Stern, *Material Culture*, 200, fig. 325,2).

who is also known from her seal.[24] It is known from other seals as well that women in Israel and Judah, including during the Persian period, could have seals, occupy government positions, and engage in commerce on their own.[25] The seller's name, Qôsnahar, seems to be Edomite, including as it does the theophoric element, Qôs. One witness' name is completely lost, another is PN son of Yaqim (perhaps ʾAbiʿadin's husband, surmises Cross) and another's name is Yehoʿezer (a clearly Yahwistic name). This provides evidence of five people associated with the four preserved seals on Samaria Papyrus 2, but there would have been ample space on the lost sections of Papyrus 2 for additional bullae.[26] It is frustrating not to be able to assign one of the surviving sealings to ʾAbiʿeden herself, but there is no evidence from ancient Israel of special styles or imagery reserved for the seals of women.

---

[24] N. Avigad, 'New Names on Hebrew Seals', *ErIsr* 12 (1975) (Hebrew) 66.1.

[25] Avigad, 'Hebrew Seals', 12, 14. Avigad has also published an impression of a woman's seal on a jar handle, excavated in Jerusalem; that the name of Hannah, daughter of ʿAzaryah appeared on a jar handle and not on a clay bulla proves that the owner of this seal was involved in a business enterprise ('A Note on an Impression from a Woman's Seal', *IEJ* 37 [1987] 18–19). Cf. Hestrin, Dayagi-Mendels, *Inscribed Seals,* 43–51.

[26] No specific reference to any officials survives in Papyrus 2. Samaria Papyrus 1 had seven sealings attached, but fewer than seven witnesses are actually named in the text; Cross considers it 'doubtful that a full list of the witnesses was normally inscribed on the documents' ('Cross, Samaria Papyrus 1', 15*).

WD 40. Kneeling Eros

(PLATE IX.1)

Mus. Inv. 937
Loose sealing
Image size: 1.6 cm x 1.1 cm
Bulla size: 1.6 cm x 1.2 cm
Clay colour: reddish brown
String preserved, some loops uncut; top and bottom of horizontal image
Papyrus imprint
Seal type: metal finger ring

A METAL finger ring with a soft oval bezel produced the impression on WD **40**. The ring's haft made its mark at the top of the impression. This bezel shape belongs in the fourth century.[1]

On WD **40**, Eros appears nude and in profile to the viewer's right, kneeling on a high groundline; one feathery wing, likewise in profile, sprouts from Eros' upper back. The large exergue may once have contained some additional detail; it would be a perfect place for an inscription, but in its current state nothing is visible. The wing is rather awkward and does not curve as might be expected to form a frame around the body. Eros' right (near) foot is tucked under his buttocks; it is difficult to say whether the far knee is also in a kneeling position or raised. Eros holds both hands out before him. The now-indistinct object of his attention (iunx wheel? knucklebones? bird? butterfly?) rested on the ground line.

Eros appears early on Greek gems.[2] Over the course of the Classical period, Eros gradually shed his years until he became a baby in the Hellenistic age.[3] On an early fourth-century scaraboid from Asia Minor he appears as a little boy, not quite a baby, sitting naked on the ground, playing with his pet goose and his knucklebones.[4]

Like Dionysos, Eros has been called 'emblematic of the [fourth] century'.[5] Numerous parallels to the kneeling Eros of WD **40** present themselves on seals and vases. Compositionally, two seals—both apparently based on statues and both from excavated contexts—and one Attic vase, come closest. On the first seal, a fourth-century gold ring from Tarentum, a nude winged figure—probably Nike, not Eros—

---

[1] Boardman, *GGFR*, p. 213/fig. 217.

[2] E.g. Boardman, *GGFR*, 333, late sixth century = Beazley, *Lewes House*, 20 (Boston).

[3] G. M. A. Hanfmann, 'Eros', *OCD* (1970).

[4] Boston MFA 27.700 = Richter, *EGGE*, no. 307 = Boardman, *GGFR*, 604 = Beazley, *Lewes House*, no. 56 = Furtwängler, *AG*, pl LXIV, 15.

[5] Herrmann, *Shadow*, 28.

kneels in profile on an Ionic capital;[6] the nude figure's arms are placed near the ground holding an uncertain object. The composition is remarkably similar to that on WD **40**, including the wings above the figure's arched shoulders. It also seems to conform to the tendency for kneeling Erotes to appear primarily on metal finger rings rather than on gems.[7] The second seal is known only in an impression on a clay token from the Athenian Agora.[8] Two crouching Erotes, seen in profile, face each other heraldically on an altar or statue base. Their wings hover over curved backs. Finally, on an early fourth-century pyxis,[9] two Erotes join two women and Aphrodite in a 'boudoir scene'; the first Eros, seen in profile, squats on the ground as he reaches out with both arms, the second runs forward in a crouch with his wings raised over his back as on WD **40**.

At the risk of making too much of a crude remnant, the possibility should be considered that this kneeling pose, repeated with numerous variations on other works of Greek art, could have originally been based on a Classical statue of Eros; such works certainly existed. There was, for example, a celebrated fourth-century Eros by Praxiteles at Parion, Eros' ancient East Greek cult centre, and statues of Eros were familiar ornaments in the gymnasia.

Eros in the fourth century was closely associated in Greek art with both Aphrodite and Dionysos; it is worth considering, then, whether the creator or owner of the WD **40** ring associated Eros with either. Both deities were connected with Phoenicia. Greeks viewed Aphrodite as having ancient and on-going ties with the Great Goddess of Cyprus whose cult had been subject to Phoenician influences since the ninth-century Phoenician colonization of the island;[10] they also recognized Aphrodite's affinities with Phoenician Astarte, Baalat and Atargatis.[11] As for Dionysos, the Greeks did not regularly equate him with any particular Phoenician deity, but Phoenicians seem to have recognized something familiar in Dionysos' followers, the satyrs. As early as the

---

[6] Richter, *EGGE*, 295 = Boardman, *GGFR*, 758, late fifth century.

[7] Five examples: On a bronze ring of the early fourth century excavated at Olynthus, Eros kneels on one leg and braces the other against the rim of the bezel to steady the aim of his bow (Robinson, 'Metal', 459, pl 26).

A contemporary bronze ring shows Eros on his knees on the ground, possibly holding a *iunx* wheel in his hands (Boardman, *Intaglios*, 80).

Another ring shows Eros squatting on the ground with a iunx-wheel and comes from Naukratis, the Greek trading colony in Egypt (Boardman, *GGFR*, 723).

The Ashmolean Museum has an early fourth-century silver ring, bought in Athens, with a kneeling Eros whose wings are raised straight up (Ashmolean/*EGFR*, 147 = museum no. 1946.262).

Somewhat earlier is a gold ring in Boston with Aphrodite weighing a pair of Erotes who crouch in the scale pans while a third tugs at her skirt (Boardman, *GGFR*, 666 = Beazley, *Lewes House*, no. 53).

[8] M. Lang, *Weights and Measures: The Athenian Agora, X.1* (Princeton, 1964) pl 32, C10 = Boardman, *GGFR*, fig. 272, 'fourth century context'. One of a group of over 600 sealings discovered in Selinus in the last century, seems to show a kneeling Eros ('Selinunte', *Notizie degli Scavi di Antichità* (August, 1883) pl X, no. CXXVII). The terminal date for these bullae is 249 BCE (Boardman, *GGFR*, p. 446).

[9] Metzger, *Représentations*, pl VI, 2, in the City Museum of Birmingham, England. In a stereotypical pose employed regularly by the Kerch painter(s), Eros kneels with one knee raised and stretches one arm straight out before him (K. Schefold, *Untersuchungen zu den Kertscher Vasen*, cf. Abb. 39, [Leningrad 494] and no. 514, pl 7 [London E45]).

[10] J. Karageorghis, *La grande déesse Chypre et son culte* (Lyons, 1977) 108–9.

[11] V. Pirenne, 'Aspects orientaux du culte d'Aphrodite à Athènes', *SP* 5 (1987) 156. Cf. also *LIMC*, s.v. 'Aphrodite'.

sixth century, Greco-Phoenician seals from Phoenician contexts carry images of satyrs (very like Bes figures),[12] and in the late fifth century, satyr heads appear on Sidonian coins.[13] Dionysian motifs—satyrs[14] and a maenad[15]—are found among the Wadi Daliyeh seal impressions.

Regardless of the ethnic background of the artist who might be Greek, Anatolian, Phoenician, or even a Samarian coin engraver/copyist, the Samarian owner of the ring possessed an object fully in the mainstream of fourth-century Greek artistic tradition.

Finally, as on WD **46**, there is evidence here of an early set of wings added to the cultural crucible that transformed *mal'akîm* (biblical 'messengers') into angels.

---

[12] Boardman, *Intaglios*, 10; many of the seals come from the Phoenician colonies on Sardinia and Sicily. Cf. also Boardman, *AG Gems*, 29.

[13] Betlyon, *Coinage*, no. 6, a 1/16 shekel.

[14] WD **2** (pl X.2), WD **5** (pl VIII.1,2), WD **21B** (pl VIII.3), WD **44** (pl X.3).

[15] WD **50** (pl IX.2).

WD 50. Dancing Maenad (?)

(PLATE IX.2)

Mus. Inv. 947
Loose sealing
Image size: 1.3 cm x 0.9 cm
Bulla size: 1.7 cm x 1.5 cm
Clay colour: reddish brown
String preserved; top and bottom of vertical image
Papyrus imprint
Seal type: scaraboid? metal finger ring?

ALTHOUGH the broad oval shape of WD **50** may indicate a scaraboid, the sealing could also come from a fourth-century metal finger ring.[1] The upper tip of the bulla has broken away, taking the very top of the seal image with it. Little of the head, upper torso, or arms of the figure has survived, and the surface retains few details.

A female figure, probably a maenad,[2] runs in three-quarter pose to the viewer's right, bending forward at the hip. The right (near) leg leads. Mirroring the legs in reverse, the left arm presses forward while the right swings back. The maenad looks in the direction in which she is running. A himation drapes, shawl-style, over the figure's left arm and swirls about her as she runs forward. A series of faint vertical lines on the torso may imply the top of a long chiton. The figure could be wearing something clinging and diaphanous to the point of transparency.

As a woman, the maenad on WD **50** is in the minority among the Wadi Daliyeh bullae. She joins three other single women—one possibly Aphrodite,[3] two or three possible Nikes[4] and four women accompanied by male figures.[5] No women appear on the purely Near Eastern impressions.

The figure is in violent motion. Her distinctive pose with the near leg forward echoes that of a well-known early fourth-century scaraboid which portrays Diomedes

---

[1] Boardman, *GGFR*, fig. 217 and p. 214, type VII.

[2] For a balanced discussion of maenads, cf. A. Henrichs' 'Greek Maenadism from Olympias to Messalina', *Harvard Studies in Classical Philology* 82 (1978) 121–65. In the second half of the fifth and the early fourth centuries, dancing maenads appeared in Greek art in considerable numbers (cf. L. B. Lawlor's 'The Maenads: A Contribution to the Study of the Dance in Ancient Greece', *Memoirs of the American Academy in Rome* VI [1927] 84). In the fifth century, the sculptor Kallimachos supposedly made a speciality of maenads carved in relief; certain distinct types of dancing maenads have traditionally been associated with him, but Ridgway (*Fifth Century*, 210–13) dismisses this is as 'pure speculation'.

[3] For Aphrodite in the Hecht Group, see pl XXIV.10. See also pl XXIV.14 for a seated Greco-Persian style figure whose gender is unclear.

[4] WD **46** (pl XI.1) and WD **I.3.22** (pl X.1). For an uncertain Nike in the Hecht Group, see pl XXIV.11.

[5] WD **6** (pl XI.3); WD **43** (pl XI.2); WD **44** (pl X.3); WD **52** (pl XII.1 [Greco-Persian]).

stealing the Trojan Palladion;[6] Diomedes' cloak also hangs over his left shoulder and arm in a manner similar to WD **50**. On WD **50**, however, the fluttering draperies which twist around the legs and fly out behind the woman, and her more pronounced forward bend suggest vigorous movement, not the guilty tip-toeing of Diomedes.

There seems to be no hint of diagnostic iconography such as a thyrsus to confirm the identification. If WD **50** does portray a running maenad, however, Classical glyptic parallels are abundant for the subject, if not the exact pose.[7] For all their wild reputation, maenads always appear clothed, however dishevelled their draperies;[8] the lines on the torso of the WD **50** figure suggest a chiton.

An early Classical scaraboid[9] supplies a possible parallel for pose and clothes. Here a dancing tambourine player runs to the right with her near leg forward; her long chiton is only lightly inscribed with a few comma shapes around her ankles indicating the swirling folds. A silver ring of the early fourth century shows a maenad in a diaphanous chiton and himation.[10] The de Clercq collection with rings of Phoenician provenance includes two Classical or early Hellenistic gold rings portraying an ecstatic maenad,[11] thus supplying evidence of other maenad seals and, perhaps, of the workshops that engraved them in the Semitic world.

Notwithstanding Dionysos' storied Phoenician ancestry, it is unlikely that there was any Near Eastern component in his earliest cult.[12] The name of Dionysos never appears in the Hebrew Bible, but the god is mentioned in the Apocrypha and Pseudepigrapha,[13] where Jews are forced to participate in the worship of Dionysos. These Hellenistic

---

[6] Boardman, *GGFR*, 596 and p. 80 = Richter, *EGGE*, 234: a large chalcedony scaraboid from Kythera (Boston MFA 27.703).

[7] Richter, MMA, pl XV: 82 (= Boardman, *GGFR*, 708), 83, 86 (Classical maenads of the late fifth and early fourth centuries); Boardman, *GGFR*, 673 'from Syria' (= Richter, *EGGE*, 257), 684–5 (= Richter, *EGGE*, 258) (finger rings); Richter, *EGGE*, 253–6, 259 (engraved gems).

[8] Although they may go bare to the waist or uncover a single breast or thigh, maenads never dance in the nude (Lawlor, 'Maenads', 82). A. Henrichs explains the differences between maenads and nymphs on vases, 'Myth', esp. 99–106.

[9] Boardman, *GGFR*, 646 and p. 211, of green glass, in East Berlin (= Zazoff, *AG*, 37,11 = Furtwängler, *Beschreibung*, no. 322).

[10] Boardman, *GGFR*, 708 (= Richter, MMA, pl XV: 82).

[11] De Ridder, *Collection*, nos. 2830–31.

[12] Although the Greeks preferred to believe that Dionysos was a late import from Asia Minor and that his cult appropriated paraphernalia from the Phrygian east where much of his myth transpires, Mycenaean Linear B texts point to his native Greek status (W. C. K. Guthrie, 'The Religion and Mythology of the Greeks,' *Cambridge Ancient History*[3], *Vol. II*, 2 [1975] p. 881, with references to the two Pylos fragments mentioning the name of Dionysos).

M. Smith ('On the Wine God in Palestine', *Salo Wittmayer Baron Jubilee Volume* [American Academy for Jewish Research, New York, 1974] 825) called attention to what he interpreted as an *oreibasia* of maidens in Judg 11:40 when Jephthah's daughter withdraws with her companions to lament her virginity on the mountain. In Judg 21:21, when the Benjaminite men kidnap the daughters of Shiloh as they dance unchaperoned in the vineyards, Smith (825) suggested an ancient Near Eastern correspondence with Dionysiac ritual. Smith's creative theories, to date, lack substantive evidence.

[13] 2 Macc 6:7 says that the abominated Seleucid king, Antiochus IV Epiphanes (175–164 BCE) forced Jews to carry ivy leaves in a procession of Dionysos. In 2 Macc 14:33 General Nicanor, Judas Maccabbeus' Seleucid counterpart, threatens to raze the temple to the ground and erect a shrine to Dionysos upon its ruins. Dionysos was Ptolemy Philopater's (221–203 BCE) patron deity and according to 3 Macc 2:29 (an Alexandrine work of the first century CE), the Egyptian Pharaoh commanded Jews to be branded with the image of an ivy leaf.

attempts to force Dionysos worship upon Jews are intriguing in light of the apparent notion in certain Greco-Roman scholastic circles that Dionysos and the god of the Jews were one and the same. Plutarch devotes some learned speculation to the correspondences between the worship of YHWH and Dionysos.[14]

Dancing maenads appear in a Phoenician context on the lower register of the purely Greek-style frieze on the 'tribune' found at Sidon.[15] Scholars debate whether the carver was Greek or a local artist skilled in Greek techniques, but they agree that the work was likely commissioned by a Phoenician philhellene (perhaps the Sidonian King Straton I [370–358]); whoever the patron, as a Phoenician, he must have read the Greek friezes on his own terms and to his own satisfaction.

What the Samarian who used this seal knew of the Greek god or thought of the figure on the seal is impossible to determine; at least four other Samarian seals are attested which have imagery (satyrs) associated with Dionysos in the fourth century.[16] It would be helpful to know whether Samarians would have grouped them together thematically as is done by the present editor.

The fourth-century context of the Daliyeh bullae and art historical principles of dating complement each other in the case of WD **50**. Greek seal rings engraved with lone maenads became popular in the last quarter of the fifth century.[17] The seal shape (if a ring), the swirling himation and the comparison with the Diomedes seal of the early fourth century should indicate a similar date for the WD **50** seal.

Excursus: The Semantics of the Near Leg Forward Pose

Figures on vase paintings shown running, fighting, or engaged in some sort of vigorous forward movement conventionally have the far leg forward. This makes artistic sense; with the far leg forward a figure is usually seen in a frontal three-quarter pose, the angle that shows off a figure to the most advantage and tells the viewer more than would a profile or rear three-quarter view.

On the occasions when the near leg is forward on a vigorously moving figure, is there any perceivable pattern of occurrence? Perhaps. The pose seems to be reserved for women, satyrs and erotes,[18] for barbarians,[19] for the less distinguished figure in a

---

[14] *Quaestiones conviviales* (4.6.1–2). Cf. M. Stern, ed., *Greek and Latin Authors on Jews and Judaism, I* (Leiden, 1974) Fr. 258.

[15] R. A. Stucky, *Tribune d'Echmoun: ein griechischer Reliefzyklus des 4. Jahrhunderts v. Chr. in Sidon, Antike Kunst*, Beiheft 13 (Basel, 1984). See also illustration in Boardman, *Diffusion*, fig. 3.11.

[16] WD **2** (pl X.2), WD **5/16B** (pl VIII.1,2), WD **21B** (pl VIII.3) and WD **44** (pl X.3).

[17] Boardman, *GGFR*, p. 216.

[18] Cf. the maenads and satyr on an early fourth-century lekanis cover in Odessa, illustrated in Metzger, *Représentations*, pl 1,3 and in Lawlor's 'Maenads', pl 17,2.

[19] Cf. the victorious Persian overwhelming his Greek opponent on an amphora of *c*.400 by the Suessula Painter in the Metropolitan Museum; the barbarian victor and the Greek victim both have their near leg forward (illustrated in G. M. A. Richter, *A Handbook of Greek Art*[6] [London, 1969] fig. 472); and the lone Persian on a Nolan amphora by the Oionokles Painter (illustrated in Boardman, *ARV*, fig. 360 [Staatliche Museen 2331, East Berlin, *ARV* 647/18]).

group[20] (such as the loser in a duel),[21] for scenes with comic elements and, perhaps, as in the case of the Diomedes scaraboid, to indicate stealth and deceit.[22]

The common denominator seems to be baseness or diminished human 'normality', where 'normality' is of course measured on a masculine standard.[23] On seals, the pose may signal the same qualities.[24] Maenads dancing in Dionysos' entourage are among the few feminine figures in Greek art who may express unladylike abandon.[25]

---

[20] On a kalyx krater by the Dokimasia Painter illustrating the Theban cycle, on the first side, Aegisthus (whom Aeschylus characterizes as a woman) can be seen dashing toward his victim, Agamemnon; both men have their near leg forward. On the second side Electra and Orestes attack Aegisthus; Electra swings an axe and runs with her near leg forward (illustrated in Boardman, *ARV*, fig. 274.1,2 [Museum of Fine Arts 63.1246, Boston, *Paralipomena* 373/34 *quater*]).

[21] Herakles fights Amazons, all of whom have their near leg forward on an Archaic volute krater by Euphronios (illustrated in Boardman, *ARV*, fig. 29 [Arezzo, Museo Civico 1465, *ARV* 15/6]). Amazons are women, they are barbarians, and they are suffering defeat in battle, hence they are triply degraded. Note also Atalanta as she wrestles Peleus on a cup by Oltos (illustrated in Boardman, *ARV*, fig. 62 [Bologna, Museo Civico 361, *ARV* 65\113]), and Aeneas' near leg is forward when Diomedes overpowers him on a kalyx krater by the Tyszkiewicz Painter (illustrated in Boardman, *ARV*, fig. 186 [Museum of Fine Arts 97.368, Boston, *ARV* 290/1]).

[22] On the same plate in Richter, *EGGE* with the Diomedes scaraboid are two seals showing male figures in a similar pose, and like Diomedes, they are doing devious deeds; a soldier is stalking an unseen enemy (Richter, *EGGE*, no. 227, 'of the fifth or fourth century'), and Eros, bow drawn, is sneaking up on some unfortunate victim of his arrow (Richter, *EGGE*, 233, 'a finished work of the fourth century' [= Boardman, *GGFR*, 633]).

[23] The pose is not one hundred percent predictable. Cf. a cup by the Triptolemos Painter on which a Persian warrior is falling to his Greek attacker. It is the Greek victor who has his near leg forward. This is unusual also in showing the victor on the right (illustrated in Boardman, *ARV*, fig. 303.1 [Royal Scottish Museum 1887.213, Edinburgh, *ARV* 364/46]).

[24] Cf. Boardman, *GGFR*, 626 and 629 for 'Classical' satyrs (p. 209) and Boardman, *GGFR*, 646 for a maenad (Ridgway, *Fifth Century*, p. 211).

[25] Similarly, goddesses such as Nike (cf. Boardman, *GGFR*, 797) and unusual female mortals such as Amazons may abandon decorum.

WD 27. Persian Dancer

(PLATE IX.3)

Mus. Inv. 924
Loose sealing
Image size: 1.5 cm x 0.9 cm
Bulla size: 1.8 cm x 1.9 cm
Clay colour: reddish brown, burnt on back
String not preserved
Papyrus imprint
Seal type: metal finger ring

THE leaf-shaped oval outline of the impression on WD **27** (common among the Wadi Daliyeh bullae) indicates that it was made by a metal finger ring of a common fifth-century type;[1] as these bullae demonstrate, in Persian territories neighbouring the Greek world, the type seems to persist into the fourth century. The full outline of the ring bezel remains intact, although the surface details have suffered the usual abrasions.

On a short groundline a Persian man in long-sleeved skirted tunic and trousers[2] seems to be dancing to the viewer's right in a three-quarters rear view with the face in profile. This is one of three such 'Persian' men who appear on the Wadi Daliyeh bullae.[3] Here the right leg is forward, but both feet are planted firmly on the ground line. The figure has a static quality despite the swing of the skirt, the flying locks of long hair and the arms flung forward.

The Classical Greek glyptic repertory includes at least one dancing male figure in Persian costume;[4] on a large Greco-Persian scaraboid in the Getty Museum, he dances the Oklasma. This was a Phrygian ritual dance which Classical sources claim came to Athens in the late fifth century as part of the cult of the Phrygian god, Sabazios; performed by women and men,[5] it was adopted by the Dionysos cult[6] and perhaps by

---

[1] Boardman, *GGFR*, type III, p. 214 and fig. 217.

[2] Only male barbarians wear long trousers (cf. Miller, *Perserie*, 256–7).

[3] Cf. WD **6** (pl XI.3) and WD **52** (pl XII.1), both showing the same subject, a Persian gentleman and his lady, but rendered in utterly dissimilar styles.

[4] Boardman, *Intaglios*, 33f., no. 88 (Getty 81.AN.76.88). Cf. also J. Boardman, 'Greek and Persian Glyptic in Anatolia and Beyond', *Études sur les rélations entre Grèce et Anatolie offertes à Pierre Demargne, Revue Archéologique*, Fasc. 1 (1976) fig. 8 and p. 50. For dancing women, especially maenads, on late fifth-/early fourth-century Greek seals cf. Richter, *EGGE*, nos. 253–9.

[5] Boardman, *Intaglios*, p. 33, citing Aristophanes, *Thesm.* 1175 and scholiasts; cf. Metzger, *Représentations*, pp. 147–53; plates XI,3; XVI,4; XXI,2.

[6] Metzger, *Représentations*, pp. 150–1.

the votaries of Demeter as well.[7] The Oklasma involved some characteristic gestures: the dancer bends forward, flexes the knees and claps his or her hands overhead, and spins like a Dervish. Possible cult associations aside, Boardman notes that Persians were 'fond of dancing',[8] and assigns the Getty seal 'to the world of Lycian reliefs, of the coinages which blend Persian and Greek, and of the Greco-Persian gems'.[9]

Unlike the Persian on the Getty scaraboid who is clearly an Oklasma dancer, the figure on WD **27** has not raised his hands above his head or flexed his torso. However, on a squat lekythos a whole troupe of Sabazios worshippers dance the Oklasma, revealing a greater variety of dance positions, including one similar to the stance of the Persian on WD **27**.[10] While it is possible that the figure on WD **27** should simply be considered as an isolated Persian dancer, the costume, the long hair and the lively pose could indicate that he, too, is performing the Oklasma.

By comparison with the Getty scaraboid, we might label the WD **27** ring 'Greco-Persian'.[11] Like the scaraboid, WD **27** shows an 'eastern' figure executed in Greek style; its provenance in a provincial Achaemenid capital is additionally suggestive; its workshop was also probably in the western Persian Empire, not excessively distant from Samaria, perhaps in southwest Asia Minor.

Excursus: Dionysian Dancers and WD 27

Without suggesting that this Persian belongs to the entourage of Dionysos—as did Boardman for the Getty's version, WD **27** was more likely created to meet a market in the Persian Empire for representations of eastern subjects—a number of parallels to the pose and clothes on WD **27** may be found on vase paintings of Dionysos and his followers who often appear in oriental costumes[12] (or what Greek artists supposed were oriental costumes). In addition to the Persian costume, the WD **27** dancer's long hair suggests he is 'oriental'. Late fifth/early fourth century vases frequently portray Dionysos[13] or his male followers with long differentiated curls or locks of hair which may, as on WD **27**, swing with the ecstatic movements of the enraptured Bacchants.

In this regard, two Attic kraters of the very late fifth or early fourth century provide helpful parallels to WD **27**. The first comes from ʾal-Mina on the north Phoenician coast[14] and shows a young male devotee dancing the Oklasma on a table top in honour of Dionysos, as the god himself looks on with a satyr and maenad. Of special interest

---

[7] *From the Lands of the Scythians, The Metropolitan Museum of Art Bulletin, Special Issue* Vol. XXXII, 5 (1973/4) cat. no. 65, a gold decorative plaque from the grave of a priestess of Demeter.

[8] Boardman, *Diffusion*, 325 n. 53, citing Athenaeus 434e.

[9] Boardman, 'Greek and Persian Glyptic', 50.

[10] Metzger, *Représentations*, pl. XIX, 1 (British Museum E. 895) and p. 148 (with references).

[11] Boardman, *GGFR*, p. 322 and Ashmolean/*ANES III*, pp. 85–6. Note most recently on this subject, Boardman, *Diffusion*, 44–5.

[12] Metzger, *Représentations*, pl XVI,4; cf. also pls II,3; XI,1,2,4; XVI,1; XXI,2. Cf. also Miller, *Perserie*, 256–7.

[13] *Inter alia*, cf. Metzger, *Représentations*, pl V, 5 and p. 75 (with references): an early fourth-century bell krater in Berlin (F 2646).

[14] Metzger, *Représentations*, pl XXI,2.

here is the combination of oriental costume, flying locks of hair and animated pose. In addition, this vase from Phoenicia gives evidence that men could tie their hair with fillets which on a seal might look like locks of hair.[15] The second vase, a bell krater from the 'beginning of the fourth century', now in Madrid,[16] again includes Dionysos and an 'oriental' dancer holding a tympanon who provides a parallel for the raised arms of the WD **27** dancer.

In addition to the bell krater from ʾal-Mina described above, two more vases from the same site show Oklasma dancers.[17] Metzger and others have cautiously speculated on the possibility that these and other vases with oriental subjects found outside Greece might have been deliberately created in Athens for an Eastern market.[18]

---

[15] For a female Oklasma dancer with flying fillets or scarf ends(?) cf. the krater in the Fogg Museum (1925.30.11; illustrated in Metzger, *Représentations*, pl XX,2).

[16] Metzger, *Représentations*, pl XVI,4 (Madrid Museum no. 11080; published by J. Beazley in *Journal of Hellenic Studies* 59 [1939] p. 32).

[17] Metzger, *Représentations*, pl XXI,1.

[18] Metzger, *Représentations*, pp. 410–13. Cf. K. de Vries, 'Attic Pottery in the Achaemenid Empire', *AJA* 81 (1977) 544–8 and G. K. Sams, 'Imports at Gordion: Lydian and Persian periods', *Expedition* (1979) 10. But note J. Boardman's cautionary article, 'The Athenian Pottery Trade: The Classical Period', *Expedition* (1979) 33–9.

WD I.3.22B. Nike (?)

(PLATE X.1)

Mus. Inv. n.a.[1]
Loose sealing; excavated in the Abu Shinjeh Cave
Image size: n.a.
Bulla size: n.a.
Clay colour: n.a.
String preserved; parallel to vertical images
Papyrus imprint: n.a.
Seal type: engraved gem in metal finger ring?
Published: Cross, 'Papyri', 28; pl 36,4 (drawing) and pl 62,b (photograph).

WD **I.3.22B** is one of two impressions on a single clay bulla[2] found by P. Lapp's team of excavators *in situ* in the Abu Shinjeh Cave itself. The pointed oval profile of the impression suggests a finger ring of a type Boardman dates to the mid-late fifth century,[3] but which appears, from the fourth century context of the Wadi Daliyeh bullae, to continue into the next century on the periphery of the Greek world.

Cross noted the poor condition of this impression, noting as well that it was 'smeared in sealing'. He described the traces of a figure of winged Nike dressed in a chiton and himation, possibly in three-quarter frontal view.[4] This would be a second example of Nike, the other being an impression of the goddess driving a frontal quadriga (WD **46**, pl XI.1), and one of only a few female figures in the Wadi Daliyeh corpus—all of them Greek or Greco-Persian, none executed in pure Near Eastern style.[5]

---

[1] Unlocated. This catalogue entry can add little to Cross's description in 'Papyri', as this bulla could not be examined personally by the present editor; the only available photographs are extremely difficult to read.

[2] The other impression, WD **I.3.22A** (pl XIX.4) seems to show a single Persian Hero with *akinakes*. As elsewhere, Greek and Near Eastern seal images appear side-by-side on the same document.

[3] Boardman, *GGFR*, fig. 217 (type III), and p. 214.

[4] Cross cites Richter, *EGGE*, pl 11.69 and parallels listed on p. 72.

[5] Besides WD **46**, the Nike of WD **I.3.22B** joins four other lone females: WD **50** (pl IX.2, a maenad), and the three women in the Hecht Group (pl XXIV.13, 10, 14)—the second may be Aphrodite; the latter bulla seems to show a seated Greco-Persian woman holding a bird, but an argument can also be made that it is Zeus with his eagle; and four women accompanied by male figures: WD **6**, pl XI.3; WD **43**, pl XI.2; WD **44**, pl X.3; WD **52**, pl XII.1 [Greco-Persian].

WD 2. Satyr and Heron

(PLATE X.2)

Mus. Inv. 958
Loose sealing
Image size: 2.0 x 1.2 cm
Bulla size: 1.4 x 1.4 cm
Clay colour: deep reddish brown
String preserved; parallel to vertical image orientation
Papyrus imprint; papyrus fragment affixed to back of bulla
Seal type: scaraboid or ring

WD 2 seems to have been made by a near-circular scaraboid or ring, deeply carved; this is a good fourth-century ring shape.[1]

A youthful satyr, nude and beardless,[2] stands looking to the viewer's right. He appears in an almost three-quarter rear view, although his head is in profile. A gouge across the figure's left shoulder and back obscures the details of his torso and left arm; because the left elbow is clear (bent behind the satyr's back) and his left hand appears just below waist-level before him, an elongated left arm must be accepted. The (apparently) feathery tail is difficult to read. The satyr's right (near) leg carries his weight, while his left leg bends at the knee with the heel of the left foot visible behind the right ankle. The stance throws the satyr's right hip forward. His hair clings like a cap to his head except at the gently curling ends.

A heron with its plumed head in profile pulls at the leash by which the satyr restrains him. The satyr grasps his end of the leash in his left hand and holds a stemmed fruit in his right hand which he extends over the bird's head as if to feed it. The heron steps forward on its right leg, trailing the other behind as it strains for the fruit with its upturned beak.

This sealing is quite clear, and the seal which produced WD 2 must have been well carved. Special care was given to the modelling of the shoulder and dorsal muscles to suggest a robust figure. There is a dimple in his left knee and a suggestion of ribs in his chest. Particularly sensitive is the attention to the different planes of the image, achieved by varying the depth of the intaglio. The youth's right (near) side is in the highest relief. A little less high is the flexed left (far) leg, behind the right. The leash seems barely cut at all, almost a scratch, but it is clearly visible; the heron is cut more deeply than the satyr's right leg, but not as deeply as the left leg and arm. However, the heron's aigrette (plume), like the leash, was only lightly incised to suggest feathers.

---

[1] Boardman, *GGFR*, fig. 217 and p. 224.

[2] The misleading photograph suggests a beard and boots which in actuality are not there.

Satyrs belong in the untamed forest world of Dionysus; they consort with maenads or nymphs[3] in the terrestrial haunts of goats, fauns, and panthers, as well as in the scarcely tamer venue of the Dionysian symposium. In earlier Greek art, satyrs often had exaggerated and grotesque features: goat legs, animal ears, thick lips, and an erect phallus. However, by the late fifth century, these were no longer essentials of satyr iconography;[4] satyrs were just as likely to strike heroic and attractive poses.[5] The satyr on WD **2** is the most 'modern' in form, then, of the several satyrs that appear in the Wadi Daliyeh corpus.[6]

The heron is the most interesting feature of this bulla.[7] According to the Homeric scholiasts, the heron (*erodios*) was regarded as a good omen, particularly on the hunt or in battle.[8] It was also sacred to Aphrodite.[9] Representations of herons are not uncommon on vase painting from the Geometric period onward, but Beazley notes that herons seldom appear on gems before the mid-fifth century; through the fourth century they were favoured subjects of gem engravers, and, one presumes, their patrons.[10] Beazley speculates that the reason for this lies in the greater interest in the life of women that becomes a 'fact of the period'.[11] On vase paintings, herons and other water birds appear primarily in feminine domestic scenes,[12] but also in depictions of mythical lovers and of symposia.

Herons interested some of the best seal engravers.[13] A lone heron is the subject of two of the four extant works signed by Dexamenos of Chios (last third of the fifth century).[14] A few heron seals of lesser quality than the 'Greek' examples (or WD **2**) fall into the somewhat vague category of 'Greco-Persian' gems, roughly dated to the

---

[3] Cf. A. Henrichs' discussion of the differences on vase paintings between maenads and nymphs in 'Myth', esp. 99–106.

[4] 'Satyrn und Silene', *Lexikon der alten Welt* (Zürich and Stuttgart, 1965) cols. 2707–8.

[5] Brommer, *Satyrspiele,* fig. 43 (Berlin F2578).

[6] Cf. WD **5/16B** (pl VIII.1,2), WD **21B** (pl VIII.3), WD **44** (pl X.3).

[7] On herons cf. Beazley, *Lewes House,* pp. 59–61. Cf. also the encyclopedic work of D'Arcy Thomson, *Glossary of Greek Birds* (London, 1936) s.v. '*Erodios*'.

[8] Thomson, *Glossary,* 103. Cf. the heron Athena sends to encourage Odysseus and Diomedes in *Iliad* 10.274. Cf. also M. Pipili, 'A Laconian Cup in the National Museum of Athens', *Oxford Journal of Archaeology* IV (1985) 233–40.

[9] Beazley, *Lewes House,* p. 60; Metzger, *Représentations,* p. 49.

[10] Beazley, *Lewes House,* p. 59; Boardman, *GGFR,* p. 195.

[11] Beazley, *Lewes House,* p. 61.

[12] Beazley, *Lewes House,* p. 60.

[13] Boardman, *GGFR,* 490 (= Richter, *EGGE,* 466). Cf. also Boardman, *GGFR,* pp. 199–200 and the following: Boardman, *GGFR,* 456 (= Richter, *EGGE,* 489), 492, 518 (= Richter, *EGGE,* 461), 519, 554, 555, 556, 557 (= Richter, *EGGE,* 465), 623 (= Richter, *EGGE* 458); Richter, *EGGE,* 459, 460, 469; *AGDS I,1* (Munich) fig. 268; Zazoff, *AG,* pl. 36,10. All are from the Classical period, and none is a metal finger ring.

F. Imhoof-Blumer and O. Keller in *Tier und Pflanzenbilder auf Münzen und Gemmen des klassischen Altertums* (Leipzig, 1889; reprinted Hildesheim, 1972) also list two coins, a didrachm of Selinus (pl VI,8) and a silver stater from Ambrakia (pl VI,9), on which a heron appears with another figure; in the first instance, with the personification of the river god Hypsas, and in the second, with Athena.

[14] Both in the Hermitage Museum; Boardman, *GGFR,* 468 = Richter, *EGGE,* 467; Boardman, *GGFR,* 469 = Richter, *EGGE,* 468; Boardman (*GGFR,* p. 195) dates them in the 'third quarter of the fifth century'.

Classical period.[15] Good 'Greek' herons appear on sealings found at the satrapal capital of Daskyleion,[16] and even in the heart of the Persian Empire, among the motifs on sealings of the Persepolis Treasury texts was a Greek-style heron.[17]

The earthbound heron on WD **2**, like many glyptic herons, rests its weight on one leg.[18] Standing herons may crook their necks to look down at the ground or curve their necks to slouch back upon their feathers. Occasionally, a heron extends its neck straight up as on the Wadi Daliyeh example.[19] This occurs particularly when the heron appears as a pet with its owner.[20]

An exact Classical period counterpart to the scene on WD **2** has yet be found. The closest is a scaraboid which belongs to a standard genre on which women feed pet birds. In this case a nude woman (Aphrodite?) in three-quarter frontal view feeds a grasshopper to her pet heron.[21] The positioning of the woman's feet mirrors that of the WD **2** satyr, and her heron similarly raises its beak for feeding. It is, perhaps, conceivable that the same artist produced the WD **2** seal.

In the search for a seal depicting a male rather than female figure with a heron, the closest Classical parallel is an unusual gold scarab in the Metropolitan Museum on which an adult Eros holds out a bunch of grapes over the head of a goose.[22] The most striking parallel to WD **2**, however, belongs to a later era: a North Italian ringstone assigned to the Roman Republican period.[23] A satyr, in a furtive 'near leg forward' pose and carrying a thyrsus, reaches out with his free hand toward a plume-headed

---

[15] Boardman, *GGFR*, 892 (possibly a heron) and 893 ('pendants group'), 934 (Bern group) (= Richter, *EGGE*, 410) fig. 308, p. 319.

[16] D. Kaptan-Bayburtluoglu, 'A Group of Seal Impressions on the Bullae from Ergili/Dalkyleion', *Epigraphica Anatolica* 16 (1990) pl 2.7,8.

[17] Schmidt, *Persepolis II*, pl 14, seal no. 67.

[18] Cf. Boardman, *GGFR*, 490, 518, 555.

[19] Boardman, *GGFR*, 518 (= Richter, *EGGE*, 461), 547, 490 (= Richter, *EGGE*, 466); *AGDS I,1* (Munich) fig. 268 (third quarter of the fifth century). Among Greco-Persian examples: Boardman, *GGFR*, 934.

[20] Boardman, *GGFR*, 547 (= Beazley, *Lewes House*, 61 = Zazoff, *AG*, pl 33,2); also, cf. J. Boardman, 'A Greek Cylinder Seal Necklace in London', *Antike Kunst* 13 (1970) 48–51, pl 27:1, early fourth century (= Boardman, *GGFR*, 595 = Victoria and Albert Museum 122–1864); and a third example (Ashmolean 1892.1598 = Boardman, *GGFR*, 640 = Ashmolean/*EGFR*, pl 22,123) from later in the same century.

[21] Boardman, *GGFR*, 547 (= Beazley, *Lewes House*, 61 = Zazoff, *AG*, pl 33,2) in the Syracuse (Sicily) Museum, 'no later than the end of the fifth century' (p. 201). Boardman (*Intaglios*, p. 22, re. no. 78) shows that the feeding motif is associated with Aphrodite and with representations of Ganymede feeding the eagle.

Other examples: A half-draped woman appears in a similar relation to her pet heron on the lovely fourth-century 'fine style' cylinder in the Victoria and Albert Museum (see above, n. 20 = Boardman, *GGFR*, 595). The Ashmolean lady with a heron (above, n. 20) is another example of the genre. On yet another seal, a chalcedony scaraboid of the late fifth century in the British Museum (72.6-4.1332, ex. Castellani coll. = Boardman, *GGFR*, 482 = Richter, *EGGE*, 297 = Walters, *BMC*, 531 = Zazoff, *AG*, pl. 33,1 = Furtwängler, *AG*, pl. 13, 20), a seminude woman (Aphrodite?) reclines in the company of a large winged ant and a pet heron which she is either feeding or fondling.

[22] Richter, *MMA*, no. 92 (MMA 21.88.166); also Boardman, *GGFR*, p. 428, listed under 'Gold scarabs with intaglios'.

[23] Sard ringstone in the Florence Archaeological Museum (sard no. 71), perhaps third century BCE, illustrated in Zazoff, *AG*, pl 70,7. Zazoff (p. 264–5) notes that the series of North Italian Republican seals under discussion derive in many respects from the Etruscan glyptic tradition.

heron which walks in front of him. WD **2** gives evidence of the antiquity of the later seal's imagery.

The composition of all the above-mentioned parallels as well as of other similar seals with women and their herons consistently show the 'human' figure and the heron in the same spatial relation to each other; the heron faces away from the human.

In Greek art it is usually women who accompany birds. Firstly, pet birds, including herons, were a part of the daily life of Greek women, and secondly, there was a prevailing trend during the last three decades of the fifth century toward merging images from the cycle of Aphrodite with scenes of the daily life of women that had appeared earlier in the century.[24] In glyptic art, the pairing of women and birds occurs most frequently in this type of scene.[25] The dated Samaria Papyri provide a mid-fourth century context for the WD **2** seal; if this satyr is dallying with the pet heron of Aphrodite or another woman, we would expect a dating in the fourth century, when satyrs abound in mythical love scenes.[26]

It would indeed be helpful to know where the seal of WD **2** was engraved. The specific subject is unique among known seals of the period; was it carved for the Greek market or for Easterners? Judging by the Greco-Persian repertoire, Persian/Anatolian taste in Greek glyptic may have favoured everyday *verité* or traditional 'hero' scenes; the Phoenicians, however, had included satyrs (although of the more grotesque type) in their artistic repertoire from at least the late sixth century[27] and were perhaps the patrons if not also the producers of the seal behind WD **2**. And the Phoenicians were surely the Samarians' seal source.

The image on WD **2** embodies some interesting aspects of Greek sexual and social attitudes. Major Olympian male gods—Zeus and Apollo—during the Classical period

---

[24] Metzger, *Représentations*, p. 36 and *passim*. For instance, Eros may accompany the woman. Is she Aphrodite or a mortal? It is not necessary to make a choice; the mythic imagination can be extremely flexible. She is one or the other or both. Cf. Boardman, *GGFR*, 716: Eros fastens a woman's sandal while a dove flutters above; Boardman, *GGFR*, 736: Eros holds out a wreath to a nude Aphrodite (?) who balances a dove on the back of her hand.

[25] Boardman, 'Greek Cylinder', pl 27, fig. 1 (= Boardman, *GGFR*, 595); cf. Boardman, *GGFR*, 482; Boardman, *GGFR*, 547; Boardman, *GGFR*, 548 (with a dove); Boardman, *GGFR*, 641 (dove?). These ladies' *déshabille* is habitual with Aphrodite, but it may also signal a boudoir scene. Considering the importance of allegory on red figure vases in the fourth century, the worlds of mortal and immortal may not be mutually exclusive (Herrmann, *Shadow*, 27).

[26] Metzger, *Représentations*, p. 30 and *passim*.

[27] Cf. discussion of WD **5/16B** p. 107, above and WD **21B** p. 110, above.

An odd parallel of a sort for WD **2** (its significance, if any, is unclear) in the Hellenized Phoenician world is an engraved bronze votive razor from third-century Carthage (Musée de Carthage, published in E. Acquaro, *I rasoi punici* [Rome, 1971] cat. no. 81 and fig. 38 [colour photograph in Moscati, *Phoenicians*, 111]). On one side Herakles (Melkart?) in a lion skin sits on a rock; on the other side, a youthful Greek man, seated on a klismos (chair), wears what looks like a leopard-skin himation and holds up, like a sceptre, what appears to be an ivy tendril. The unexpected detail here is the long-legged water bird, balancing on one leg behind the chair. The seated man may originate in Phoenician lore or may be Dionysos (or a combination?). He holds a leash or rope-like vine in his hand which is either attached to the bird or which the bird tugs at with its beak. Cf. C. Picard, *Sacra Punica. Étude sur les masques et rasoirs de Carthage: Karthago* 13 [1966] 87 and Boardman, *Diffusion*, 62.

have iconographic birds,[28] but in general a male figure will accompany birds only in certain contexts. A bird was not an appropriate companion for an adult man; in art, when a man is seen with a live bird, he usually fails in some manner to qualify as an adult in the full social dignity of his maleness.[29] Thus vases and seals can show a male child or Eros, the boy-god, with a bird,[30] in scenes that often refer implicitly to Eros as the go-between in both homo- and heterosexual courtship. Go-betweens, as well as the lovers themselves, could offer a cock or heron as a love gift.[31]

These scenes relate both to Aphrodite, the goddess of love, and/or Dionysos, the lord of the symposium, two divinities capable of 'unmanning' their victims and whose spheres of influence overlap. Here is where satyrs[32] and Pan,[33] another semihuman figure, fit into the category of man-with-bird scenes. Physically, satyrs belong in the liminal area between man and beast; functionally, they drink and debauch in Dionysos' honour and, by the late fifth century, they also attend love scenes.[34] The heron on WD 2 may suggest that the satyr, by nature a Dionysian figure, is simply playing the part of a gift-bearing lover.

---

[28] Greek divinities had signature birds: Athena's owl, Zeus' eagle, Aphrodite's doves; the swan belonged both to Apollo and Aphrodite, particularly on Attic vases of the fourth century (Metzger, *Représentations*, p. 175, for Apollo: p. 173; for Aphrodite: p. 61; Roscher, *Lexikon*, 'Apollon', col. 144).

[29] Apollo's is an interesting case in this regard. Though he has love affairs, some early details of his mythology show that he may have been viewed as a god who must remain forever an adolescent. This is the mythic compromise which suspended the cycle of divine patricide; Apollo will not kill his father Zeus.

The Asiatic moon god Mên, whose constant companion in late Classical art is his rooster, is another example of a male deity whose masculinity was suspect; he was foreign and only foreigners in Attica worshipped him. Perhaps owing to the fact that for Greeks the Moon was always female, Attic sculptors portrayed Mên in a 'decidedly androgynous' manner (Herrmann, *Shadow*, no. 7, p. 20, a two-sided votive relief to Helios and Mên, *c*.340).

Admittedly, on a few Greco-Persian gems men appear with birds, usually in a clearly domestic setting with a woman (Boardman, *GGFR*, 892). But for the chronically xenophobic Greeks, Persians were a troublesome human category. Their presence in a scene signals a Never-never Land exempt from Greek social mores.

Winged things could hold particular terrors for Greek men. In Homer, birds appear vividly as eaters of human carrion on the battlefield. On Archaic gems, winged beings carry off the *psyche*. Excluding the special trio of Nike, Eros and Iris, the winged creatures of Greek mythology are horrifying and usually female: the Harpies, the Gorgons, the Sirens, the Stymphalian birds, the Sphinx. When they depicted the Sphinx, a particularly dangerous beast, Greek artists preferred to depict the winged female variety of Anatolia and Syria to the original Egyptian male sphinx modelled on the Pharaoh's male gender.

[30] Note the frequent pairing of small boys or Eros with certain birds. On *choes* jugs of the spring Anthesteria festival, little boys play with pet songbirds or geese (H. Rühfel, *Kinderleben im klassischen Athen*, Kulturgeschichte der antiken Welt 19 [Mainz, 1984] figs. 80, 82–3). On another vase, a child with a pet goose scurries along at the side of a Dionysiac procession (A. E. Klein, *Child Life in Greek Art* [New York, 1932] 27 [= BM 533]). Among Greek seals there are such scenes as Eros with his pet goose (Richter, *EGGE*, 307; 'fifth-fourth century', Boston MFA 27.700), or two erotes with roosters (Boardman, *GGFR*, 746), or Eros alone with a dove (Boardman, *GGFR*, 738).

[31] Metzger, *Représentations*, p. 49 and G. F. Pinney and B. S. Ridgway, *Aspects of Ancient Greece: an Exhibition Organized by the Allentown Art Museum* (Allentown, PA, 1979) 34.

[32] For satyrs, cf. Henrichs, 'Myth', 94–9 and references.

[33] P. Borgeaud, *Récherches sur le dieu Pan*, Bibliotheca Helvetica Romana, XVII [Rome, 1979]; P. H. von Blanckenhagen, 'Easy Monsters', in A. Farkas *et al.*, eds., *Monsters and Demons*, 91–4.

[34] Sexuality is a factor in this discussion. Eros is sexually immature, while Pan and satyrs, however eager their amours, are characterized by sterility (Borgeaud, *Récherches*, 118). Eratosthenes (I.40) (275–194 BCE) reports that the expression 'to honour Pan' means to practice male homosexuality.

Another, very tentative suggestion, is that WD **2** is actually a sly hybrid combining scenes of women with pet birds and images of hunters and their dogs,[35] as suggested by another unusual detail of WD **2**, the leash.[36] If dogs are suitable pets for a man and a water bird for a woman,[37] the image on WD **2** may be playing with ideas of sexuality and role-reversal.

---

[35] Boardman, *AG Gems*, 285, 286 (ex-Cesnola, from Cyprus); Richter, *EGGE*, 218, a green plasma scaraboid 'about 450' in the British Museum (92.11–28.1) found in Cyprus; and Richter, *EGGE*, 224, a chalcedony scaraboid of the end of the fifth century in the Fitzwilliam Museum, Cambridge. Another possible parallel in this category is a cornelian 'lion gem' which Boardman dates to the fourth century (Boardman, *Intaglios*, 37, now Getty Museum); a youth (Apollo? a hero?) with his left hand on his hip reaches out with his right in which he holds something like a leaf over a small seated dog-like lion. The pose and arrangement of the figures is almost a mirror image of WD **2**, although the image must derive from the hunter scenes.

[36] Leashed birds are unusual; note a) an uncertain example on a bell krater (probably Attic) of the fourth century in London; Dionysus presides over the usual assortment of satyrs and maenads, while on the base line a crawling Eros tugs at his end of a ribbon or leash as a goose pulls on the other with his bill (Metzger, *Représentations*, pl XVII). 2); b) the third-century votive razor from Carthage (see note above).

The hunters on seals listed above seem not to use leashes, but the hunter on a marble relief of *c*.460 (Berlin, Staatliche Museen, Antikenabteilung, no. 1871) restrains his dog firmly on a rope lead (illustrated in Boardman, *GA*, fig. 115). The Amasis Painter depicted a hoplite with a dog on a chain (panel-amphora, Louvre F 25, illustrated in A. F. Stewart, 'Narrative, Genre, and Realism in the Work of the Amasis Painter', in J. Paul Getty Museum, *Papers on the Amasis Painter and his World* [Malibu, 1987] fig. 13). On another late sixth-century red figure cup by Apollodoros (BM E 57), the man has a pet panther cub on a leash. A group of idlers on a late sixth-century statue base (Athens, National Museum 3476) watch an encounter between a leashed cat and dog (Lullies-Hirmer, *Sculpture*, pls 64–5). Cf. J. K. Anderson, *Hunting in the Ancient World* (Berkeley, 1985) 46.

Ancient Near Eastern cylinder seals for over 1000 years could symbolically represent authority by means of the leash by which a divinity controls a lion or mythical monster. Cf. Collon, *First Impressions*, fig. 151, an 'Anatolian Group' cylinder of the late second millennium (Brussels 01396), and fig. 351, Neo-Assyrian, *c*.700 (BM 105111). For a biblical example, note Job 41:2, 5 (English).

[37] Boardman, *ARV*, p. 215.

WD 44. Knucklebone (*Astragaloi*) Players

(PLATE X.3)

Mus. Inv. 941
Loose sealing
Image size: 0.7 cm x 1.1 cm
Bulla size: 1.4 cm x 2.1 cm
Clay colour: reddish brown
String preserved; left and right of horizontal image
Papyrus imprint
Seal type: metal finger ring, probably silver

WD **44** is a horizontal oval impression, slightly pointed at the left and right ends. This is a fourth-century ring bezel shape.[1] The somewhat carelessly engraved border is almost unique among the Wadi Daliyeh impressions which have few decorated borders or groundlines, although not unknown on Classical finger rings.[2] It consists of two parallel lines with occasional dots or hatching between them. In the impression, the border is almost complete.

Two figures sit on the ground facing each other, on the right, a woman, apparently nude, and on the left a goat-legged satyr.[3]

Classical seals with two figures are unusual;[4] WD **44** is one of four two-figure Greek images in the Wadi Daliyeh corpus.[5] The complex, if crude, composition is preserved in its entirety. The deeply drilled figures are awkwardly executed with oversized heads and bulbous bodies which are too heavy for their thin legs and arms. The overall shape of the composition echoes the curve of the outline but seems cramped in its small space, and there is a general confusion of arms and legs.

The bearded satyr, with his right leg tucked under him and his left knee raised, sits back on his thick haunches. The woman, presumably a nymph,[6] squats rather than sits, crouching with her left foot flexed under her buttocks and her right knee raised before her just like the satyr. She extends her left hand while raising her right hand before her to chin height. Both of the satyr's arms are bent at the elbow, with his hands kept at the level of his chest. The figures' attention is focused on five small round objects in the air between them, two above the level of their knees and three below.

---

[1] Boardman, *GGFR*, fig. 217, type V.

[2] Cf. Boardman, *GGFR*, 704, 785, 821.

[3] Other Wadi Daliyeh satyrs: WD **2** (pl X.2), WD **5/16B** (pl VIII. 1, 2; pl XXII.1d), WD **21B** (pl VIII.3; pl XXII.2b).

[4] Boardman, *Intaglios*, p. 14.

[5] WD **43** (pl XI.2); WD **6** (pl XI.3); WD **52** (pl XII.1). A man and a woman appear together on all four.

[6] Cf. A. Henrichs' discussion of the differences between maenads and nymphs in Dionysiac scenes on vases, 'Myth', esp. 99–106.

The squatting, facing position of the satyr and woman is typical of *astragal* (knucklebone)[7] players. The five dots are the *astragals*, and the two figures on WD **44** are probably playing *pentalitha* ('five stones', Pollux IX 126). *Astragals* like modern jacks could be 'thrown up and caught on the back of the hand without losing those already caught'.[8] They were also used for games of chance along the lines of craps shooting.[9] Girls and boys[10] and women[11] played knucklebone games in the Hellenic world from the Classical through Roman periods. Opponents squatted opposite each other on the ground precisely as we see them on WD **44**. From the position of the woman's arms, it would seem to be her toss.

Already by the second half of the fifth century large-scale works of art were portraying scenes similar to the one on WD **44**. The most famous knucklebone players were the two daughters of Pandareios playing in the Underworld in a wall painting by Polygnotos, the *Nekyia* in the Knidian Lesche at Delphi.[12] In sculpture, Polykleitos is said to have created a celebrated bronze group of two boys playing knucklebones.[13] Pairs of knucklebone players served as the subjects of mass-produced free-standing miniature terracotta groups, which were very popular in the fourth century.[14] On an

---

[7] 'Knucklebones' (*astragaloi*) is an inaccurate term for the small bones found within the tarsal joint of hooved animals. Cf. J. Dörig's extensively documented, 'Tarentinischen Knöchelspielerinnen', *Museum Helveticum* XVI (1959) 29–58, and H. B. Walters, ed., *A Guide to the Exhibition Illustrating Greek and Roman Life* (British Museum; London, 1929) 200–203.

Players at *astragals* used sheep and goat bones, but clay, ivory, metal and stone *astragals* also exist (cf. Klein, *Child Life*, 18, nos. 238–9 and A. F. von Pauly, *Paulys Real-Encyclopädie der klassischen Altertumswissenschaft* (Stuttgart, 1894–1963) 'astragalus'. Hundreds of bone *astragaloi* were found during excavations at Olynthus, 191 in a single grave. Excavators also report five of solid lead (one inscribed) and two of bronze (D. M. Robinson, 'Metal', 503).

Astragals could also be presented as votive offerings and dedications in cultic contexts. Cf. W. H. D. Rouse, *Greek Votive Offerings* (Princeton, 1975 [reprint of 1902 edition]) 249, 397.

[8] Klein, *Child Life*, 18.

[9] *OCD*, 'astragalus'. Excavators at Delos discovered a 'loaded' (weighted) *astragal* (Robinson, 'Metal', 503).

[10] R. Schmidt, *Die Darstellung von Kinderspielzeug und Kinderspiel in der Griechischen Kunst*. Exhibition catalogue, Österreichischen Museum für Volkskunde (Vienna, 1977) 55, cat. nos. 76–97. Children going about their daily lives in Attic vase painting are seldom without their bag of *astragals* (cf. H. Rühfel, *Kinderleben im klassischen Athen, Kulturgeschichte der antiken Welt 19* (Mainz, 1984) 48, figs. 24, 26). The Palatine Anthology includes a verse celebrating Konnaros, a clever boy whose superior penmanship won him eighty knucklebones as a prize (*Anth. P.* 6.308).

[11] Schmidt, *Darstellung*, 45. Pollux (IX.126) says that 'five-stones' is primarily a woman's game. (Cf. also Plato *Lysis* 206e, *Anth. P.* 6.276 and the summary of a paper read by G. F. Pinney at the 87th General Meeting of the Archaeological Institute of America, *AJA* 90 [1986] 218).

[12] Schmidt, *Darstellung*, 45; cf. Pausanias 10.30.2. A wall-painting from Herculaneum of the first century CE (Naples Museum no. 9562) may preserve some idea of Polygnotos' work (Dörig, 'Tarentinischen', 30–31, fig. 1; also Schefold, *Klassischen*, fig. 220). Signed by Alexandros of Athens and based on a Greek painting of *c*.430, it shows the daughters of Niobe and Leto playing *astragals*. The girl crouching on the right resembles the WD **44** nymph.

[13] Schmidt, *Darstellung*, 45. Cf. Pliny *Hist. Nat.* 34.5. The Museum of Fine Arts, Boston (01.8203) owns a fragment of a Roman copy in marble of an Attic work of the early fourth century that may have shown a woman leaning over to pick up or throw an *astragal* (Herrmann, *Shadow*, 17, cat. no. 2).

[14] Schmidt, *Darstellung*, 48, 55, cat. nos. 79–80; Dörig, 'Tarentinischen', 29–58; Klein, *Child Life*, no. 246. McCallum (*re*. cat. no. 133) in G. Pinney and B. S. Ridgway, eds., *Aspects of Ancient Greece* (Allentown, 1979) 272 includes an extensive bibliography on these terracottas.

even smaller scale knucklebone players appear on vase paintings,[15] in jewellery,[16] on coins[17] and seals.

Solitary players[18] are found on seals, but there is the occasional example with two figures; among the latter a gold ring from the Oxus Treasure (boy and girl)[19] and a late fifth-century oval carnelian ring stone in Berlin (two youths).[20] The most remarkable parallel, however, is a silver ring of the fourth century from Asia Minor (now in the Getty Museum) on which a pair of chubby babies play *astragals*;[21] the pronounced stylistic similarities between this ring and WD **44**, namely, crude bulbous figures, the arrangement of the players, the 'combination linear and dotted border' and almost identical bezel size, allow for once, in this catalogue, an assignment to the same workshop, perhaps even the same hand. WD **44**, too, may have been produced by a silver ring. Nothing more can be said of the workshop location beyond the likelihood that it was in 'the East' (i.e. Asia Minor to the Levant).

Albeit on a miniature scale, WD **44** suggests in its falling *astragals* and in the movement of the nymph an aspect of later Classical and Hellenistic art, namely the tendency toward compositions that capture a particular moment in time, an uncompleted gesture or act heightening the effect of a scene. Clearly the motif of a satyr and nymph playing knucklebones is not unusual in the fourth century. As Herrmann notes, the subjects of fourth century sculpture could be 'decidedly lightweight: knucklebone players, satyrs or demigod shepherd boys like Ganymede'.[22]

Astragals were, indeed, the everyday playthings of ordinary women and children, but it is worth noting that knucklebones and knucklebone games also had symbolic resonances of fate, sexuality, death, and transition, not understood today.[23]

---

[15] Schmidt, *Darstellung*, nos. 76–7. Cf. Webster, *Potter*, 235, 237; Dörig, 'Tarentinischen', fig. 3 (ex. Tyszkiewicz; auctioned by Sotheby's, Monaco, December 5, 1987, lot. 147).

[16] I.e. gold earrings in Berlin of the second quarter of the fourth century depicting Nike, about to throw dice or knucklebones in H. Hoffmann and P. F. Davidson, *Greek Gold, Jewelry From the Age of Alexander*. Exhibition Catalogue, Museum of Fine Arts (Boston, 1966) no. 20.

[17] An electrum stater of Cyzicus (440–330) has on its obverse a youth throwing knucklebones (Museum of Fine Arts, Boston 58.347 = Herrmann, *Shadow*, cat. no. 115 and M. Comstock and C. Vermeule, *Greek Coins, 1950–1963* [Boston, 1964] no. 150). Tarsus in Cilicia minted a stater (*c*.370) with an animated maiden playing astragals (Kraay, *Coins*, 1042). No coins with two gaming figures are known; however, coins with *astragaloi* players clearly were being minted fairly close to Phoenicia proper.

[18] A kneeling girl tosses knucklebones on an early fourth-century gold seal ring once in the Museum of Fine Arts, Boston (Boardman, *GGFR*, 726, 'from Kythnos', cat. no. 625); on a much-published chalcedony scaraboid: an infant Eros plays with knucklebones and a pet goose; it is said to come from Asia Minor (Richter, *EGGE*, 307 = Boardman, *GGFR*, 604 = Beazley, *Lewes House*, 56, pl 4 = Lippold, *Gemmen*, pl 28,1 = Furtwängler, *AG*, pl 54.15).

[19] Boardman, *GGFR*, cat. no. 659, p. 421 (British Museum, Western Asiatic Department; illustrated in O. M. Dalton, *The Treasure of the Oxus* [London, 1965] pl 15.101).

[20] *AGDS II* (Berlin) Inv. FG 328, fig. 153, 'from Asia Minor' = Boardman, *GGFR*, 543, pp. 201, 291, and catalogue no. 165 (p. 410). See also Boardman, *GGFR*, p. 234; fig. 272, p. 235 and 286, and Lang, *Agora X,1* (Princeton, 1964) 76ff., 'in a fourth-century context'.

[21] Spier, *Ancient Gems*, no. 58.

[22] Herrmann, *Shadow*, 15.

[23] Why else in the late sixth century would a giant inscribed knucklebone cast in bronze and weighing 212 pounds be considered a worthy dedication to Apollo at his oracle at Didyma? Apparently, the Persians carried it off to Susa where French excavators found it and sent it to the Louvre (L. H. Jeffery, *Local Scripts of Archaic Greece*

Did Samarians play knucklebones or use them in games of their own? Knucklebones had a place in ancient Near Eastern gaming traditions. They appear in both Egypt and Mesopotamia; the Egyptian board game of Hounds and Jackals used three *astragals* as dice for determining moves;[24] the Oriental Institute in Chicago has six or more knucklebones from seventh–sixth century Egypt and eleven dated as early as 2300 from Tell Asmar in Iraq,[25] all apparently used for gaming. Excavations at Persian period Shiqmona on the Mediterranean coast south of Carmel uncovered a set of four knucklebones.[26] The Samarians were probably not very different from their coastal neighbours in indulging in games of chance.

Would this image of semidivine figures playing knucklebones, however, with its nuances (for Hellenes) of capricious fate, the unpredictability of love, possibly even immortality, have meant anything to the wealthy Samarian who was probably the owner of the seal? It is impossible to know whether the imagery was the source of anything more than aesthetic delight and/or the prestige of owning something exotic.

Nevertheless, it must have been clear to the owner of the WD **44** ring that the two figures were playing a game, and games involve luck. If Ecclesiastes reflects some of the concerns of the time it was written (sometime between the fifth and third centuries),[27] then some Yahwists at least, like their Hellenic contemporaries, contemplated the vagaries of fate: Time and chance befall them all (Eccl 9:11).

[Oxford, 1961] 334 and references). Pausanias tells of a cult cave of Herakles at Bura in Achaia, where, by tossing four knucklebones conveniently provided (for a fee), visitors might learn their own futures (7.25.10). E. Vermeule alludes to the link between sex, death, and *astragals* in her discussion of late fifth-/early fourth-century vases in the form of knucklebones (*Aspects of Death in Early Greek Art and Poetry* [California, 1979] 156, fig. 10). See the discussion of this subject in M. J. Leith, *Greek and Persian Imagery in Pre-Alexandrine Samaria* (Ph.D. diss., Harvard University, 1990) 280–83.

[24] *IDB*, 'games, O.T.' mentions a set from 12th Dynasty Thebes and from the time of Tutankhamun (14th century). Note also cat. no. 375 in Boston Museum of Fine Arts, *Egypt's Golden Age: The Art of Living in the New Kingdom 1558–1085 B.C.* (Exhibition Catalogue, 1982).

[25] Robinson, 'Metal', 503 n. 70.

[26] J. Elgavish, *Archaeological Excavations at Shiqmona: Field Report 1, The Levels of the Persian Period, Seasons 1963–5* (Haifa, 1968) (Hebrew) pl LXIV,179.

[27] J. Kugel, 'Qohelet and Money', *CBQ* 51 (1989) 32–49, esp. 46.

E.   OTHER COMPLEX SUBJECTS

WD 46. Nike in Facing Quadriga

(PLATE XI.1)

Mus. Inv. 943
Loose sealing
Image size: 1.3 cm x 0.9 cm
Bulla size: 1.5 cm x 1.5 cm
Clay colour: reddish brown
String preserved; top and bottom of vertical image
Papyrus fragments on back
Papyrus imprint
Seal type: scaraboid? ring?
Published: Cross, 'Papyri', 29, pl 63,o.

WD **46** is an broad oval sealing equally suggestive of a scaraboid or a ring of the fourth century.[1] The odd proportions and evidently crude workmanship of the device suggest the original seal may have been of less than first quality, perhaps even of glass or wood. The top and bottom of the bulla have broken away; the outline of the seal appears only on the upper and lower right. Elsewhere, the edges of the seal seem never to have made their mark in the clay; the sealer must have been hasty. Only the broadest outlines of the complicated image are legible.

The impression shows a frontal quadriga driven by a single figure who towers over the four horses.[2] Behind the charioteer's left shoulder there seems to be a wing; that there does not appear to be sufficient room for the matching wing over the other shoulder is explained by careless sealing which both warped the bulla and left parts of it blank. Tiny slashes here and there on the wing are probably meant to depict feathers. This is the goddess Nike, personification of both military and athletic victory.[3]

The chariot, invisible behind the horses, is stationary. The four horses stand with their stumpy forelegs ranged in a straight row. While the two middle 'yoke' horses look

---

[1] Boardman, *GGFR*, fig. 217 and p. 214, somewhere in the range of types V–VIII.

[2] Horses appear on a number of other Wadi Daliyeh bullae. In the Rockefeller Museum group they are all pairs, Near Eastern in style and execution (WD **18**, pl XVI.1; WD **34** pl XVI.2). All horse images in the Hecht Group are Greek (two examples are in pl XXIII.7, 8). H. Frankfort (*Art*, 152) stressed that views taken of the subject in the artistic repertoire of various ancient cultures 'differ . . . completely. The Assyrian saw in the horse as a rule a labouring draught-animal; the Egyptians a noble creature, prancing with curved neck and hollow back; the Mycenaeans a miracle of fleetness hardly touching the soil'.

[3] See also WD **I.3.22B** (pl X.1), perhaps also Nike. Nike's enduring popularity began in earnest at the time of the Persian Wars in the first half of the fifth century. In addition to WD **I.3.22B**, the Nike of WD **46** joins four other lone females: WD **50** (pl IX.2, a maenad), three women in the Hecht collection (pl XXIV.10, 13, 14 [uncertain gender]; pl XXIV.11 has been identified as female but this is also uncertain); and four women accompanied by male figures: WD **6**, pl XI.3; WD **43**, pl XI.2; WD **44**, pl X.3; WD **52**, pl XII.1.

directly ahead, both outer 'trace' horses turn their muzzles to their left. Ornamental topknots possibly adorn the horses' heads. Nike's attire is indeterminate. Like the yoke horses, she seems to look directly out at the viewer and has only the sketchiest of facial features. The pillow-shaped headdress is probably meant to be a plumed helmet, seen from the front. Some attempt has been made to indicate foreshortening in the charioteer's arms and hands from which three sets of reins are still visible. The yoke horse on the viewer's left is the only one of the horses whose reins can be made out in front. They form an inverted 'V' across his chest.

Chariots were a fact of warfare and an artistic subject in both the ancient Near East[4] and Greece. On WD **46** Nike and her chariot are purely Greek;[5] frontal chariots never appear in Near Eastern art.

Greek artists working in two dimensions—vase painting, architectural relief, seals, coins—generally shunned frontality.[6] In a few rare instances, frontal quadrigas appear in Greek glyptic art, mostly in the Archaic period.[7] A frontal quadriga quite similar to WD **46** and noteworthy for its indisputably Persian provenance also exists only in impression—on a single tablet from the Persepolis Treasury.[8] The charioteer of the stationary quadriga might be Athena, but this is uncertain.[9] She looks to her left as the streamers on her plumed Corinthian helmet flutter behind her in the opposite direction. Her shield appears on her left. The horses look in the expected directions,[10] and their knobby drilled legs line up below nicely modelled foreparts. As (perhaps) on WD **46**, the horses have head ornaments or hairlocks; there is a similar discrepancy in scale between the horses and their gigantic master.

A Classical ivory scaraboid in Berlin with frontal quadriga and anonymous driver belongs to the mid-late fifth century.[11] This seal with its zigzag exergue and hatched border has a vaguely Phoenician flavour. The Phoenician-style exergue and border, as well as the fact that the seal is of ivory, much of which came through Phoenicia from its Syrian hinterlands as well as from Egypt, suggest a possible Phoenician hand in

---

[4] M. A. Littauer and J. H. Crouwel, *Wheeled Vehicles and Ridden Animals in the Ancient Near East* (Leiden, 1979).

[5] G. Hafner, *Viergespanne in Vorderansicht* (Berlin, 1938) remains a useful source.

[6] Cf. P. Erhart, *The Development of the Facing Head Motif on Greek Coins and its Relation to Classical Art* (New York/London, 1979).

[7] For an early example cf. J. Boardman, *Island Gems, A Study of Greek Seals in the Geometric and Early Archaic Periods* (London, 1963) 125, no. F18, 'mid-sixth century'. Boardman, *AG Gems*, 324, 'Group of the Beazley Europa', belongs to the transitional period between late Archaic and Classical (= Furtwängler, *AG*, pl 9,10 = Bibl.Nat. 1867A = *Viergespanne*, no. 143, p. 33f. [see above, n. 5]). A magnificent gold finger ring from the Crimea provides a late Classical parallel; Nike drives a frontal biga, grasping a set of reins in each hand. Here, and on WD **46**, the upper curve of Nike's wings rise barely higher than her head, and her wings are spread in full display (Boardman, *GGFR*, 727 and p. 223 [Leningrad I.O. 30] = Furtwängler, *AG*, pl 10,47).

[8] Schmidt, *Persepolis II*, pl 12, no. 45, from Persepolis Treasury Text 6 134.

[9] So identified by Schmidt in *Persepolis II*. The face is indistinct and Athena's breasts, which are usually indicated are not apparent. For comparisons, consult *LIMC*, 'Athena', and the subcategory, '*Athena en char*' (p. 974).

[10] The canonical arrangement in the Archaic and Classical periods was for yoke horses to look inwards, and trace horses to look outwards.

[11] *AGDS II*, 166b (Berlin, Inv FG 173 = Furtwängler, *AG*, pl 10,6), mid-fifth century.

commission or execution. As more is learned about the Achaemenid East, cultural ambidexterity on the part of its artists merits serious contemplation.[12]

The subject of chariots would naturally appeal to Easterners among whom chariots symbolized prestige and power. Even maritime Sidon, hardly renowned for its land-based exploits, minted a silver four-shekel piece showing a figure who looks like the Persian King standing in a chariot drawn by two horses in elaborate headgear.[13] A few seals classed as Greco-Persian (made for Easterners?) show Persians in chariots but never frontally.[14] On these seals, too, the horses have topknots.

Two series of coins issued two centuries apart also bear discussion. The first series was minted in Chalcis in the second half of the sixth century.[15] On the obverse a charioteer, possibly Hera, drives a frontal quadriga.[16] The second series comes from Cyrene on Africa's Mediterranean shore; the city minted a series of coins with frontal quadrigas driven by Nike between 331 and 322.[17] This gold stater bears a notable resemblance to WD **46**. Nike faces the viewer, her wings unfurled behind her to the left and right. She towers over her steeds as she grips the reins. The arrangement of Nike's hair appears to match that of the figure on WD **46**, as do the columnar legs of the horses.

Do WD **46** and the Cyrenaian gold stater relate to one another? Obviously, the bulla must antedate the coin. Chariot groups, admittedly in profile, but often driven by Nike, were popular across the Hellenized world in the fourth century and appeared occasionally on seals and frequently on coins, most notably a famous group of Syracusan decadrachms.[18] It is a motif that certainly underwent cross-fertilization between the numismatic and glyptic arts. Most of Cyrene's quadriga coinage followed the Syracusan model; however, in this one instance, someone in the fourth century, perhaps the magistrate Jason whose name the gold stater bears, chose a different model.

It is improbable that the Nike device found both on the Cyrenaic stater and the WD **46** seal was reinvented in the middle of the fourth century. After its heyday in the Archaic period, the frontal quadriga maintained a thin thread of continuity in South

---

[12] See INTRODUCTION, p. 27 and *passim* and references to M. C. Root's work.

[13] Kraay, *Coins*, pl 61: 1054, 1056, 1058 (late fifth century). The identification of the figure in the chariot is disputed. Cf. Betlyon, *Coinage*, 5, pl 4.

[14] Note Boardman, *GGFR*, 928 (Leningrad 428) from Kerch, on which the Persian winged sun disc hovers over a charioteer and his bow-wielding master in a galloping quadriga, and Boardman, *GGFR*, 864 (= Richter, *EGGE*, 502 = British Museum 1911.4–15.1) in the 'Greek style' of the mid-late fourth century found in Mesopotamia which shows, in profile, a Persian horseman chasing two men in a chariot drawn by a pair of horses.

[15] Kraay, *Coins*, pl 15: 262, 263; cf. also Erhart, *Development*, 90ff.

[16] Euboea was sacred to Hera; her head appears in profile on some of these coins, and Pausanias (9.39,5) reports of the oracle of Trophonios in neighbouring Boeotia that initiates sacrificed to Hera Heniochê ('holding the reins,' i.e. 'the charioteer'). Cf. also Erhart, *Development*, 97.

[17] E. S. G. Robinson, *BMC Coins* v. 29 (Cyrene) pl XIII,10 and p. lxxix. See also L. Naville, *Les monnaies d'or de la Cyrenaique 450–250 avant J.C.* (Geneva, 1951) nos. 22–4, p. 23ff. and Jenkins, *Coins*, fig. 312.

[18] Richter, *EGGE*, p. 24 and nos. 335–7; Boardman, *GGFR*, p. 210, pl 639. The motif begins earlier, in the fifth century. Cf. Kraay, *Coins*, pl 48, 815 (Syracuse, *c*.390); pl 51, 871 (Thermae, *c*.340). Nike's first appearance on a coin seems to be in 510 on an Olympian issue (A. R. Bellinger and M. Alkins Berlincourt, *Victory as a Coin Type*, American Numismatic Society Monographs No. 149 [1962] 4).

Italian vase painting[19] and on coins and gems; enough of a continuity for an old motif to be put together with the newer one of Nike driving a chariot, as attested by the Cyrenaic coin and the Wadi Daliyeh bulla.

It is unknown on what models the engravers of the coin and seal patterned their work. Most likely the model was on a small scale and easily transportable—another seal or perhaps an as-yet-undiscovered coin.[20] Thanks to L. Woolley's discovery of the collection of clay bullae in the coffin at Ur,[21] and E. Porada's clever theory that they belonged to a seal engraver,[22] we can speculate that the creator of WD **46** may have provided his clientele with a 'catalogue' in the form of clay impressions from both coins and gems. Perhaps the creator of WD **46**, a relatively unsophisticated engraver, worked from this sort of prototype.

Why might there be a Nike seal in fourth-century Samaria? If only as an artistic image, chariots had long enjoyed the favour of Near Eastern ruling classes to which the Samarians, as administrators for their Persian overlords, certainly belonged. Nike's wings would not have worried them; the Near East favoured representations of fantastic winged monsters and divinities. They appear on other bullae from Wadi Daliyeh. It remains uncertain whether the owner of the facing quadriga seal also recognized Nike or simply wanted to follow fashion by owning something Greek.[23]

Possibly Nike, as a winged charioteer, was 'read' as a Phoenician war goddess such as Astarte. We might also consider another identification within the known parameters of contemporary post-exilic Jewish imagery. The most familiar aspect of Ezekiel's sixth century vision of God's *kabod* 'glory' are the four-winged, four-headed human figures attached to wheels, essentially anthropomorphic winged chariots (Ezek 1; 3:12-14). Zechariah, the late sixth-century prophet of Jerusalem (heavily influenced by Ezekiel's restoration programme) saw two winged women lift up the *ephah* of wickedness and take it to Babylon (Zech 5:9). Presumably these women served in the heavenly court of YHWH along with YHWH's messengers, the prophets, and other attendants such as the six-winged seraphim of Isaiah 6 (an eighth-century text). As post-exilic Jewish factions, for a variety of theological reasons, made new use of the ancient imagery of YHWH's divine court, the heavenly population exploded, as it were, with new

---

[19] *Viergespanne*, pl 2, (see above, n. 5) a fourth-century South Italian krater in Ruvo (Coll. Jatta, Catalog 431, no. 1088).

[20] Cyrene is an intriguing area in which to find a parallel to WD **46**. S. Applebaum (*Jews and Greeks in Ancient Cyrene, Studies in Judaism in Late Antiquity* 28 [Leiden, 1979] 130) finds evidence in the fourth century of a Jew in a list of soldiers deposited in the temple of Zeus. He mentions Crete, Lycia and Cyprus as trading with Cyrene in the Classical period (127), a possible mechanism by which a Cyrenaean coin could travel to the eastern Mediterranean region. A great many fourth-century Carthaginian coins are found in Cyrene (128) thus placing Cyrene in the range of Phoenician trade. Applebaum also suspects (129) that Cyrene exported seal stones (already engraved?).

[21] Legrain, *Ur*, nos. 701–832.

[22] Porada, 'Greek Coin', 230.

[23] The quadriga motif was to enjoy a long life in Palestine. One example, a coin from Aelia Capitolina (Jerusalem) of the early third century CE, shows a facing quadriga carrying the sacred stone ('betyl') of Elagabalus (*SNG-ANS, Part 6*, figs. 625–6). When, in the early Byzantine period, the elders of the synagogue at Beth Alpha in Galilee commissioned a mosaic floor, the central image of the magnificent zodiac was a facing Helios (or Apollo) driving a frontal quadriga (*EAEHL*, 'Beth Alpha', illus. p. 189).

messengers and extra-terrestrial intermediaries. Nike driving her chariot might well have fit right in among the ever-expanding host of YHWH, as a distant ancestress of the Christmas tree angel.

F. OTHER MALE AND FEMALE FIGURES

WD 43. Achilles and Penthesilea (?)

(PLATE XI.2)

Mus. Inv. 940
Loose sealing
Image size: 1.4 cm x 1 cm
Bulla size: 1.6 cm x 1.6 cm
Clay colour: reddish brown
String preserved, loop uncut; top and bottom of vertical image
Papyrus fragments on back
Papyrus imprint
Seal type: metal finger ring?

WD **43** is an oval impression taken probably from a metal finger ring.[1] There is a slight indication of the transition from bezel to ring shaft at the top of the deeply impressed image. The bulla suffers from overall surface abrasion; a papyrus fibre, which pressed into the unfired clay bulla and later fell away, left a small gash in the lower right edge. The very bottom of the image has crumbled off.

The bulla shows two warriors in plumed helmets. On the left, in profile, a bearded man with a chlamys knotted at his throat leans over (to the viewer's right) to support a second warrior who has collapsed to a kneeling position, with the torso in three-quarter view. This is one of the most ambitious of the Wadi Daliyeh seal devices; indeed, Boardman notes that two-figure groups are rare on Classical seals,[2] and compositions with two figures of equal narrative weight are even rarer. Including WD **43**, there are four examples in the Wadi Daliyeh corpus.[3]

As the soldier on the left grasps the wounded warrior under the armpits, elevating the right shoulder, the fallen figure's head slumps forward and slightly to the left; the right arm falls limply to the side, slightly overlapped by the supporting warrior's flexed right leg. The kneeling figure's left arm also hangs down uselessly. Abrasions have eliminated all trace of the second figure's facial features. The standing figure's beard establishes his sex, but the poor condition of the impression prevents us from determining the barbarian's gender.

The fallen warrior wears elaborate armour—plumed helmet, tunic, and corselet, from the bottom of which dangles a row of rectangular tabs (pteryges). The apparent flexibility of the corselet and the shape of the shoulder guards suggest this is a linen corselet.[4] An additional piece of the wounded warrior's equipment, a pelta, appears to

---

[1] Boardman, *GGFR*, fig. 217/type VII, fourth century.

[2] Boardman, *Intaglios*, p. 14.

[3] WD **44** (pl X.3); WD **6** (pl XI.3); WD **52** (pl XII.1). A man and a woman appear together on all four.

[4] Several figures on the Parthenon Frieze (*c*.445) wear the linen corselet. For a clear illustration of this type of corselet over a longer tunic, see Lullies-Hirmer, *Sculpture*, pl 55, a detail from the north frieze of the Siphnian

the figure's left. The pelta was a crescent-shaped shield associated with a variety of barbarians in Greek art.

The arched back of the standing man and the curve of the wounded warrior's helmet-plume fit neatly within the oval of the seal itself. WD **43** bears no artistic or stylistic relation to the many bullae of anonymous warriors from Wadi Daliyeh. It somewhat resembles WD **5/16B** (pl VIII.1,2) in leaving only a minimal amount of empty background space.

Notwithstanding the unfortunate condition of the impression, the composition still conveys a sense of pathos in the contrast between the raw vigour of the supporting figure and the slump of the fallen warrior's head and arms. The supporting warrior's slightly upward glance over his fellow's head suggests uncomprehending grief. The subject of WD **43** appears to be Achilles with Penthesileia, the dying Amazon queen. Support for this identification requires some further discussion.

The 'Helper Group'

In both motif and execution, WD **43** presents a well-known Greek sculptural motif. It first appeared in the mid-fifth century, possibly as part of the Amazonomachy on the outside of the shield of the Athena Parthenos.[5] The popularity of this motif, called by E. Bielefeld 'the Helper Group', continued, with numerous variations in style and subject, down into the Hellenistic and Roman periods.[6] The Helper Group is regularly found in an assortment of well-populated scenes, primarily Amazonomachies,[7] but also in battles between Greeks and Persians, and in distinctly savage episodes—city-sackings and massacres.

Most often in Helper Groups the fallen figure is lifted from behind, the limp body curving like the letter C, or is held from the side with one leg extended.[8] A reasonably close parallel to WD **43** occurs on an early fourth-century relief vase depicting the *Ilioupersis*.[9] The similarity lies in the disposition of the sound warrior's right leg alongside the companion's limp arm, although on the relief vase the supporting figure is frontal as he supports his slumping friend essentially from behind, rather than from the side; on the bulla the visible leg is in profile.

---

treasury at Delphi (*c*.520). For a summary description of Classical Greek armour with useful bibliography, see Emeline Hill Richardson, 'The Muscle Cuirass in Etruria and Southern Italy', *AJA* 100 (1996) 91–120, esp. pp. 92–3; Richardson reports (p. 93) that the linen corselet is also found on Etruscan bronze warriors of the fourth century. See also WD **32** (p. 74 above).

[5] D. von Bothmer, *Amazons in Greek Art* (Oxford, 1957) 209–14 and pl LXXVII,6. Besides the Helper Group associated with the shield of the Athena Parthenos, the Helper Group on the Bassai frieze (British Museum B 542) of the late fifth or early fourth century should be noted (illustrated in Ridgway, *Fifth Century*, fig. 65).

[6] E. Bielefeld, *Amazonomachia*, Hallische Monographien 21 (Halle, 1951) 24ff. and 'Liste A', 67–72. This compositional scheme was later appropriated by artists of the Christian West for the Deposition of Christ.

[7] There were three Amazonomachies in Greek tradition: the Trojan, the Athenian, and the Themiskyrian involving, respectively, Achilles, Theseus, and Herakles.

[8] Von Bothmer, *Amazons*, pl LXXXVIII and 215–16, an Amazonomachy in the reconstruction of the marble frieze of the Temple of Apollo Epikouros at Phigalia (421–418 BCE).

[9] Herrmann, *Shadow*, no. 36, a relief vase in Boston (00.350), dated to the first quarter of the fourth century; a Trojan supports a dead or dying compatriot.

No Helper Groups among Classical Greek gems or finger rings compare fully with WD **43** although Etrusco-Italic oval ringstones of the third to second century and later sometimes portray one or more warriors supporting a wounded comrade.[10] W. Martini cautions against specific identification of these scenes and suggests they are general representations of comradeship in war.[11]

Identification and Dating

The pelta helps considerably in narrowing down the possible subjects of WD **43**; in Greek iconography the pelta marks the fallen warrior as a 'barbarian'—Amazon, Scyth or Persian. In this composition, in contrast to the fallen figure, the nudity of the supporting warrior suggests he is Greek.[12] The contrast would appear to be deliberate, the artist signalling that the standing soldier is Greek, the fallen one a barbarian.

The Helper Group motif itself informs us that the standing warrior is in sympathy with the fallen figure. Where in Greek lore is there an episode in which a Greek warrior feels remorse for a fallen barbarian? Precisely such a moment occurs in the *Aithiopis* which notably includes an Amazonomachy, one of the artistic subjects in which the Helper Group frequently appears.[13] The *Aithiopis* tells of the Amazons who come to aid the Trojans after the death of Hektor. In the ensuing conflict, the greatest Greek hero, Achilles, slays Penthesilea, queen of the Amazons; just as he kills her, he realizes his love for her.[14] This is the scene depicted on WD **43**. The fallen warrior's costume poses no problems; Amazons wear helmets, tunics, corselets and peltas.[15]

From the late seventh century the customary presentation of Achilles and Penthesilea, especially on bronze shieldband reliefs, showed them in combat as the Greek hero struck his mortal blow.[16] Occasionally—but more often on Hellenistic and Roman monuments[17]—they are seen a moment later when, according to late written sources, Achilles realizes he loves her and can only attend her helplessly as she dies.[18]

---

[10] Cf. *AGDS II* (Berlin) 318–21 identified as Menelaos and Patrokles, Ajax and Odysseus with the dead Achilles, Ajax with the dead Achilles.

[11] W. Martini, *Die Etruskische Ringsteinglyptic* (Heidelberg, 1971) 82, n. 246a.

[12] Only 'suggests' since Greek artists occasionally portrayed nude barbarians, and in that case WD **43** would portray a pair of anonymous male barbarian comrades-in-arms.

[13] *The Aithiopis* exists only in Proclus' fifth-century CE summary (*Hesiod, the Homeric Hymns and Homerica* [Loeb Edition, Cambridge, 1977]).

[14] G. Nagy (*Best of the Achaeans* [Baltimore, 1979] 70) has observed that the names 'Penthesilea' and 'Achilles' mean the same thing (*akhos* and *penthos* both mean grief; *laos*, people); by killing the Amazon queen, Achilles symbolically kills himself. Not long after, Achilles falls to Paris' fatal arrow.

[15] Vase painting: Von Bothmer, *Amazons*, 177, no. 30, a squat red figure lekythos in Boston [95.48] pl LXXVII, 6; relief: Von Bothmer, *Amazons*, 209–14, pl LXXVII,1–2.

[16] K. Schefold, *Frühgriechische Sagenbilder* (Münich, 1964) 86. Listed and selectively illustrated in *LIMC*, 'Achilleus', 162–3. Cf. Von Bothmer, *Amazons*, 1–5. Exekias seems to have felt a special interest in the subject; he twice illustrated it (Boardman, *ABV*, p. 230 and fig. 98 [British Museum B 210]).

[17] R. Glynn, 'Achilles and Penthesilea: An Iconographic Study of an Engraved Gem', *Oxford Journal of Archaeology* I (1982) 169.

[18] Quintus Smyrnaeus 1.48–61; 659–74 (fourth century CE). In Proclus' summary of the *Aithiopis* he says only that Thersites mocks Achilles for being in love with Penthesilea (*Hesiod, the Homeric Hymns and Homerica*, p. 507).

At Olympia, Panainos' late fifth century painting of the *Ilioupersis* may have included this second episode.[19]

Although the subject of Achilles as the agonized lover was treated in a lost large-scale Hellenistic sculpture,[20] surviving works of Greek art pre-dating the Panainos painting do not depict it. The episode apparently does not occur on black or red figure vases of the sixth-fifth centuries.[21] The one pre-Hellenistic gem which clearly depicts the Greek and Amazon, a late Archaic sard scaraboid in Boston, shows them duelling.[22]

However, South Italian vases, particularly a series of Apulian volute kraters from the first half of the fourth century, provide good parallels for both the subject and composition of WD **43**.[23] The arrangement of the two figures is strikingly similar, particularly on a volute krater in the Adolphseck Collection.[24] Penthesilea is dying, her knees have buckled, her head droops; on her right, Achilles in helmet and chlamys is leaning over her. With his right hand, he grips her under her right shoulder. For romantic emphasis, Aphrodite and Eros hover in the background as interested spectators.

It is perhaps significant for an understanding of the typological tradition of the Wadi Daliyeh bulla that on the South Italian vases, as on WD **43**, Achilles is essentially nude (he wears greaves, helmet, and chlamys), while Penthesilea is fully outfitted in varying combinations of Greek and 'Phrygian' battle gear. The regularity of costume on these vases is unusual; generally, Amazons and their adversaries on Greek vases wear an impressively unpredictable variety of dress and undress.[25] South Italy in the fourth century, although beginning to move in its own artistic directions, still had close ties to

---

It is difficult to determine whether the love story is truly late or if the *Aithiopis* told of Achilles' doomed love, or if Proclus simply took the tradition for granted in his summary.

[19] On the fence surrounding the statue of Zeus enthroned. Cf. *LIMC*, 'Achilleus', p. 165, and Pausanias 1.17.2–3.

[20] E. Berger, 'Der neue Amazonenkopf im Basler Antiken Museum—Ein Beitrag zur hellenistischen Achill-Penthesileagruppe', *Gestalt und Geschichte: Festschrift Karl Schefold* (Bern, 1967) 61–75.

[21] *LIMC*, 'Achilles und Penthesilea'.

[22] Beazley, *Lewes House*, no. 31, pl 2 (MFA 27.682) = Boardman, *AG Gems*, 255 = Richter, *EGGE*, 150 ('from Cyprus').

Achilles and Penthesilea appear on Etruscan and Italian seals and in poses that are related to but not exactly like the scene on the Wadi Daliyeh bulla (Lippold, *Gemmen*, pl XLI,1,7,11,12; 'Krieger' and 'Achille' in index to Martini, *Etruskische Ringsteinglyptik*). Particularly well known is a banded agate scarab in London (Walters, *BMC*, no. 634 = Zazoff, *AG*, pl 57,6), until recently assumed to be Etruscan of the mid-fifth century and thus the earliest known depiction of Achilles supporting Penthesilea. Recently, however, R. Glynn demonstrated that it is actually an Etruscanizing work of the third century BCE or later (Glynn, 'Achilles and Penthesilea'). Notwithstanding the later dating, it is reminiscent of the Wadi Daliyeh bulla. Achilles, with frontal torso and profile head and right leg, lifts Penthesilea's right arm; the Amazon sinks to her knees in front of Achilles, obscuring his lower body and left leg. For the older opinion on this scaraboid, cf. Horster, *Statuen*, 10–12.

[23] *LIMC*, 'Achilleus', nos. 740/1; p. 465, no. 186.

[24] *LIMC*, 'Achilleus', no. 740 (Adolphseck, Schloss Fasanerie 178).

[25] Von Bothmer, *Amazons*, *passim*. On the late Archaic Boston seal with Achilles and Penthesilea (see above n. 21), Achilles wears a helmet and chlamys while Penthesilea is clothed in a tunic. On the other hand, on the third century Etrusco-Italic gem discussed by Glynn ('Achilles') both figures wear armour. Perhaps the distribution of clothing on this seal is an additional clue to its distance from a Classical period visual convention.

Greek artistic tastes and trends,[26] so a South Italian source for the proposed subject of WD **43** need not be postulated.[27] It is probable that WD **43** and the South Italian vases derive from the same Greek prototype: a sculpture perhaps, or painting.[28]

On the other hand, it is difficult to say where the WD **43** ring may have originated. WD **43**, although small in scale, is an ambitious work. A tentative suggestion would be that WD **43** might have some connection to the workshop or shops (in Sidon?) which produced the series of Greek-style royal sarcophagi[29] and the reliefs on the strange 'Tribune' or podium found in the Sidonian Temple of Eshmun.[30] Gable C of the Alexander Sarcophagus includes a Helper Group episode as part of a battle between Greeks and Persians.[31]

The late fourth-century date for the Alexander Sarcophagus need not trouble us if, as von Greave believes, the Alexander Sarcophagus derives from a Sidonian workshop of long standing (from at least the second quarter of the fourth century and probably earlier) whose artists may or may not have been Greek. Sidon in the fourth century was a wealthy Phoenician city and, although the city's relations with Greece remain unclear, evidently had a very hellenized governing class.[32] The unusual subject matter of WD **43** might also direct us to a Phoenician workshop. Boardman, in discussing the de Clercq collection with its Phoenician provenances, notes that the subjects of these gold rings in Greek style tend to be rare and sometimes unique.[33]

WD **43** represents an unexpected and valuable addition to the corpus of Greek glyptics, even if, ultimately, the identification of the two figures on WD **43** as Achilles and Penthesilea cannot be conclusively determined. The motif of two warriors, even two male warriors, is so rare on Greek seals that good comparanda simply do not exist.[34] If this is indeed a scene of Achilles and his Amazon, it would be one of the earliest examples of a motif that became more common in Hellenistic and Imperial art.[35]

---

[26] E. M. W. Tillyard, *The Hope Vases* (Cambridge, 1923) 18.

[27] Note that South Italy had long-standing trading ties with the Punic world.

[28] Horster, *Statuen*, 12.

[29] See Hitzl, *Sarkophage*.

[30] R. Stucky (*Tribune*) reports that excavators found this thoroughly Greek work below an ash layer which contained Attic sherds of the second half of the fourth century. Cf. also E. Will, 'Un problème d'*interpretatio graeca*: la pseudo-tribune d'Echmoun à Sidon', *Syria* 62 (1985) 105–24 and Boardman, *Diffusion*, 57.

[31] Von Graeve, *Alexandersarcophag*, pl 66,1 and 67,1.

[32] Elayi, 'Phoenician Cities', 20, 22 and 23. Cf. E. Will, 'Un problème d'*interpretatio graeca*', 110.

E. Berger ('Der neue Amazonenkopf') discusses a late marble copy of an Achilles-Penthesilea group in the Beirut Museum found in 1939 at Byblos (Berger, 66 and pl 26). Of course, it is probably only a coincidence that one of the few surviving sculptural examples—and a late one, at that—of the theme under consideration should come from Phoenicia, but it is an interesting coincidence.

[33] Boardman, *GGFR*, p. 221.

[34] In his chapter on Greco-Persian gems Boardman lists a seal (British Museum; Western Asiatic Department) from the Oxus Treasure (Boardman, *GGFR* 851) which shows two Greek warriors in combat, one victorious, the other crumpled on the ground. The composition resembles the Achilles and Penthesilea gem in Boston mentioned above. The figures on both the Oxus gem and the piece in Boston occupy much less of the field than the two figures on WD **43** and bear no stylistic resemblance to them.

[35] Lippold, *Gemmen*, pl 41, nos. 1 and 7.

The ring shape, the frequency with which Helper Groups appear in Greek art of the late fifth century/early fourth century,[36] as well as the careful modelling of the standing warrior's leg and the logic of the pose suggest a comparable mid-late Classical date for the WD **43** seal ring. Its pathos-laden scene anticipates the spirit of Hellenistic art.

---

[36] Bielefeld, *Amazonomachia*, Liste A, 67–72, and see above.

WD 6. Persian Man and Woman

(PLATE XI.3)

Mus. Inv. 961
Loose sealing
Image size: 1.4 cm x 1.2 cm (as preserved)
Bulla size: 1.8 cm x 1.8 cm
Clay colour: deep reddish brown
String preserve; left and right of vertical impression
Papyrus imprint
Seal type: scaraboid?

WD **6** bears a seal impression of oblong oval shape that could denote a scaraboid or a ring bezel with a fourth-century profile.[1] In the process of sealing, the extreme upper portion of the image failed to register in the clay and consequently the heads of the two figures are missing. The remainder of the bulla is fairly clear. There is a ground line but no encircling outline.

This is one of four Greek or Greco-Persian images from Wadi Daliyeh portraying a man and woman, a rare subject in the already unusual category of Classical two-figure seal compositions.[2] A man and woman face each other, fully clothed and positioned literally toe-to-toe, he on the left, she on the right. They stand just above a ground line bisected in the middle by an inverted 'V' shape which seems to hang on the line. Simple, unbroken single ground lines are the general rule for Greek gems of the Classical period, but the inverted 'V' hanging over the line on WD **6** is unparalleled. The strange mark may denote a knot in a rope border, or perhaps, a Greek *lambda*; might it be the artist's monogram or the initial of the owner?[3]

Both figures appear in a modified three-quarter view. The man sets his weight solidly on both feet, with the left leg a step ahead of the right and both knees locked. The lady, by contrast, sways in an elegant contrapposto. The right leg carries her weight, her left leg is bent slightly back. Her bare feet are carefully carved. Even the

---

[1] Boardman, *GGFR*, ring type VII (fig. 217) and p. 214. The scaraboid was the seal type favoured by Greek seal carvers and patrons in the Classical period (Boardman, *GGFR*, p. 191).

[2] Boardman, *Intaglios*, p. 14. The three other bullae are WD **43** (pl XI.2); WD **44** (pl X.3); WD **52** (pl XII.1).

[3] The possibility that it is a fourth-century formal Aramaic *gimel* is remote. Boardman discusses various linear devices—Lydian, Aramaic, Greek—on stamp seals from the western satrapies of the Persian Empire in 'Pyramidal', 19–45. An inverted 'V' is no. 54 on his list (fig. 3) but he says only that it is derived from Greek and may be a monogram (p. 24). The device does not occur as a countermark on Achaemenid coins (fig. 4), nor in fact do these symbols ever decorate the ground line of the stamp seals but are placed haphazardly in the field of the image. The linear devices Boardman discusses seem in general to appear earlier than the fourth century-date of WD **6**. Elsewhere Boardman informs us that '[t]he strange linear devices on Lydian Achaemenid stamps appear otherwise only on some wholly Greek gems, not on Graeco-Persian' (Boardman, *GGFR*, p. 327).

toes of her left foot are visible. While the man caresses the chin or cheek of his lady with his right hand, she holds his right wrist in her left hand.[4] The mood of the scene is intimate yet dignified.

The artist has attempted to represent the volume of both his subjects' bodies under the folds of their clothing, rather more successfully in the case of the woman. There is a delicacy of line in the woman's drapery reminiscent of large-scale Classical relief, while the lines indicating her companion's clothing seem less carefully, even hastily, executed. The difference, intentional perhaps, highlights the woman's femininity beside the more robust man. The lady is reminiscent of Timarista on the late fourth century grave relief of Timarista and Krito from Rhodes;[5] it is even possible that the WD **6** seal comes out of an East Greek tradition of relief sculpture.

Most intriguing here is the clothing and, in particular, the nationalities implied by it. The male figure wears standard Persian attire as conceived by Greek artists (in actuality it is Median): leggings, short tunic, shoes, possibly long sleeves, and if the top of the sealing were extant, perhaps a soft leather hat.[6] Tucked into his belt, it is just possible to discern a short dagger (*akinakes*) with a round pommel. The woman is bare-armed; she has folded her peplos over at the waist so that its folds fall longer in the back than in the front. The skirt is bunched into pleats in the front which fall neatly to the top of the lady's feet.[7]

When comparable images are sought out on Greek, Achaemenid, or Greco-Persian seals this international couple proves to be unusual. In fact, a survey of the Greek and Persian glyptic evidence reveals nothing quite like the 'mixed marriage' of WD **6**. In the art of Greece after the Persian wars, Persian men—as warriors and hunters—made their appearance in all manner of media,[8] from monumental wall painting (the Battle of

---

[4] The gesture suggests the pair are courting or actual lovers. Cf. Boardman, *ABV*, p. 211 and fig. 124, a black figure amphora by the Phrynos Painter, *c*.550–540 (Würzburg University Museum, 241). Cf. also cat. no. 20 in National Gallery, *The Human Figure in Early Greek Art* (Exhibition catalogue; Washington, D.C., 1988), a seventh-century oenochoe from Crete (Herakleion Museum 6971) on which a young man caresses the face of his sweetheart, while she (affectionately?) holds his wrists.

The wrist-holding gesture appears on an early fifth-century Ionian Six's technique thymiaterion excavated at Phokaia (in Turkey, north of Ismir), now in the Louvre (E. Langlotz, *Studien zur nordostgriechischen Kunst* [Mainz, 1975] pl 68, p. 500), and in vase paintings of weddings where the groom clasps the bride's hand or wrist; cf. a fifth century red-figure kalyx krater from Tanagra (Athens 1388) discussed in R. F. Sutton, Jr., *The Interaction Between Men and Women Portrayed on Attic Red-Figure Pottery* (Ph.D. diss., University of North Carolina, Chapel Hill, 1981) 177. More work remains to be done before the full connotations and development of the gesture on WD **6** are understood, especially in the Archaic Period.

[5] Rhodes Archaeological Museum 13638 (illustration in Lullies-Hirmer, *Sculpture*, pl 185).

[6] The truly Persian formal outfit consisted of a long chiton-like robe with loose sleeves and folds at the middle of the skirt. Cf. G. Thompson, 'Iranian Dress in the Achaemenian Period: Problems Concerning the *Kandys* and other Garments', *Iran* III (1965) 121–6; cf. also Miller, *Perserie*, 249–66. See also the summary of D. Stronach's paper, 'Notes on Iranian Dress in the Achaemenid Period', read at the 88th General Meeting of the Archaeological Institute of America, in *AJA* 91 [1987] 309, and H. Koch, *Es kündet Dareios der König . . . Vom Leben im persischen Grossreich* (Mainz am Rhein, 1992) chap. V, 'Kleidung'.

[7] For a similar chiton arrangement cf. the grave relief with Timarista and Krito from Rhodes (see above, n. 5).

[8] Good sources on this subject are: W. Raeck, *Zum Barbarenbild in der Kunst Athens in 6 und 5 Jahrhundert v. Chr* (Bonn, 1981); A. Bovon, 'La représentation des guerriers perses et la notion de barbare dans la Ière moitié du Ve siècle', *Bulletin de Correspondance Hellénique* 87 (1963) 579–602; Miller, *Perserie*; K. Schauenburg, 'Siegreiche

Marathon in the Stoa Poikile) and reliefs (the Nike Temple on the Acropolis) to vase painting and, occasionally, seals.[9] On the other hand, indisputably Persian women are all but non-existent in 'mainstream' Greek art of the Classical period.

Achaemenid artists as a general rule did not consider women a suitable artistic subject; there are no women on the Persepolis reliefs.[10] Greco-Persian gems are one of the few sources for depictions of Persian women.[11] Often executed in a Greek style, Greco-Persian seals are thought to have been produced by artists working in western Anatolia for patrons within the Persian Empire;[12] on these seals, the women reflect the 'Persian preference for full breasts and buttocks'.[13] WD **52** (pl XII.1) presents the stereotypical example of the 'Greco-Persian' type of female figure, but this is not the manner in which the woman on WD **6** has been portrayed. Her elongated figure draped in an elegant chiton fits the Greek, and not the Persian, canon of beauty.[14]

Intimate scenes of daily life on seals were apparently never popular in Persia itself; nevertheless, the Greeks had created a taste for naturalistic imagery among the Great King's western subjects, and some artists—Persian? native? Greek?—seem obligingly to have supplied the demand.[15] Ethnically matched 'conversations' between a Persian man and Persian woman do appear on Greco-Persian seals;[16] in fact, WD **52** (pl XII.1) is a

---

Barbaren', *Athenische Mitteilungen* 92 (1977) 91–100; H. Schoppa, *Die Darstellung der Perser in der griechischen Kunst bis zum Begin des Hellenismus* (Heidelburg, 1933).

[9] For example, a late fifth-century scaraboid showing a Persian leaning on his spear, a work which Boardman calls 'thoroughly Greek in style' and assigns to the hand of an East Greek artist working for a Greek patron. The Persian on the scaraboid shares a certain kinship with the Persian on WD **6** (Boardman, *GGFR*, 532 = Furtwängler, *AG*, pl 13.5 (in St. Petersburg, from Kerch); cf. Boardman, *GGFR*, p. 201.

[10] Boardman, *GGFR*, p. 324 and Cook, *Persian Empire*, 165.

[11] A. Spycket's, 'Women in Persian Art' (in D. Schmandt-Besserat, ed., *Ancient Persia: The Art of an Empire* (Malibu, 1980) 43–6 serves to show how little information is known on the subject. H. Koch has addressed the question most recently in *Dareios*, 241–9. See also the entry for WD **52**, p. 157.

[12] On the subject of Greco-Persian gems (and bibliography) see Boardman, *GGFR*, chap. VI; Marvin, *Studies*; Root, 'Heart', esp. 13–22 and Boardman, *Diffusion*, 39–47. The ethnic identity of the seal carvers remains a subject of theoretical debate.

[13] Boardman, *GGFR*, p. 310. Boardman believes these seals were produced by Greeks working in the East. It is becoming increasingly probable that Eastern artists were capable of producing works in a variety of styles, including Greek (cf. discussion of WD **43**, p. 149).

Cf. also Boardman, *Intaglios*, 87 (pl 29.2); Boardman, *GGFR*, fig. 283 = Richter, MMA, no. 133 (MMA 25.78.98), a late fifth-century chalcedony scaraboid in New York; it is carved in a very Greek manner but the lady is a buxom Persian in a very full chiton-like robe with elaborate folds and long batwing sleeves. She wears sandals and carries an ointment jar. Like all the other Persian women on these seals, she has braided her hair in a single waist-length pigtail ornamented with little knobs at its end.

[14] Marvin observes that although seal carvers seem to have been able to work in both the Greek and Near Eastern styles, the two modes of representation do not appear on the same seal (Marvin, *Studies*, 34–5). WD **6** does not contradict her observation; the male figure, although in Persian attire, is portrayed in Greek style. 'Persians' are the subject of a number of Greek (as opposed to Greco-Persian) seals (cf. Boardman, *GGFR*, 525, 681).

[15] Boardman, *GGFR*, p. 324 and Root, 'Heart', 19–22.

[16] Boardman, *Intaglios*, 87; also Boardman, *GGFR*, 891 = Richter, *EGGE*, 503 = Zazoff, *AG*, pl 41.5, a Persian man on a pink chalcedony pendant (in the British Museum, from Cyprus) facing a Persian lady and resting his left arm on her right shoulder in 'unPersian familiarity' (Boardman, *GGFR*, p. 316). They both wear Persian garb as expected on Greco-Persian gems; the lady is plump and has a long knob-end pigtail. On the reverse are a seated Persian mother and her child, a typically Greek motif.

good example. Although Persian men and women appear together on seals, Greek-style women are not known to consort with Persian men.[17] Stylistically, WD **6** does not belong in the Greco-Persian category.[18] Precedents must be sought for elsewhere.

Persian men appear frequently and in a variety of scenes on Greek vases.[19] Usually, Persians do battle against Greeks; they also hunt and feast in oriental splendour.[20] Their costume varies, but usually entails a jacket with sleeves, trousers, a knee-length chiton, shoes, and several types of headdresses;[21] they are never nude. The outfit of the Persian on WD **6** has numerous counterparts on these vases. Neither 'Persian' nor 'Greek' women figure in scenes of battle or the hunt.

The most likely parallel to the scene on WD **6** is a variant on another conventional scene in Greek vase painting, the 'warrior's farewell'.[22] The motif first appears in the mid-fifth century and declines in popularity by century's end.[23] The 'Persian' variation shows a Persian warrior accompanied by a fully-clad lady holding a phiale or oenochoe. Although scholars have attempted to interpret the Persian warrior and peplos- or chiton-clad lady (or ladies) on red-figure vases as pouring a drink offering to the Persian Great King, or as actors in Greek drama, or even, in the case of a lekythos in Frankfort,[24] as personifications of Persia and Greece solemnizing the Peace of Kallias,[25] Raeck demonstrates that the scene is a transposition of a favourite subject of vase painters[26] to an exotic Persian milieu.[27]

Additional Greco-Persian 'conversation' scenes are Boardman, *GGFR*, 880 = Richter, *EGGE*, 510 = Zazoff, *AG*, 41.4; Boardman, *GGFR*, 892; Boardman, *GGFR*, 950; Boardman, *GGFR*, fig. 297.

[17] One possible Archaic exception in Boston: an 'orientalizing' pyramidal stamp probably from East Greece which Boardman dates to approximately the late sixth or early fifth century, earlier than the Greco-Persian group, (Boardman, 'Pyramidal', 27, pl 2,18). The dating of this group of stamp seals is not firm, however.

[18] If the portrayal of Persian women on the Greco-Persian gems is accepted as approaching authenticity, we must recognize the different artistic traditions at work in Attic vase painting and Greco-Persian glyptic. The absence from Attic vase painting of the big and buxom Persian women as found on Greco-Persian gems would serve to confirm the theory that the gems were made for Persians or Easterners, and not for Greeks.

[19] Cf. especially Raeck, *Barbarenbild*, *passim*.

[20] A well-known Apulian volute krater, the name-piece of the Darius Painter (Naples 3253), shows the Persian court in a dramatic scene, probably from the *Persai* of the fourth-century dramatist, Phrynichos. Persians there are aplenty on this vase, but none are women.

[21] Raeck, *Barbarenbild*, 108; cf. also Miller, *Perserie*, chap. 4, for a discussion of Greeks wearing Persian fashions.

[22] Cf. W. Wrede, 'Kriegers Ausfahrt in der archaischgriechischen Kunst', *Athenische Mitteilungen* 41 (1916), 222–374; Webster, *Potter*, 220ff; Raeck, *Barbarenbild*, 138–44.

[23] Raeck, *Barbarenbild*, 138.

[24] Raeck, *Barbarenbild*, no. P565 and p. 140.

[25] Raeck, *Barbarenbild*, 138–40 with references.

[26] Raeck, *Barbarenbild*, fig. 61. T. Hölscher claims that '. . . auf Vasenbildern . . . die das Leben der damaligen Krieger betreffen, gerade im fünften Jahrhundert der Abschied von der Familie viel häufiger dargestellt wird als der Kampf' ('Ein Kelchkrater mit Perserkampf', *Antike Kunst* 17 [1974] 84).

[27] Raeck, *Barbarenbild*, 138–45. Just as Amazons (in Greek or foreign costume) and other non-Greeks appeared on vases in scenes typical of warriors, so might Persians.

Raeck listing: P565, P567, P585, P591, P593, P594, P598. P594 is a lekythos from the workshop of the Kleophon Painter (*c*.430) found on Cyprus and cited by K. deVries as an example of a vessel made in Athens for export to the Eastern market ('Attic Pottery in the Achaemenid Empire', *AJA* 81 [1977] 546–7).

Not surprisingly, the attempt to represent Persians at home fell short of ethnographic accuracy; there were few if any eyewitness accounts of Persian domestic life, and Greek ignorance of Persian women and the harem would have been total. On vases, the degree of 'Persianness' and general details may vary, but in every case the women wear Greek clothing 'occasionally supplemented with orientalizing details'.[28] Costumes to the contrary, the women must be 'read' as Persian.[29] Thus, WD 6 could be a glyptic version of the 'Persian's farewell', and the woman should be interpreted as Persian.[30]

Since WD 6 includes neither weapons nor offering vessel, we should also consider a few alternative explanations. Another possible reading of WD 6 fits the imagery and 'romantic' mood of much fourth century art. It became customary among Greek vase painters, after the Persian wars and well into the fourth century, to regularly portray certain figures from Greek mythology as Easterners.[31] WD 6 is quite similar to such illustrations, particularly scenes with Paris. Paris, as an Asiatic prince in 'judgement' scenes and in tableaux with Helen, often wears a sumptuous Eastern costume very like the 'Persian' outfit with fancy leggings, short tunic, long sleeves, a Phrygian hat, and shoes.[32] Helen, as befits a Greek princess, wears jewels, and her clothes are embroidered, but they are nonetheless Greek.[33] Although, as noted, there are no such scenes in the known glyptic repertoire, it is not impossible that WD 6 shows Paris and Helen, or some comparable combination.[34]

One last interpretation of WD 6 derives from Persian culture. M. Marvin and P. Calmeyer independently proposed that the Greco-Persian 'conversations' might illustrate a popular Iranian romance, the tale of Zariandres and Odatis.[35] According to Chares of Mytilene, chamberlain to Alexander the Great, scenes from the love story decorated the walls of Achaemenid temples, palaces, and private homes.[36] Depending on variant Iranian traditions, Princess Odatis gave Prince Zariandres either a gold cup or a flower.[37] Marvin suggests that the unchanging set of details on the Greco-Persian

---

[28] Raeck, *Barbarenbild*, 144.

[29] Note the superficial orientalizing details of the Persian lady's costume on an oenochoe in the Vatican (Raeck P591, fig. 58 = Vatican 16536).

[30] The only example found of a glyptic warrior's farewell is a mid fifth-century Etruscan work (Walters, *BMC*, 651 = Zazoff, *AG*, pl 57.7 = Furtwängler, *AG*, pl 16.2.3).

[31] Metzger, *Représentations*, pp. 172, 269, 274, 280, 284, 313, 340. Other 'Asiatics' include Dionysos (with Ariadne), Artemis and Andromeda. Anchises, another Trojan, appears in Phrygian cap, chitoniskos, trousers, boots, and a cloak in a scene with his paramour, the goddess Aphrodite. She is half-nude, draped from the waist down in a mantle (Herrmann, *Shadow*, no. 16, p. 29, a squat lekythos [*c*.400] from the Peloponnese).

[32] Metzger, *Représentations*, pp. 269, 274, 280, 284; pls 37, 41. These scenes begin in the second half of the fifth century.

[33] *LIMC*, 'Alexandros', pp. 505ff; *LIMC* II,2, pp. 384–5, figs. 46–48, 50.

[34] WD **43** (Achilles and Penthesileia) might constitute a related example of an 'ethnically mixed' couple on a seal.

[35] Marvin, *Studies*, 146–7; P. Calmeyer, 'Textual Sources for the Interpretation of Achaemenian Palace Decorations', *Iran* 18 (1980) 60–61.

[36] Calmeyer, 'Textual Sources', 60. Cook (*Persian Empire*, 256) suggests tapestries as a possible medium for the story.

[37] Calmeyer, 'Textual Sources', 60–61.

'conversations' could imply a 'special woman recognized by purchasers'.[38] Perhaps WD **6** shows a Greek interpretation of this Achaemenid scene of which WD **52** is the more standard Greco-Persian example.

On the basis of parallels from Greek vase painting and from Greco-Persian seals, the scene may illustrate, in diminishing order of probability: a Persian warrior's farewell, Paris and Helen (or similar couple of different nationalities from Greek myth), or an old Persian tale. The motif of the warrior's farewell, however, should not be too strictly defined, especially when dealing with cross-cultural influences. The latter two possibilities are not necessarily excluded from the first category, and it is not impossible that in the fourth century, WD **6** and WD **52**, the 'Greco-Persian' conversation, would have been understood as depicting the same scene.

To conclude, WD **6** comes from a fourth-century scaraboid (or maybe a ring), perhaps engraved in East Greece or western Anatolia. Alternatively, a Sidonian workshop might be the source,[39] the woman on WD **6** has counterparts on the 'Mourning Women' sarcophagus (mid fourth century)[40] and among the maenads who parade across the contemporary 'tribune' found at the Temple of Eshmun.[41]

---

[38] Marvin, *Studies*, 146.

[39] See INTRODUCTION, p. 11.

[40] See R. Fleischer, *Der Klagenfrauensarkophag aus Sidon* (Tübingen, 1983); illustrated in Boardman, *Diffusion*, p. 56.

[41] See R. Stucky, *Tribune d'Echmoun: ein greichischer Reliefzyklus des 4. Jahrhunderts v. Chr. in Sidon, Antike Kunst*, Beiheft 13 (Basel, 1984); illustrated in Boardman, *Diffusion*, p. 57.

WD 52. Persian Man and Woman

(PLATE XII.1)

Mus. Inv. 949
Loose sealing
Image size: 1.5 cm x 1.1 cm
Bulla size: 1.7 cm 1.8 cm
Clay colour: reddish brown, back burnt black
String not preserved; string holes visible at top and bottom of image
Papyrus fibres on front
Papyrus imprint
Seal type: scaraboid mounted in a ring?

WD **52** suffered partial burning which blackened the back of the bulla and destroyed the string although the string holes remain. The sealing shows a man and a woman within the broad oval outline of the sealing. The shape and the fine raised ridge preserved on the right edge of the sealing suggest an engraved gem (a scaraboid?) possibly set in a ring or other mount.[1] Part of the man's head, right arm, and lower limbs are almost totally indistinguishable. Much surface detail has also disappeared. Parallels cited below suggest WD **52** had a ground line although this is no longer apparent.

A man dressed in Median style with a cowl headdress (the *tiara*[2]), sleeved coat, trousers, and soft shoes[3] stands in a modified three-quarter view, his chest almost frontal. He looks at his female companion with his head in profile. In an affectionate gesture,[4] the man reaches out with his left hand to touch his female companion's shoulder or chin. His right hand rests on or behind his hip. He stands with his left leg forward, the knee very slightly bent; his straight right leg carries his weight.

The buxom barefoot lady is fully in profile, standing erect with her right foot a little in advance of the left. Her Persian robe has deep batwing sleeves and folds at the front

---

[1] For a gem mounting other than a ring, cf. Johns, 'Excavations', pl XIV.629 and fig. 49, a Greco-Phoenician scarab set in a swivel mounting.

[2] Koch, *Dareios,* 216, and *idem, Achämeniden Studien* (Wiesbaden, 1993) 130–33.

[3] Generally, the long robe with flowing sleeves worn by Persian kings, soldiers, and dignitaries on the Persepolis reliefs is considered 'Persian', while the outfit with sleeved jacket and trousers is labelled 'Median'. However, it has been pointed out that these costumes do not always mark the ethnicity of the wearer since Persians appear to have worn both; usually the robe for formal occasions, the trousers for more strenuous activities (Koch, *Dareios,* chap. 5, 'Kleidung', and A. Shapur Shahbazi, 'Costume and Nationality: Remarks on the Usage of the "Median" and "Persian" Costumes of the Achaemenid Period', *AMI Ergänzungsband* 6 [1979] 195; Boardman, *GGFR,* p. 310).

[4] Cf. discussion in WD **6** p. 151, above, and note Boardman, *ABV,* 211 and fig. 124 = P. E. Arias, *One Thousand Years of Greek Vase Painting* (New York, 1962) fig. 52, p. 296, a black figure amphora by the Phrynos Painter, *c.*550–540 (Würzburg University Museum, 241).

of her waist, falling in pleats to her feet. The robe ends in a short train.[5] She has arranged her hair in a long braid terminating in a tassel ornament.[6] She extends one hand on either side of her companion's raised arm.

WD **52** reproduces a conventional composition found on a number of Greco-Persian engraved gems and is one of two identifiable Greco-Persian images from Samaria.[7] On WD **52** the woman, in particular, whose clinging dress accentuates the ample proportions supposedly prized in the Persian harem,[8] is a twin to the Persian women portrayed on a number of very characteristic Greco-Persian seals.[9] Especially comparable is a pear-shaped pendant seal of pink chalcedony in the British Museum,[10] reportedly from Cyprus, with a Persian couple similar in clothing and composition to WD **52**. A second Greco-Persian scaraboid now in the Getty Museum presents the

---

[5] O. M. Dalton (*The Treasure of the Oxus* [London, 1965] 103) suggests that this robe illustrates the term, *helkesipeplos*, 'trailing the robe/ long-trained' (*Iliad* 6.442).

[6] The single braid is all but unknown in Greek art. One possible Greek example occurs on a late Archaic lekythos in Brussels (Musées Royaux A 1019) by the Nikon Painter. The tall, buxom lady with a braid(?) looks a little like the Greco-Persian ladies (illustrated in Boardman, *ARV*, fig. 365). Furtwängler believed it was a fashion indigenous to Asia Minor (Furtwängler, *AG* iii, p. 123). The 'Lydian Shrine' (*c.*540–30) from Sardis depicts women with what looks like single braids in the 'stepped wig' style (G. M. A. Hanfmann and N. Ramage, *Sculpture from Sardis: the Finds through 1975* [Cambridge, MA, 1978] figs. 33–4, 40–41). However, since essentially the same hairstyle is worn earlier by both male and female figures on Neo-Assyrian cylinders (cf. Collon, *First Impressions*, figs. 351, 379, 561) it is even more likely to derive from a Mesopotamian tradition.

[7] The seated Persian in the Hecht Group (pl XXIV.14) resembles the WD **52** woman in dress, but the gender of this figure remains uncertain.

[8] As Koch points out, clothing often worn by male Persian dignitaries scarcely differs from the ladies' outfits on the seals (*Dareios,* 244ff.). Xerxes and Darius wear the same chiton-like robe with batwing sleeves on the frieze of the Persepolis Treasury (Frankfort, *Art*, pl 184.a). On a Samarian silver obol (Meshorer-Qedar, *Coinage of Samaria*, no. 21) a four-winged male deity resembling the Persian king could be mistaken for a Greco-Persian woman were it not for his beard and crown; indeed, he looks fully as plump as any Persian lady.

Perhaps the reason the Persian ladies on these seals have such prominent features is due not only to (male) preference (Boardman, *GGFR*, p. 310) but also to the availability of true Chinese silk (Miller, *Perserie*, 214ff; cf. G. M. A. Richter, 'Silk in Greece', *AJA* 33 [1929] 27–33); Koch, *Dareios*, 209–10. Greek delight in the new Oriental fabric which Athenians associated with Persia may have been responsible for the new 'wet look' at the beginning of the 430s in Athenian art (Miller, *Perserie*, 214).

The image of the Persian woman reflected in Greco-Persian gems does not belong in the largely Attic-influenced Greek artistic tradition. When an Athenian vase painter wished to show a Persian lady he selected details from his mental file of such 'Persian trappings' as were familiar to Athenians: sleeves, fancy embroidery, fans, rhyta, etc. (Miller, *Perserie*, chap. 4; cf. also T. Linders, 'The Kandys in Greece and Persia', *Opuscula Atheniensa* XV:8 [1984] 107). Ethnographic accuracy did not interest the Greek artists who had a definite cultural agenda in mind when they depicted Persians on their pots. Artists in East Greece and Anatolia had better opportunities for observing Persian woman at first hand; Iranian soldiers retired to estates all over the Persian Empire. Lydian Sardis was home for large numbers of Persian land grantees who also settled on the Hellespont (Daskyleion) and in Phrygia, Magnesia, Caria, Lycia, Cappadocia, Syria, and Babylonia (Miller, *Perserie*, 197–8, 203). It is assumed that many of these men brought along their Persian wives.

[9] Boardman, *GGFR*, 879 = Richter, *EGGE* , 508 = Walters, *BMC*, 434; Boardman, *GGFR*, 880 = Richter, *EGGE,* 510 = Zazoff, *AG*, pl 41.4; Boardman, *GGFR*, 891 = Richter, *EGGE* , 503 = Zazoff, *AG*, pl 41.5 = Walters, *BMC*, 436; Boardman, *GGFR*, 903 = Richter, *EGGE*, 507 = Walters, *BMC*, 433. For impressions from fourth- and third-century contexts, cf. Rubensohn, *Elephantine*, impression 26 (from a papyrus dated 284/3) and 'Selinunte,' *Notizie degli scavi di Antichità* (August, 1883) pl X, fig. CIV.

[10] Boardman, *GGFR*, 891 = Richter, *EGGE* , 503 = Zazoff, *AG*, pl 41.5 = Walters, *BMC*, 436.

same image, called 'a typical family group' by Boardman.[11] As on WD **52** and the British Museum pendant, the man has his hand on his hip and wears the expected Median outfit, including the cowl headdress. His other arm stretches straight out to rest proprietarily on his female companion's left shoulder. The lady with a long braid is again in profile and dressed in the familiar clinging gown. She holds out a flower to her companion.

The scene on WD **52** does not belong to any Phoenician glyptic tradition. Boardman interprets these Greco-Persian 'conversations' as scenes from daily life, observing that the sorts of images associated with 'Greco-Persian' gems—hunts, women, children—do not appear on Achaemenid Court Style seals which tend toward the hieratic or heraldic or obviously mythological. M. Marvin theorized that the seals—mostly scaraboids— with the buxom Persian ladies may be traced to Cilicia and possibly a Tarsian workshop of the first half of the fourth century.[12] She also proposes that artists in Cilicia could work in the Court Style of their overlords or in a more Greek mode. During the Persian period, Phoenicia and Cilicia enjoyed close economic and political ties;[13] indeed, the next stop after Phoenicia on the coastal trade route to Ionia and beyond was Tarsus.

Boardman points to the 'un-oriental familiarity' of the Greco-Persian couples as additional evidence that the source of the imagery on Greco-Persian gems is Greek.[14] However, the pedigree of this type of scene may be more complex. No doubt the background of the scene is partly East Greek, but pairs of human figures are not common in Greek glyptic of the late fifth/fourth centuries.[15] Zazoff notes that both the Cypriote and Etruscan glyptic traditions—unlike that of mainland Greece—favour scenes with mythological content and multiple figures,[16] a tendency he traces to the influence in both areas of Ionian artists.[17] Three other Wadi Daliyeh bullae show a man and woman together;[18] is this merely a matter of chance or possibly a pattern reflecting Eastern taste in seals? More specifically, could the Greco-Persian 'conversation' motif on WD **52** (and secondarily, on WD **6**) also boast some more essentially Eastern ancestry?

There is a striking compositional resemblance between the ubiquitous Persian Court Style motif of the Persian Hero confronting a winged animal or lion on the one hand

---

[11] Boardman, *Intaglios*, p. 33, fig. 87, blue chalcedony (Getty 81.AN.76 + 87).

[12] Marvin, *Studies*, 144. Marvin used Boardman's general Greco-Persian categories as the starting point for her examination of the problematic group. Her unpublished study remains the most rigorous examination of these seals.

[13] For example, from 350 or 345 BCE onwards, Mazaios was satrap not only of Cilicia, but also of Abarnahara which included north Syria, Phoenicia and Palestine (Cook, *Persian Empire*, 264, n. 30; *CHJ I*, 76; Elayi, 'Phoenician Cities', 27). He, in fact, appears to have allowed Samaria to mint coins in his name modelled after Cilician issues (Meshorer-Qedar, *Coinage of Samaria*, nos. 14, 16, 21, 48). The Persian kings, in their preparations for campaigns against the Greeks or Egypt, usually mustered their navy off the Cilician coast, a navy that consisted of Phoenician and Cypriote mariners and Persian marines.

[14] Boardman, *GGFR*, p. 316.

[15] Boardman, *Intaglios*, p. 14.

[16] Zazoff, *AG*, p. 104.

[17] Zazoff, *AG*, p. 106–7.

[18] WD **43** (pl XI.2) (Achilles and Penthesilea), WD **44** (pl X.3) (knucklebone players), WD **6** (pl XI.3) ('Persian' man and 'Greek' woman).

and the Greco-Persian couples on WD **52** and its parallels on the other. Two examples of this Court Style contest scene appear in the Wadi Daliyeh corpus (WD **4**, pl XVIII.2 and WD **8**, pl XVIII.3) as well as on many fourth-century Samarian coins.[19] The subject is the natural result of centuries of Mesopotamian and North Syrian development of the so-called 'Gilgamesh' motif. Just as on the Greco-Persian 'conversations', in a contest scene the male hero appears in a three-quarter stance with his left arm (in impression) extended straight out before him to grasp his animal adversary by the horn or neck. With his other arm the hero holds his sword or club either swung down and back to begin the trajectory of the thrust or actually delivering the death blow. Sometimes the victim (in profile) faces away from its captor, but frequently (again in profile) it faces in the warrior's direction. This latter scheme produces a composition of uncanny similarity to the Greco-Persian 'conversations.' Even the disposition of the Persian ladies' arms in these domestic scenes matches that of the animals' forelegs which usually claw at the King's/hero's extended arm. When the enemy faces away, wings frequently fill the same compositional space before the hero's extended arm.[20]

This 'conversation' motif thus seems to be an example of Greek artistic subject matter grafted onto an ancient Near Eastern compositional scheme. It is tempting to find an expression of ancient views on gender relations in this peculiar correspondence between a scene of battle and a scene of human intimacy in which the woman's placement makes her equivalent to the dangerous but soon-to-be-defeated monster.

WD **52** and WD **6** (pl XI.3), viewed as a pair, illustrate the broad artistic range of the world beyond the borders of Samaria. These two seals with essentially the same subject executed in distinctly different styles, highlight the issue of artists and patrons in the Persian Empire, particularly in Asia Minor and the Levant. What sort of scenes did the seal engravers think they were creating? What did patrons think they were getting? No doubt, patrons often 'saw' something different from the carver's intentions. Could WD **6** and WD **52** be Hellenized variations on the (apparently popular) Persian story of Zariandres and Odatis?[21] Does WD **52** present us with an orientalizing Aphrodite and Adonis, or Perseus and Andromeda?

The very real possibility that artists working in the Persian Empire knew how to do the equivalent of today's market survey, and were ready to create an image to the taste and specifications of a variety of patrons, must be left open. South Italian vase painters, working in another area exposed to different artistic styles, could paint one side of a vase with a restraint native to Attica and on the other side employ the flowery

---

[19] Meshorer-Qedar, *Coinage of Samaria*, nos. 16, 44–5, 48–50. See also Legrain, *Culture*, 939, 941, 947, and most of pl LVIII for numerous examples of this image on tablet sealings in the archives of the Murashu banking concern active in Persian period Nippur (studied most recently by Bregstein in *Seal Use*).

The consensus now leans toward seeing the Persian Hero as the king or as the king 'in the role of' the hero. Such conclusions are the result of research into the iconography of Achaemenid kingship by Root (*King*, 303 n. 15, and 303–7). The figure appears on ten of the fifteen known seal types found at Persepolis inscribed with the name of the Achaemenid king and is thus the motif most often chosen (Root, *King*, 303).

[20] If Persian Court Style 'hero' scenes lie behind the Persian conversations, questions are raised about the sexual implications associated with the theme of man and his 'prey' and of the 'threatening weapon'. Would such a transformation of an artistic motif have unconsciously evoked such underlying resonances?

[21] Cf. discussion of WD **6**.

Kertsch style.[22] A wealthy Persian landowner/chancellory official (and there were plenty of them scattered from the Black Sea to Syria) might want the woman on the seal he commissioned to conform to native ideals of beauty, or, just as likely, might have seen enough of the world to be attracted to images in the Greek style. The fourth-century sarcophagi from the royal cemetery at Sidon[23] and some of the objects with relief carving from the Sidonian temple of Eshmun[24] show that the Phoenicians commissioned reliefs which included Greek-style women, in addition to the more traditional Phoenician women/goddesses of the Phoenician ivories.[25]

WD **52** is one of the few impressions from Wadi ed-Daliyah to belong to a readily identifiable glyptic category, whether labelled Greco-Persian, Cilician, or Anatolian.

---

[22] E. M. W. Tillyard, *The Hope Vases* (Cambridge, 1923) 18.

[23] Cf. von Graeve, *Alexandersarcophag*.

[24] Cf. Stucky, *Tribune*.

[25] The Phoenician ivory-carving traditions seem to persist into the third and second centuries, but it is true that by the fifth and fourth centuries, Greek artistic influences gain the upper hand in the Phoenician and Punic worlds. For a third- or second-century female figurine in ivory, cf. Moscati, *Phoenicians*, 417 (in the Musée de Carthage). Cf. also S. Lancel, 'Ivoires Phénico-Puniques de la Nécropole Archaïque de Byrsa, Carthage', *Atti del I congresso internazionale di studi fenici e punici, 1979* (Rome, 1983) 687–92.

WD 47. Nude Hero (Herakles?) vs. Two Inverted Lions

(PLATE XII.2)

Mus. Inv. 944
Loose Sealing
Image size: 1.6 cm x 1.1 cm
Bulla size: 1.9 cm x 1.35 cm
Clay colour: reddish brown
String preserved; top and bottom of vertical image
Papyrus fragments stuck to sides of bulla
Seal type: Metal finger ring

THE image on WD **47** is badly worn, pitted, and incomplete. Most of the left third of the impression is indistinct or non-existent. The general outlines suggest that the bulla was produced by a broad, leaf-shaped metal finger ring of Boardman's Type V or VI (late fifth-early fourth centuries);[1] the lower edge of the impression makes a gentle point, and the ring haft may have left a nick in the clay just below the point.

WD **47** displays the familiar 'Master of Animals' motif. The slim, frontal nude hero with his head in profile to his right is flanked by a pair of inverted animals, probably lions, each of which he holds by one hind leg. On the original ring, the flanking animals were probably mirror images of each other. The general outlines of the creature on the viewer's right are sufficiently preserved to show the curve of its torso, one front leg resting on the ground and its head curled back as if to look up at the hero. Of the animal on the left, a faint outline of the torso and the hind paw of the leg gripped by the hero can be discerned. The static heraldic symmetry of the two animals is somewhat offset by the assymetrical stance of the hero. As on another, cruder Daliyeh seal, represented in several impressions,[2] the hero seems to have just stepped to his right.

The rather scrawny proportions of the male figure's torso suggest that the ring was a provincial product, perhaps made of bronze. Gold and silver, as precious metals, may have merited the exclusive attention of the most talented artists in a workshop setting, while apprentices or provincial artists focussed on cheaper bronze. Even when freshly impressed, the image could well have lacked clean definition.

The design on WD **47** is reminiscent of the numerous Achaemenid period stamps and impressions found from Mesopotamia to Egypt showing the 'Persian Hero' as

---

[1] Boardman, *GGFR*, p. 214.

[2] WD **3A**, WD **10A**, WD **11B**, WD **12**, WD **24** (pl XIX.1–3).

Master of Animals;[3] indeed, there are three such images among the Daliyeh bullae.[4] The 'Persian Hero' on some examples, although not those from Daliyeh, seems to assume a pose similar to that of the WD **47** figure; arms out, but elbows flexed, one leg extended.[5] On many of these seals good parallels are also found which help to identify the slender animals on WD **47** as lions; often the hero handles them in exactly the same fashion as the figure on WD **47**.[6]

However, the figure on WD **47** is nude, a condition never contemplated by the 'Persian Hero' or his Mesopotamian glyptic ancestors. The influence on WD **47** of Near Eastern/Achaemenid glyptic conventions is obvious, but the nudity in addition to the more vigorous stance of the hero on WD **47** also suggests Greek precedents. For example, an identification of the WD **47** figure as Herakles is slightly bolstered by the peculiar 'rays' of hair that project from the back of his head. These resemble the tufts of fur on Herakles' head, visible on WD **39** (pl VI.2), which represented the head of the Nemean lion.[7] A number of Greek-influenced Phoenician scarabs depict clearly identifiable nude Herakles figures wrestling a single animal.[8]

There are also precedents for seeing the WD **47** figure in the guise of Herakles as Master of Animals. A Greek scarab of the Archaic period shows Herakles wearing the lion skin on his head and grasping flanking winged horses.[9] The Master of Animals, however, is not always Herakles. At least one Archaic Greek seal shows an anonymous nude Master of Animals.[10]

The most compelling interpretation of WD **47** is that it shows Herakles, but in a hybrid composition related to sixth- and fifth-century Phoenician and Greco-Phoenician glyptic representations of the Egypto-Phoenician god Bes.[11] On some seals, Bes, who is often but not always nude, may appear like Herakles smiting or wrestling the lion;[12] on others, he is Master of Animals, flanked by a variety of creatures.[13] A

---

[3] Cf. Legrain, *Culture*, pl LVII; Bregstein, *Seal Use*, nos. 1–51; Boardman, 'Pyramidal', pp. 33ff., nos. 106–15, pl 5; Petrie, Mackay, Wainwright, *Meydum*, pls 35–6, no. 25.

[4] WD **17**, WD **36**, WD **51** (pl XVII.1–3).

[5] Legrain, *Culture*, pl LVI.905; pl LVII.911, 923

[6] Legrain, *Culture*, pl LVI.901, 903, 905, 906.

[7] For other examples of Herakles in the lion skin, see discussion of WD **39**, p. 90ff.

[8] Cf., for example, Moscati, *Phoenicians*, p. 518 and cat. no. 846, from Ibiza, Spain.

[9] Boardman, *AG Gems*, no. 80 and pp. 49–50.

[10] Richter, MMA, 38 = Richter, *EGGE*, 98 = Boardman, *AG Gems*, 135, a nude youth holding flanking, rearing horses, which Richter compares to a similar motif on a Clazomenian sarcophagus in the British Museum.

[11] See *LIMC*, 'Bes', and 'Bes (Cypri et in Phoenicia)'. Cf. also Boardman, *AG Gems*, chap. 4, *passim*; and Walters, *BMC*, p. xxx; V. Wilson, 'The Iconography of Bes with Particular Reference to the Cypriote Evidence', *Levant* 7 (1975) 77–103. Cf. also discussion of WD **5/16B** (p. 107, above) and WD **21B** (p. 110, above).

[12] Walters, *BMC*, 368; *LIMC*, s.v. 'Bes', p. 111. Cf. Walters, *BMC*, 279, a green jasper scarab, which is reminiscent of WD **42**; Richter, MMA, 16, green jasper; *ibid.*, 17, carnelian scarab; all from the sixth century.

[13] Cf. de Ridder, *Collection*, nos. 2767–8 carnelian, 'from Phoenicia', and de Ridder, *Collection*, no. 2772, green jasper from Byblos; Johns, 'Excavations', pl XIV, 935 = fig. 85, green jasper; R. D. Barnett and C. Mendleson, eds., *Tharros*, (British Museum, London, 1987) pl 59, b8/18 = Walters, *BMC*, 368, green jasper. Cf. *LIMC*, 'Bes', p. 111; Boardman, *AG Gems*, no. 64; Walters, *BMC*, 348, from Cyprus (note that the position of Bes' legs is similar to that on WD **47**). Cf. an unprovenanced Archaic chalcedony scaraboid in Paris (Boardman, *AG Gems*, no. 65 [Bibliothèque Nationale]); the Bes-like creature holds apart inverted lions and stands in the same position as the

glass scarab, reportedly found at Ashkelon provides an interesting comparison; here a naked Bes grasps flanking inverted lions of the same sort seen on WD **47**.[14]

A final curious parallel is provided by a Phoenician scarab ('fifth/fourth century') from Ibiza on which a bearded warrior in a tunic advances to his right, just as on WD **47**.[15] Unlike the WD **47** warrior's symmetrical adversaries, the objects this warrior grasps in his extended arms—a severed head and an axe—do not 'match', but the overall composition is strikingly similar.

Thus WD **47** is most likely an glyptic palimpsest, combining elements of Mesopotamian, Phoenician and Greek traditions. The Phoenicians were especially prone to such scramblings in their artistic creations. Perhaps WD **47** preserves an example of Phoenician workmanship. If WD **47** comes from a (cheaper) bronze ring, it might reflect a local, even Samarian, work, produced away from an artistic center like Sidon, but dependent on it for prototypes and patterns.

WD **47** comes from a fourth-century finger ring, possibly produced in Palestine from bronze.

---

figure on WD **47**. Note the cylinder impressions from Nippur (Bregstein, *Seal Use*, nos. 206–7, 210). See also Spier, *Ancient Gems*, nos. 103–4.

[14] L. Y. Rahmani, 'A Phoenician Scarab from Ashkelon', *'Atiqot* [English Series] XI (1976) 110–11, pl 31.3.

[15] Moscati, *Phoenicians*, cat. no. 840, steatite, in a silver mount.

G.   SINGLE ANIMALS

WD 45. Winged Boar Protome

(PLATE XII.3)

Mus. Inv. 942
Loose sealing
Image size: 1.7 cm x 1 cm
Bulla size: 1.7 cm x 1.4 cm
Clay colour: reddish brown
String preserved; left and right of horizontal image
Papyrus imprint
Seal type: metal finger ring

THE profile of the broad, leaf-shaped bezel of a metal finger ring is easily discerned on WD **45**. This is a late-fifth/early fourth century bezel type[1] found frequently among the Wadi Daliyeh bullae.

Although much obscured by abrasion and misleading losses, WD **45** portrays the winged forepart (protome) of a boar flying in profile to the viewer's left. The boar extends both forelegs sharply forward. Below the long snout a curved tusk emerges from the short lower jaw. Just under the upper edge of the impression faint traces of the mane bristles that no Greek or Greco-Persian boar lacks may still be seen. In place of normal hindquarters, this boar has two wings arranged 'scissors fashion' and curling gently upward at the ends. Each wing seems to have two parallel ranks of feathers, although the feathers survive only on the lower rank of the upper (near) wing.

Traditionally hostile creatures of the forests and mountains, boars wreak havoc in numerous Greek myths and fragments of legendary lore.[2] The fact that in some variants a boar deals death to both Attis and Adonis, two 'Oriental' figures from the Greek point of view, is intriguing but probably insignificant here.[3]

Archaic and Classical Greek coins often displayed truncated versions of real and supernatural creatures.[4] In fact, a lion forepart appears on two fourth-century Samarian

---

[1] Boardman, *GGFR*, p. 214.

[2] Both Artemis and Ares are associated with boars. The most famous is probably the Kalydonian boar, sent as an agent of destruction by Artemis (*Iliad* IX. 538ff). As a boy on Mt. Parnassus, Odysseus was gored by a wild boar, the cause of his famous scar (*Odyssey* XIX. 439).

[3] Attis: Paus., VII, 17. 10–12; Arnobius, *Adv. Nat.* V, 5ff. For the birth and death of Adonis: Apollod., *Bibl.*, III, 14, 4; Ovid *Met.* 10.298ff. J. G. Frazer's *Adonis Attis Osiris* (London, 1903) is still a fascinating work. The Lydian King Croesus' son was killed during a boar hunt on Mt. Olympos in Mysia (Herodotus 1.34ff); his name was Atys.

[4] Winged protome of a griffin: Jenkins, *Coins*, 195 (a hekte of Phokaia, *c*.460); winged protome of a horse: Jenkins, *Coins*, 190 (a gold stater of Lampsakos, 450–430; cf. Kraay, *Coins*, 74, a similar image on an electrum stater, *c*.500); a winged lion forepart: Jenkins, *Coins*, 48 (*c*.480, a gold hekte of Lesbos).

issues, and a horse protome appears on one.[5] The forepart of a winged boar appears on the obverse of coins minted in Asia Minor in the late sixth century.[6] Both wingless and winged boar foreparts appeared on Lycian coins of the early fifth century.[7] While the boar on WD **45** differs from those on the coins in being more elongated to fit within the leaf-shaped oval of the ring,[8] it is identical to the numismatic device, notwithstanding the fact that these parallels antedate the Samaria Papyri by over a century.

Two Archaic or early Classical Greek seals,[9] one a scaraboid, the other of unknown form, depict the forepart of a winged boar.[10] The same design appears on a group of Archaic scarabs whose provenances in East Greece and the Aegean islands mirror the distribution of the motif on coins.[11]

Boardman dubs the winged boar foreparts on these gems a 'special problem', wondering if 'the Ionian preference for winged demons may have suggested this type',[12] and noting that the design appears on Etruscan[13] as well as some Greco-Phoenician green jasper scarabs from Phoenicia and Tharros.[14] More recently he has

---

[5] Meshorer-Qedar, *Coinage of Samaria*, nos. 13–14 (lion); no. 24 (horse). Meshorer cites coins of Cypriote Amathus as possible prototypes for the lions (34).

[6] Polykrates, tyrant of Samos, issued a series of drachms with the forepart of a winged boar on the obverse (Kraay, *Coins*, 96–7). Cf. also coins minted around 500 by Mytilene on Lesbos (Jenkins, *Coins*, 53; electrum hekte [one-sixth of a stater]) and (probably) by Ialysos on Rhodes (Kraay, *Coins*, 94) and Klazomenae on the central coast of Asia Minor (Jenkins, *Coins*, 24, silver didrachm [= Kraay, *Coins*, 112]); a winged boar was said once to have ravaged the territory of Klazomenae (Aelian *Hist. anim.* 12.38, a late source).

[7] Kraay, *Coins*, 983 (wingless); Hill, *BMC Coins*, 18 (Lycia), pl 6, 16.

[8] Cf. Boardman, *AG Gems*, 376, a winged lion forepart with similarly elongated wings.

[9] Boardman, *AG Gems*, p. 152.

[10] Boardman, *AG Gems*, 558 (= *AGDS* I.1 [Munich], no. 172 [A 1370], bought in Rome); Boardman, *AG Gems*, 559, unknown form and location (= Lippold, *Gemmen*, pl 82.13).

   Cf. also Boardman, *AG Gems*, 560, scaraboid showing the forepart of a winged boar attached to one human leg and male genitals (= Boardman, *GGFR*, fig. 196 = Richter, *EGGE*, 179 = E. Babélon, *Collection Pauvert de la Chapelle . . . Bibliothèque Nationale* [Paris, 1899] no. 44).

   Cf. also *Ashmolean/EGFR*, 56 (1941.113) (= J. Boardman, *Island Gems* [London, 1963] 231) a serpentine lentoid depicting a winged boar forepart which Boardman dates to the second half of the sixth century.

[11] Boardman, *GGFR*, 399 (Basel, Dreyfus Coll.) and Richter, *EGGE*, 179 (= Boardman, *AG Gems*, 500 = *AGDS* II [Berlin], no. 103 = Furtwängler, *Beschreibung*, 166, from Mytilene). In his entry on the lentoid stamp seal (*Ashmolean/EGFR*, 56), Boardman notes both the Dreyfus carnelian scarab and another similar—apparently unpublished—scarab in the Seyrig Collection. Cf. also Boardman, *AG Gems*, 498–9, 501 (= *AGDS* II [Berlin], no. 102 = Furtwängler, *Beschreibung*, 165, from Kythera).

[12] Boardman, *AG Gems*, pp. 146–7.

[13] Boardman, *AG Gems*, p. 147 n. 11.

[14] Boardman, *AG Gems*, p. 147 n. 10, 11.

   For the Greco-Phoenician gems, cf. C. W. Mansell, (n.t.), *Gazette Archéologique* IV (1878) 50–53, three figs. on p. 50. The first, 'de Phénicie même', is in the Cabinet des Médailles, Bibliothèque Nationale, Paris, Collection de Luynes no. 292. The two others, one a green jasper, the other a carnelian scarab, came from the cemetery at Tharros on Sardinia. By the Persian period at least, boars had entered Phoenician iconography. Another green jasper scarab, in the Metropolitan Museum (Richter, *MMA*, 16 [37.11.7]), shows Bes with a lion slung over his shoulder and an inverted boar clutched in one hand.

   There appear to be two 'boar' items among the excavated Tharros material in the British Museum: a bone amulet from Grave 9 which 'should perhaps be considered a Sicilian or Greek import' (Barnett-Mendleson, *Tharros*,

stated that the device of joined animal foreparts or 'animal whorls' (a category to which winged boar foreparts belong) is a Greek motif, copied occasionally by the Phoenicians.[15] There is some disagreement over the date of the Phoenician green jasper scarabs; Acquaro suggests the fifth and fourth centuries, while Boardman opts for the Archaic period (sixth and early fifth centuries).[16]

Whether or not the motif originated in the East Greek world, the presence during the Persian period of winged boar foreparts on Phoenician seals in the 'green jasper series' raises the possibility that the ring behind WD **45** came to Samaria from Phoenicia. While it repeats a motif found on the 'green jasper series', WD **45** belongs to a different seal tradition. The ring shape places WD **45** beyond the Archaic period, and there is no reason to doubt it was produced in the early to mid-fourth century, contemporary with the Samaria Papyri.[17]

Might the appearance of WD **45** in Persian Palestine (and originally Phoenicia?) reflect Persian cultural influence in the area?[18] The boar apparently had a special significance in Persia. In a prophecy, Cyrus the Great was described as an animal 'more courageous than a boar'.[19] Later, it was associated with the god Mithra and figured as a royal symbol on Sassanian seals.[20]

On Greco-Persian gems of the Classical period, one finds several portraits of single boars,[21] also scenes of hunters in Median dress attacking wild boar on foot[22] and from

---

115, cat. no. 9/37), and a green jasper scarab with the forepart of a boar joined to the inverted forepart of a lion (cat. no. 31/19 = Walters, *BMC*, 421). Barnett also mentions a green jasper scarab showing a boar discovered in Tomb 2 of Canon Spano's nineteenth century excavations at Tharros (p. 31). Cf. also the serpentine scarab in Hanover with a lion fighting a boar (*AGDS* IV [Hanover], 13 [K1843]).

Petrological analysis of the 'green jasper' (actually greenstone facies) scarabs has demonstrated that the stone has the same 'fingerprint' regardless of whether a scarab comes from the eastern or western Mediterranean (Boardman, 'Scarabs', p. 100). Thus, although some scholars believe that the workshop was on Sardinia, questions about the location of the actual 'green jasper workshops' remain unanswered. Cf. S. Moscati and A. M. Costa, 'L'origine degli scarabei in diaspro,' *Rivista di Studi Fenici* 10 (1982) 203–11.

[15] Boardman, 'Scarabs', 102.

This may well be true, but could the animal 'whorls' on Neo-Babylonian and Achaemenid seals perhaps have been a prior influence on the eastern Greek motif? Cf. Legrain, *Culture*, 872–85.

[16] Barnett-Mendleson, *Tharros*, 43.

[17] This might support Acquaro's later dating of the 'green jasper series'. On the other hand, the lack of any seals in the 'green jasper series' at Daliyeh could also indicate that this tradition had died out by the fourth century, giving way to a preference for finger rings.

[18] Older sources, such as Mansell (see above n. 14) mention that the Syrians called the month which ended with the summer solstice *Khaziran* ('boar') and celebrated the death of Adonis at this time, the idea being that a celestial boar devours the sun. The present editor is reluctant to make much of the Adonis-boar connection in view of the lateness of the sources on Adonis and also in view of the fact that little of a concrete nature is known about the earlier manifestations of the god, including his real name.

[19] Athen. 14, 633e. Cf. *Wörterbuch der Mythologie*, H. W. von Haussig, ed. (Stuttgart, 1961) 'Eber', and K. Erdmann, 'Eberdarstellung und Ebersymbolic in Iran', *Bonner Jahrbücher* 147 (1942) 345 ff.

[20] *Wörterbuch der Mythologie*, H. W. von Haussig, ed. (Stuttgart, 1961) *s.v.* 'Eber'.

[21] Boardman, *GGFR*, 914, 945; Boardman, *GGFR*, 897 shows a boar attacked by two dogs. On the back of Boardman, *GGFR*, 628 (= Galling, 'Bildsiegel', no. 42) a two-sided scaraboid without recorded provenance (its whereabouts are ambiguous as well; Galling says it is in the British Museum, but Boardman records it as being in Leningrad), appears a galloping boar surrounded by an inscription in Aramaic. Galling admits his reading is questionable but records the inscription as *mtrṣtd hmd nk* [..]. The element *mtr* indicates it probably belonged to a

horseback.[23] Boars do not really enter the Mesopotamian-style[24] cylinder seal repertoire until the Persian period when a number of cylinder seals, stylistically related to the Greco-Persian series and probably of Lydian origin,[25] show a hunter confronting a boar.[26] This motif also appears on a series of stylistically different cylinder seals with provenances in North Mesopotamia and Susa;[27] this more linear tradition is probably descended from Neo-Elamite styles[28] which are perhaps the ultimate source for the Greco-Persian image.

As is well known, among many Semitic peoples swine seem to have been more or less taboo; it is proverbial in the Bible.[29] Apparently the Egyptians also had dietary laws relating to swine,[30] and the sow was a popular Egyptian fertility symbol.[31] As animals sacred to various gods of Babylon, swine were eaten only during selected

---

Persian. Boardman groups *GGFR*, 628 with his 'plain eastern gems' and suggests, without much evidence, a source in the Syria-Palestine (Boardman, *GGFR*, p. 209).

A limestone sarcophagus, *c.*470–460, from Golgoi on Cyprus (now in the British Museum) is decorated with a low relief frieze of Cypriot(?) warriors, dressed as Greek hoplites, and hunting a bull and a boar (illustrated in V. Tatton-Brown, *Ancient Cyprus* [British Museum, London, 1987] fig. 80).

[22] Boardman, *GGFR*, 926 (= Richter, *EGGE*, 498 = Athens, National Museum, numismatic section inv. 890), a chalcedony scaraboid. Also cf. Boardman, *GGFR*, 885, 972.

[23] Boardman, *GGFR*, 905, 924–5, fig. 290, no. 132 (not illustrated). Cf. the list on p. 440.

[24] Boars seem much more significant in Indo-European than in Semitic cultures. Note that E. Herzfeld (*Iran in the Ancient East* [Oxford, 1944]) mentions a Jemdet Nasr (fourth millennium) stamp seal with a boar from Tepe Giyan in Iran (p. 70, fig. 135). There are no boars on any of the numerous Mesopotamian cylinder seals published in Legrain, *Culture* before the Persian period.

J. G. Frazer collected boar-related rituals and symbolism in *The Golden Bough, Part V, Spirits of the Corn and of the Wild, Part II* (London, 1980 [repr. 3rd ed., 1913]).

[25] Collon, *First Impressions*, 93, *re*: no. 427.

[26] Wiseman, *Cylinder*, 111 (British Museum 89144 [= Collon, *First Impressions*, 698]); Collon, *First Impressions*, 922, from Babylon (Berlin VA 6967), p. 155; Boardman, *GGFR*, 850 (Boston Museum of Fine Arts 03.1011); Boardman, *GGFR*, no. 141 (Cooke Collection). Cf. the cylinder seal impressions from Nippur in Legrain, *Culture*, 987, 990 (impressions from Nippur) and in Bregstein, *Seal Use*, nos. 145–51 and 178. See also A. Goetze, 'Three Achaemenian Tags', *Berytus* 8 (1944) 99 (seal b, from Telloh in southern Mesopotamia?) and pl 11, b; also Schmidt, *Persepolis II*, pl 10, no. 34.

For stamp seal impressions cf. Legrain, *Culture*, 819, 824–5; also Legrain, *Ur*, 803, the impression of a 'lozenge-shaped ring stone' decorated with a lion and boar; also Schmidt, *Persepolis II*, pl 14, no. 73 (a single attacking boar).

The same motif, a mounted hunter accompanied by his dog and attacking a boar, appears on a Phrygian limestone stele in Istanbul dated to the end of the fifth century (illustrated in Turkish Ministry of Culture, *Anatolian Civilisations: Vol.II* [Istanbul], B 146).

[27] P. Amiet, *Glyptique Susienne* (Paris: 1972) no. 2204, found in the French excavations at Susa; Collon, *First Impressions*, no. 426 (= Wiseman, *Cylinder*, 99 = British Museum 102557).

[28] Collon, *First Impressions*, p. 93.

[29] Lev 11:7; Deut 14:8.

[30] Swineherds seem to have been the 'untouchables' of Egypt (Herodotus 2.47); cf. also, *inter alia*, Josephus *Ap.* 2.13.

[31] Barnett-Mendleson, *Tharros*, p. 115. The boar, on the other hand, seems to have no place in Egyptian iconography.

festivals.[32] Lucian, in the early second century CE, notes that pigs were taboo at the Syrian holy city of Hierapolis.[33]

Wild boar posed a real threat to growing crops in Palestine and supplied the metaphor in Ps 80:13 for an enemy who has laid Israel waste.[34] In the nineteenth century, naturalist H. B. Tristram described the ravages of the herds of wild boar who lived in the 'reedy marshes and thickets along the banks of the Jordan from Jericho to the Lake of Gennesaret'.[35] Samarians in the fourth century were no doubt acquainted with wild boar and would have known perfectly well what the strange creature on WD **45** was supposed to be.

In view of biblical Israelite taboos, it is surprising to find a boar device here and also possibly on WD **23**. But the supposed Israelite horror of swine is actually less than monolithic. For example, according to 1 Chr 24:15, חזיר ('swine', 'boar') seems to have been the eponym of an Aaronid priestly house in Jerusalem.[36] The preponderance of Jewish names in the Samaria Papyri increases the likelihood that the seal ring behind WD **45** may have belonged to a YHWH-worshipping citizen of Samaria. However, it remains an open question whether designs on seal rings from this time and place reflect religious conviction or practice in any way; WD **23** and WD **45** may ultimately tell us nothing about kosher laws in the early Second Temple Period.

In summary, even though no metal finger rings comparable to WD **45** have been found, there are abundant precedents for the winged boar forepart on Archaic Greek coins from Asia Minor, including Rhodes and Lycia. In addition, the motif is found on Archaic and early Classical engraved gems in both the Greek and Greco-Phoenician idioms. When the Greek examples have provenances, they seem to come from Ionia and southern Asia Minor.

The apparent gap between these parallels and the presumed early/mid fourth-century date of the WD **45** ring is not troubling. In the first place, too little is still known about the period for such a 'gap' to be very worrisome. Furthermore, the glyptic parallels themselves lack firm dates, provenances and archaeological contexts. The presumed gap is lessened somewhat by a gold clothing ornament found in a fifth century Scythian tomb.[37] It is an almost exact replica of the winged boar forepart on the late-Archaic Greek coins. Finally, there is always the argument that like the

---

[32] *Interpreter's Dictionary of the Bible*, s.v. 'Swine.'

[33] Lucian, *De dea Syria* 54. A sow appears on a late Punic stele from Carthage next to a knife and an altar, suggesting that at this time, the sow was a sacrificial animal (S. Moscati, *I fenici e cartagine* [Turin, 1972] 279).

[34] See *ABD*, s.v. 'Zoology'.

[35] H. B. Tristram, *The Natural History of the Bible*[9] (London, 1898) 54.

[36] F. M. Cross kindly drew this passage to my attention. The Chronicler is probably writing in the Persian period; the list of priestly families in 1 Chronicles 24 has no parallel in Samuel-Kings and probably should be understood as post-Exilic material. There clearly seems to have been such a family in Jerusalem in the time of Ezra when a 'chief of the people' named Ḥēzîr one of the signatories to Ezra's covenant (Neh 10:21). A well-known landmark in Jerusalem's Kidron Valley is the Hellenistic Tomb of the priestly family, the Bene Hezir.

[37] *From the Lands of the Scythians: Ancient Treasures from the Museums of the USSR, 3000 B.C.–100 B.C.* = *Metropolitan Museum of Art Bulletin*, XXXII, no. 5 (1973–74) [Special Issue] pl 9, cat. no. 51, from Taman, Seven Brothers, Kurgan 2; cf. M. I. Artomonov, *The Splendor of Scythian Art* (New York, 1969) figs. 43–4, 46–50. Other such ornaments also seem to copy Greek numismatic devices, such as the owl of Athens.

Scythian ornament, the WD **45** ring came from a provincial workshop still using old patterns that had disappeared from 'mainstream' glyptic art.

WD 55. Lion Scratching His Ear

(PLATE XIII.1)

Mus. Inv. 952

Loose sealing

Image size: 1.2 cm x 1.5 cm

Bulla size: 1.8 cm x 1.9 cm

Clay colour: black (burnt)

String not preserved; string holes left and right of image

Papyrus imprint

Seal type: ringstone? scaraboid?

THIS broad oval sealing has survived in its complete circumference. The shape and raised outline suggests a shallowly carved seal, perhaps set in a metal ring mount. The overall condition of the sealing is fairly good although there is a deep gash across the lion's haunch.

WD 55 is one of the most charming of the Wadi Daliyeh impressions. It depicts a shaggy-maned lion scratching himself behind the ear with his right rear paw. The contrast between the innate majesty of lions and this homely, doglike activity animates the tiny composition.

The scratching lion motif also appears on at least three bullae in the Hecht Group of Samarian sealings, none duplicating WD 55 and all carved more deeply and more crudely. Two are duplicates of each other and come from a more narrowly horizontal seal than WD 55;[1] the third bulla probably came from a seal carved in the same workshop as the seal which produced the duplicate bullae. This is thus a design attested in three versions in fourth-century Samaria.

The reclining lion's bristly back, seen essentially from the side, arches across the centre of the sealing and repeats the shape of the outline of the seal. The lion's broad head is seen frontally and from above. His long, tufted tail curls casually around his left leg. There is nothing hieratic here, nor are there any decorative anatomy patterns to suggest oriental parallels. The style is Greek; Boardman would perhaps say the lion was behaving in a Greek manner.[2]

On a number of Archaic Greek coins, animals curve around to scratch or lick themselves.[3] However, while mules, cows, and dogs may stoop to such undignified

---

[1] Pl XXIII.11; see also Stern/Hecht, 'Hoard', drawing pl 1.7, 8, 10.

[2] Boardman, *GGFR*, p. 314. Cf. Boardman's discussion of Greek, Court Style, and Mixed Style animals in Boardman, *GGFR*, p. 312. There is a possibility that there are Phoenician traits in the background of WD 55. A seventh-century Phoenician ivory from Nimrud of a crouching calf with its head curling toward its hind feet does not seem terribly different in concept from WD 55 (Moscati, *Phoenicians*, cat. no. 99 [British Museum WA 118140].

[3] *The Garrett Collection II* [Auction catalogue, October 16–18, 1984; Bank Leu, Zürich] lot no. 213), a cow scratching her nose with her hind leg on a rare Euboian silver tetradrachm of *c*.500 (see also Kraay, *Coins*, 269–71).

behaviour on official coinage, lions generally do not.[4] Scratching animals do show up on Archaic Greek seals; indeed, the motif seems to go as far back as Minoan glyptic art.[5] Especially during the Archaic period, Greek artists seem to have enjoyed fitting the rounded contours of scratching animals into the circular or oval frame of a seal.[6] Two Greco-Persian tabloid (multi-faced) seals in Munich assigned to the fifth century include a scratching dog among their various animal and human subjects.[7]

Cyprus is the putative source of Boardman's late Archaic 'Group of the Cyprus Lions',[8] a group of seals which includes two scratching felines. The provenances of this category (c.500) are Cypriote and Phoenician, with parallels 'in green jasper, the Phoenician material, but Greek in style [.]'[9] The first of these 'Cyprus Lions' is in the de Clercq collection.[10] The second, a ringstone in Nicosia whose shallow engraving recalls the style of WD **55**, also includes a large murex shell, the source of Phoenician purple dye.[11] Both lions arch their backs, curl their tails and extend their left leg downward in exactly the same manner as the WD **55** lion. The elongated legs on these two lions are like those of WD **55**; the heads are viewed frontally and from above as on WD **55**.

There are some subtle differences in style, if not pose, between these 'Cyprus Lions' and WD **55**. The two 'Cyprus Lions' mentioned above have sketchy manes and elongated, almost emaciated bodies, particularly around the shoulder and chest— several ribs protrude clearly on both. By contrast, the WD **55** lion seems sturdier, with muscular shoulders, a broader head and a rich mane. However, damage to the sealing surface makes it impossible to say whether there were once any visible ribs. On the other hand, the two 'Cyprus Lions' seals differ from each other in that the first has a hatched border making it look more archaic than the second, which lacks any indication of border at all.

A mule turns back to lick its right hind leg on a Lycian silver stater of the mid-fifth century dynast Kprlli (Hill, *BMC Coins,* 28 [Lycia] pl IV.10, and Mørkholm-Zahle, 'Coinage', pl III, nos. 93–7).

[4] But note that by the Classical period, Greek artists depicted lions only on second-hand evidence. G. M. A. Richter (*Animals in Greek Sculpture* [New York, 1930] 8) recognized that dogs provided the model for most Classical lions. Boardman suggests as perhaps Greco-Punic the unusual motif of a lion with its head turned back to inspect its genitals (Boardman, *AG Gems*, 401 and p. 128, with references to two Greco-Punic seals from Sardinia).

[5] *AGDS* II, Berlin, no. 40, a late Minoan II chalcedony lentoid with a lion scratching himself on the head with his hind paw (= Furtwängler, *Beschreibung*, pl I). For similar late Helladic II and Late Minoan II lentoid seals, see *AGDS* I,1, Munich, nos. 61–2.

[6] Boardman, *AG Gems*, 569; Boardman, *GGFR*, 521 (Moscow Historical Museum 10561); Legrain, *Ur*, no. 830, impression of a Persian period metal finger ring; Boardman, *GGFR*, 400 = Boardman, *AG Gems*, no. 529, an Archaic scarab from Cyprus (Nicosia Museum no. 1964).

[7] Boardman's 'Arndt Group'; cf. Boardman, *GGFR*, p. 314, fig. 289 = *AGDS* I,1, Munich, no. 249, pls 28–9: red jasper; *AGDS* I,1, Munich, no. 250, pls 28–9: a cornelian pyramidal seal with a pair of boars, a running goat, a dog scratching itself and a fox.

[8] Boardman, *GGFR*, p. 152. Cf. also Boardman, *AG Gems*, pp. 130ff.

[9] Boardman, *GGFR*, p. 152. For example, Boardman, *AG Gems*, no. 478, a green jasper scarab bought in Athens, now in Boston (Boston MFA 27.679): a bull scratches his nose with his hind leg.

[10] Boardman, *GGFR*, 385 = Boardman, *AG Gems*, no. 424, pl 30 = de Ridder, *Collection*, 2794: a chalcedony scaraboid from Beirut; a lion (or panther?) scratches his nose with his hind leg as a cock and an Ethiopian look on, from Beirut with a Cypriote inscription. Boardman thinks the 'animal mixture' may derive from hieroglyph devices.

[11] Carnelian, Boardman, *GGFR*, 386 = Boardman, *AG Gems*, no. 425, pl 30 (Nicosia Museum no. 1960).

It should be noted that these two 'Cyprus Lions', which Boardman assigns to the same hand,[12] are carved in different materials and appear on similar, but not identical, seal types. Boardman also believes the same artist carved a third seal in the 'Cyprus Lions' group: a black jasper scaraboid from Cyprus depicting a pair of symmetrically positioned fighting lions.[13] The heads of both lions on this seal are a little stockier than those of the two scratching lions and are held at the same angle, in relation to the body and extended forelegs, as the WD **55** lion. The duelling felines are more like WD **55** in that they are sleeker, without the emaciated look of the scratching lions. Also strikingly similar are the bristles down to the middle of the back, and the way the herringbone manes on both the WD **55** lion and the two fighting lions are cut away on the shoulder. As with the two scratching 'Cyprus Lions' and the WD **55** lion, these two lions have very long legs and like the 'Cyprus Lions', WD **55** could have come from a scaraboid or a ringstone. The fighting lions seal provides the connection to WD **55** and leads to the ascribing of WD **55** to the same workshop or, at least, artistic tradition.[14] Boardman includes in his fourth century 'Common Style' category a lion with prey which looks very similar to the 'Cyprus Lions' and may relate to WD **55**.[15]

With its many Archaic period parallels, it is possible that WD **55** may have been an heirloom sealstone of the first half of the fifth century. On the other hand, the cited unexcavated parallels cannot be solidly dated and could be later, or WD **55** and its associated bullae in the Hecht Group could be examples of the survival into the fourth century of an Archaic seal motif, a phenomenon suspected in the case of other Wadi Daliyeh seals. It is possible that the WD **55** lion is an 'import' from Phoenicia proper or Cyprus, while a local Samarian workshop produced the other two seals from Samaria with scratching lions.[16]

---

[12] Boardman, *GGFR*, p. 185, entry for 384.

[13] Boardman, *GGFR*, 384 = Boardman, *AG Gems*, no. 423 = Zazoff, *AG*, pl 24.1 = Richter, *EGGE*, 201 = Walters, *BMC*, no. 450 (British Museum 1909.6–15.1): inscribed in Cypriote script with the Greek name, Aristokles.

[14] A carnelian seal from Carthage in the Musée de Carthage with a scratching horse (Moscati, *Phoenicians*, no. 273, '4th–3rd century B.C.') gives evidence that the motif continues to appear in Phoenician contexts for several centuries.

[15] Boardman, *GGFR*, 619, an agate scaraboid in the Péronne Danicourt Collection. The herringbone mane, rib incisions and curly tail recall both WD **55** and the 'Cyprus Lions'.

[16] Lions were apparently popular in Samaria; they appear several times on seals (WD **37** and WD **55**; the Hecht Group lions [pl XXIII.10–12]; cf. Stern/Hecht, 'Hoard', drawings pl 1) and on Samarian coins (Meshorer-Qedar, *Coinage of Samaria*, nos. 13–14, 22, 42, 54, 62). The lions on the coins and sealings look quite different from each other, and it seems unlikely that the various engravers of any of the lion coins worked on the seals with lion designs.

WD 37. Lion

(PLATE XIII.2)

Mus. Inv. 934
Loose sealing
Image size: 1.1 cm x 1.4 cm
Bulla size: 1.3 cm x 1.5 cm
Clay colour: reddish brown
String preserved; left and right of horizontal image
Papyrus fragments on back
Papyrus imprint
Seal type: scaraboid? metal finger ring?

ONLY the general outlines of the design on WD **37** remain. A slight imprint of the seal rim appears at the bottom centre of the impression; otherwise no edges survive to indicate whether the original seal was a ring or an engraved gem. The shallow impression was probably never very distinct. The duplicate sealing of WD **37** in the Hecht Group (Pl XXIII.9) is too fragmentary to provide any supplementary details.

The single lion on WD **37** stands in profile to the right with his head turned frontally toward the viewer. His substantial mane may once have been quite impressive, covering his right (near) shoulder and extending almost to the middle of his back. Of the lion's two forelegs only one paw is still clearly visible, and it is difficult to tell to which leg it belongs. The hind legs are clearer, with the lion's (near) right leg placed a little behind the left. Only the tail is absolutely unambiguous, trailing down behind him and terminating in a tiny tuft.

Lions are a common subject in both eastern and western glyptic art. The naturalistic depiction of the lion on WD **37** most probably puts it stylistically in the Greek, Greco-Persian, or Greco-Phoenician rather than purely Near Eastern glyptic tradition.[1] However, a Samarian predisposition for the lion motif would be logical in view of the strong Syro-Palestinian—including Israelite—Iron Age tradition of seals with lions.[2]

---

[1] The categories are very fluid and include Greco-Persian, Greco-Phoenician, Orientalizing, East Greek, etc. Cf. Boardman, *GGFR*, 844, 866, 889, 907, 909, 959, 995 (all categorized as Greco-Persian); Boardman, 'Pyramidal', pl 3; pl 6. 140 and pl 8. 194 (East Greek, Lydian, 'Orientalizing', etc.).

[2] See in particular the well-known lost seal of Shema' servant of Yarob'am found at Megiddo (Hestrin, Dayagi-Mendels, *Inscribed Seals,* no. 3 = Galling, 'Bildsiegel', no. 17); cf. Galling, 'Bildsiegel', nos. 18–22; A. Lemaire, 'Nouveau sceau nord-ouest sémitique avec un lion rugissant', *Semitica* 29 (1979) 67–9; *idem,* 'Trois sceaux inscrits inedits avec lion rugissant', *Semitica* 39 (1990) 13–21; Avigad, 'Seals and Sealings', *IEJ* 14 (1964) 190–93; *idem,* 'A Group of Hebrew Seals from the Hecht Collection', *Festschrift Reuben Hecht* (Jerusalem, 1979) no. 2; *idem,* 'A New Seal Depicting a Lion', *Michmanim* 6 (1992) *33–6; and Ashmolean/*ANES III*, p. 40. O. Keel describes the roaring lion as originally a north Syrian motif adopted in Phoenician- and Aramaic-speaking circles (Keel-Uehlinger, *Göttinnen,* 214).

With at least five seals depicting single lions attested between the Wadi Daliyeh[3] and Hecht Group bullae,[4] and five different versions of lions on Samarian coinage,[5] lions would appear to have been particularly favoured by the Samarians.

Achaemenid Court Style lions on seals[6] occasionally appear alone, but usually in full profile and with stylized linear ornamentation on their shoulders and ribs.[7] A crude version of this Court Style lion appears on a Samarian coin of the Persian period.[8] The WD 37 lion's mane seems more naturalistic than the bristly, almost sparse Achaemenid version.[9] Although their heads may be frontal, the seated lions on Phoenician green jasper seals also differ from WD 37.[10]

In Achaemenid art, lions may appear with frontal heads but almost exclusively in scenes where they are shown attacking another animal.[11] This convention carried over into Archaic and Classical Greek art, including seals.[12] A number of lions with frontal heads on Classical seals are shown surprised in the process of eating, and are eyeing the viewer warily.[13] On the foregoing examples of frontal headed felines, the animals are in action: attacking, eating, suckling, stalking. The WD 37 lion does not seem involved in any special enterprise. He simply stands and turns his head frontally.

Studies of single animals in profile,[14] some posing passively, appear on ring impressions from Nippur and also on Greco-Persian scaraboids and rings. The bull on

---

[3] WD **37**, WD **55** (pl XIII.1).

[4] See pl XXIII. 9–12.

[5] Meshorer-Qedar, *Coinage of Samaria*, nos. 13–14 (lion forepart), 22 (Court Style striding lion), 42 (seated Court Style lion), 54 (seated Court Style lion), 62 (frontal lion).

[6] Boardman, *GGFR*, 908 (Paris, BN 6000), a blue chalcedony scaraboid.

[7] Boardman, 'Pyramidal', p. 34. Cf. also Legrain, *Ur*, nos. 793 (impression of a conoid stamp), 794 (impression of a leaf-shaped ring bezel).

[8] Meshorer-Qedar, *Coinage of Samaria*, no. 22, a silver hemiobol from the Nablus Hoard; on the reverse the Persian king kneels with bow and spear.

[9] Cf. the lions on the Persepolis reliefs and on the glazed brick lion frieze at Susa. Legrain, *Culture*, no. 820 is an impression from Nippur of a leaf-shaped metal finger ring (the cuneiform text apparently mentions that it was a gold ring) showing a lone roaring lion walking in profile beneath a winged sun disk. Cf. also Legrain, *Ur*, for fragments of clay casts of Achaemenid metal cups elaborately decorated with abstract designs and figures, including lions (nos. 834, 836).

Stern ('Seal Impressions', 6–16 and in *Material Culture*, 209–13) discusses a group of bullae from Persian period contexts which show single lions, either seen horizontally in profile, or rampant; the latter are accompanied by Persian-style incense burners. The seals were probably of local manufacture and very crude. Stern suggests, probably correctly, that the motif was taken from more elaborate compositions on Persian seals; see Keel's comments on the subject in *Göttinnen*, 446–8. The lion on WD **37** comes from a different tradition.

[10] Moscati, *Phoenicians*, cat. nos. 655–6, 848.

[11] The best examples are the reliefs from Persepolis. Cf. Legrain, *Ur*, no. 797.

[12] Cf. Boardman, *AG Gems* (*inter alia*), 365, 391, 409, 413; Boardman, *GGFR*, 696–7, 935.

[13] Boardman, *GGFR*, 693, a gold ring, in Boston (MFA 98.785). Cf. also Boardman, *GGFR*, 619, and the design on a (Greek-style?) ring impression from Achaemenid Ur (Legrain, *Ur*, no. 803). The lion devouring his prey also appears in the de Clercq group of Phoenician rings (de Ridder, *Collection*, no. 2870 = Boardman, *GGFR*, fig. 224) and in the Hecht Group of Samarian bullae (pl XXIII.12).

[14] Legrain, *Culture*, 820 = Bregstein, *Seal Use*, no. 280; Legrain, *Culture*, 818 = Bregstein, *Seal Use*, no. 281; also Bregstein, *Seal Use*, nos. 279, 282–5 (all the above except Bregstein, *Seal Use*, no. 282 are impressions from gold or bronze rings).

a Greco-Persian 'Mixed Style' scaraboid in the Ashmolean Museum is shown in a stance like that of the WD **37** lion.[15] Stylistically, the Daliyeh lion differs from the bull whose knobby body results from free use of the drill. Nevertheless, the WD **37** lion probably fits best in the vague Greco-Persian category which allows for local workshops imitating 'pure' Greek styles as well as creating hybrids of their own. The WD **37** seal was perhaps produced purposely for a Syro-Palestinian clientele with a history of lion seals.

Finally, a possible numismatic parallel may be adduced here. This is a Siculo-Punic silver four-drachma coin of the mid-fourth century.[16] On the reverse, the bushy-maned lion who stands before a palm tree and looks out at the viewer might have provided the model for our lion on WD **37**. It is possible that the lion on this Punic coin, as well as on WD **37,** is to some degree a descendant of the Iron Age lions found on so many Syro-Palestinian seals.

---

[15] Boardman, *GGFR*, 911 = Ashmolean/*EGFR*, 181, a blue chalcedony scaraboid (Oxford 1892.1544), and Boardman, *GGFR*, pp. 317–18. Boardman dates it to the end of the fifth century and states that its engraver has made an awkward attempt at showing a frontal face.

[16] Kraay, *Coins*, 876. Kraay calls this coin 'a masterpiece'. The location of the mint of these coins is uncertain.

Gold Ring A. Eagle

(PLATE XIII. 3)

Mus. Inv. 782[1]
Seal type: Gold finger ring, narrow leaf-shaped bezel

GOLD RING A (hereafter, GR-A) was one of two gold rings with intaglio decoration purchased with the Wadi Daliyeh papyri and bullae. Frank Cross reported that there was an impressive amount of jewellery and coins offered in association with the papyri,[2] but he was able to acquire only a representative selection of the 'treasure'.

In its narrow leaf-shaped bezel, GR-A corresponds to Boardman's Type II,[3] which he locates in the mid- to late-fifth century. He notes, however, the tendency for older ring types to persist beyond the Hellenic world proper and mentions in particular his 'de Clercq Group' of gold rings with Phoenician provenances.[4] In addition, excavators at Olynthus in northeastern Greece uncovered numerous examples of bronze finger rings of the same shape as GR-A; they belong to the first half of the fourth century.[5]

Nearest the bezel, the closed hoop of the ring is carinated toward the outside, forming a triangle with the point at the top in the cross-section. As the hoop curves farther away from the bezel, it seems to flatten into a lozenge-shaped cross section. On the evidence of the photograph, there seems to be a slightly raised rib running along the middle of the inside of the hoop. The minutely elevated ridge of the bezel itself marks the transition from hoop to bezel.

The unusual border around the image[6] consists of a chain of what in more modern contexts might be called bellflowers. This chain runs more or less parallel, just inside the edge. Similar borders can occasionally be seen on coins.[7] The form of the border, which may be due to the careless use of a gouge or similar tool, along with the crudeness of the image, may signal a local source for the ring in nearby Phoenicia or even in Samaria itself which had historically, at any rate, sustained a population of craftspeople.[8]

---

[1] Currently unlocated. All discussion of GR-A is based on a single photograph. Data such as size, colour, detail of the back of the bezel, the join of the hoop to the bezel, etc. is unavailable.

[2] F. M. Cross, personal communication.

[3] Boardman, *GGFR*, fig. 217, pp. 213–15; cf. also Boardman, *GGFR*, 657–61.

[4] Boardman, *GGFR*, p. 221. Boardman, *GGFR*, 695 is an example of another fourth-century ring in a similar shape; this one from South Russia.

[5] Robinson, 'Metal', pl XXVII.

[6] Metal rings seldom had borders in the Classical period.

[7] Cf. Jenkins, *Coins*, no. 380, a tetradrachm of Messana, 425–420.

[8] Stern, 'Phoenician', 211–12.

A considerable amount of empty space surrounds the image of an eagle in profile facing to the viewer's left. The relatively narrow neck and low placement of the wings here argue against identifying the bird as a falcon, although in view of the inferior workmanship a falcon cannot be ruled out.[9] The body of the eagle is worked in an angular style with a minimum of detail. Three tail-feathers emerge below the folded wing which is defined by two smaller 'feathers' under a single larger 'feather'. The eagle's (far) right leg with one talon visible seems to be a little in advance of the left, with two rather crude and oversized talons. This bird has a bulbous eye and an equally outsized, down-curved beak.

By the Classical period, the eagle was well established as the bird of Zeus and a symbol of majesty and power. On seals, however, eagles rarely appear, although a poorly preserved bronze ring from Olynthus dating to the first half of the fourth century with a shape similar to GR-A may show an eagle posed in profile.[10]

The eagle was an especially common motif on Greek coins which were liable to be copied by other mints[11] and by gem engravers as well.[12] For example, a very crude eagle on a fifth- or fourth-century black jasper scaraboid in the Metropolitan Museum is compared by Richter to the coins of Elis. This piece also seems to have indications of a rather vestigial border that looks similar to the outline on GR-A.[13]

Possible numismatic parallels to GR-A may come from Akragas,[14] halfway between Gela and Selinus on the southern coast of Sicily, which minted eagle coins from the late sixth through the third century.[15] Of particular relevance here is a series of didrachms and tetradrachms minted in the fifth century[16] which show an eagle remarkably similar to that on GR-A. With its head erect, it (usually) looks in profile to the viewer's left. Its (far) right leg is in advance of the left with the talons of variable distinctness, depending on the issue. The tail feathers visibly separate from the wing as on GR-A. The Historisches Museum, Frankfort-am-Main, has one unimpressive Acragan didrachm which, in fact, could almost be the twin of GR-A.[17] Closer to

---

[9] Nothing about the ring or its design suggests any Egyptian elements.

[10] Robinson, 'Metal', pl XXVII, 484.

[11] Samarian coins of the fourth century imitate Sidonian and Cilician issues in particular (Meshorer-Qedar, *Coinage of Samaria*, 20).

[12] Porada, 'Greek Coin'.

[13] Richter, MMA, 128. Cf. also a Greco-Persian scaraboid at Oxford (Ashmolean/*EGFR*, no. 196 [1921.1231]) of the late fifth century displaying a bird of indeterminate species, possibly an ibis or an eagle.

[14] Jenkins, *Coins*, 140; *SNG-ANS* III, pls 26 and 28; G. K. Jenkins discusses the early Acragantine coins in *The Coinage of Gela: Antike Münzen und geschnittene Steine* II (Berlin, 1970) 162–4; cf. G. Förschner, *Münzen*, nos. 377f.

[15] In the fifth century Acragas was an active participant in the economic and political give-and-take between Greeks, native Phoenician merchants, and Punic Carthaginians as they struggled for control of the island or carried out the more day-to-day functions of Mediterranean trade. Cf. A. C. Tusa, 'Rapporti tra Greci e Punici in Sicilia attraverso l'evidenza numismatica', in *Atti del I congresso* (see above) 143; Tusa's conclusions are summarized in Moscati, *Phoenicians*, 204–5.

[16] Jenkins, *Coins*, 140. See Förschner, *Münzen*, nos. 377–80. Cf. pls 27 and 28 of *SNG-ANS* III for a good representation of the eagle series.

[17] Förschner, *Münzen*, no. 378, a silver didrachm of 500–490.

Phoenicia and Samaria, the late fifth-century Lycian dynast, Kherêi, may have copied the Akragantine eagle for the reverse of a Lycian stater.[18]

It would not be surprising for a Greek coin to be copied by a seal engraver, whether Phoenician or otherwise. The Italian numismatist, A. Tusa, has suggested that occasionally in the fifth century, Punic and Greek towns may have shared coin-die cutters or workshops.[19] One characteristic of the de Clercq rings from Phoenicia is 'animal devices which repeat common Classical motifs'[20] (although there are no eagles in the de Clercq collection). GR-A could well belong with this group. Boardman ascribes the de Clercq rings to Greek artists. This is a possibility, but it need hardly be the only one, since it seems clear that by the fourth century artists all around the eastern Mediterranean and even deep inside the Persian Empire could work in a variety of styles.[21]

The excavated context of GR-A gives it a *terminus ante quem* in the third quarter of the fourth century. The evidence of the fifth century Acragantine coins could conceivably date GR-A to the fifth century. On the other hand, the image on the ring could have been based on a fifth century Acragantine coin, kept as a model in a fourth-century Phoenician or Samarian workshop, for example, or GR-A could be a descendant of such a ring. That the ring is gold and apparently not significantly worn might tip the balance in favour of a fourth-century date.

---

[18] Kraay, *Coins*, 986, *c*.420. Lycian coins often copy from other issues, cf. Mørkholm-Zahle, 'Coinage', 57–113 (esp. 107–10) and 'The Coinage of the Lycian Dynasts Kheriga, Kherêi and Erbbina', *Acta Arch* XLVII (1976) 47–90.

[19] Tusa, 'Rapporti', 136; the towns in question are Punic Motya and Greek Segesta, Panormus (Palermo), and Acragas.

[20] Boardman, *GGFR*, p. 221.

[21] Root, 'Heart', 1–29, esp. 17–22. Cf. Porada, 'Greek Coin', 228–34; Von Graeve, *Alexandersarcophag*; Marvin, *Studies, passim*; G. Lefebvre, *Le tombeau de Petosiris* (Paris, 1923); W. S. Smith, *Interconnections in the Ancient Near East* (New Haven, 1965); Stern, 'Phoenician', 211–12; for the evidence of the Samarian coins see Meshorer-Qedar, *Coinage of Samaria*.

WD 30. Running Quadruped

(PLATE XIV.1)

Mus. Inv. 927
Loose sealing
Image size: 0.65 cm x 1.3 cm
Bulla size: 1.7 cm x 1.9 cm
Clay colour: reddish brown, burnt black on back
String not preserved (string imprint only); left and right of horizontal image
Papyrus imprint
Seal type: metal finger ring

MANY of the sealings from Wadi Daliyeh appear to have been made carelessly, resulting in only partial impressions of the designs. Sometimes the bulla seems to have been mishandled while the clay was still soft, so that it looks as if soft clay has been folded over part of the image. WD **30** has suffered this and more; the bulla appears to have been impressed twice, as if the seal owner's hand slipped. The resulting image is a blur of shapes which are it difficult to decipher. That the original seal design was probably rather undistinguished only adds to the difficulties.

It is at least clear that the original seal was a metal finger ring with a broad leaf-shaped bezel, a common ring type at Samaria judging from the Wadi Daliyeh and Hecht Group bullae. The outline of the bezel is easily traced despite the 'foldovers' of clay at the top and bottom of the impression, and the haft of the ring has left a clear impression on the right side of the horizontal image. By Boardman's classification, this is a Type II or III found in the mid- to late-fifth century but persisting into the fourth century in places like Phoenicia.[1]

There are no comparable images among the Daliyeh or Hecht bullae to consult for clarification. WD **30** seems to show some sort of quadruped running or reclining, facing to the viewer's right. The double sealing created a flurry of extra fore- and hind legs which mislead the eye into seeing frenzied forward motion where originally there was probably an animal at rest. A clear absence of wings suggests a true-to-life rather than mythical creature.[2] Traces of a groundline of connected dots appear under the animal's forelegs, but the line disappears under the fold of clay that obscures the lower edge of the impression and seems worn away on the left side. Short horizontal strokes

---

[1] Boardman, *GGFR*, fig. 217 and pp. 212–13, 221.

[2] Possible comparisons may be made with Boardman, *GGFR*, 527, a stalking(?) lion on a fifth-century sliced barrel; Boardman, *GGFR*, 576, a Classical scaraboid with a lioness; Boardman, *GGFR*, 833, a dog beneath a winged sun disk; Boardman, *GGFR*, 941, a reclining stag; and Boardman, *GGFR*, 948, a stag which Boardman places in his Greco-Persian group.

over the creature's head might be horns or perhaps the long ears of a hare[3] or even a calf,[4] a fawn[5] or a goat.[6]

To venture beyond this brief description would merely be groundless speculation. On the basis of the ring shape the design could have been Greek, Greco-Persian, or even Phoenician. All three traditions include single animals in their glyptic repertoire. It may or may not be relevant to the discussion of WD **30** that among the Daliyeh bullae almost all of the 'Greek' images are vertical, and all those recognizably 'Near Eastern' are horizontal.

---

[3] Jenkins, *Coins*, 381 (cf. Kraay, *Coins*, 772–3, 775–8), a Messanian tetradrachm, *c*.425–420. Coins minted both by the Sicilian city of Messana and by the South Italian town of Rhegium (Kraay, *Coins*, 781) in the fifth century show a running hare. For a hare on an Achaemenid cylinder seal, cf. Collon, *First Impressions*, no. 419 (Baltimore, Walters Art Gallery). For a running hare on two Greek rings, cf. Boardman, *GGFR*, 707, a fourth-century gold ring from Crete = Marshall, *BMC*, 113, and Boardman, *GGFR*, 869 = Marshall, *BMC*, 128 (a late Classical gold ring).

[4] Boardman, *GGFR*, 574, a fifth-century scaraboid from Cyprus.

[5] Boardman, *GGFR*, 630, in the Walters Art Gallery, Baltimore, a 'Plain Eastern Gem'.

[6] Jenkins, *Coins*, 308, on the reverse of a quarter stater issued by Evagoras I of Salamis (Cyprus), *c*.411–374.

WD 23. Boar (?) with Inscription

(PLATE XIV.2)

Mus. Inv. 973
Loose sealing
Image size: 1 cm x 1.4 cm (as preserved)
Bulla size: 1.45 cm x 1.5 cm
Clay colour: pinkish brown
String preserved; left and right of horizontal image
Papyrus imprint
Seal type: metal finger ring (or oval ringstone??)
Publication: Cross, 'Dâliyeh', 47, n.4 (no. 4); Cross, 'Papyri', 18, n. 10 (no. 4).

THE extreme left edge of WD **23** has broken away, but the remainder of the horizontal oval sealing is preserved. The gently pointed right edge of the impression indicates it was probably made by a leaf-shaped metal finger ring. This ring bezel shape appears repeatedly on the bullae from Daliyeh. Unfortunately, the clearest part of WD **23** is the outline of the ring. The design and the inscription below are both frustratingly faint. It is impossible to determine which of the Samaria papyri was sealed by WD **23**.

The Inscription

WD **23** is one of four bullae in the known corpus of Samarian sealings with a preserved and legible inscription.[1] Like the so-called 'Sanballat' seal, WD **23** appears to be in palaeo-Hebrew script. The first three letters are reasonably distinct: ליש-. The final letter appears to be an *ʿayin*; the circle of the *ʿayin* is missing on the right side where there is some surface loss, but the reading is reasonably certain. Between the *šin* and the *ʿayin* there is sufficient space for an additional character, but the bulla has sustained a triangular break which took with it the letter that might have been in the space.[2]

Circumstantial evidence suggests reconstructing a *waw* in the break.[3] The reading would then be לישוע. Samaria Papyrus 14 mentions *[ys]wʿ* -(or *[yd]wʿ*)- בר סנאבלת ('Yešuaʿ, son of Sanballat) and could supply the *waw*. Another papyrus fragment reads, לישוע בר סנאבלת חנן סגנא ([ʿbefore Yeš]uaʿ son of Sanballat (and) Ḥanan the prefect'), again, perhaps indicating a *waw* on WD **23**. Finally, there is WD **22**, affixed to Papyrus 5 (*c*.358–338) and inscribed, like WD **23**, in palaeo-Hebrew. According to Cross's

---

[1] The others are WD **22** (the 'Sanballat' impression), WD **54** (pl V.2); and the 'Ishmael' bulla in the Hecht group (pl XXIII.2). WD **18** (pl XVI.1) might have been inscribed.

[2] On the basis of the photographs, without recourse to the actual sealing, it may be possible to detect the upper portion of a *waw* and possibly even the tail.

[3] The following information on the readings of the papyri is contained in Cross, 'Dâliyeh', 47 and Cross, 'Papyri', 46–7.

reconstruction it reads *[yš‘?] yhw bn [sn’]blt pht smr[n]*, ('Yešu‘/Yeša‘yahu, son of Sanballat, the governor of Samaria').[4] The text of Papyrus 5 mentions *[__]yhw_bn [sn’]blt pht smr[n]*, [. . .], probably '[Yeša‘]yahu, son of [San]ballat, governor of Samaria.'[5] Taken all together, the proposed *Yešua‘* on WD **23** might well be the same figure as the possible Yeša‘yahu, son of Sanballat, the governor of Samaria.[6]

Why would the governor have had two different seals? Perhaps his apparent ownership of two different seals indicates that *Yešua‘* held a variety of official posts, represented by various seals, or he may have simply used two different seals, perhaps one for personal transactions, the other for official ones. Perhaps his subordinates were issued seals in his name for their use when acting on his behalf. It is known that this was standard practice elsewhere in the Persian Empire.[7]

WD **22** and WD **23** contain the only palaeo-Hebrew inscriptions among the Daliyeh bullae; the use of this national script during the Persian period may have signalled the public and official nature of the document upon which it appeared.[8] The actual papyrus documents, however, were written in 'everyday' Aramaic. WD **22** and (to a lesser degree) WD **23** are also the only Daliyeh bullae that indisputably belong to the long-running glyptic tradition of Iron Age Judah and Israel.[9] As conservative survivals, WD **22** and WD **23** are just the sort of seals that might be expected to belong to the hereditary governor of what was once Israel; he would be ruling at the dispensation of the Persians whose foreign policy fostered, admittedly to a limited degree, the national identities of its subject peoples.

WD 23: The Ring and its Design

During the Iron Age, almost without exception official and private seals in Israel and Judah took the form of scarabs and scaraboids. Judging by the shape of the impression, WD **22** was also produced by a stone scaraboid. On the other hand, WD **23** probably came from a ring; thus it is an exception to the dominant Israelite glyptic tradition. In addition, most Israelite seals were arranged into registers by horizontal dividing lines

---

[4] For a photograph and drawing of WD **22**, cf. Cross, 'Papyri', pl 61; cf. also p. 18.

[5] Cross, 'Dâliyeh', 46–7.

[6] 'The alternation of caritatives and formal names is not unexpected in this period' (Cross, 'Dâliyeh', 47 n. 4).

The fourth-century governors of Samaria have been extensively studied by Cross. In addition to the two articles on the Samaria Papyri cited above, see Cross, 'Samaria', 148–58; F. M. Cross, 'A Reconstruction of the Judean Restoration', *JBL* 94 (1975) 4–18 (a slightly revised version of this paper appeared in *Interpretation* 29 [1975] 187–203); Cross, 'Aspects'.

[7] R. T. Hallock, 'The Use of Seals on the Persepolis Fortification Tablets', *Seals and Sealings in the Ancient Near East, Bibliotheca Mesopotamica* 6, eds. McGuire Gibson and R. D. Biggs (1977) 127.

[8] F. M. Cross ('Report', 21 and 'Samaria', n. 50) is seconded by J. Naveh and J. C. Greenfield ('Hebrew and Aramaic in the Persian Period,' in *CHJ* I, 114–29), who similarly believe that the use of palaeo-Hebrew arose after the middle of the fourth century when the Tennes Rebellion occurred, and reflects 'a national awakening in Judea and Samaria' (Naveh and Greenfield, 'Hebrew and Aramaic', 125). This is not impossible, but it is also an *argumentum ex silentio*. The role of Samaria and Judah, if any, in the Tennes Rebellion is unknown, and the evidence from this period is too scanty to dismiss the possibility that palaeo-Hebrew was in use in Samaria before the mid-fourth century and with the blessing of the Persians.

[9] Cf. Hestrin, Dayagi-Mendels, *Inscribed Seals*, 53–120, with ample illustrations of Iron Age (First Temple) Hebrew seals.

(as on WD **22**),[10] but no dividing line separates the image on WD **23** from the inscription below it. This may be less of an anomaly than the unusual appearance of a palaeo-Hebrew inscription on a ring, however, since on some Israelite and Judaean seals the line dividing a design from the inscription does not appear.[11]

As noted above, the shape of the ring bezel impressed on WD **23** suggests a common type of ring at Samaria. On the evidence of the Wadi Daliyeh and Hecht Group of Samarian bullae, many of the rings with this shape have Greek imagery while a few look Phoenician; a majority of these rings could have come from workshops in Phoenicia. Was the WD **23** ring a local product in imitation of a ring from a Greek or Phoenician workshop but inscribed in Hebrew?

The likelihood that the WD **23** seal came from a local workshop is hardly diminished by the fact that of all the Samarian bullae, WD **23** has arguably the most crudely executed design. The image is extremely obscure. WD **23** appears to show an animal in profile, running to the viewer's right. The animal has a long snout, a heavy body, and short legs which look incapable of carrying the animal's bulk. On close inspection the tiny rear hoof appears to be cloven, something of a surprise on this crude work.

The animal could be any mammal with four legs, but the swaybacked, heavy body, long snout, insubstantial legs and hoof suggest a boar. This is not impossible. Another bulla from this corpus, WD **45**, came from a ring portraying the forepart of a winged boar. WD **23** might be compared with a two-sided scaraboid with no recorded provenance and of indifferent workmanship that nonetheless surpasses that of WD **23**.[12] Boardman groups this scaraboid with his 'plain eastern gems', suggesting a source in Syria-Palestine. On the back of the scaraboid appears a galloping boar surrounded by an inscription in Aramaic which seems to mention a Persian.[13] This boar was probably based on a Persian or Greco-Persian depiction of a boar,[14] but it is vaguely similar to the animal on WD **23**.

E. Stern has isolated two motifs—a roaring lion and a rampant lion before an incense burner—which appeared on numerous locally produced Judaean seals dated

---

[10] Cf. Hestrin, Dayagi-Mendels, *Inscribed Seals*, nos. 3 and 45. On the use of registers in glyptic art, cf. A. Lemaire, 'Essai sur cinq sceaux phéniciens', *Semitica* 27 (1977) 29ff. and *Ashmolean/ANES III*, p. 38.

[11] Hestrin, Dayagi-Mendels, *Inscribed Seals*, no. 34, from Jerusalem, seventh century (note the remarkable similarity between this seal and the third-century Punic coins of Cadiz [illustrated in Moscati, *Phoenicians*, p. 473]); see also Hestrin, Dayagi-Mendels, *Inscribed Seals*, no. 41 (from Samaria, eighth century).

[12] Boardman, *GGFR*, 628 (= Galling, 'Bildsiegel', no. 42) and p. 209; its whereabouts are ambiguous as well; Galling says it is in the British Museum, and Boardman records it as being in Leningrad.

[13] Galling ('Bildsiegel', entry for no. 42) admits his reading is questionable but records the inscription as *mtrṣtd hmd nk*. The element *mtr* is suggestive of a Persian owner.

[14] Note that a late sixth-century Macedonian issue with a boar in profile was found at Akko (Stern, *Material Culture*, 218, fig. 365). See the entry for WD **45**, p.167ff., above, with a discussion of boars on cylinder seals, on Greco-Persian gems, and on coins from eastern Greek and Lycian cities from the late sixth century.

In fairness, it should be noted that boars were also part of the Phoenician glyptic repertoire during the Persian period. They appear on a number of green jasper seals found in both the eastern and western Mediterranean contexts (references in entry on WD **45**, p. 167ff.). Because boars do not appear on Phoenician seals before the Persian period it is reasonable to assume Persian or Greek influence.

between the end of the sixth to the end of the fifth century.[15] Both motifs, Stern shows, derive from Achaemenid cylinder seal imagery, and he believes the seals belonged to officials connected with the administration of the Persian province of Judah.[16] If the animal on WD **23** is a boar, the original seal similarly may have been a copy of an Achaemenid motif. The boar seems to have had a special symbolic value in Persian culture, and it appears on cylinders and stamps of the Persian period;[17] furthermore, in spite of the biblical rejection of the swine family, there are occasional indications, even in the Bible, that suggest a less uncompromising attitude.[18] Perhaps the engraver of WD **23** was copying an Achaemenid boar in the same way that the Judaean seal carvers created their local version of Persian lions. The lions on the Judaean sealings and the (possible) boar on WD **23** seem to be equally debased versions of Achaemenid glyptic motifs.

---

[15] Stern, 'Seal Impressions', 6–16; cf. also Stern, *Material Culture*, 209–13. For his latest view of the dating, cf. p. 211; see also O. Keel's comments in *Göttinnen,* 210–14.

[16] Stern, 'Seal Impressions', 14–16.

[17] See references in entry for WD **45**, p. 167ff.

[18] See discussion of this subject in the entry for WD **45**, p. 169.

WD 35. Winged Hippocamp (with Rider?)

(PLATE XIV.3)

Mus. Inv. 932
Loose sealing
Image size: (preserved) 0.9 cm x 0.8 cm
Bulla size: (preserved) 1.5 cm x 2.1 cm
Clay colour: reddish brown
String preserved; left and right of horizontal image
Papyrus imprint
Seal type: oval gemstone mounted in metal ring (?)

THE original seal which produced WD 35 seems to have been an almost round oval seal stone set in a ring or other mount; a slight ridge along the right side of the impression could have been caused by a minute space between the stone and its mount. The upper third of the image is missing, and was possibly undecorated. There is no ground line or border. In addition, the original seal may have been cracked; a zigzag line descends diagonally across the sealing from upper left to lower right.

WD 35 seems to show an animal in profile facing towards the viewer's right.[1] Beyond this general reading, there are only two clear details. The most distinct, on the left near the edge of the sealing, is a fish tail with some indication of scales. It is also possible to see an upturned sickle-shaped wing in the centre of the image, curving back to the viewer's right. Most of the tail and much of the lower part of the wing appear to have chipped away. The animal's head remains, but only barely; nevertheless it is almost certainly the horse head of a hippocamp. The fish tail and wing in combination with the vague profile of the middle section calls to mind a well-known series of Tyrian coins minted between 400 and 332 depicting a hippocamp and rider.[2] The amorphous 'blob' above the wing could be a rider.

---

[1] The bulla itself has substantially deteriorated since the photograph in pl XIV.3 was taken in the mid-1960s.

[2] Jenkins, *Coins*, 328, a Tyrian double-shekel, *c*.400; cf. Betlyon, *Coinage*, pls 5 and 6, and pp. 44–59; Hill, *BMC Coins*, 26 (Phoenicia), pl XXVIII,16–17 and pl XXIX,1,5,6–8,12,15–16; *SNG-ANS, Berry Collection*, I, pl 55,1446–8 and pl 56,1454–5. Also illustrated in Moscati, *Phoenicians*, 465 and cat. no. 134. Cf. E. S. G. Robinson, 'The Beginnings of Achaemenid Coinage', *Numismatic Chronicle* (1958) 187–193. The figure carrying a bow and riding the hippocamp on the Tyrian coins most resembles the Persian King or Persian Hero as heroic archer on satrapal gold darics and silver sigloi (cf. Hill, *BMC Coins* 28 [Arabia, Mesopotamia, Persia], pls 24–7; Jenkins, *Coins*, 111, 116–22).

The same design appears on a stater of Tarsus which probably copies the Tyrian issues (Kraay, *Coins*, 1034). Kraay believes this issue consciously imitates the Tyrian coins because an unnamed satrap in Tarsus was using the Tarsian staters (so labelled in Aramaic) to pay sailors in Persia's Phoenician fleet (p. 281). He conjectures a date of *c*.410, which is too early, according to Betlyon's dates, for the Tarsus coin to be a copy. Kraay's date should probably be lowered to the early fourth century.

Most significantly, the Samarian mint imitated the Tyrian issues when it produced a silver hemiobol of its own.[3] This coin is known only from an extremely worn example, but it seems to bear a decided likeness to WD **35**, especially in the upward flip of the fish tail and the long, upcurved wing. The hippocamp on the Samarian coin would appear to be riderless. The tentative restoration of the horse head on WD **35** is based on the Tyrian and Samarian hippocamps.

On the other hand, some problems with an absolute identification of WD **35** with the Tyrian image must be acknowledged. In the first place, even if there were a rider on WD **35**, the shape which might be a rider is rendered on a much larger scale than the marine bowman from Tyre who leans comfortably back into the curve of his steed's wing. Where the Tyrian figure's head reaches only a little higher than his mount's, the WD **35** rider's head would tower above his/her hippocamp. A second difference; the wing on WD **35** does not extend as far back as that on the Phoenician coins.

The possibility that this is a riderless hippocamp should at least be considered. A riderless winged hippocamp in a Phoenician context appears in the exergue of some fourth-century Byblian issues.[4]

Whether the hippocamp of WD **35** has a rider or not, the subject is familiar in the Phoenician cultural sphere.[5] The sixth-century Phoenician workshops on Sardinia offered both winged and wingless hippocamps, with and without riders.[6] The only known Archaic Greek gems with hippocamps come from Sicily, Magna Graecia,[7] and

---

Although numismatists usually identify the hippocamp rider as the Tyrian god Milqart (*milk-qart*, 'king of the city') there is neither textual nor iconographical evidence for the equation (cf. Betlyon's discussion, p. 46 and nn. 44–7 to chap. 2). Milqart was, in fact, not the chief god of Tyre. That position was apparently occupied by Baʿal Šamem (R. A. Oden, 'Baʿal Šamem and ʾEl', *CBQ* 39 [1977] 457–73).

Milqart, who came to be known in the ancient world as the Tyrian Herakles, has no apparent connections to the sea. By the fourth century he was identified with Mesopotamian Nergal, the ruler of the Underworld (Betlyon, *Coinage*, n. 45) and in the Punic world, at least, with Rasap (Reshef), lord of the underworld city of the dead (Betlyon, *Coinage*, n. 45, and J. M. Solá-Solé, 'Miscelánea púnico-hispana. I. 3. HGD, ʾRSF y el pantheon fenico punico de España', *Sefarad* 16 [1956] 341–55). Recent attempts to grapple with the question of Milqart's identity include M. Fantar, *Le dieu de la mer chez les Phéniciens et les Puniques*, Studi Semitici 48 (Rome, 1977) and C. Bonnet, *Melqart: cultes et mythes de l'Héraclès Tyrien en Méditerranée*, SP 8 (1988). Cf. also C. Bonnet-Tsavellas, 'Le dieu Melqart en Phénicie et dans le bassin Méditerranéen: Culte national et officiel', *SP* 1/2 (1983) 195–207 and M. Yon, 'Cultes phéniciens à Chypre: l'interpretation chypriote', *SP* IV [1986] 127–52.

[3] Meshorer-Qedar, *Coinage of Samaria*, no. 76 (ex. Samaria Hoard).

[4] Betlyon, *Coinage*, pl 8.8 and 9.2; also cf. Hill, *BMC Coins*, 26 (Phoenicia), pl XI,9–15.

[5] After the man-fish, the hippocamp is the second most common type of sea monster in pre-Hellenistic Greek art (K. Shepard, *The Fish-Tailed Monster in Greek and Etruscan Art* [New York, 1940] 25). No Near Eastern versions of hippocamps antedate the Greek examples; it is conceivable that these mythical sea-horses were actually Greek variations on Oriental *Mischwesen*. For Assyrian fish creatures, cf. A. Green, 'A Note on the Assyrian "Goat-Fish," "Fish-Man" and "Fish-Woman"', *Iraq* 48 (1986) 25–30. Note the illustration in Collon, *First Impressions*, fig. 229 (Old Babylonian) and also the (different) motif of a man in a fish skin, Collon, *First Impressions*, figs. 351, 356, 357 (Neo-Assyrian). For additional discussion of the Near Eastern background to the hippocamp, consult entry on WD **35** in Leith, *Imagery*, 384–5.

[6] Shepard, *Monster*, 26. Cf. Walters, *BMC*, 398, a green jasper scarab from Tharros with a rider on a wingless hippocamp; cf. also Furtwängler, *AG*, pl XV. 35, green jasper, a riderless winged hippocamp.

[7] Shepard, *Monster*, 27.

Cyprus;[8] all these areas, to varying degrees, were in touch with Phoenicians. Around 500, Tarentum minted coins with a sickle-winged (Achaemenid style) hippocamp,[9] and in the ensuing decades several Sicilian cities issued coins with hippocamps.[10] By the Classical period, 'Greek' hippocamp wings usually have the 'natural' appearance of birds' wings rather than the stylized Phoenician or Achaemenid curve visible on WD **35**.[11]

Ultimately, however, the rough similarities between WD **35** and Tyrian and Samarian coins must surely have some significance. It is indeed unfortunate that both WD **35** and the Samarian coin are so indistinct.

---

[8] Richter, MMA, 58, a winged hippocamp on an agate scarab of the early fifth century.

[9] Shepard, *Monster*, 27 and Hill, *BMC Coins* (Italy), 166–7 and *SNG-ANS* I, pl 22.831–42 and 845–8. Most of Tarentum's Classical and later coinage shows a nude rider on a horse or dolphin. The hippocamps, however, never carry any riders. Until the late fifth century Pegasos' wings on Corinthian coins were of the curved sickle type (O. Ravel, *Les 'Poulains' de Corinthe* [Chicago, 1979 (reprint)] 26, 39 and all plates).

[10] Shepard, *Monster*, 41: Panormos (Hill, *BMC Coins* [Sicily], 247); Akragas (*ibid*, 15–16, nos. 93ff); Himera (*ibid*, 81, no. 48); Messana (*ibid*, 104, no. 48; *SNG-ANS* IV, pl 13.380).

[11] Richter, *EGGE*, 365 = Boardman, *GGFR*, 788 = Marshall, *BMC*, 84, a gold ring in the British Museum from Reggio. Other riderless winged hippocamps: Boardman, *GGFR*, 789, a silver ring in Dresden (Z.V. 1461); Boardman, *GGFR* 979 (Leningrad 571 ['Graeco-Persian']). For a Classical wingless hippocamp with rider, cf. Boardman, *GGFR* 652, a green glass seal in Leningrad (500) with a bearded man riding a wingless hippocamp, and Richter, *EGGE* 332 = Boardman, *GGFR*, no. 162 (with extensive bibliography), a carnelian scarab in the Bibliothèque Nationale with a youth riding the hippocamp.

WD 53. Winged 'Persian Hero' Sphinx

(PLATE XV.1)

Mus. Inv. 950
Loose sealing
Image size: approx. 1 cm x 1.3 cm
Bulla size: 1.5 cm x 1.7 cm
Clay colour: reddish brown
String not preserved; string holes left and right of horizontal image
Papyrus fragment on back
Papyrus imprint
Seal type: scaraboid?

IT is impossible to determine from the bulla whether a ring or a stamp produced the very worn image on WD **53**. The outlines of the seal have faded away, and are indistinguishable now from the surrounding unimpressed clay. Comparable works, discussed below, suggest the original seal was a stone scaraboid.

Although faint, the design on the bulla is clearly that of a winged sphinx with the crowned and bearded head of the 'Persian Hero'.[1] He is running to the viewer's right while at the same time he looks back, in profile, over his shoulder. His fore- and rear legs are extended in the so-called 'flying gallop' position, suggesting rapid movement. The knobby knees and toes of his forelegs give clear indication of the use of the drill. His sickle-shaped wing curves in the direction of his head; the tail has disappeared.

This same species of sphinx, which Boardman and others have dubbed the 'royal sphinx',[2] appears on WD **3A** (pl XIX.1), WD **48** (pl XXI.2) and possibly WD **31** (pl XV.2); similarly the pair of winged scorpion men on WD **25** (pl XXI.1) have the head of the 'Persian Hero'. The creature with its human head, lion body and fantastic wings belongs in the traditional Persian Court Style menagerie, usually in a symmetrical arrangement with its mirror image.[3]

The Achaemenid 'royal sphinx' is most likely to appear alone on scaraboids, for example, a red-and-yellow jasper Persian Court Style scaraboid in the Ashmolean Museum,[4] and a similar blue chalcedony scaraboid in Berlin.[5] The excavators of the Persepolis Treasury published a third such scaraboid, apparently worn as an amulet.[6]

---

[1] The photograph in pl XV.1 belies the relative clarity of the image upon actual inspection.

[2] Boardman, 'Pyramidal', p. 34. On the 'Persian Hero', see entry for WD **4**, p. 214ff.

[3] Cf. entry for WD **3A**.

[4] Boardman, *GGFR*, 837 (Oxford 1965–362).

[5] Richter, *EGGE*, 493 = *AGDS II* (Berlin), no. 202 = Furtwängler, *Beschreibung*, 187 = Furtwängler, *AG*, pl 11.20; said to come from Sparta.

[6] Schmidt, *Persepolis II*, pl 17, PT 767; note also two ring impressions with a single, seated, Persian Hero-headed sphinx from Nippur in Bregstein, *Seal Use*, nos. 460–61.

The three scaraboids depict the sphinx in regular profile, walking on all fours. The Berlin sphinx has drilled knees and feet which resemble those on WD **53**. Boardman classifies these works as western Court Style, partly on the basis of the scaraboid shape which is essentially Greek.[7] Probably related to the images discussed by Boardman are at least two bullae excavated at the satrapal city of Daskyleion (near the Hellespont) which show the running figure of a single 'royal sphinx.'[8] They appear to have been made by stamp seals, but of undetermined types.

A (probably) fifth-century pyramidal stamp seal in Boston shows the sphinx in a complex composition with several figures;[9] its interest here lies in the 'flying gallop' position of the legs. The over-the-shoulder profile is attested for sphinxes with the 'Persian Hero' head, but only, apparently, in cases where the sphinx is in a symmetrical arrangement.[10] However, a scaraboid which Boardman labels Greco-Persian does show a solitary winged bull looking over his shoulder, reminiscent of WD **53**.[11]

---

[7] Boardman, *GGFR*, p. 306. Two ring impressions from Ur show seated winged sphinxes in profile (Legrain, *Ur*, pl 41.779–80); both sphinxes share the space with an incense burner, a compositional detail which puts the rings in a different category from the scaraboids and WD **53**.

[8] Balkan, 'Inscribed Bullae', pl 33c and d.

[9] Boardman, 'Pyramidal', 126 (Boston MFA 03.1012).

[10] I.e. Boardman, 'Pyramidal', 122.

[11] Boardman, *GGFR*, 919 (Cambridge, England) and pp. 317–18.

WD 31. Seated Winged Sphinx

(PLATE XV.2)

Mus. Inv. 928
Loose sealing
Image size: 1.4 cm x 1 cm
Bulla size: 1.6 cm x 2.2 cm
Clay colour: black, badly burnt
String not preserved
Horizontal image
Papyrus imprint
Seal type: oval ring or scaraboid?

THE oval outline of this badly burnt clay impression is unusual among the Wadi Daliyeh bullae. It is a shape more often associated with Classical scaraboids or other forms of engraved gems than with rings, although by the fourth century, this was also a metal finger ring profile.[1] The soft edges of WD **31** could have come from a gem with rounded sides. Intense burning left the bulla extremely friable; much of the right side of the image has peeled away.

WD **31** shows a sphinx seated in profile looking to the viewer's right with its left (far) paw raised.[2] A sickle wing with the familiar multi-register Achaemenid feather pattern curves back toward the sphinx's head; the tail curls up over the sphinx's haunches. Whether the head was human or animal remains uncertain; in view of the relatively large number of Persian Hero-headed[3] sphinxes among the bullae from Samaria[4], this form would seem likely.

If the Persian Hero's head did appear on the WD **31** sphinx, its precise parallels can be found in the very heart of the Persian Empire among the images conveying the message of imperial might at Persepolis.[5] A pair of winged Persian Hero sphinxes with

---

[1] Boardman, *GGFR*, fig. 217, types V–VII, fifth-fourth centuries.

[2] This entry substantially revises the discussion in Leith, *Imagery*, 477. Note also the fragmentary sphinx in the Hecht Group (pl XXIII.6).

[3] See discussion of the 'Persian Hero' in entry for WD **4**, p. 214ff. The alternative term for 'Persian Hero' Sphinx is the 'Royal Sphinx'.

[4] Cf. WD **53** (pl XV.1), WD **3A** (pl XIX.1), WD **48** (pl XXI.2); the pair of winged scorpion men on WD **25** (pl XXI.1) similarly have the Persian Hero head.

[5] Root (*King*) analyzes the programmatic use by the Persians of symbols and images to promote the interests of the Empire.

raised paws cap the central panel of the eastern stairway of the Apadana,[6] for example, and they appear on the facade of the Palace of Darius.[7]

The raised paw of the winged sphinx seems to be a gesture of power in Imperial Persian art. An unprovenanced cylinder seal in Paris belonging to a Persian official shows a pair of Persian Hero headed sphinxes with raised paws below the 'Ahura Mazda' symbol.[8] The motif also appears on Persian decorative elements such as a gold textile ornament in the form of a winged, horned lion with raised paw found probably at Hamadan-Ecbatana;[9] the winged lion provides an alternative restoration for the sphinx's head on WD **31**.

The winged sphinx with raised paw on the ring impression of a Babylonian official of the Persian King[10] preserved on one of the Murashu texts from Nippur provides a good glyptic parallel to WD **31**. Elsewhere, pairs of the same sphinxes 'salute each other' on a number of pyramidal stamp seals from Achaemenid Anatolia.[11]

WD **31** takes its place beside the many other good examples of the Persian imperial Court Style found in the corpus of sealings from the Wadi Daliyeh. It is tempting to assign it to a Samarian serving as an official of the Persian administration, but the unpredictable patterns of seal images and types used by similar officials and 'civilians' at Nippur shows how difficult it is to make such assumptions.[12]

---

[6] E. Porada, *Art*, fig. 83.

[7] M. C. Root, 'Circles of Artistic Programming', *Investigating Artistic Environments in the Ancient Near East*, ed. A. C. Gunter (Madison, Wisconsin, 1990) 126, fig. 9.

[8] Bordreuil, *BN*, no. 128 (Cabinet des Médialles), inscribed 'seal of Mithriš, son of ŠʿY'.

[9] Porada, *Art*, pl 52.

[10] Bregstein, *Seal Use*, no. 460; and pp. 154–5; seal of the *ustarbar* official, 419 BCE.

[11] Boardman, 'Pyramidal', nos. 5, 116–28; p. 34. There is one singleton sphinx in the group, no. 128. Note also Boardman, *GGFR*, 834 = Boardman, 'Pyramidal', no. 5.

[12] This is the conclusion of Bregstein in *Seal Use*.

WD 38. Winged Bull (?)

(PLATES XV.3 AND XXIII.5 [?])

Mus. Inv. 935
Loose sealing
Image size: 1 cm x 1.5 cm
Bulla size: 3 cm x 2 cm
Clay colour: reddish brown
String preserved; left and right of horizontal image
Papyrus imprint
Seal type: oval engraved gem in mounted in a ring?

THE seal which produced WD **38** may have been an engraved gem set in a heavy metal ring; the imprint of what looks like a thick ring mount is visible around the oval gem impression. Only faint remnants of the image itself, a Persian Court Style winged bull, have survived. Although the correlation is not certain, a bulla in the Hecht Group with the same subject (pl XXIII.5) is probably a duplicate sealing and has supplied additional details.

WD **38** depicts a winged bull of rather lean proportions in profile facing to the viewer's right. An Achaemenid sickle wing curls above the animal's back curving to the right in the direction of the head. The animal is shown in a 'flying gallop', the two forelegs extending forward, both rear legs and tail straight back. Just visible at the head are the horn and an ear. Beyond some faint wing-feather patterning, no decorative details of the sort expected on an Achaemenid animal are visible.

The winged bull reappears in a Samarian context on WD **8** (pl XVIII.3), a contest scene in which the bull succumbs to the Persian Hero. It also appears on the obverse of a Samarian silver hemiobol.[1]

Beyond Samaria, the winged bull is found—primarily in contest scenes—on seal impressions on dated clay tablets of the Persian period excavated at Nippur and Ur.[2] Among the Nippur sealings there is also a ring impression dating to the late fifth century of a single leaping winged lion, an animal quite similar in profile and posture

---

[1] Meshorer-Qedar, *Coinage of Samaria*, no. 63 (in the Ashmolean Museum, Oxford). It has been suggested that the design on this coin derives from Achaemenid seals; see p. 32.

[2] Legrain, *Culture*, no. 947 = Bregstein, *Seal Use*, no. 138, a cylinder impression; Legrain, *Culture*, 943 = Bregstein, *Seal Use*, 136, cylinder impression; Legrain, *Culture*, 944 = Bregstein, *Seal Use*, 139, a stamp impression; Bregstein, *Seal Use*, 137, a stamp impression.

The winged bull also appears, forepart only, in animal whorl designs on stamp impressions; cf. Legrain, *Culture*, 869 = Bregstein, *Seal Use*, 420; Legrain, *Culture*, 875 = Bregstein, *Seal Use*, 413.

Ur sealing: Legrain, *Ur*, pl 41,784. This sealing comes from the group of over 200 clay bullae deposited in the bottom of a clay coffin. They may have been samples and records from a seal-cutter's workshop (Porada, 'Greek Coin', 230).

to the winged bull.[3] In the course of his excavations at Memphis, Sir Flinders Petrie discovered a silver finger ring engraved with a running winged bull which he reports as coming from an Achaemenid context.[4] Boardman observes that winged bulls are unusual in Greek art, and when they do appear are probably borrowed from the east.[5]

---

[3] Legrain, *Culture*, no. 829 = Bregstein, *Seal Use*, no. 398.

[4] W. M. F. Petrie, *The Palace of Apries: Memphis II* (London, 1909) 16, pl 26.9 (= *Ashmolean/ANES III*, 578 [1909.1091]).

[5] Boardman, *AG Gems*, p. 146; cf. the winged bull foreparts, nos. 491–4.

H. FLANKING HORSES, GRIFFINS

WD 18. Flanking Winged Horses

(PLATE XVI.1)

Mus. Inv. 969
Loose sealing
Image size: 1 cm x 1.3 cm
Bulla size: 1.7 cm x 1.7 cm
Clay colour: reddish brown
String preserved; top and bottom of horizontal image
Papyrus imprint
Seal type: stone stamp seal (scaraboid suspended from string or chain?)

ALMOST the entire outline of an egg-shaped seal impression is preserved on WD **18**. Unique to WD **18**, two curious indentations just to the left and right of centre on the lower edge of the impression might have come from a suspension device, possibly strings threaded through a scaraboid seal. WD **18** is also unusual in being one of the few bullae from Wadi Daliyeh whose string lay perpendicular to a horizontal image. The impression itself is quite worn, and the finer details of ornamentation that must have embellished the design are missing.

The horizontal oval impression on WD **18** shows two recumbent sickle-winged horses in profile with their legs tucked under their bodies. They hover over a double ground line. It is possible that the area below the ground line was originally not empty; there is ample space for additional elements, possibly even an inscription. One can see stiff, cropped manes and head ornaments like tall top knots on both horses.[1] Traces of feathers have survived on the wing of the horse to the viewer's right. Paradoxically, perhaps, in view of these animals' supernatural nature, they wear the bridles and reins of domesticated horses. A conical stamp seal impression from Persian period Nippur[2] shows the foreparts of a winged horse wearing bridle and bit, although the Nippur horse is of the 'normal', unwinged, variety.[3]

The horses may or may not have flanked a central element fanning open like a papyrus plant in the triangular space above where their two foreheads almost meet. There are precedents for the papyrus detail in Phoenician and more generically 'Levantine' glyptic art from the Iron II through the Achaemenid periods.[4] The ground line, too, belongs in the Phoenician tradition.

---

[1] For a good illustration of equine 'parade dress' in Achaemenid art, cf. the horses brought by the Lydian delegation, on the eastern stairway of the Apadana at Persepolis, in Porada, *Art*, pl 43.

[2] Legrain, *Culture*, no. 883 (= 882) = Bregstein, *Seal Use*, no. 346.

[3] Pegasos, the most famous winged horse of all wears a bridle on Corinthian coins of the late sixth and early fifth centuries (Kraay, *Coins*, nos. 220–48). The bridle starts to disappear around the time Pegasos's wings change from the earlier sickle-shape to 'natural' pointed wings about the middle of the fifth century.

[4] Cf. *Ashmolean/ANES III*, 263–4, 272, 501–2.

Although Boardman notes that winged horses are better known to Greek than eastern artists in the Persian period,[5] they also belong in the Near Eastern repertoire; winged horses can be found in the Neo-Assyrian period on cylinder seals,[6] and on Persian period seals from Nippur.[7] The pose of the horses with forelegs tucked under their chests may be an Achaemenid trait. The joined animal foreparts which acted as decorative column capitals at Persepolis and Pasargadae fold their forelegs under their chests in exactly the same way;[8] and while many of these capitals seem to have been in the form of bulls, at least one capital fragment, found at Pasargadae, was of a horse.[9] Unfortunately, too little of the Pasargadae horse capital is preserved to see if it, like the bulls on the capitals and the horses on WD **18**, had a short, cropped mane.[10] The bulls which topped the Persian columns wore ornamental trappings which resemble the bridle and cheek piece of the right-hand horse on WD **18**. The sculptural style of WD **18** gives the impression of not looking at 'real' or living animals, but rather, at statues of winged horses.

A possibly related work in the round belongs to the Walters Art Gallery.[11] This is a tiny lapis lazuli bead in the shape of a (wingless) bull attributed to the Achaemenid period. Like the horses on WD **18**, it reclines with fore- and hind legs neatly tucked under its body and has also been compared to the Persian column capitals.

WD **18** belongs essentially to the Persian Court Style with possible Phoenician mediation. The image seems to have demonstrable affinities to Persian sculpture, and the symmetrical arrangement of the horses is at once characteristically Near Eastern and common to Court Style glyptics. The presence of the sickle wings on a seal with a good fourth-century context probably also signals an 'eastern' source. By this time sickle wings had disappeared from 'Greek' coins and seals. Notably, Persian-style animal protome column capitals and bases are also attested in the Phoenician homeland, discovered in the late sixth/fifth century remains of what some scholars suspect was the palace of the Persian governor at Sidon. Another group of bull protome capitals were discovered in the ruins of the Sidonian Temple of Eshmun, and, like the Daliyeh bullae, are presumed to date to the end of the Persian period.[12] Seal engravers in Phoenicia presumably had first-hand exposure to such examples of large-

---

[5] Boardman, 'Pyramidal', p. 29.

[6] N. Yalouris, *Pegasus, Ein Mythos in der Kunst* (Mainz am Rhein, 1987) nos. 3–5. Cf. L. Delaporte, *Catalogue des cylindres orientaux et des cachets Assyro-Babyloniens, Perses et Syro-Cappadociens de la Bibliothèque Nationale* (Paris, 1910) pl 22.324.

[7] Bregstein, *Seal Use*, no. 400, a ring impression from the late fifth century of a recumbent winged horse; no. 401, a stamp impression of a striding winged horse; Legrain, *Culture*, 869 = Bregstein, *Seal Use*, no. 420, a winged horse protome in a whorl design from a stamp seal which includes two other members of the Court Style menagerie, a winged lion and winged bull.

[8] Stern, *Material Culture*, fig. 64. Cf. Porada, *Art*, 145–6, 156, fig. 79. Cf. also Frankfort, *Art*, 221–5, pl 180c.

[9] E. Herzfeld, *Iran in the Ancient East* (Oxford, 1941) pl XXXIX.

[10] Cf. also the Achaemenid rhyton in the form of a lion monster with the same short mane, Porada, *Art*, pl 47.

[11] J. V. Canby, *The Ancient Near East in the Walters Art Gallery* (Baltimore, 1974) cat. no. 51 (42.221). As with many other works cited as coming from Iran, the bead lacks a secure provenance.

[12] Stern, *Material Culture*, fig. 79. See M. Dunand, review of G. Contenau, *La civilisation phénicienne* (Paris, 1926), *Syria* 7 (1926) 276, pl 5 and Stern, *Material Culture*, 60, 66.

scale Achaemenid sculpture, although whether or how they reacted to it remains an unresolved question.

Several other Samarian bullae with horse imagery merit passing mention in a discussion of WD **18**. The first, WD **34** (pl XVI.2), superficially resembles WD **18** in showing a pair of animals which are probably horses. However, they are of the normal unwinged variety, semirampant and depicted in a much more 'naturalistic' style than the formally hieratic winged horses of WD **18**. The WD **18** horses barely fit into their allotted space, while the WD **34** horses have more than ample room in which to cavort. Several bullae from the Hecht Group (pl XXIII.7–8) also depict individual 'real-life' horses in a decidedly 'Greek' style.

WD 34. Two Horses

(PLATE XVI.2)

Mus. Inv. 931
Loose sealing
Image size: 1.1 cm x 1.8 cm
Bulla size: 1.4 cm x 1.9 cm
Clay colour: burnt black
String not preserved (imprint only); left and right of horizontal image
Papyrus imprint
Seal type: metal finger ring

THE outline of a metal finger ring with a broad leaf-shaped oval bezel is the clearest aspect of WD **34** although only the left side of the bezel imprint and a small portion of the opposite end are actually preserved. The shape reflects the most common ring bezel type found among the Wadi Daliyeh bullae.[1]

Within the ample field of the ring bezel, two apparent horses in profile confront each other. There is always the possibility that they are lions or griffins, but the bodies appear to be equine, and the head of the right-hand (and more complete) animal appears to be that of a horse. On the left side, a small stony inclusion obscures the animal's head. The two horses do not appear to be precisely symmetrical, although both torsos line up along the central horizontal axis of the ring bezel. On the other hand, the animals were possibly mirror images and the sealing has distorted the design on the actual ring. Both horses appear to rear up on their hind legs. The placement of their forelegs is a matter of conjecture. The surrounding field looks suspiciously bare on this bulla; could there have been more detail, now lost?

Horses appear alone,[2] with riders,[3] drawing chariots[4] and as prey[5] on Greek and Greco-Persian gems. Symmetrical flanking animals are more familiar in Near Eastern art, although horses figure less in such compositions than do other species of real and imaginary creatures.[6] At Nippur, symmetrical rearing horses appear on impressions of

---

[1] Boardman, *GGFR*, fig. 217, types II–III, mid/late fifth century, persisting into the fourth century outside the Greek world.

[2] Boardman, *GGFR*, 559 (= Richter, *EGGE*, 415), a chalcedony scaraboid of the late fifth century in the Royal Cabinet of Coins and Gems, The Hague. See also Boardman, *GGFR*, 473, 612, 644.

[3] Boardman, *GGFR*, 672, 882, 886.

[4] Boardman, *GGFR*, 790.

[5] Boardman, *GGFR*, 867.

[6] Note the design on a Phoenician silver gilt bowl in the Walters Art Gallery (57.705), supposedly from the seventh century, which includes numerous horses arranged in a decorative pattern (illustrated in Canby, *Ancient Near East*, cat. no. 27).

stamp seals and one cylinder but not on rings.[7] On at least three of these there is a plant detail, a possibility, although remote, on WD **34**. Additional horses of both Near Eastern (WD **18**, pl XVI.1) and Greek lineage (pl XXIII.7–8)[8] appear among the Samarian bullae.

From what little remains of the animals and the design on WD **34**, it can only be tentatively observed that the flanking horses resemble the symmetrical horses from Nippur, and that they seem more naturalistic than stylized.

---

[7] Legrain, *Culture*, 842 = Bregstein, *Seal Use*, no. 326, a cylinder impression; see also Legrain, *Culture*, 843 = Bregstein, *Seal Use*, no. 325, a stamp impression; Legrain, *Culture*, 845 = Bregstein, *Seal Use*, no. 312, a stamp impression; Bregstein, *Seal Use*, no. 324, a stamp impression.

[8] Bullae from the Hecht Group.

Gold Ring B. Flanking Griffins

(PLATE XVI.3)

Mus. Inv. 782[1]
No preserved bullae impressed by Gold Ring B
Size: n.a.
Seal type: gold ring with narrow hoop and leaf-shaped bezel

WHILE a significant amount of jewellery was associated with the Samaria Papyri, Gold Ring B (hereafter, GR-B) and Gold Ring A (GR-A) (pl XIII.3) were the only pieces which Cross was able to purchase. Both rings have an intaglio design on the bezel, but there are no known bullae from Samaria with impressions of either ring.

GR-B appears to be heavier than GR-A, with a broader oval leaf-shaped bezel. Also, unlike GR-A, no design element marks the transition from bezel to hoop. The bezel on GR-B is in a continuous line with the outer side of the hoop, and is not raised higher than the hoop. The hoop itself seems to have been constructed of a flat piece of metal folded into uneven thirds, the two loose ends meeting inside the hoop.

GR-B looks like a combination of Boardman's Types III and V,[2] both attributed to the fifth century. The evidence of these two rings from Samaria indicates that the types were still current in the fourth century.[3] A number of gold rings from the de Clercq collection, acquired primarily in Lebanon, also have similar bezels and are only vaguely dated by art historical criteria. The de Clercq and Wadi Daliyeh material might be evidence of a provincial Phoenician workshop or workshops; on the other hand, out of context, some of the Daliyeh material might be classified as 'mainstream' Greek. Most of the gold and silver rings which supply the evidence for Classical ring typology lack a good stratigraphic context crucial for dating, or even a vague provenance. Methodologically it seems premature to know which works can be dismissed from classification on the basis of 'provinciality'. 'Provincial' areas might well be producing 'mainstream' goods and therefore should not be excluded from typological considerations. (Bronze rings from fourth-century Olynthus have this shape,[4] but bronze rings, usually of lesser quality and subject to more variations, belong in a separate, if related category).[5]

Gold is a soft metal, and not surprisingly, GR-B is fairly worn. Nevertheless, the image is quite clear. Over all, the design is very simple, yet it is constructed in a

---

[1] Currently unlocated. The following discussion is based on photographs.

[2] Boardman, *GGFR*, pp. 212–15; cf. pl 711.

[3] Admittedly, the two gold rings might be heirlooms, but GR-A may best be compared to fourth-century coins and there is no compelling reason to assume GR-B was any earlier than the fourth century.

[4] Robinson, 'Metal', pl XXVII. Olynthus was destroyed in 348 BCE.

[5] Boardman, *GGFR*, pp. 212, 230–32.

remarkably subtle way. An elegant pair of sickle-winged, horned griffins with attenuated bodies sit facing each other in profile; they flank a trefoil lotus blossom. Their torsos and wings are more deeply engraved than their extremities.

A griffin is a winged creature with the body of a lion and a horned head ranging on the animal spectrum from eagle to lion. The Greek griffin's head is more aquiline or serpentine,[6] while the Near Eastern griffin looks more like a horned lion, often with lion forelegs and talons for hindlegs.[7] The griffin on a Phoenician ivory of the eighth century has a raptor's head, somewhat like an falcon.[8] The Greek or Greco-Persian griffins with 'natural' wings on three Samarian bullae in the Hecht Group (pl XXIII.1–3) differ substantially from the pair on this ring. On GR-B the griffins' heads have suffered the most over time, and it is difficult to determine whether they tend to the aquiline or leonine and whether their mouths are open or closed. The expected upcurled tails are not visible in the working photograph.

Legs, feet, and horns do not quite—or just barely—connect to their bodies giving the griffins a jointless aspect which contributes to the airy effect of the design. This disjointedness is intentional; indeed, the shape of the animals' bodies is secondary to the overall pattern of the image. Between the griffins, the trefoil blossom consists of a tiny teardrop petal flanked by two longer petals, each indicated by a delicate arc; this blossom floats over a tiny vestigial teardrop-shaped stem on either side of which branches out a horizontally arcing tendril. Thus, the three elements of which the blossom is constructed are repeated below it in a flattened mirror image. At the same time, each of the two longer blossom elements doubles as a half-raised griffin leg, while the (far) front and rear feet and lower legs of the griffins may also be 'read' as extensions of the floral element. Very cleverly, the artist plays with reflections in both vertical and horizontal directions and creates pleasing ambiguities within the overall design.

The GR-B griffins are closer to the Persian Court Style griffins than to the Greek variety, and the complex symmetrical design of GR-B is more likely to have come out of the Near Eastern than the Greek world. The lightness of style compares with that of a Phoenician scarab in the Getty Museum.[9] GR-B might also be compared to a Phoenician gold ring of the Persian period found at Gibeon.[10] Although the cartouche shape of the ring differs from GR-B, it is engraved with flanking animals, depicted in a loose, sketchy style vaguely akin to that of GR-B.

The flower pattern supplies additional evidence for the Phoenician identity of GR-B.[11] I. Winter has observed that Phoenician flowers tend to have volutes, that is,

---

[6] Boardman, *GGFR*, p. 198, pl 511–12; 838–41; Kraay, *Coins*, 893, stater of Teos, *c.*470.

[7] Legrain, *Culture*, 855 = Bregstein, *Seal Use*, no. 432. Cf. also Collon, *First Impressions*, 420 (Ashmolean 1889.360).

[8] Moscati, *Phoenicians*, 406 and cat. no. 86, from Nimrud, now in Brussels (Musées Royaux d'Art et d'Histoire [O 3009]). Cf. *Ashmolean/ANES III*, p. 41; Galling, 'Bildsiegel', pl 5.1–11.

[9] Spier, *Ancient Gems*, cat. no. 97 (Mus. no. 83.!N.437.3), blue frit, attributed vaguely to 'late sixth-fifth century B.C.'

[10] J. B. Pritchard, *Gibeon Where the Sun Stood Still* (Princeton, 1962) 116, figs. 77–8 = Stern, *Material Culture*, 199, fig. 322.

[11] Note that none of the de Clercq rings resembles GR-B, nor do any of the gems and rings in the Greco-Persian category of Boardman, *GGFR*. GR-B is also far removed stylistically from the Phoenician 'Green Jasper' tradition.

tendrils at the stem juncture (the point where the flower joins the stem).[12] The stem juncture on GR-B may not be emphasized, but a case could be made that the horizontal arcs are vestigial volutes. Furthermore, it was a Phoenician stylistic trait of long standing to combine animals and stylized plants in complex patterns,[13] just as they appear on GR-B.[14]

---

[12] I. Winter, 'Phoenician and North Syrian Ivory Carving in Historical Context: Questions of Style and Distribution', *Iraq* 38 (1976) 6.

[13] Moscati, *Phoenicians*, 406.

[14] Cf. Moscati, *Phoenicians*, ivories: cat no. 86; cat no. 89; cat. no. 97, an ivory plaque depicting griffins and a sacred tree of the seventh century (British Museum, WA 118157); metal bowls: cf. p. 438.

I. PERSIAN HERO

WD 17, WD 36, WD 51. Persian Hero Fights Flanking Inverted Lions

(PLATES XVII.1–3)

WD 17
Mus. Inv. 968
Image size: 1.2 cm x 1.4 cm
Bulla size: 1.7 cm x 2.2 cm
Loose sealing
Clay colour: reddish brown
String preserved; top and bottom of horizontal image
Papyrus fragments on back
Papyrus imprint
Seal type: cylinder
Published: Cross, 'Papyri', 28, pl 62.f

WD 36
Mus. Inv. 933
Loose sealing
Image size: 1.7 cm x 1.5 cm
Bulla size: 2.2 cm x 1.8 cm
Clay colour: reddish brown
String preserved; top and bottom of horizontal impression
Papyrus imprint
Seal type: cylinder

WD 51
Mus. Inv. 948
Loose sealing
Image size: 1.6 cm x 1.8 cm
Bulla size: 1.8 cm x 1.8 cm
Clay colour: reddish brown
String preserved; top and bottom of image
Papyrus imprint
Seal type: cylinder
Published: Cross, 'Papyri', 228–9, pl 62.g

WD 17, WD 36 and WD 51[1] display the same design, but were produced by different seals. While the Near Eastern ancestry of the 'Master of Animals' pose is well known,[2] the Achaemenid version here with the 'Persian Hero' grappling flanking animals first

---

[1] Possibly also WD 3B (pl XVIII.1).

[2] Cf. S. M. Paley, 'Inscribed Neo-Assyrian and Neo-Babylonian Seals', *Insight Through Images*, ed. M. Kelly-Buccellati (Malibu, 1986) 214–18.

appears on seals in the reign of Darius I (522–486);[3] at Persepolis, thus far, the name of the king has appeared only on seals of this type.[4] It is the motif found most often on the cuneiform tablets from Nippur dated in the reigns of Artaxerxes and Darius II.[5] This design, and the common variant (also found in the Daliyeh corpus[6]) showing the hero fighting a single adversary adorned countless cylinder and stamp seals produced in the Persian Empire from the late sixth to the late fourth century.[7] As an emblem of imperial power, the image played a potent role in Persian propaganda.[8]

WD **36** and WD **51** look very similar. In their current state of preservation, if the hero's head were not facing in different directions on the two bullae it would be tempting to assign them to the same seal.

The same image appears on two fourth-century Samarian silver obols[9] and on other Wadi Daliyeh bullae. WD **3B** (pl XVIII.1; in a very poor state of preservation and of indeterminate type) was attached to Papyrus 14; it is unclear what sort of creatures the hero is fighting. A debased, possibly local, version of the motif appears on at least five bullae (WD **3A**, WD **10A**, WD **11B**, WD **12**, WD **24**; pl XIX.1–3) impressed by the same seal ring.[10]

The Question of Cylinder Seals

This motif and related compositions with the hero battling other monsters, appear on both Achaemenid cylinders and stamps. Cylinders were rapidly disappearing during the Persian period, as papyrus replaced clay as the preferred writing surface. As a general rule, Persian officials used cylinders for government business and stamps for their private transactions.[11]

---

[3] Zettler, 'Chronological', 260. As a sidelight on this motif, P. Calmeyer discusses its later transformation, in Middle Eastern Christian and Muslim folk art, into a traditional representation of Daniel in the lion's den, 'The Persian King in the Lion's Den', *Iraq* 45 (1983) 138–9.

For a discussion of the hero's costume, cf. entry on WD **4**.

[4] Zettler, 'Chronological', 263.

[5] Legrain, *Culture*, 903 = Bregstein, *Seal Use*, no. 10 and Legrain, *Culture*, 910 = Bregstein, *Seal Use*, no. 23. See also nos. 901–23 and Bregstein, *Seal Use*, nos. 1–51.

[6] Cf. WD **4** (pl XVIII.2) and WD **8** (pl XVIII.3).

[7] In addition to the Nippur sealings, the following seals and sealings from controlled excavations resemble WD **17**, WD **36**, and WD **51**: Legrain, *Ur*, pl 40.757; Petrie, Mackay, Wainwright, *Meydum*, pl 36.30 (rampant winged lions from a cylinder seal), 31 (rampant lions from a stone stamp seal); Schmidt, *Persepolis II*, pl 3.2,3; pl 4.4–7; pl 5.9–13. Of these, nos. 3 and 6 show the hero battling inverted wingless lions.

For unprovenanced examples, see Delaporte, *Catalogue*, nos. 501 (= Bordreuil, *BN*, no. 129), a cylinder and 636, a stamp; Bordreuil, *BN*, no. 129 (see Delaporte, above) and no. 138, a cylinder; works (exclusive of those already noted above) cited in Boardman, 'Pyramidal', nos. 107 (= *AGDS* [Munich, I] no. 236); 108 (at Oxford); 109 (British Museum, WA 115551); 110 (at Oxford); 111 (Metropolitan Museum, NY, no. L.46.25.8); 113 (at the Bibliothèque Nationale, Paris); B. Teissier, *Ancient Near Eastern Cylinder Seals from the Marcopoli Collection* (Beverly Hills, 1984) nos. 289–93.

[8] For a discussion of Persian Hero iconography, see the entry on WD **4**, p. 214ff. Cf. also Zettler, 'Chronological', 257–270, and Root, *King, passim*.

A common variant of this motif shows the hero battling a single monster (cf. entries on WD **4** and WD **8**).

[9] Meshorer-Qedar, *Coinage of Samaria*, nos. 59–60.

[10] Cross, 'Papyri', 29.

[11] Moorey, 'Metalwork', *CHI II*, 864.

The archaeological evidence from Palestine confirms the trend toward stamp seals in the Persian period. Controlled excavations in Palestine have unearthed only one Achaemenid cylinder seal, a small (2.4 cm high) carnelian cylinder from a fifth-century context at Tell el-Heir in northwest Sinai (nearer Egypt than the Palestinian 'heartland').[12] This seal shows the Persian Hero as Master of Animals repelling flanking griffins.

As for impressions of Achaemenid cylinder seals, although Stern claims that none have been found in Palestine,[13] he illustrates at least one bulla that may have been impressed by a cylinder.[14] This bulla, discovered at Shechem, depicts an archer drawing his bow; behind him is a winged disk, and behind the disk is what appears to be a piece of palm tree branch or monster wing. This latter detail might belong to the object of the archer's aim, in which case, this must be a cylinder impression. If the incomplete object is a tree, that, too, would indicate a cylinder rather than a stamp; such trees appear only on cylinders.

Another probable cylinder impression—it is catalogued as such, in fact—was discovered at Samaria.[15] The fragmentary image was originally about 2 cm high and consisted of the Persian Hero battling at least one winged lion.[16] The horizontal wave detail at the top of the design would be more appropriate on a cylinder than on a stamp seal where a ground line would be expected, not a 'sky' line. Reisner believed the clay fragment to have come from a clay tablet,[17] another good (if not definitive) reason to believe the imprint came from a cylinder.

It would have been tricky to employ a cylinder on the small clay bullae attached to the Samaria papyri, and the vertical dimensions of the sealings (1.2 cm, 1.7 cm, 1.6 cm) might seem exceedingly tiny for a cylinder. On the other hand, there are hints of horizontal edges at the top and bottom of WD **17**, WD **36** and WD **51** that suggest they might have come from cylinders, and both WD **36** and WD **51** show incomplete images, as if there had not been room for the cylinder to make a complete revolution. Achaemenid cylinders in particular are known for their minute size, more like beads than cylinders.[18] Considerable evidence on this point is provided by seals and

---

[12] E. Oren, 'The 'Migdol' Fortress in Northwest Sinai', *Qadmoniot* 10 (1977) (Hebrew) 76 (= Collon, *First Impressions*, 423 = Stern, *Material Culture*, fig. 316 and p. 198).

[13] Stern, *Material Culture*, 197–8.

[14] Stern, *Material Culture*, fig. 317 (and cover photo) = G. E. Wright, *Shechem, The Biography of a Biblical City* (New York-Toronto, 1965) 168, fig. 94.

[15] Reisner, Fisher, Lyon, *Harvard*, pl 57h.1–2; cf. Stern, *Material Culture*, 197.

A third related impression was also found at Samaria, but this bulla probably came from a large scaraboid seal (over 2 cm high); it depicts the 'Persian Hero' battling a griffin which stands on a 'royal sphinx' (Crowfoot, Crowfoot, Kenyon, *Samaria-Sebaste*, 88, pl 15.42).

[16] In the published photograph (Reisner, Fisher, Lyon, *Harvard*, pl 57h.2) the hero's right arm is not clearly visible; if it were horizontal, there should be another lion on the hero's other side; if the arm were lowered, it would hold a weapon with which to dispatch a single lion.

[17] Since Reisner noted when impressions carried the imprint of papyrus documents, calling them 'letter seals', it is plausible that he is correct in supposing the impression was part of a clay document. He notes that the impression seemed to be next to the rounded edge of the putative tablet.

[18] Moorey, 'Metalwork', 864.

impressions from Nippur[19] and Persepolis.[20] Numerous cylinders seem to have been about 2 cm high, and not a few cylinders measure less.

Without actually seeing the Palestinian bullae cited above, it is impossible to say that they definitively came from cylinders rather than stamps; nor can it be claimed that the evidence for cylinders in the Daliyeh material is conclusive. Nevertheless, the possibility should not be dismissed that in the first half of the fourth century at Samaria, cylinders may still have been used occasionally, even though the documents they sealed were papyrus, not clay tablets.

At Nippur, many of the owners of cylinder seals with Persian Hero contest scenes were middle-level public officials, among them men with Babylonian, Egyptian and Jewish names.[21] Despite the attractiveness of the theory that, at Samaria, ownership of a Court Style cylinder seal indicated official status in the Persian administration, a recent study of Nippur sealings found that there was no correlation between a seal owner's office and his seal imagery.[22]

E. Akurgal who published two uninscribed Daskyleion bullae[23] says the cache of bullae[24] at Daskyleion on the Hellespont had traces of papyrus and string on the back, but it is unclear whether all bullae carried such traces of having been affixed to papyrus documents. If all the Daskyleion bullae came from papyrus rolls, then the presence of the cylinder sealings mentioned somewhat contradictorily by K. Balkan, the co-publisher of the bullae,[25] would indicate that Persian officials could seal papyrus documents as well as clay tablets with cylinders.[26] If, as Balkan proposes, these bullae came from a satrapal archive, it would seem that official satrapal documents written on papyrus could be sealed by either stamps or cylinders.

---

[19] A random sampling of cylinder seal measurements for twenty-four Persian Hero contest scenes provided in Bregstein, *Seal Use* (nos. 7–30) finds twelve cylinders (i.e. half) with both dimensions less than two cm, the same approximate size as the three impressions under discussion here.

[20] Schmidt, *Persepolis II*, pl 2, PT6 3; pl 8, no. 25; pl 10, no. 33 (which resembles the Shechem sealing [see above]) and no. 34; pl 11, no. 40. Actual cylinder seals less than 2 cm high: pl 15: PT5 266, PT5 743, PT3 111; pl 16: PT6 51.

[21] Bregstein, *Seal Use*, cat. nos. 1–51.

[22] Bregstein, *Seal Use*, 206–7.

[23] Akurgal, 'Fouilles', p. 23 and pl 12.

[24] 300 bullae, according to Akurgal ('Fouilles', 23) but more recently calculated at 400 (Bregstein, *Seal Use*, 64).

[25] Balkan, 'Inscribed Bullae', 128.

[26] Moorey ('Metalwork', 864) echoes current scholarly consensus that 'cylinder seals were largely used for official purposes, whilst private individuals preferred stamp seals and signet rings'.

WD 3B. Persian Hero Contests Flanking Animals

(PLATE XVIII.1)

Mus. Inv. 779[1]
Papyrus 14: lease or sale of storechambers[2]
Image size: n.a.
Bulla size: n.a.
Clay colour: n.a.
String preserved; left and right of horizontal image
Seal type: oval stamp or scaraboid?

ALTHOUGH the outline impression of the oval rim of the seal is well defined and complete, WD **3B** is the least clear of the five related images of the Persian Hero battling flanking animals found at Daliyeh.[3] The oval shape and the depth of the impression suggest the original seal was an engraved stone seal such as a scaraboid, a ringstone specially prepared for mounting in a metal ring or a ring with a raised bezel. There are no signs of a nick from a ring bezel.

Still faintly visible in the smoothly worn impression are the Persian Hero's left arm raised in the characteristic manner to grip the head or hind leg of an opponent and a piece of the vertical line of the hero's cloak. Traces of an indeterminate type of animal, probably winged, appear on the right side of the bulla. The presence of an animal on the left can be assumed on the basis of the hero's central placement in the composition.

---

[1] The following description is based on a single photograph. WD **3B** was unavailable for inspection.

[2] F. M. Cross, personal communication.

[3] WD **3A** (pl XIX.1–3)—also attached to Papyrus 14, WD **17** (pl XVII.1), WD **36** (pl XVII.2), WD **51** (XVII.3). Also related are the scenes of the 'Persian Hero' battling a single opponent: WD **4** (pl XVIII.2), WD **8** (pl XVIII.3), WD **19** (pl XX.1). For discussion of the motif, see entry for WD **4**, p. 214ff.

WD 4. Persian Hero Battles Rampant Winged Lion

(PLATE XVIII.2)

Mus. Inv. 959
Loose sealing
Image size: 1.9 x 1.7 cm
Bulla size: 1.9 x 1.7
Clay colour: deep reddish brown
String preserved; visible at top and bottom of impression
Papyrus imprint
Seal type: stone stamp (?)
Published: Cross, 'Papyri', 28, pl 62; Cross, 'Dâliyeh', 51, fig. 37.

THE bottom edge of WD **4** has cracked into two pieces barely held together by the string, but in general the large round image is crisp and covers the entire surface of the bulla. The edges of the impression, however, are not visible, and the left edge of the bulla has been chipped away. Because the surface of the impression is slightly concave—like an inverted bowl[1]—the sealing might have been made by a circular stone stamp seal with a convex surface, a scaraboid,[2] perhaps, or a Neo-Babylonian-style conoid in blue chalcedony, a type favoured in the Achaemenid period.[3]

WD **4** shows the Persian Hero battling a single animal,[4] a motif of Mesopotamian ancestry[5] which in its Persian incarnation became one of the most conventional of all Achaemenid images in the official Court Style.[6] On WD **4** the bearded Persian Hero[7] (turning to the viewer's right) wears a cylindrical, fluted crown on his head[8] and the flowing long-sleeved Persian robe fastened by cords or lappets over the breast and

---

[1] WD **8** (pl XVIII.3) with a similar design is a convex sealing from a seal with a concave surface.

[2] Keel, 'Tell Keisan', cat. no. 21, a scaraboid with a closely related design.

[3] Boardman, *GGFR*, p. 305, 323.

[4] Note WD **17** (pl XVII.1), WD **36** (pl XVII.2) and WD **51** (pl XVII.3) show the Persian Hero contesting two animals.

[5] E. Porada, review of Schmidt, *Persepolis II*, 68. Cf. also A. Sachs, 'The Late Assyrian Royal-Seal Type', *Iraq* XV (1953) 167–70. For a seventh-century Phoenician example, clearly influenced by the Assyrian type, cf. Bordreuil, *BN*, no. 18, the scaraboid seal of 'Mikaʾel'. Cf. also S. M. Paley, 'Inscribed Neo-Assyrian and Neo-Babylonian Seals', *Insight Through Images*, ed. M. Kelly-Buccellati (Malibu, 1986) 214–18.

[6] On the Court Style, note Boardman, *GGFR*, pp. 305–9; Root, *King, passim* (and see below); E. Porada, *Corpus of Ancient Near Eastern Seals in North American Collections, I: The Collection of the Pierpont Morgan Library* (Washington, 1948) nos. 819ff.

[7] Another term applied to this figure is 'Royal Hero'; see discussion below.

[8] There has been considerable discussion over the nomenclature and meaning of the Persian crown or crowns. Koch, *Dareios*, 212–13, provides a judicious summation of the problems. For a bibliography on the subject see Leith, *Imagery*, 400.

worn over a long underskirt with gathered folds.[9] This probably ceremonial outfit appears on the Persepolis reliefs as well as on numerous Persian Court Style seals. Here the hero's opponent is a hefty, winged, horned lion who rears up on his hind legs to paw at the hero's left arm and waist. The hero throttles the monster's throat with his left hand. Clutching a short sword (the *akinakes*[10]) in his lowered right hand he prepares to plunge it into the lion's belly.

Close parallels to WD **4** come from Samaria, greater Syro-Palestine and the western Persian Empire. WD **8** (pl XVIII.3) is a near double of WD **4**. In Samaria itself, Reisner discovered a clay fragment, possibly of a clay tablet, bearing a seal impression of the Persian Hero fighting a winged lion very like WD **4**.[11] Crowfoot and Kenyon excavated a clay bulla bearing the cylinder seal impression of an Achaemenid seal on which the Persian Hero battles a griffin.[12] A green oval scaraboid with this scene comes from Phoenician Tell Keisan.[13]

Similar images, produced by both stamps and cylinders appear in the two richest corpora of dated seal impressions from the Persian period: on the tablets of the Murashu Archives from Nippur (455–405)[14] and on Persepolis Treasury and Fortification texts (*c.*515–424).[15] Galling's compilation of inscribed seals from first millennium Syria-Palestine includes three cylinders with the long-skirted, flat-footed, frontal Persian Hero, arms outstretched, battling rampant monsters.[16]

Sealings of the fifth century excavated at Ur[17] and at Persian Daskyleion[18] on the Hellespont should also be mentioned. J. Boardman has published several Persian

[9] Koch, *Dareios*, 203–11; T. Linders, 'The Kandys in Greece and Persia', *Opuscula Atheniensia* XV:8 (1984) 107–14; B. Goldman, 'Origin of the Persian Robe', *Iranica Antiqua* 4 (1964) 132–52; P. Beck, 'A Note on the Reconstruction of the Achaemenid Robe', *Iranica Antiqua* 9 (1972) 116–22; Boardman, 'Pyramidal', 31–2.

[10] On the *akinakes*, cf. A. Farkas, 'Is There Anything Persian in Persian Art?', *Ancient Persia: The Art of an Empire*, ed. D. Schmandt-Besserat (Malibu, 1980) 19, with references.

[11] Reisner, Fisher, Lyon, *Harvard*, pl 57.h2. According to the report, the impression came from a small cylinder seal 20 mm high, not an unusual size for Achaemenid cylinders (see entry for WD **17**).

[12] Crowfoot, Crowfoot, Kenyon, *Samaria-Sebaste*, pl 15.42.

[13] Keel, 'Tell Keisan', cat. no. 21.

[14] I.e. Legrain, *Culture*, 941 = Bregstein, *Seal Use*, no. 90, cylinder impression, 17 mm x 17 mm.

[15] Schmidt, *Persepolis II*, pl 13, no. 60. Note also M. Garrison's forthcoming publication of these impressions, drawing from his Ph.D. dissertation, *Seal Workshops*.

[16] Galling, 'Bildsiegel', p. 196, pl 11.162–4. At more than two cm in height, all three cylinders are larger than the proposed stamp seal of WD **4**. Galling (p. 164) notes that the workshop for these cylinders was probably Mesopotamian and that the seals should date to the fifth century. Of less certain provenance, there is a conoid agate stamp seal 'from Damascus' in Berlin published in L. Jakob-Rost, *Die Stempelsiegel im Vorderasiatischen Museum* (Berlin, 1975) no. 477. The Bibliothèque Nationale's collection in Paris includes a number of stamp seals with this motif (Delaporte, *Catalogue*, pl XXXVIII.639, 642 [with Lydian inscriptional device], 644).

[17] Legrain, *Ur*, nos. 751–5. The motif is similar on these Ur stamp seal impressions, but the style is not. Porada describes them as 'Graecizing' in *JNES* XX (1961) 68–9, and the warrior's costume is not definitively Persian. No. 757, which shows the Persian Hero in a long tunic fighting off flanking Bes animals seems closer in artistic spirit to WD **4**.

[18] Balkan, 'Inscribed Bullae', pl 33.b (also pl 33.a). Balkan (125) reported that 'the number of bullae containing this scene amounts to thirty. Exactly the same scene [as on his pl 33.a] is found on 86 more complete or fragmentary bullae but without the [Old Persian] inscription'. The Old Persian cuneiform inscription read 'I am Xerxes, the king'. Balkan's pl 33.b is an uninscribed example. The bulla in pl 34.a displays a very similar image produced by a

period Lydian stamp seals with this device[19] which he dates no later than the early fifth century.

A series of fourth-century Sidonian silver half- and sixteenth-shekels[20] are of particular interest in relation to WD **4** and Samaria; they show the Persian Hero confronting a rampant—although unwinged—lion. Except for the missing wings, WD **4** and the coins have the same image. Samaria minted a number of coins based on these Sidonian models.[21] Meshorer has noted: 'The strong influence of the Sidonian coinage is due to the fact that the Sidonian currency was dominant in the region of Samaria, indicating strong commercial connections with the Phoenician economy'.[22] Thus, the image on a seal, possibly belonging to a local official of the Persian administration in the territory of Samaria, matches in its essential motif that on fourth-century coins clearly in use and perhaps even minted there. However, the theory that ownership of a Court Style cylinder seal at Samaria indicated official status in the Persian administration is rendered less persuasive by a recent study of Nippur sealings which found that there was no correlation between a seal owner's office and his seal imagery.[23]

That this image embodied Achaemenid ideals of royal power as well as possessing certain apotropaic powers is succinctly demonstrated in the heart of Persia. Door jambs in the palace of Darius I (522–486) at Persepolis were carved with reliefs showing the Persian Hero battling a rampant winged lion-monster.[24]

The precise symbolic content of the scene on WD **4** (and WD **8** and the related images from Samaria) derives ultimately from such essentially Mesopotamian traditions as the 'Gilgamesh' heroes slaying a monster. M. Root, who made an extensive study of the nuances of Achaemenid royal imagery, found the motif of the 'royal hero' stabbing a rampant lion, lion monster, bull or griffin monster on ten of the fifteen known official royal seal types inscribed with the name of the Persian king discovered at Persepolis.[25] It also appears on numerous uninscribed seals as here in the case of WD **4**. Root summarizes the various scholarly interpretations of the scene: the hero is the king; the hero is a mythical figure distinct from the king; the hero is the king acting for Ahura Mazda; the hero is a god.[26] On the basis of Assyrian analogies, Root tentatively favours the king acting on behalf of his god, Ahura Mazda.

---

stamp seal with an Aramaic inscription. In an earlier report from Daskyleion, E. Akurgal published two other uninscribed Daskyleion bullae ('Fouilles', pl 12). All the foregoing images show the Persian Hero grasping the rampant monster by the horn, but there is also a landscape element: a date palm.

[19] Boardman, 'Pyramidal', p. 30ff, pl 4.76–102 (83 = Delaporte, *Catalogue* [above] pl XXXVIII.642; 86 = Boardman, *GGFR*, 824).

[20] Hill, *BMC Coins*, (Phoenicia), pl XVIII.5,7 (inscribed *'b*); pl XIX, 9–11; pl XX.5; pl XXI.3 (inscribed *mz* for Mazdai/Mazaeios, satrap of Cilicia and, after 347 BCE, governor of Sidon), and see below. Betlyon suggests that this motif persisted on Sidonian coinage from *c*.435–347, especially on silver half-shekels (Betlyon, *Coinage*, pls 1–3).

[21] Meshorer-Qedar, *Coinage of Samaria*, nos. 16, 44–5, 48–51.

[22] Meshorer-Qedar, *Coinage of Samaria*, 23.

[23] Bregstein, *Seal Use*, 206–7.

[24] Porada, *Art*, pl 44, and note also her comments on p. 159.

[25] Root, *King*, 303; cf. also pp. 118–22 and chap. 8, part B.

[26] Root, *King*, p. 303.

In Assyrian art, the king—in human form—killed real animals, not mythical ones; only gods, genii and mythical figures battled the fantastic creatures. On the other hand, the Achaemenid hero battles real and fantastic animals alike.[27] What the Achaemenid commissioners of these seals may have wanted to imply, then, would be the new concept that the Persian king was simultaneously the human king as well as the super-human hero of Assyrian scenes with fantastic animals.[28] Darius' boast on the Naqsh-i-Rustam inscription somewhat bears this out, 'I was a better rider; as archer I was a better archer, whether on foot or horseback. As spearthrower, I was superior, whether on foot or horseback'.[29]

---

[27] Root, *King*, p, 304–5. Cf. also Porada, (n. 24 above) p. 68.

[28] Root, *King*, p. 305. Cf. also Porada, *JNES* 20, 68. Root's basic thesis is that the Persian royal ideology adapted the time-honoured Mesopotamian/Egyptian model of the king as conqueror of subject nations to a somewhat more benign ideal of the king as adored and supported by his people. Ethnic identities were clearly portrayed in artistic representations of the king with his subjects. The Persian king as hero was subduing danger rather than alien nations, singlehandedly protecting his subjects. Root makes the case for the hero on the Persepolis reliefs as the king representing the idea of the 'Persian Man', a phrase which appears on the Behistun inscription. She concludes that the crowned figure on the seals derives directly from Assyrian/Mesopotamian traditions.

[29] J. Borchhardt, 'Bildnisse Achaimenidischer Herrscher', *AMI Ergänzungsband* 10 (1983) 208; R. G. Kent, *Old Persian Grammar, Texts, Lexicon* (2nd. ed.; New Haven, 1953) 140.

WD 8. Persian Hero Battles Winged Bull

(PLATE XVIII.3)

Mus. Inv. 963
Loose sealing
Image size: 1.5 cm x 1.8 cm (as preserved)
Bulla size: 1.9 cm x 2 cm
Clay colour: dark reddish brown
String preserved; top and bottom of horizontal image
Papyrus fragment affixed to back; papyrus fibres on back and image surface
Papyrus imprint
Seal type: stamp seal

WD **8** was produced by a deeply concave round stamp seal, a Neo-Babylonian cone, perhaps. The engraved surface area of this seal would have been slightly larger than that of the Greek-style rings and stamps which impressed so many of the Daliyeh bullae. The plain curved edge outline of the notably convex sealing survives only on the right side.[1] The top of the bulla has broken away. In addition, the original lump of clay was insufficiently prepared to receive the full impression of the stamp, so that the lower portion of the image never appeared on the clay. Only the central portion of the fairly crisp image remains.[2] The apparent shape and the Achaemenid design suggest the seal was perhaps an import to Samaria from farther east.

WD **8** represents yet another example from Samaria of the Persian Court Style.[3] Among the Wadi Daliyeh bullae, the design of WD **4** (pl XVIII.2) is most similar. On both bullae we see the same bearded Persian Hero wearing the high Persian crown and a flowing long-sleeved robe over a long underskirt or tunic; the expected chignon hairstyle is indicated at the nape of his neck.[4] In the case of WD **8**, the hero's opponent is a slender, winged bull in profile facing the hero;[5] the bull rears up on its hind legs as the hero grabs its topknot—or horn or forehead fringe—(this is unclear) with his outstretched left hand. Careless sealing has truncated the hero's left arm; however, the motif is familiar enough to allow for confident restoration of the lowered right hand gripping the dagger to dispatch the rather unthreatening beast. The animal has upcurled wings with feathers patterned into two ranks. In an unusual variation on the

---

[1] Note by contrast that WD **4** (pl XVIII.2), a similar sealing, has a concave surface.

[2] The photograph is particularly misleading in the case of WD **8**.

[3] Note WD **17** (pl XVII.1), WD **36** (pl XVII.2) and WD **51** (pl XVII.3) show the Persian Hero contesting two animals.

[4] See entry on WD **4**, above, p. 214ff., for discussion of the Persian Hero, his costume and the iconography of the motif.

[5] A single winged bull may also appear on WD **38** (pl XV.3).

norm, both wings are shown, scissors-fashion. There is also a short, cropped horselike mane.[6] The animal's hooved forelegs flail the air before him, and his tail trails behind.

In addition to WD **4**, glyptic parallels to WD **8** are to be found at Samaria[7] and across the western Persian Empire.[8] The large corpus of impressions from Nippur in southern Mesopotamia includes a number of Persian Hero contests against a winged bull, although the bull has one wing and consistently turns away from the Hero rather than facing him as on WD **8**.[9] Examples of Court Style representations of the Persian Hero contesting two-winged opponents are rarer, but the British Museum owns an unprovenanced Court Style cylinder seal inscribed in Aramaic showing the Persian Hero battling a two-winged bull-man and a two-winged lion as the Ahura Mazda figure hovers overhead.[10]

In addition, the Persian Hero battles a single opponent—a lion—on coins, including issues from Sidon[11] which Samaria imitated for its own coinage.[12]

To conclude, WD **8**, like WD **4** which it resembles, comes from a well-executed stone stamp seal in Achaemenid Court Style. The traditional motif on WD **8** appears on seals from the sixth through the fourth centuries.

---

[6] Many winged bulls on the Nippur sealings have similar manes. Cf. Legrain, *Culture*, no. 944 = Bregstein, *Seal Use*, no. 139; Legrain, *Culture*, no. 875 = Bregstein, *Seal Use*, no. 413.

[7] On actual stamps and cylinders as well as impressions. For a more detailed discussion, with references, see the entry on WD 4, above, p. 214ff.
    An unprovenanced Achaemenid cylinder in the Bibliothèque Nationale, inscribed *'dry* in Aramaic, shows the Persian Hero battling flanking bulls, one winged and the other wingless (Galling, 'Bildsiegel', no. 164 = Delaporte, *Catalogue*, no. 501). Cf. also the conoid stamp showing the Persian Hero fighting a wingless bull which is very like WD 8 (Delaporte, *Catalogue*, no. 639).

[8] Schmidt, *Persepolis II*, pl 5, no. 8; pl 11, no. 37.

[9] Legrain, *Culture*, no. 946 = Bregstein, *Seal Use*, no. 96; Legrain, *Culture*, no. 952 = Bregstein, *Seal Use*, no. 97; Bregstein, *Seal Use*, nos. 98–9.

[10] Galling, 'Bildsiegel', no. 163. The two-winged variation may be a survival of an older Mesopotamian tradition; cf. Collon, *First Impressions*, nos. 866 and 894.

[11] See entry for WD 4, above, p. 214ff.

[12] Meshorer-Qedar, *Coinage of Samaria*, nos. 16, 44–5, 48–51.

WD 3A, WD 10A, WD 11B, WD 12, WD 24.
Hero Flanked by Winged Sphinxes

(PLATE XIX.1–3)

WD 3A

Mus. Inv. 762[1]

Papyrus 14: lease or sale of storechambers[2]

Image size: 0.8 cm x 1.5 cm (measurement assumed)

Bulla size: n.a.

Clay colour: n.a.

String preserved; left and right of horizontal image

Additional bulla attached to Papyrus 14: WD **3B**

Published: Cross, 'Papyri', 29, pl 63.j

WD 10A

Mus. Inv. 763

Loose sealing

Image size: 0.8 cm x 1.5 cm (estimate)

Bulla size: n.a.

Clay colour: n.a.

String preserved; left and right of horizontal image

Additional bulla found in association with WD **10A**: WD **10B**

Published: Cross, 'Papyri', 29, pl 63.k

WD 11B

Mus. Inv. 765

Papyrus 1, slave sale, dated March 19, 335.[3]

Image size: 0.8 cm x 1.5 cm (measurement assumed)

Bulla size: n.a.

Clay colour: n.a.

String preserved; left and right of horizontal image

Additional bullae found with WD **11B** on Papyrus 1: WD **11A–G**[4]

Published: Cross, 'Papyri', 29, pl 63.l

---

[1] WD **3A**, WD **10A**, WD **11B** are discussed only on the basis of photographs; they were unavailable for examination.

[2] F. M. Cross, personal communication.

[3] Cf. Cross, 'Samaria Papyrus 1'; corrections in Cross, 'Report'; Gropp, *Samaria Papyri*, 1–37.

[4] The Papyrus 1 bullae have not actually been examined by the present editor. Tiny photographs of WD **11A** which may show flanking winged sphinxes, WD **11E**, depicting a mature Greek man draped in a himation, and WD **11D**, WD **11F** and WD **11G**, which remain illegible, were made accessible as were two photographs of WD **11B** and of WD **11C**, which shows Herakles.

WD 12

Mus. Inv. 965

Loose sealing

Image size: 0.8 cm x 1.5 cm

Bulla size: n.a.

Clay colour: dark reddish brown

String preserved; left and right of horizontal image

Papyrus fibres on front and back

Papyrus imprint

Published: Cross, 'Papyri', 29, pl 63.m

WD 24

Mus. Inv. 921

Loose sealing

Same image as WD **3A**, WD **10A**, WD **11B**, WD **12**.

Image size: 0.8 cm x 1.5 cm

Bulla size:

Clay colour: reddish brown, burnt black in some places

String not preserved

Papyrus imprint

Published: Cross, 'Papyri', 29, pl 63.n (upside down)

Seal type: metal finger ring

THESE five bullae come from the same seal, probably a metal finger ring with a flattened oval bezel; the imprint of the hoop of the ring is visible on the right side of WD **3A** and WD **24**. Because this seal is represented by sealings attached to three different papyri, and because the only name repeated in all three was that of the Samarian Yehonur, 'a wealthy slaveholder',[5] Cross suggests that perhaps the seal belonged to him,[6] although this is impossible to prove. The five bullae vary in clarity and state of preservation; WD **12** is the most complete, but none is particularly well preserved; perhaps the original seal was already worn when it was put to use.

An irregular border of tiny dots circles the design close to the outer edge of the impression. The image is probably a provincially manufactured variant of the well-known Achaemenid motif, the Persian Hero battling flanking animals. Including WD **3A**,[7] there are at least five such images among the Wadi Daliyeh sealings.[8] In this example, the hero threatens a pair of winged sphinxes with Persian king heads, complete with chignon, beard and dentate crown, a creature often called the 'royal

---

[5] Cross, 'Report', 18.

[6] Cross, 'Papyri', 29.

[7] For convenience, the whole group of duplicate sealings will be termed 'WD **3A**'.

[8] See entries on WD **17** (pl XVII.1), WD **36** (pl XVII.2), WD **51** (pl XVII.3), WD **3B** (pl XVIII.1); cf. also the variant of this motif in which the hero is depicted with only one adversary: WD **4** (pl XVIII.2), WD **8** (pl XVIII.3) and WD **19** (pl XX.1).

sphinx'.[9] A single curved wing is visible over the back of each animal as he sits on his haunches with his tail raised behind him. The sphinxes seem unconcerned by the figure between them. The bearded hero, who wears a short tunic, is larger in scale than the sphinxes. He seems to have short hair, or is perhaps wearing a flat cap. Turning to his right, he raises his fully extended right arm toward the sphinx in a menacing gesture. His left arm is lowered behind him. *Contra* Cross who mentions a scimitar,[10] it appears that the hero carries no weapon in either hand.

A parallel to the hero's odd, bent knees is found in a plasma scaraboid with a vague Cypriot provenance.[11] As on WD **3A**, the scene is one of a hero flanked by animals. In this example, a youth with bent knees similar to those on WD **3A** stands between a pair of rearing horses. Boardman assigns this work stylistically to a group of Archaic East Greek seals.[12] However, this scene of a hero flanked by horses differs from the other works in Boardman's group in its broadly horizontal composition and in its multiple figures. These aspects of the scaraboid are characteristic also of many sixth-century Cypriot seals.[13] In addition, the decorated border and multiple figures of the plasma scaraboid would not be out of place in Phoenician work of the Archaic period. WD **3A**, however, probably came from a ring of the late fifth or early fourth century, not of the Archaic period.

The scene on WD **3A**, although conventional, deserves some discussion. There are two other Samarian bullae (WD **15A**, pl XXI.3 and WD **53**, pl XV.1) on which Persian 'Royal Spinxes' make an appearance; the same head type also appears on the flanking scorpion men of WD **25** (pl XXI.1). However WD **3A** is the only bulla on which sphinxes are clearly portrayed as the hero's adversaries.[14] This circumstance, while not unusual in Achaemenid glyptic art, may strike the viewer as rather bizarre in view of the sphinxes' royal heads. Why would the Hero fight creatures with the royal countenance? However illogical the scene on WD **3A** may seem, antecedents as well as contemporary parallels come readily to hand, not from Egyptian art, but on Mesopotamian seals.

In its Egyptian homeland, the sphinx was a protective being—the Pharaoh's guardian whose face was often that of the reigning Pharaoh; as an embodiment of the Pharaoh's might, sphinxes are represented smiting the enemies of Egypt.[15] Phoenician

---

[9] I.e. Boardman, 'Pyramidal', p. 34.

[10] Cross, 'Papyri', 29.

[11] Boardman, *AG Gems*, 135 = Richter, MMA, 38 = Richter, *EGGE*, 98 (ex. Cesnola), said to come from Cyprus.

[12] Boardman, *AG Gems*, p. 65.

[13] Boardman, *AG Gems*, 70–73, pp. 45–7.

[14] WD **19** (pl XX.1) might show the Persian Hero attacking a sphinx.

[15] A. Dessenne, *Le Sphinx, étude iconographique des origines à la fin du second millénaire* (Paris, 1957); R. D. Barnett, *Catalogue of the Nimrud Ivories in the British Museum*, 2nd ed. (London, 1975) p. 83 ff.; Winter, 'Phoenician', 1ff.; M. Trokay, 'Le bas-relief au sphinx de Damas', *SP* IV [1986] 99–118; G. Markoe, *Phoenician Bronze and Silver Bowls from Cyprus and the Mediterranean* (University of California, 1985) 34 ff.; cf. also Ashmolean/*ANES* III, p. 41.

Cf. also H. G. Fischer's, 'The Ancient Egyptian Attitude Towards the Monstrous', *Monsters and Demons*, eds. A. Farkas, *et al*. (Mainz, 1987) 13–26, esp. 14. Fischer stresses that in Egypt, composite creatures such as sphinxes were 'hieroglyphic composites, products of a style of representation that was hieroglyphic from its inception, at the

sphinxes of the Iron Age for the most part reflect the positive, protective Egyptian concept of the sphinx.[16] Moving inland, away from Phoenicia to Tell Halaf in northern Syria, apotropaic sphinxes in the ninth century decorated and protected gateways.[17]

On the other hand, for Mesopotamians, sphinxes appear to have been another exotic item of hero fodder.[18] In the Neo-Assyrian period, for example, cylinder seals show the four-winged Assyrian genius battling a winged sphinx,[19] and the royal huntsman hunting a sphinx.[20] A Neo-Assyrian faience cylinder from the Mari excavations shows the latter scene; its cataloguer comments that the head of the hunter's prey is very like that of the hunter.[21] The Achaemenid Empire absorbed this Mesopotamian concept of the sphinx (as did the Greeks, who viewed the sphinx as a malevolent *daimon*[22]). Apparently, Achaemenid seal cutters working in the Court Style blithely depicted the Persian Hero killing beasts whose heads were fashioned on the same pattern as his own.[23] In all fairness, however, it should be noted that these artists, sensitive to the paradoxical logic of religious symbols, also illustrate the protective (apotropaic) and supportive aspects of such sphinxes; on many Achaemenid seals they are found supporting, variously, the Persian Hero or the so-called 'symbol of Ahura Mazda' or sometimes, both.[24]

The fact that WD **3A** comes from a ring and illustrates a rather crude version of a standard Court Style scene suggests a provincial source; even Samaria cannot be completely ruled out. The non-Phoenician sphinx type, however, suggests that the model for the WD **3A** ring came from an area closer to Mesopotamia or the Persian heartland. This theory is sustained by the fact that, first, as noted above, excavated seal impressions which show the Persian Hero/royal hunter battling a royal sphinx who is

---

beginning of the Dynastic Period' (13). This aspect prevented the creatures from being truly 'monstrous' in a negative sense; it is especially true of 'human-headed animals that embody the might and majesty of the king' (14).

[16] Cf. a seventh century Phoenician bowl from Idalion (Cyprus) on which is depicted a sphinx resting its paws on a fallen enemy (Moscati, *Phoenicians*, p. 442, cat. no. 128 [Louvre]).

[17] Collon, *First Impressions*, p. 83; Frankfort, *Art*, 177.

[18] Sphinxes appear on cylinders of the Akkadian period, but do not become common until the first millennium (Collon, *First Impressions*, p. 186).

[19] Collon, *First Impressions*, 964 (British Museum 130807).

[20] Collon, *First Impressions*, p. 75 and no. 380 (British Museum 89800).

[21] H. Kühne, et al., *Das Rollsiegel in Syrien* (exhibition catalogue, Eberhard-Karls-Universität, Tübingen, 1980) no. 90 (= Damascus Museum no. 1421). Cf. also Collon, *First Impressions*, no. 356, from the Nimrud excavations, dating to the late seventh century.

[22] *OCD*, *s.v.* 'sphinx'; as is usually the case with frightening beasts, sphinxes in Greece not only terrorized victims, but also protected sacrally charged spaces such as sanctuaries and graves.

[23] Legrain, *Culture*, no. 912 = Bregstein, *Seal Use*, no. 47; see also Wiseman, *Cylinder*, no. 104 (= Collon, *First Impressions*, 421 [British Museum no. 89781]); and Schmidt, *Persepolis II*, pl 4.4,5.
Similarly perplexing is the curious scene on a Samarian silver obol in which identical Persian Hero/King figures seem to confront (or embrace?) each other in the traditional 'contest scene' pose; each carries a dagger in his right hand (Meshorer-Qedar, *Coinage of Samaria*, no. 54); the obverse shows a Phoenician galley.

[24] Wiseman, *Cylinder*, no. 106 (British Museum no. 89352). This chalcedony cylinder with a very elaborate design is particularly notable; three different types of beings on this one seal have the identical Persian Hero head, namely, the 'Hero' himself, a pair of sphinxes, and the figure in the flying circle.

his facial twin have Mesopotamian and Persian provenances, and that second, this image appears not only on stamps but on cylinders, a seal-type native to Mesopotamia.[25]

---

[25] It would be helpful to know if this motif appears on any of the unpublished bullae excavated at Daskyleion (Akurgal, 'Fouilles', 20–4 and Balkan, 'Inscribed Bullae', 123–31).

WD I.3.22A. Persian Hero (?)

(PLATE XIX.4)

Mus. Inv. n.a.[1]
Loose sealing; excavated in the Abu Shinjeh Cave
Image size: n.a.
Bulla size: n.a.
Clay colour: n.a.
String preserved; parallel to vertical images
Papyrus imprint: n.a.
Seal type: engraved gem in metal finger ring?
Published: Cross, 'Papyri', 28; pl 36.4 (drawing) and pl 62.a (photograph)

WD **I.3.22A** is one of two impressions on a single clay bulla[2] found by P. Lapp's team of excavators *in situ* in the Abu Shinjeh Cave. Traces of a vertically oriented oval outline suggest a finger ring of a type Boardman dates to the mid-late fifth century,[3] but which appears, from the fourth-century context of the Wadi Daliyeh bullae, to continue into the next century on the fringes of the Greek world; a similar survival is attested to by the de Clercq group of finger rings from Phoenicia.[4]

Cross emphasizes the poor condition of this impression, noting that it was 'smeared in sealing'.[5] Apparently, the Persian Hero stands in profile to the viewer's right, preparing to despatch an animal now detectable only in traces. The image probably resembled that on WD **4** (pl XVIII.2).

---

[1] Unlocated. This entry can add little to Cross's description in *DWD*, as examination of this bulla has not been possible; the only available photographs are extremely difficult to read.

[2] The other impression, WD **I.3.22B** (pl X.1), seems to depict a winged Nike. As elsewhere, Greek and Near Eastern glyptic imagery appears side-by-side on the same document. The data does not exist to determine if there was any pattern of seal choice by social status or religious inclination on the part of the Samarians who sealed the Samaria Papyri.

[3] Boardman, *GGFR*, fig. 217 (type III), and p. 214.

[4] Boardman, *GGFR*, p. 221; de Ridder, *Collection*, pls 19–20.

[5] Cross, 'Papyri', 28.

WD 19. Persian Hero Attacking One Opponent

(PLATE XX.1)

Mus. Inv. 970
Loose sealing
Image size: 0.8 cm x 1.2 cm (as preserved)
Bulla size: 0.9 cm x 1.3 cm
Clay colour: reddish brown
String preserved; top and bottom of horizontal image
Papyrus fragments on reverse
Papyrus imprint
Seal type: metal finger ring

WD **19** appears to have been made by a metal finger ring, slightly smaller in size than most of the other Wadi Daliyeh bullae. The edge of a leaf-shaped bezel appears in impression on the left side of the bulla. Although the horizontal orientation of an image on a finger ring of this shape is unusual, it is not unknown; several Samarian bullae from metal finger rings have a similarly horizontal design.[1] Careless sealing left the right edge of the image unimpressed in the bulla; the remaining right half of the impression has sustained abrasions which erased the figure which filled the space. Only the left half of WD **19** still makes any visual sense.

There is no difficulty in recognizing the figure on the left side of WD **19** as the Persian Hero. The costume is consistent with the numerous examples of Persian Court Style seals found all over the western Persian Empire;[2] it is the same crown, hair style, beard, cloak, and full-length underdress found on WD **4** (pl XVIII.2), **8** (pl XVIII.3), **17** (pl XVII.1), etc. Both the heroes on WD **19** and WD **4** are armed with identical daggers which they hold in the same conventional retracted position from which to despatch their opponents.

Just what or who the WD **19** figure's opponent might be is unclear; it seems rather large in relation to the hero. A tentative suggestion in view of the ample available space on the bulla is that the hero is battling a sphinx.[3] A rather nondescript oval stamp seal found in the French excavations at Susa and dated to the Achaemenid period might be comparable.[4] On this seal a small *'personnage'* stands still before a seated sphinx depicted on a much larger scale. The indifferent workmanship of this seal makes it hard to relate to anything else, but it is the only seal the present editor has found with

---

[1] Cf. WD **44** (Greek; pl X.3); WD **48** (Phoenician? pl XXI.2); Gold Ring B (Phoenician? pl XVI.3).

[2] Cf. the discussion of the Persian Hero's costume in entry for WD **4**, p. 214ff.

[3] Cf. E. Møller, 'Cylinder Seals from the Horniman Museum, London', *Iraq* 48 (1986) no. 12, pl 12, a Neo-Babylonian carnelian cylinder seal showing a hero threatening a sphinx; cf. also Collon, *First Impressions*, no. 380 (British Museum 89800), another Neo-Babylonian cylinder depicting a sphinx in a more conventional context.

[4] P. Amiet, *Glyptique Susienne* (Paris, 1972) no. 2216.

an incongruity of scale similar to that of WD **19**, and it does come from a good Persian period archaeological context.

On the other Daliyeh examples, as well as on most Persian Hero Court Style contest scenes, the hero stands frontally with both feet firmly on the ground in a static hieratic posture. The artist implies that no creature, however horrible, could intimidate the hero into a defensive or even excessively offensive stance; the figure is the epitome of unruffled heroic calm. By contrast, the hero on WD **19** rushes forward to meet his adversary. Leading with his (far) left leg, the hero has swung his fully extended left arm upward—it is difficult to determine if the 'blob' at the end of the arm is the left hand or a mace—while he readies the dagger in his lowered right hand. Overall, the hero's body forms a sinuous 'S' shape, unlike the resolute verticals of the usual Persian Hero scenes. In another deviation from the normal Persian Court Style, the hero's garment bunches slightly over his bent right knee.

These anomalies of pose and modelling might be due to Greek stylistic influences on the (Near Eastern?) engraver of the WD **19** ring; conversely, the ring may have been carved by a worker more familiar with Greek styles who was commissioned to produce a Court Style image. An unusual comparison is provided by an Achaemenid cylinder seal, reportedly found at Borsippa in the early nineteenth century, on which two heroes each confront a different adversary.[5] The delicate drilled design elements and elegant animals call to mind the Persian Persepolis and Susian reliefs,[6] but Collon and others have noted signs of 'Hellenistic Greek influence' on this seal;[7] the pose of the Persian Hero on the left is much more animated than usual as he determinedly advances forward, dangling a lion by its hind leg. As on WD **19**, his long skirt clings and wrinkles around the trailing right leg and knee.

Persian Court Style single animal contest scenes on seals need not always involve a hero dressed in the Persian Hero costume, nor need these variant contest scenes be always as static as the Persian Hero contests. A number of sealings from Nippur show a hero in a stance related to that of the Persian Hero, but whose costume—a short tunic, sometimes worn under a long garment with a split skirt—owes more to Neo-Babylonian than Persian conventions, not surprising, perhaps in view of the Mesopotamian provenance of the tablets. On some examples, these contests have more animation than the standard Persian Hero duels.[8] Scholars have noted the greater dynamism of Neo-Babylonian glyptics relative to earlier styles;[9] perhaps the Nippur

---

[5] Collon, *First Impressions*, no. 428 (British Museum 89337 [Rich Coll., 1825]); cf. Wiseman, *Cylinder*, pl 105.

[6] This is not the place to discuss the intriguing issue of Greek influence on Persepolis or vice-versa. It is well known that Ionian Greeks as well as craftsmen from other subject lands worked on Persian building projects. The ideas in G. Richter's seminal article, 'Greeks in Persia', *AJA* 50 (1946) 15–30 have since been supplemented and qualified; cf. C. Nylander, *Ionians in Pasargadae, Uppsala Studies in Ancient Mediterranean and Near Eastern Civilizations*, I (Uppsala, 1970); Frankfort, *ArtOrien*, 225–8; A. Farkas, *Achaemenid Sculpture*, Uitgaven van het Nederlands Historisch-Archeologisch Instituut XXXIII (1974); J. Boardman, *The Greeks Overseas* (London, 1980) 102–9; Root, 'Persepolis', 9–11; M. C. Root, 'The Parthenon Frieze and the Apadana Reliefs at Persepolis: Reassessing a Programmatic Relationship', *AJA* 89 (1985) 103–20; Boardman, *Diffusion*, 24–48.

[7] Collon, *First Impressions*, p. 93.

[8] Legrain, *Culture*, 945 = Bregstein, *Seal Use*, no. 140; Legrain, *Culture*, 943 = Bregstein, *Seal Use*, no. 136; Legrain, *Culture*, 944 = Bregstein, *Seal Use*, no. 139.

[9] Collon, *First Impressions*, p. 83.

sealings under discussion represent a perpetuation of Neo-Babylonian stylistic elements into the Persian period. Sealings produced by both cylinders and stamps from the Persepolis Treasury texts also include images of heroes wearing the split tunic with the leading leg bare, who are making a running assault on their monster foes.[10]

The costume of the figure on WD **19** clearly marks him as the Persian Hero, and thus WD **19** does not fall precisely into this variant quasi Neo-Babylonian category.[11] Nevertheless, it is important to recognize that 'animation' as an artistic quality need not be attributed exclusively to Hellenic influence. WD **19** is a curious image, and without a clearer idea of the entire seal design, it would be premature to conjecture extensively.

---

[10] Schmidt, *Persepolis II*, pl 11, seal 38; pl 13, seals 59–60.

[11] A Persian cylinder seal impression that depicts the Persian Hero in unusually naturalistic circumstances might be noted here; on a bulla excavated at Ur, two Persian Heroes on a hunt, accompanied by their lively dogs subdue a wounded lion bristling with arrows (Legrain, *Ur*, pl 40.759). Is this work influenced by Greece or is it 'purely' Near Eastern? A cylinder seal in the British Museum inscribed with the name of King Darius I himself may belong to the same tradition (cf. the wounded lion).

J.   FLANKING SPHINXES

WD 13 and WD 41. Flanking Persian Royal Sphinxes with Double Crown of Egypt

(PLATE XX.2—3)

WD **13**
Mus. Inv. 966
Loose sealing
Image size: 1.5 cm x 1.7 cm
Bulla size: 1.5 cm x 1.7 cm
Clay colour: dark reddish brown
String preserved; top and bottom of horizontal image
Papyrus fibres on front and back
Papyrus imprint
Seal type: circular (conical?) stamp

WD **41**
Mus. Inv. 938
Loose sealing
Image size: 1.5 cm x 1.7 cm
Bulla size: 1.6 cm x 1.7 cm
Clay colour: reddish
String preserved, loop uncut; top and bottom of horizontal image
Papyrus imprint
Seal type: circular (conical?) stamp

WD **13** and WD **41** are essentially the same size, and they look almost exactly the same. Both were produced by the same type of circular stamp seal. The only detail that suggests they came from two different seals is the ground line on which the winged sphinxes recline. On WD **13** this consists of two parallel horizontal lines regularly connected by perpendicular hatch-lines, rather like a ladder set on its side; the ground line on WD **41** is a double version of that on WD **13**. The exergues of both sealings appear empty; however, since the lower portions of both bullae have sustained damage and breaks, this is not absolutely certain. These two bullae can probably be assigned to the same workshop and possibly to the same seal engraver as well.

Except for the differing ground lines, the same description applies to both WD **13** and WD **41**. A pair of recumbent sickle-winged sphinxes appear in profile, facing each other. They extend their forepaws toward each other on the ground before them without quite touching. Both have tucked their two hind paws on their near side.[1] Their tails float upward with a slight curl at the end.

---

[1] Cf. the sixth—fourth century basalt crouching lion from Byblos whose hind legs are tucked around in a similar manner (Moscati, *Phoenicians*, p. 285, cat. no. 13 [Louvre AO 4950]).

The most interesting feature of these sphinxes is their headgear. Their faces are familiar from other Wadi Daliyeh sealings and from many examples of Persian Court Style sculpture showing the Persian Hero himself as well as animals with the head and crown of the Persian Hero.[2] On WD **13** and WD **41,** the usual Persian Hero beard, hair bunched at the nape of the neck, the hooked nose, and large frontal eye are present. However, rather than the expected dentate crown these sphinxes wear the double crown of Egypt. The tall white crown (*hedjet*)—somewhat truncated, but recognizable nonetheless—is fitted into the red crown (*deshret*) with its distinctive high back and frontal curl.[3] The curl of the sphinxes' tails echoes that of the red crowns; indeed, the entire design is an essay in parallel and reversed curves.

The design on these two sealings is apparently unique. Given the variety of Achaemenid creatures, even among the Daliyeh bullae, who appear with the Persian Hero's head, it should not be surprising to find it on the sphinxes of WD **13** and WD **41**. However, it is quite unexpected to find the Persian Hero/Royal Sphinx (Boardman's term)[4] crowned like an Egyptian Pharaoh. WD **13** and WD **41** together clearly illustrate how incomplete knowledge of ancient Near Eastern imagery remains to this day.[5]

A Phoenician workshop was the probable source of the seals behind WD **13** and WD **41**. The Phoenicians readily absorbed and reworked Egyptian artistic motifs,[6] and they were more likely than Egyptians to place wings on sphinxes or to portray flanking monsters, a design more familiar along the Tigris-Euphrates than the Nile.[7] The arrangement of the sphinxes' tails on WD **13** and WD **41** is Phoenician, rather than Egyptian.[8] Furthermore, Phoenician artists tended to distribute the double crown of Egypt rather indiscriminately; Phoenician ivories from Arslan Tash (ancient Khadatu, mid-ninth century) show Hapy (the Nile god), protective winged goddesses and ram-headed, winged sphinxes, all wearing the double crown.[9] An eighth-century ivory plaquette from Nimrud shows a winged sphinx wearing the double crown and standing

---

[2] Cf. entry on WD **4** (above, p. 214) for general discussion of the Persian Hero motif; the Persian Hero on the Wadi Daliyeh sealings: WD **4** (pl XVIII.2), WD **8** (pl XVIII.3), WD **17** (pl XVII.1), etc.; other sphinxes: WD **48** (pl XXI.2) WD **3A** (pl XIX.1), WD **15A** (pl XXI.3), WD **53** (pl XV.1); 'Royal' scorpion men: WD **25** (pl XXI.1).

[3] For a clear picture of the separate regalia, cf. the Narmer Palette.

[4] Boardman, 'Pyramidal', 34.

[5] Had it appeared on the art market, an unprovenanced seal with this image might conceivably have been dismissed as an ignorant forgery.

[6] H. Frankfort says of Phoenician art, '[t]he hallmark of the Phoenicians is the lavish use of bungled Egyptian themes' (Frankfort, *Art*, 188).

[7] Cf. the detailed discussion of Phoenician sphinxes in R. D. Barnett, 'Phoenician and Syrian Ivory Carving', *PEQ* (1939) 16–17, and *idem, A Catalogue of the Nimrud Ivories* (London, 1957) 31–62.

[8] Gubel, 'Syro-Cypriote', 205, 208.

[9] Frankfort, *Art*, pl 168.A–D; cf. also pp. 191–5. Neither Hapy nor the protective winged goddesses (Isis, Nephthys, Neith and Selkis) as a rule wear the double crown when they appear in true Egyptian—rather than Egyptianizing—contexts.

on all fours among long-stemmed palmettes.[10] Phoenician green jasper scarabs of the Archaic period show the wingless sphinx wearing the double crown.[11]

Quite close in its details to the WD **13** and WD **41** sphinxes is a reclining winged sphinx on an alabaster panel from Aradus in Phoenicia; the bullae and the panel show the sphinx with the double crown (a rather short, white crown on the panel) and the same elevated, curled tail.[12] The most securely dated image of a sphinx somewhat comparable to that on WD **13** and WD **41** appears on the earliest series of coins of Byblos (425–410).[13] The Byblian sphinx has the double crown and lies with its chest fully on the ground, but unlike the seated sphinxes on WD **13** and WD **41**, it is wingless.

It is tempting to correlate the Egyptian crown worn by these sphinxes with Persian Hero faces with the brief period during the fourth century when the Persians regained control of Egypt (343–337; slightly later, Darius III reconquered Egypt just in time for Alexander to lay claim to it). In the late sixth century, for example, when Persia controlled Egypt, four imposing red granite stelae commissioned by Darius I and erected in the Wadi Tumilat (Lower Egypt) provided an Egyptian royal titulary for Darius as son of the goddess Neith, image of Ra, etc.[14] These stelae, along with a monumental Egyptianizing statue of Darius I found at Susa (but intended for Egypt),[15] constitute evidence which M. Root cites to demonstrate that the Achaemenid programme of royal propaganda consisted in many instances of deliberate cultural assimilation, rather than cultural imperialism.[16] Might the fact that on WD **13** and WD **41** the Persian royal sphinxes wear the Egyptian crowns suggest that somewhere in the

---

[10] Moscati, *Phoenicians*, 407 and cat. no. 88 (British Museum, Western Asiatic 132991); note also a Phoenician ivory plaquette of the seventh century from tomb 79 at Salamis (Cyprus) with a similar crowned sphinx in the Cyprus Museum, Nicosia (illustrated in Moscati, *Phoenicians*, 158).

[11] Walters, *BMC*, 378–9, both from Tharros on Sardinia.

[12] Moscati, *Phoenicians*, p. 300, cat. no. 18 (Louvre AO 4836). The cataloguers of *Phoenicians* date this work to the sixth/fifth centuries; I. Winter gives it a third-century date and labels it Phoenician (Winter, 'Phoenician', 7 n. 41); D. Harden cites it as eighth/seventh century (D. Harden, *The Phoenicians*, 2nd. rev. ed. [Baltimore, 1971] 182, fig. 57]).

Other winged sphinxes, all standing and wearing the double crown and shown with raised, curled tails from Levantine contexts include: the bas relief of a winged sphinx on a basalt orthostat [ninth century?] found reused in a wall of the Ummayad mosque in Damascus (M. Trokay, 'Le bas-relief au sphinx de Damas', *SP* IV [1986] fig. 1); a sphinx on an ivory from Samaria of the early first millennium (J. W. and G. M. Crowfoot, *Early Ivories from Samaria* [London, 1938] 20, pl V.1) and the aforementioned ivories from Arslan-Tash, also of the early first millennium (F. Thureau-Dangin, *et al.*, *Arslan-Tash* [Paris, 1931] 89–90, 102 ff., pl XXVII.22 and pl XXVIII.23–5).

[13] Kraay, *Coins*, 1051; Betlyon, *Coinage*, p. 112, pl 8.1–3, silver didrachms and various portions of a sheqel. The type was not repeated after 410 BCE. Betlyon points out the association of the sphinx with royal and/or divine thrones in the Levant and suggests the image on the coins might be an allusion to the throne of Baʿal Šamem one of the chief deities of Byblos (p. 112 n. 18).

[14] A. T. Olmstead, *History of the Persian Empire* (New York, 1948) 145–7; J. M. Cook, *The Persian Empire* (New York, 1983), 65–6; W. Hinz, 'Darius und der Suezkanal', *AMI* 8 (1975) 115–21.

[15] Initial publication by D. Stronach, 'Une statue de Darius découverte à Suse', *Journal Asiatique* 260 (1972) 241–6.

[16] P. Calmeyer, 'Ägyptischer Stil und reichsacheimenidische Inhalte auf dem Sockel der Dareios-Statue aus Susa/Heliopolis', *Achaemenid History* VI (1991) 285–303; Root, 'Persepolis', 12 and figs. 2–3. Cf. also Root, *King. passim*.

Persian Empire (Egypt? the Levant?) the Persian 'Royal Hero' or Persian King had already been represented in other artistic media wearing the Egyptian crowns, perhaps as a symbol of Persia's claim on Egypt? In Achaemenid art not only the Persian Hero (or Persian Royal Hero) and Persian King (in unambiguous contexts), but also sphinxes and scorpion men share the same face, hair and crown,[17] so that a certain fluidity in iconography could be expected between 'human' hero and 'monster' sphinx.

On the other hand, if the white crown as well as the other Egyptian crowns worn by Phoenician bronze smiting warrior figurines (identified variously as Resheph or Baʿal)[18] may be understood as a marker in Phoenicia of divinity or of the god's kingship, there is justification in speculating that the Egyptian crown had assumed a purely Phoenician significance separate from its Egyptian origins. As noted, in Phoenician art the presence of Egyptian royal regalia need not be seen as a reflection of Egyptian political influence nor of any Phoenician claims *vis-à-vis* Egypt.[19] Tempting although it may be to see in these sphinxes evidence for a new wrinkle in Persian imperial propaganda of the fourth century, it is much more probable that the sphinxes on WD **13** and WD **41** are simply hybrids born of a Phoenician imagination crossed with a vigorous strain of Persian Court Style imagery.

---

[17] See entry on WD **3A**, p.220ff.

[18] D. Collon, 'The Smiting God: A Study of a Bronze in the Pomerance Collection in New York', *Levant* 4 (1972) 111–34; O. Negbi, *Canaanite Gods in Metal. An Archaeological Study of Ancient Syro-Palestinian Figurines* (Tel Aviv, 1979); A. M. Bisi, 'La diffusion du "Smiting God" syro-palestinien dans le milieu phénicien d'occident', *Karthago* 19 (1980) 5–14; H. Seëden, *The Standing Armed Figurines in the Levant* (Munich, 1980); A. M. Bisi, 'Le "Smiting God" dans les milieuux Phéniciens d'occident: un réexamen de la question', *SP* IV (1986) 167–87; illustrations in Moscati, *Phoenicians*, cat. nos. 107 (combination of white crown and west Semitic horns), 110 (Atef crown), 655 (Atef crown).

[19] Barnett, 'Phoenician and Syrian Ivory Carving', 16–17.

WD 25. Flanking Royal Scorpion-Men

(PLATE XXI.1)

Mus. Inv. 922
Loose sealing
Image size: 1 cm x 1.5 cm
Bulla size: 1.9 cm x 1.8 cm
Clay colour: black (burned)
String not preserved; string holes left and right of horizontal image
Papyrus imprint
Seal type: engraved stone, mounted in a ring?
Published: Cross, 'Papyri', 29, pl 62.e.; Cross, 'Dâliyeh', 51 and fig. 39

WD **25** is an exceptionally clear sealing produced probably by an oval finger ring.

Two scorpion-men appear in profile, facing each other in a symmetrical arrangement which is duplicated on many Achaemenid cylinder and stamp seals. They have the bodies and tails of scorpions, generic eastern sickle wings and the legs and feet of a stick-figure. The heads and faces of the scorpion-men are indistinguishable from that of the Persian Hero, having the same beard, dentate crown, and hair worn bunched at the nape of the neck found also on WD **4** (pl XVIII.2), WD **8** (pl XVIII.3), WD **17** (pl XVii.1), **53** (pl XV.1), etc.[1] WD **25** is unusual among the Wadi Daliyeh sealings in having an outline; a delicate, twisted rope device.

The scorpion and scorpion-men had a long history in ancient Mesopotamian art.[2] A common figure especially in late Neo-Assyrian art, the human-headed, scorpion-tailed, bird-footed figure was regarded as a beneficent spirit who averted the malice of evil demons.[3] Artists in the Achaemenid Empire produced a new variation on the Mesopotamian scorpion-man by giving him the head of the Persian Hero, a guise in which the Persian king also appears.[4] Usually a pair of scorpion-men face each other in a symmetrical arrangement as on WD **25**. Occasionally, a scorpion-man appears alone (on seal rings) or accompanied by the human figure of a king or hero.

---

[1] See entry on WD **4** (above, p. 214ff.) for further discussion of the Persian Hero.

[2] Collon, *First Impressions*, p. 187. For recent discussion of the *qirtablilu* and *zuqaqipu*, with references, cf. A. Green, 'Neo-Assyrian Apotropaic Figures', *Iraq* 45 (1983) 87–96; *idem*, 'A Note on the "Scorpion-Man" and Pazuzu', *Iraq* 47 (1985) 75–82; E. D. van Buren, *The Scorpion in Mesopotamian Art and Religion, Archiv für Orientforschung* 12 (Berlin, 1937–9); 'Scorpion-People' in J. Black and A. Green, *Gods, Demons and Symbols of Ancient Mesopotamia, An Illustrated Dictionary* (British Museum, London, 1992).

[3] A. Green, 'A Note on the "Scorpion-Man"', 76.

[4] Legrain, *Culture*, no. 897 (and see below). For discussion of the Persian Hero head on fantastic animals, see entry on WD **3A**, p. 220ff., above.

Glyptic parallels from controlled excavations include Persian period sealings from Nippur (stamps on clay tablets)[5] and Memphis[6] (Egypt) (sealing of unspecified type on papyrus), a bronze ring from Persepolis[7] and, closer to Samaria, a cylinder seal found in the excavations at Tell Jemmeh, twenty kilometres south of Gaza.[8]

Boardman does not include any scorpion-men in his publication of pyramidal stamps, most of which seem to come from Court Style workshops in eastern Anatolia,[9] and scorpion-creatures seem rare in the Phoenician glyptic repertoire.[10]

Although the scorpion-men of WD **25** with the head of the Persian Hero are technically a Perso-Babylonian motif, a lone Persian Hero scorpion-man appears in another good Samarian context, namely on a silver hemiobol probably minted by Samaria in the fourth century.[11] Clearly, this is an image at least nominally significant to Samarians. The coin, in fact, has a border on both obverse and reverse which resembles the border outline of WD **25**.

WD **25** appears to be a classic example of the Persian/Mesopotamian type and derives from artistic circles familiar with Persian Court Style iconography. Perhaps there was a conscious omission of Persian religious symbolism in the case of WD **25**. Most of the pairs of scorpion-men on the Nippur stamp, cylinder, and ring sealings flank an altar or incense burner, and even when the space between is empty,[12] there is often a religious symbol such as a crescent or winged disk above the figures.

The design on WD **25** comes from the east, but its appearance on a Samarian coin with a border nearly identical to that on WD **25** suggests local production as a possible source for the WD **25** seal. The same hand that produced the coin could well be responsible for the seal.[13]

---

[5] Legrain, *Culture*, 897 = Bregstein, *Seal Use*, no. 533. See also Legrain, *Culture*, 893 = Bregstein, *Seal Use*, no. 521; Legrain, *Culture*, 894 = Bregstein, *Seal Use*, no. 518; Legrain, *Culture*, 895 = Bregstein, *Seal Use*, no. 516. The scorpion-men on Legrain, 893–4 have 'Persian Hero' heads; the scorpion-men on the other sealings wear low peaked caps, a holdover from Neo-Babylonian traditions.

[6] Petrie, Mackay, Wainwright, *Meydum*, pl 37.46 and p. 43.

[7] Schmidt, *Persepolis II*, pl 17.PT5 283, bronze ring with a round bezel.

[8] Stern, *Material Culture*, 196–7. Note also an unprovenanced cylinder seal with a scorpion-man and an Aramaic inscription (Bordreuil, *BN*, no. 30).

[9] Boardman, 'Pyramidal'.

[10] From the Phoenician green jasper series of scarabs (sixth–fifth century) comes a mutation of the motif, a scorpion woman with the head of Isis (Richter, MMA, 15 [Metropolitan Museum 31.11.14], 'from Ibiza').

[11] Meshorer-Qedar, *Coinage of Samaria*, no. 63 (from the Nablus Hoard, now in Oxford). The obverse shows a leaping winged bull.

[12] Legrain, *Culture*, 897 = Bregstein, *Seal Use*, no. 533, a crescent hovers over the scorpion-men's heads. On the other hand, perhaps additional details were regularly omitted from rings; the ring impressions from Nippur show only scorpion-men with no other elements. Cf. also Galling, 'Bildsiegel', no. 172 and p. 165 (a cylinder seal inscribed *dśthn*, in the Louvre).

[13] Meshorer (Meshorer-Qedar, *Coinage of Samaria*, 32) proposes that the 'designs on [coin 63] derive directly from Achaemenid seals'.

WD 48. Flanking Winged Sphinxes

(PLATE XXI.2)

Mus. Inv. 945
Loose sealing
Image size: 0.6 cm x 1 cm
Bulla size: 1.1 cm x 1.7 cm
Clay colour: light beige
String preserved, loop uncut; left and right of horizontal image
Papyrus imprint
Seal type: metal finger ring? engraved ringstone in ring mount?

WD **48**, like many other Wadi Daliyeh bullae, was impressed carelessly and was probably never a complete sealing; the upper right quarter of the horizontal oval composition is missing. Abrasions and breaks have further obscured most of the overall surface details, particularly on the right side and the upper edge. A crude outline border is only partially preserved. The loop of string over which WD **48** was affixed is still uncut, presumably because the original unopened papyrus document deteriorated and the bulla became separated from it.

What sort of seal produced WD **48** is unclear. The slightly flattened horizontal oval shape of the image probably indicates a ring. The thickly engraved solid border line which surrounds the two animals appears, if only occasionally in the Classical period, on both all-metal rings and engraved ringstones set in metal rings.

The left half of WD **48** is sufficiently distinct to make out the figure of a seated, sickle-winged sphinx. The vague outlines that survive on the other half of the bulla suggest a second sphinx symmetrically mirroring the first. Whether anything ever appeared in the limited space between the two creatures is doubtful. From its horizontal position on the ground, the left-hand sphinx's curiously long tail makes an awkward 90-degree turn to rise vertically up to the height of the sphinx's wing. Unfortunately, only the faintest traces of the sphinxes' heads survive. On analogy with the other Wadi Daliyeh sphinxes and winged *Mischwesen*,[1] restoration of the animals as royal sphinxes, with the chignon, hooked nose, beard, and tiara of the Persian Hero is tentatively suggested.

If the animals on WD **48** are royal sphinxes, there are good parallels for this standard Persian Court Style motif not only from Samaria but also from such widely separated locations in the western Persian Empire as Egypt,[2] Sardis (Asia Minor),[3] and

---

[1] Sphinxes with the Persian Hero head: WD **3A** (pl XIX.1–3), WD **15A** (pl XXI.3), WD **53** (pl XV.1); sphinxes with Persian Hero faces: WD **13** (pl XX.2), WD **41** (pl XX.3); scorpion men with Persian Hero heads: WD **25** (pl XXI.1); seated sphinx, paw raised: WD **31** (pl XV.2).

[2] Boardman, 'Pyramidal', pl 5, no. 122, from Egypt.

[3] Boardman, 'Pyramidal', pl 5, nos. 121 and 123, from Sardis.

Kerch (Russian Crimea).[4] At least one comes from Persepolis itself.[5] More securely excavated examples come from Daskyleion[6] (on the Hellespont) and from Nippur (Babylonia).[7] Boardman has isolated a Lydian series of flanking royal sphinxes (mostly without good provenances) on pyramidal stamp seals which he dates to the fifth century.[8]

There is some variation among all these seals and bullae. The sphinxes often raise one front paw to each other. They may flank an incense burner, flower (as on WD **15A**), or 'tree of life'. Occasionally a winged disk or a crescent hovers over the animals. Sometimes only one of the two creatures is a royal sphinx and the other is a griffin or similar monster. Theoretical restorations of WD **48** include: (a) the animals saluting each other, touching raised inner paws (as on WD **31**, pl XV.2), and/or (b) dissimilar animals.

In contrast with all of these other examples where, at most, a horizontal ground line is found, WD **48** shows the sphinxes encircled by a continuous border line. This border seems to consist of a continuous line of tiny flattened circular blobs. The influence of coin engraving may be seen in this type of border, perhaps specifically Phoenician coin engraving.[9] Indeed, the dotted border is a common feature on Samarian fourth-century issues which as a whole betray particular dependence on Phoenician and Cilician prototypes.[10]

Phoenicia is a likely source for the WD **48** ring. WD **13** and WD **41** may supplement the evidence that Phoenician artisans did work in the Persian Court Style idiom which included royal sphinxes. However, without a clearer picture of the design on WD **48**, it is difficult to make any very definitive pronouncements on its style or workshop location.

---

[4] Boardman, *GGFR*, 834 (= Boardman, 'Pyramidal', pl 1, no. 5), from a Kerch burial of the late fifth century.

[5] Schmidt, *Persepolis II*, pl 3, no. 1.

[6] Balkan, 'Inscribed Bullae', pl 33.c and d (single royal sphinxes).

[7] Legrain, *Culture*, nos. 888 = Bregstein, *Seal Use*, no. 507 (iron ring); Legrain, *Culture*, 889 = Bregstein, *Seal Use*, no. 501 (stamp seal); Legrain, *Culture*, 891 = Bregstein, *Seal Use*, no. 499 (cylinder). No. 888 (from a ring) is similar in shape to WD **48**.

[8] Boardman, 'Pyramidal', no. 5 (= Boardman, *GGFR*, 834); also nos. 116–25. Cf. pp. 34, 37–8.

[9] Jenkins, *Coins*, 328, a Tyrian double-sheqel, *c*.400; cf. the Tyrian coins in Betlyon, *Coinage*, pl 6.nos. 2, 5, 7–9.

[10] Meshorer-Qedar, *Coinage of Samaria*, 20 and *passim*.

WD 15A. Sphinxes Flanking a Flower

(PLATE XXI.3)

Mus. Inv. 775[1]
Papyrus 6[2]
Image size: n. a.
Bulla size: n. a.
Clay colour: n. a.
String preserved; left and right of horizontal image
Seal type: engraved stone (conoid? scaraboid?)

HORIZONTAL and vertical cracks have exacerbated the already poor legibility of WD **15A**. The edge of the original oval sealing has disappeared along the lower portion of the bulla; there is some distortion on the left side of the image, probably from uneven sealing pressure. It is difficult to make more than a guess as to the original seal type— perhaps a stamp seal or a scaraboid.[3] There is no border design, and probably no ground line.

The general outline of the design on WD **15A** is clear. A pair of male sickle-winged sphinxes face each other essentially in profile. Their chests are in a modified three-quarter view that leaves both forelegs visible. The sphinxes' long necks give them a surprised look; they seem to wear their hair bunched in a chignon on the nape of their necks in the fashion of the Persian Hero. The two animals were probably identical, but on the bulla, the sphinx on the viewer's right is much clearer. His wing feathers are articulated in two ranks, and he carries his tail upright and curled slightly outward at the end. Both sphinxes have long legs and knobby, drilled paws. Other details are difficult to determine. The sphinxes may be bearded. Are they crowned? There seems to be some sort of headdress, perhaps a fillet in the Assyrian manner which also appears in Achaemenid art.[4] The Persian high dentate crown is a less likely possibility. The sphinx on the right might be sitting on its haunches, but the image in that area is very faint. The photograph of WD **15A** strongly suggests that the left-hand sphinx is up on all fours, and on that basis, it is presumed that its companion is its mirror image; perhaps the pose is a semicrouch similar to that of the winged monsters on

---

[1] The following discussion is based only on a photograph. The bulla was unavailable for examination.

[2] Papyrus 6 documents the sale of two slaves, one named ʾAbi-Luḥay (possibly a north Arabic name in the opinion of Cross [personal communication]); the names of the other slave and the interested parties as well as the number of witnesses and the date are not preserved (Gropp, *Samaria Papyri*, 102, 104). Also still affixed to Papyrus 6 was WD **15B** (pl III.3), a ring impression in the 'Greek' style showing a nude youth seated on a rock.

[3] Cf. Ashmolean/*ANES III*, 464 (oval conoid), 465 (scaraboid).

[4] Boardman, 'Pyramidal', p. 32; Legrain, *Culture*, 902 = Bregstein, *Seal Use*, no. 53; Legrain, *Culture*, 950 = Bregstein, *Seal Use*, no. 55.

Gold Ring B (pl XVI.3). The sphinxes flank a long-stemmed chest-height lotus blossom or palmette with two abbreviated down-turned tendrils.

It is difficult to place WD **15A** stylistically. It seems unrelated to any of the various sphinxes on the Wadi Daliyeh bullae,[5] and no sphinxes at all appear on Samarian coins. The sickle wings of the sphinxes on WD **15A** are the common Achaemenid type. One comparison is provided by a pyramidal stamp seal in Paris[6] which shows two standing sphinxes, one of the Persian Hero type with the high crown, the other with a fillet, perhaps like the sphinxes on WD **15A**. Also in Paris is an Achaemenid conoid stamp showing a winged disc hovering over a pair of seated sphinxes with fillets who flank a trefoil flower.[7] The trefoil flower on a stem is attested on Achaemenid seals such as the Paris conoid, above, and on cylinders where it again divides pairs of monsters[8] as on WD **15A**. The blossom on Gold Ring B (pl XVI.3) is another variant.

On the other hand, WD **15A** also could be viewed as having Phoenician characteristics. I. Winter notes that Phoenician flowers tend to have volutes, that is, double downturned curling tendrils at the stem juncture (the point where the flower joins the stem).[9] It is difficult to determine if the two tendrils on the WD **15A** flower curl or not, but they do appear on a slant rather than at right-angles with the trefoil blossom as is common on the Achaemenid examples. Long legs are also characteristic of Phoenician sphinxes.[10] The upcurled tail[11] as well as the sickle wings appear regularly on Achaemenid works but could also be Phoenician.

The design on WD **15A** fills the field less fully than most related Court Style seals. The angle at which the sphinxes' chests are seen is rare in Persian Court Style work which prefers a stricter profile view. In Achaemenid glyptics, unlike WD **15A**, the profile of the neck is often obscured by hair and beard. If the WD **15A** sphinxes are standing, this, too, is less common on Persian period seals.

WD **15A** might be Persian or Phoenician. Its sphinxes also bear comparison with a single sphinx on a Greco-Persian scaraboid in Geneva;[12] the male sphinx, which Boardman calls 'Greek',[13] has the long neck, curved wing, and tail of the WD **15A**

---

[5] Cf. WD **53** (pl XV.1); WD **31** (pl XV.2); WD **3A** (pl XIX.1–3); WD **13** (pl XX.2); WD **41** (pl XX.3); WD **48** (pl XXI.2).

[6] Boardman, 'Pyramidal', 125 (Bibliothèque Nationale M6560).

[7] Delaporte, *Catalogue*, 632. Cf. Delaporte, *Catalogue*, 633 = Boardman, 'Pyramidal', 116. Sometimes, this flower becomes a similarly triangular fire altar or incense burner.

[8] Delaporte, *Catalogue*, 399, seated royal sphinxes flank a lotus, surmounted by the human-headed, winged 'Ahura Mazda' figure; D. J. Wiseman, *Cylinder Seals of Western Asia* (London, 1959) no. 106 (British Museum 89352) = Collon, *First Impressions*, 864. Cf. also the conoid stamp seal in the Ashmolean Museum with Persian Hero-headed sphinxes flanking a plant (Ashmolean/*ANES III*, 464 (no. 1891.337).

[9] Winter, 'Phoenician', 6.

[10] Winter, 'Phoenician', 7.

[11] Cf. Gubel, 'Syro-Cypriote', 205, 208.

[12] Boardman, *GGFR* 956 (= M.-L. Vollenweider, *Catalogue raisonnée des sceaux, cylindres et intailles I* [Musée d'Art et d'Histoire de Genève] [Geneva, 1967] 208). A more straightforwardly Greek version of the male sphinx appears on a rock crystal scaraboid 'from Rethymnon' (Boardman, *GGFR*, 580). Richter (*EGGE*, p. 103) notes that while monsters and hybrid creatures tend to fade from the scene during the Classical period, they do continue to appear on gems.

[13] Boardman, *GGFR*, 319.

sphinxes, but appears in true profile, wears a Greek *pilos* and an individuality which contrasts with the more decorative qualities of the WD **15A** sphinxes. Nevertheless, this scaraboid demonstrates the stylistic fluidity of traditional motifs in the western Persian Empire.

On balance, because of the Phoenician flower and the curled tails, and because Phoenician art is stylistically so eclectic, the present editor is inclined to label WD **15A** as Phoenician.

INDEX OF WADI DALIYEH NUMBERS

Wadi Daliyeh Seal Impressions by WD Number

18	969	XVI.1	199	Flanking Winged Horses
19	970	XX.1	226	Persian Hero Attacking One Opponent
20	971	VII.3	102	Frontal Male Figure in Himation
21A	781	XXII.2A	——	Illegible
21B	767	VIII.3	110	Dancing Satyr
		XXII.2B		
21C	778	XXII.2C	——	Illegible
21D	780	III.2	55	Standing Nude Youth
		XXII.2D		
22	972	——	3 n. 2	Sanballat Inscription
23	973	XIV.2	184	Boar (?) with Inscription
24	921	XIX.2	220	Hero Flanked by Winged Sphinxes
				(= WD 3A, 10A, 11B, 12)
25	922	XXI.1	235	Flanking Royal Scorpion-Men
26	923	IV.2	64	Nude Hoplite with Shield and Spear
27	924	IX.3	121	Persian Dancer
28	925	II.1	49	Nude Youth with Himation
29	926	II.2	50	Nude Youth with Himation and Branch (?)
30	927	XIV.1	182	Running Quadruped
31	928	XV.2	193	Seated Winged Sphinx
32	929	V.1	74	Warrior with Spear, Shield, and Sack
				(Perseus?)
33	930	IV.3	66	Smiting Nude Warrior
34	931	XVI.2	202	Two Horses
35	932	XIV.3	188	Winged Hippocamp (with Rider?)
36	933	XVII.2	209	Persian Hero Fights Flanking Inverted
				Lions
37	934	XIII.2	176	Lion
		= XXIII.9		
38	935	XV.3	195	Winged Bull (?)
		= XXIII.5?		
39	936	VI.2	90	Herakles in Lionskin with Club
40	937	IX.1	114	Kneeling Eros
41	938	XX.3	231	Flanking Persian Royal Sphinxes with
				Double Crown of Egypt
42	939	VI.3	92	Herakles (with Club) vs. Nemean Lion
43	940	XI.2	145	Achilles and Penthesileia (?)
44	941	X.3	131	Knucklebone (*Astragaloi*) Players
45	942	XII.3	167	Winged Boar Protome
46	943	XI.1	137	Nike in Facing Quadriga
47	944	XII.2	162	Nude Hero (Herakles?) vs. Two Inverted
				Lions
48	945	XXI.2	237	Flanking Winged Sphinxes
49	946	I.3	47	Hermes (?)
50	947	IX.2	117	Dancing Maenad (?)

SUBJECT INDEX

Satyr   WD 2; WD 16B; WD 21B; WD 51
Scorpion men (winged)   WD 25
Sphinx   WD 3A; WD 11B; WD 13; WD 15A; WD 24; WD 31;
                                      WD 41; WD 48; WD 53; XXIII.6

Stag   XXIII.3
Warrior (Greek)   WD 1; WD 16A; WD 21D; WD 26; WD 32; WD 33;
                                      WD 43; WD 54; WD 56; XXIV.6

Woman (see Female Figure)
Youth: nude, unarmed (Greek)   WD 7; WD 14; WD 15B; WD 28; WD 29; WD 49;
                                      WD 57; XXIV.1, 2, 3, 4, 5, 9

Zeus   XXIV.12

PLATES

UNLESS so noted in the catalogue entry, all drawings were executed on the basis of personal examination of each bulla. Many details on the bullae which the eye can detect are often invisible on the photographs, or would only appear in their totality if several photographs from different angles were provided, a desideratum, but an excessively costly one.

Plates I–XXII present Wadi Daliyeh (WD) bullae located in the Rockefeller Museum, Jerusalem. The numbers following the WD number denote photographs taken by the Palestine Archaeological Museum (PAM), now known as the Rockefeller Museum. For example, on Plate I, WD **7**, the Rockefeller Museum number assigned to that bulla, is followed by 43.923, which is the PAM photograph number. These numbers appear as listed in S. A. Reed and M. J. Lundberg with M. B. Phelps, *Dead Sea Scrolls Catalogue: Documents, Photographs and Museum Inventory Numbers* (SBL Resources for Biblical Study 32; Scholars Press, Atlanta, Georgia, 1994).

Plates XXIII and XXIV present a significant selection of related bullae formerly in the collection of Reuben and Edith Hecht, and now in the collections of the Israel Museum, Jerusalem (IM) and the Reuben and Edith Hecht Museum, the University of Haifa (HM). Photographs of the bullae on plates XXIII and XXIV may be obtained from the appropriate museum.

PLATE I

 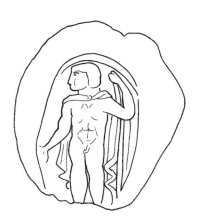

WD 7 (43.923)

WD 14 (43.932)

 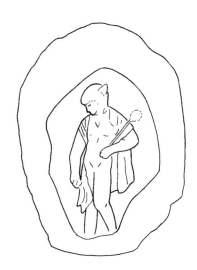

WD 49 (44.034)

PLATE II

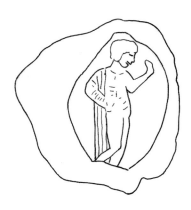

WD 28 (44.023)

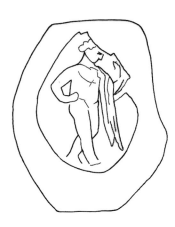

WD 29 (44.024)

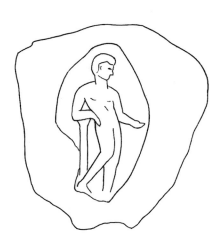

WD 57 (44.042)

PLATE III

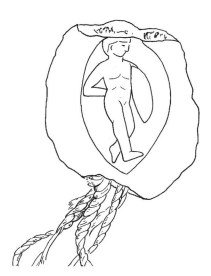

WD 1 (43.916)

WD 21D (43.911)

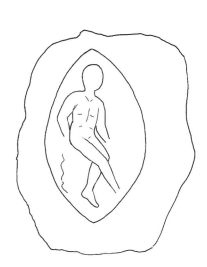

WD 15B (43.933)

PLATE IV

WD 16A (43.936)

WD 26 (44.022)

 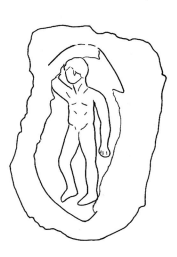

WD 33 (44.026)

PLATE V

 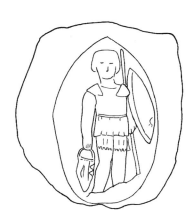

WD 32 (44.025)

WD 54 (44.039)

WD 56 (44.041)

PLATE VI

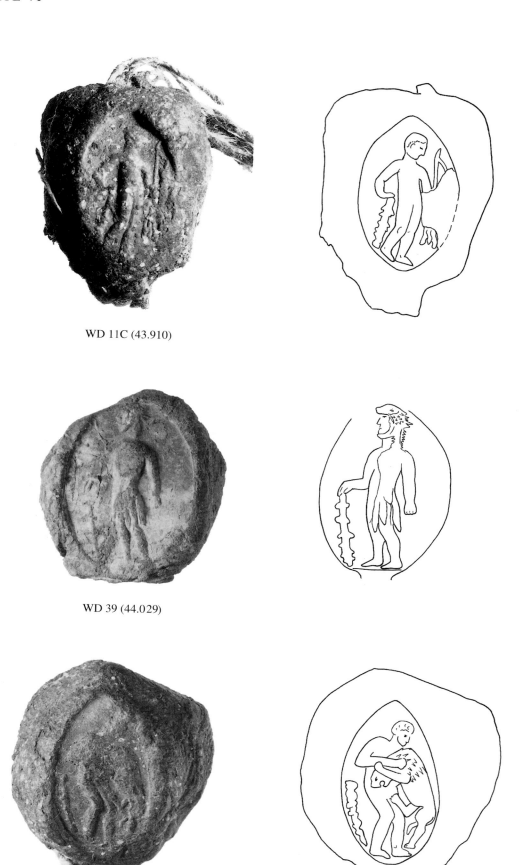

WD 11C (43.910)

WD 39 (44.029)

WD 42 (44.030)

PLATE VII

WD 9 (43.925)

WD 11E (43.910)

WD 20 (43.940)

PLATE VIII

WD 16B (43.935)

WD 5 (43.921)

WD 21B (43.911)

PLATE IX

WD 40 (44.029)

WD 50 (44.035)

WD 27 (44.023)

PLATE X

WD I.3.22B

WD 2 (43.917)

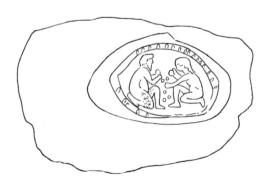

WD 44 (44.031)

PLATE XI

WD 46 (44.032)

WD 43 (44.031)

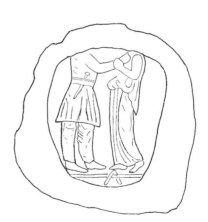

WD 6 (43.922)

PLATE XII

WD 52 (44.037)

WD 47 (44.033)

WD 45 (44.032)

PLATE XIII

 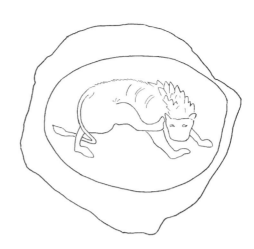

WD 55 (44.040)

WD 37 (44.028)

GR-A (44.019)

PLATE XIV

WD 30 (44.024)

WD 23 (44.020)

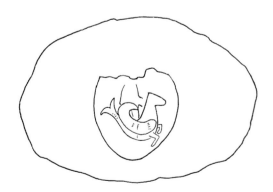

WD 35 (44.027)

PLATE XV

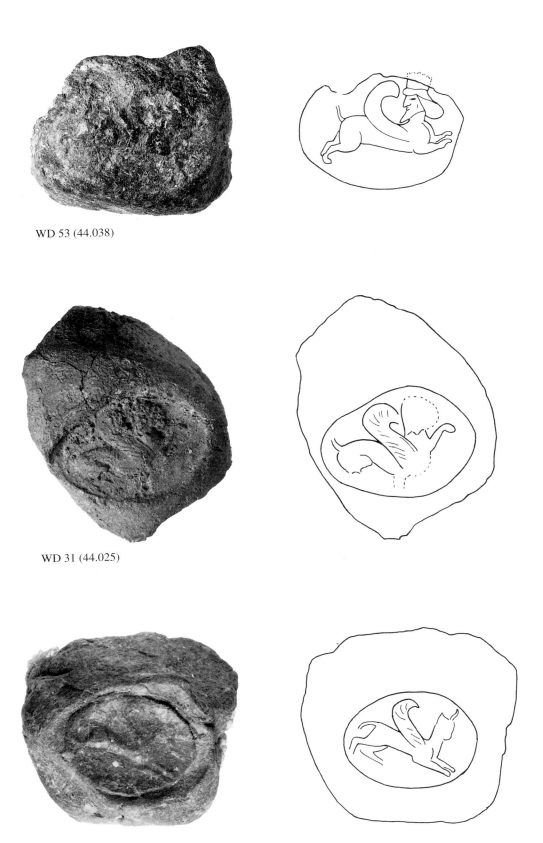

WD 53 (44.038)

WD 31 (44.025)

WD 38 (44.028)

PLATE XVI

WD 18 (43.938)

 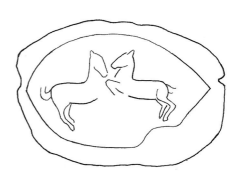

WD 34 (44.026)

GR-B (44.019)

PLATE XVII

WD 17 (43.937)

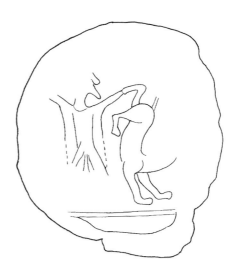

WD 36 (44.027)

WD 51 (44.036)

PLATE XVIII

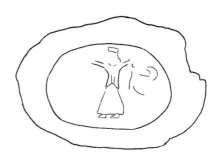

WD 3B (43.918)

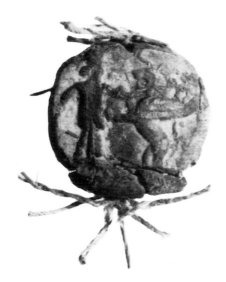

WD 4 (43.920)

WD 8 (43.924)

PLATE XIX

WD 3A (43.919)

WD 24 (44.021)

WD 11B (43.928)

WD I.3.22A

PLATE XX

WD 19 (43.939)

WD 13 (43.931)

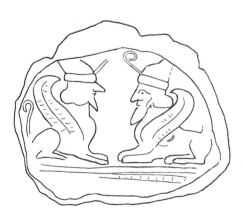

WD 41 (44.030)

PLATE XXI

WD 25 (44.022)

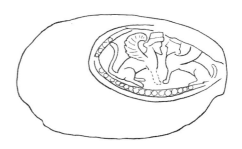

WD 48 (44.033)

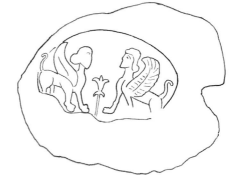

WD 15A (43.934)

PLATE XXII

WD 16A-D attached to WDSP 3 (43.936)

WD 21A-D attached to WDSP 2 (43.911)

PLATE XXIII

1. IM 82.19.919

2. HM K63.L

3. IM 82.19.925

4. IM 82.19.942

5. IM 82.19.941

6. HM K63.R

7. HM K63.F

8. HM K63.I

9. HM K63.K

10. HM K63.J

11. HM K63.N

12. IM 82.19.922

13. HM K63.Q

14. HM K63.S

For references see TABLE OF PLATES

PLATE XXIV

1. HM K63.V

2. HM K63.A

3. HM K63.X

4. HM K63.P

5. IM 82.19.930

6. IM 82.19.920

7. IM 82.19.231

8. HM K63.B

9. IM 82.19.926

10. IM 82.19.939

11. IM 82.19.923

12. IM 82.19.928

13. IM 82.19.945

14. IM 82.19.934

For references see TABLE OF PLATES